RISK MARKERS FOR SEXUAL VICTIMIZATION AND PREDATION IN PRISON

In 2003, the US Senate and Congress passed the Prison Rape Elimination Act (PREA), prompting a number of research projects that cumulatively began to broaden and deepen our understanding of this complex aspect of prison life. *Risk Markers for Sexual Victimization and Predation in Prison* contains the results of Dr. Warren and Dr. Jackson's study, and it extends the literature on prison rape in important and distinct ways. Their research, which encompasses the full continuum of sexual behavior among incarcerated individuals, succeeds in identifying multi-layered predictive models for different types of sexual behavior across and within genders. The process by which the authors came to their study design, their experiences while implementing it, and the nature and significance of their findings, represent the content of this book.

Janet I. Warren, DSW, is Professor of Psychiatry and Neurobehavioral Sciences in the University of Virginia School of Medicine and Director of the *Restoring Youth©* program at the Institute of Law, Psychiatry, and Public Policy at the University of Virginia. She is the University of Virginia liaison to the Behavioral Sciences Unit of the FBI and a member of the FBI National Center for the Analysis of Violent Crime Research Advisory Board. She is an associate of Park Dietz and Associates (PD&A) and a practicing psychoanalyst in Charlottesville, Virginia.

Shelly L. Jackson, PhD, is Assistant Professor of Psychiatry and Neurobehavioral Sciences, School of Medicine, Institute of Law, Psychiatry, and Public Policy, University of Virginia. Dr. Jackson was a post-doctoral fellow in the Psychology and Law program at the University of Nebraska-Lincoln. Subsequently, Dr. Jackson was awarded the Society for Research in Child Development Executive Branch Policy Fellowship and membership in the American Association for the Advancement of Science. For three years she was a Social Science Analyst with the National Institute of Justice, US Department of Justice, in the Violence and Victimization division.

International Perspectives on Forensic Mental Health

A Routledge Book Series

Edited by Ronald Roesch and Stephen Hart, Simon Fraser University

The goal of this series is to improve the quality of health care services in forensic settings by providing a forum for discussing issues related to policy, administration, clinical practice, and research. The series will cover topics such as mental health law; the organization and administration of forensic services for people with mental disorder; the development, implementation and evaluation of treatment programs for mental disorder in civil and criminal justice settings; the assessment and management of violence risk, including risk for sexual violence and family violence; and staff selection, training, and development in forensic systems. The book series will consider proposals for both monographs and edited works on these and similar topics, with special consideration given to proposals that promote best practice and are relevant to international audiences.

RISK MARKERS FOR SEXUAL VICTIMIZATION AND PREDATION IN PRISON

Janet I. Warren and Shelly L. Jackson

Routledge
Taylor & Francis Group

NEW YORK AND LONDON

First published 2013
by Routledge
711 Third Avenue, New York, NY 10017

Simultaneously published in the UK
by Routledge
27 Church Road, Hove, East Sussex BN3 2FA

Routledge is an imprint of the Taylor & Francis Group, an informa business

Library of Congress Cataloging in Publication Data
Warren, Janet I.
Risk markers for sexual victimization and predation in prison / Janet I. Warren &
Shelly L. Jackson.
    p. cm.
Includes bibliographical references and index.
1. Prison violence—United States.
2. Rape—United States.   3. Sex crimes—United States.
4. Prisoners—Sexual behavior—United States.
5. Prisoners—Violence against—United States.   6. Criminal behavior,
Prediction of—United States. I. Jackson, Shelly L. II. Title.
HV9025.W37 2012
365'.6—dc23

                                                    2012019497

ISBN: 978-0-415-89726-6 (hbk)
ISBN: 978-0-415-64128-9 (pbk)
ISBN: 978-0-203-08117-4 (ebk)

Typeset in Bembo
by RefineCatch Limited, Bungay, Suffolk, UK

Certified Sourcing
www.sfiprogram.org
SFI-00453

Printed and bound in the United States of America
by Edwards Brothers, Inc.

CONTENTS

TABLES

FIGURES

ACKNOWLEDGMENTS

This research was funded by grant #2004-RP-BX-0004 by the National Institute of Justice, Office of Justice Programs, US Department of Justice, to the University of Virginia. Points of view expressed in this document are those of the authors and do not necessarily represent the official position or policy of the US Department of Justice. We delight in paying special tribute to our colleagues, Ann Booker Loper, PhD, who also served as co-principal investigator on the original project and co-author of the final report, and Mandi Burnette, PhD, our statistician, who served as a co-author on the final report.

We are grateful to the Ohio Department of Rehabilitation and Correction and to the Texas Department of Criminal Justice for providing us with access to inmates. We would like to give a special thank you to Gayle Bickle, Chair of the Human Subjects Research Review Committee at the Ohio Department of Rehabilitation and Correction. In Texas, we would like to thank Doug Dretke, Dimitria Pope, Jennifer Geffken, and Karen Hall for facilitating our research.

We are sincerely grateful to the wardens in both Ohio and Texas who gave their permission for us to collect data at their various institutions. We are also appreciative of the assistance provided by Warden's Assistants at each institution. They were instrumental in setting up logistics and providing assistance on a daily basis while we were visiting the institutions.

We would like to thank the inmates in Ohio and Texas for taking the time to talk to us. We are also grateful to the correctional staff for providing assistance in transferring inmates to and from the interview and providing protection during our visits. We recognize the disruption our presence created in the institution. Specifically in Texas, we would like to thank the Safe Prisons officers at each unit we visited.

The authors would like to thank Sarah Berson for her administrative assistance on this project.

We would like to extend a sincere thank you to the graduate students who conducted interviews with the inmates and for their goodwill and clinical sensitivity while in the field interviewing inmates and coding "combo" interviews. In Ohio, these students included: Lauren Ashbaugh, Sarah Daoust, Bernice Joo, Irina Komarovskaya, George Loper, Jennifer Sturek, and Philip Wickline. At Sam Houston State University, graduate students included: Amanda McGorty, Jeremy Johnson, Amber Simpler, Bethany Young, Chantal VanReeyuk, Claire Sauvagnat, Kristy Lawson, Cynthia Mundt, Jennifer Sanders, and Carol Woods. We would also like to acknowledge the contribution made by Daniel Murrie, PhD, who provided training and oversight during data collection in Texas.

We also wish to thank Adriane Li Mullins, Robert Dillard Lytle III, Alison Marie Brooks, Caitlin Duffy, and Roberta J. Reiman for their assistance with file reviews in Ohio. File reviewers in Texas included Danielle Linders and Chantal VanReeyuk.

We would like to thank Irena Bocarnea for assistance with the literature review and Ashley Engels Dibble for assistance with manuscript preparation. We are also grateful to Matthew Morrison and Johnson Mei for their assistance with data entry.

Finally, we would like to thank Andrew Goldberg, our grant manager at the National Institute of Justice, for his support of our research.

ABOUT THE AUTHORS

Janet I. Warren, DSW, is Professor of Psychiatry and Neurobehavioral Sciences in the University of Virginia School of Medicine and Director of the *Restoring Youth©* program at the Institute of Law, Psychiatry, and Public Policy at the University of Virginia. She is the University of Virginia liaison to the Behavioral Sciences Unit of the FBI and a member of the FBI National Center for the Analysis of Violent Crime Research Advisory Board. She is an associate of Park Dietz and Associates (PD&A) and a practicing psychoanalyst in Charlottesville, Virginia. Dr. Warren has received research grants from the National Institute of Justice (NIJ), the Office of Juvenile Justice and Delinquency Prevention (OJJDP), the Virginia Department of Criminal Justice Services (VDCJS), and has collaborated for many years with the Behavioral Sciences Unit of the FBI on their research regarding serial rapists, sexual sadists, and serial killers. Her current research interests include the nature of sexual behavior in prison, the recording activities of serial killers, maternal responses to child sexual abuse, the structure of personality disorders and psychopathy in male and female inmates, and the outcomes of juvenile competence restoration services. Dr. Warren obtained her bachelor and master degrees from the University of Manitoba and her doctorate from the University of California, Berkeley. She received her psychoanalytic training through the New York Freudian Society in Washington, DC.

Shelly L. Jackson, PhD, is Assistant Professor of Psychiatry and Neurobehavioral Sciences, School of Medicine, Institute of Law, Psychiatry, and Public Policy, University of Virginia. Dr. Jackson received her doctorate in Developmental Psychology from the University of Vermont, her master's degree in Applied Developmental Psychology from Portland State University, and a Bachelor of Science degree in Psychology from Rutgers University. Dr. Jackson was a post-doctoral fellow in the Psychology and Law program at the University of Nebraska-Lincoln. Subsequently, Dr. Jackson was awarded the Society for Research in Child Development Executive Branch Policy Fellowship and membership in the American Association for the Advancement of Science. For three years she was a Social Science Analyst with the National Institute of Justice, US Department of Justice, in the Violence and Victimization division. Since coming to the University of Virginia, her research and teaching interests have focused on family violence across the lifespan, the sexual behavior of incarcerated individuals, and juvenile competency. In collaboration with colleagues, she has been awarded two grants from the National Institute of Justice.

1

AN INTRODUCTION TO THE PRISON RAPE ELIMINATION ACT

Our research emerged in the context of a federal initiative to study and address the problem of prison rape among both male and female inmates. While initially overestimated in terms of prevalence, this national attention nonetheless spawned a number of research projects that cumulatively began to broaden and deepen our understanding of this complex aspect of prison life. Our research, which chose to encompass the full continuum of sexual behavior among incarcerated individuals, succeeded in identifying multi-layered predictive models for different types of sexual behavior across and within genders. The process by which we came to our study design, our experiences while implementing it, and the nature and significance of our findings represent the content of this book.

Historical Context of the Prison Rape Elimination Act (PREA)

The PREA legislation reflected a culmination of efforts that emerged both in the context of human rights advocacy, both inside and outside of Washington DC, and the legal thrust of the United States Supreme Court coupled with amendments to federal law concerning civil rights litigation by prisoners.

Human Rights Advocacy

With the passage of PREA in 2003, federal and state correctional institutions were required to engage seriously in activities designed to eliminate prison rape. Part of the impetus for the PREA legislation emerged in the context of human rights law and the ratification of two international treaties, the *International Covenant on Civil and Political Rights*, adopted in 1976, and the *Convention against Torture and Other Cruel, Inhumane and Degrading Treatment or Punishment*, adopted in

1987. Both of these declarations require the United States (US) to protect prisoners from sexual violence. Along with the *Universal Declaration of Human Rights* (1948), these statements define basic human rights, which include protection against cruel, degrading, or inhumane treatment or punishment along with the accessibility of individuals to remedies for the violation of these rights. The decision to address prison rape within this human rights perspective helped to separate the issue from the criminal arena and the specifics of the crimes for which these victims had been incarcerated. Vulnerability to infection with the AIDS virus further aligned the issue to the basic principle of human rights and the avoidance of a death sentence that had not been imposed by the court.

It was this human rights perspective that came to define the mission and purpose of Just Detention International (JDI), an organization established in 1980 by Russell Dan Smith. Smith, an inmate who had experienced a sexual assault in prison, began the grassroots organization, People Organized to Stop the Rape of Imprisoned Persons, to "deal with the problems of rape, sexual assault, sex slavery, and forced prostitution in the prison context" (http://www.justdetention.org/en/spr_history.aspx). Shortly thereafter, the organization was renamed Stop Prison Rape, and in 1994 was incorporated by Stephen Donaldson, who went on to serve as the President of the organization until his death.

In 1973, Stephen Donaldson was arrested for trespassing after participating in a prayer-in at the White House which was advocating for peace in Vietnam. Mr. Donaldson was a Quaker activist who refused to post a $10 bond on moral grounds and was sent to a Washington, DC jail. Mr. Donaldson was behind bars for two nights, during which time he was gang raped approximately 60 times by various inmates. When Mr. Donaldson was released, he became a prolific and committed activist, writing many editorials and appearing on national television before his death in 1996 from AIDS, believed to have been contracted as a result of his assaults in the Washington, DC jail.

After his death, the Stop Prison Rape staff was active in advocating for the passage of the Prison Rape Elimination Act, and after its passage, the implementation of its legislative mandates in a meaningful and effective manner. In 2008, the name of the organization was changed to Just Detention International. Currently located in Los Angeles, California, the organization identifies three core goals for its work: To ensure governmental accountability for prisoner rape, to transform ill-informed public attitudes about sexual assault in detention, and to promote access to resources for individuals who have experienced sexual assault while confined in a penal institution. It is currently active in advocating for protections of detainees in US immigration centers.

A second wave of human rights involvement emerged in 2001 when Michael Horowitz, Director of the Hudson Institute's Project for Civil Justice Reform and Project for International Religious Freedom, turned his attention to prison rape based upon his earlier work with the *International Religious Freedom Act* of 1998, followed by the *Victims of Trafficking and Violence Protection Act* of 2000. A human rights coalition had been formed to pass these two legislative mandates, and after completion of these advocacy endeavors, the question of "what next?" remained. According to Mr. Horowitz, he raised this question informally with Linda Chavez of the Center for Equal Opportunity, and a member of the coalition, and she replied "You know, prison rape has always troubled me." At that point, the coalition identified this as their next legislative goal and, based upon their prior experience, they began convening both conservative and liberal groups who had been working on prison rape, a group that collectively became known as the "Prison Rape Coalition." Initially made up of 18 members including a congressman, congressional aides, academic researchers, religious leaders for prison reform, a victim of prison rape, and a philanthropic CEO, the group gradually expanded to 58 members by the time the bill passed in 2003. The group sponsored congressional hearings, drafted legislation, and procured sponsorship from four congressmen (Michael Horowitz, personal communication, October 18, 2006). One commentator, who was central to the negotiations that transpired during this time period, observed that the swiftness with which the legislation obtained bipartisan support reflected a rather unexpected blending of concern about the conditions and rehabilitation of incarcerated individuals on the one hand, and an ideological commitment to eradicating homosexual behavior on the other (Bobby Vassar, personal communication, October 2, 2006).

Farmer v. Brennan (1994), United Supreme Court

Perhaps the most significant Supreme Court case relevant to prison rape litigation is *Farmer v. Brennan* (1994). Dee Farmer was a pre-operative transsexual who had undergone unsuccessful black market surgery to remove her testicles. At the time of her 20-year imprisonment for multiple counts of credit card fraud, she had a noticeable feminine appearance with silicone breast implants, hormone replacement therapy, and a manner of dress that was designed to portray a feminine appearance. Due to the rules concerning gender determinations and custody in the Federal Bureau of Prisons, she was sentenced to serve her time in an all-male prison.

On March 9, 1989, Ms. Farmer was transferred from the Federal Correctional Institute at Oxford, Wisconsin, to a maximum security penitentiary at Terre Haute, Indiana, after she was found guilty of ordering fruit baskets and flowers with a stolen credit card over the prison telephone. She was initially placed in administrative segregation but on March 23, 1989, she was released into general population based on earlier challenges she had made for pertinent medical treatment and safe housing that did not involve segregation. On April 1, 1989, Ms. Farmer was approached by another inmate "demanding" sexual intercourse with her. When she refused she was punched in the face, kicked, and raped at knife point with the assailant threatening to kill her if she reported it to prison officials. One week later, Ms. Farmer reported the incident to the prison and, acting without counsel, filed a complaint against the Federal Bureau of Prisons requesting transfer to a mixed gender facility and compensatory damages. The district court and the Court of Appeals for the Seventh Circuit granted the defendant's motion for summary judgment and Ms. Farmer acting pro se petitioned the Supreme Court successfully for certiorari.

In June of 1994, the Supreme Court ruled unanimously and unambiguously that prison officials had a duty under the Eighth Amendment to protect prisoners from harm at the hands of other prisoners. The court applied the standard of "deliberate indifference" identified in cases involving medical care thus broadening the "malicious and sadistic" standard applied to prior cases of physical violence perpetrated by prison officials against prison inmates. The Supreme Court vacated the lower court decision and remanded Ms. Farmer's case with Justice Blackmun's statement that the court's decision "creates no new obstacles to prison inmates to overcome and sends a clear message to prison officials that their affirmative duty to provide for the safety of inmates is not to be taken lightly." In upholding this decision, the court accepted the argument that the Federal Bureau of Prisons was aware of Ms. Farmer's transsexual status and demonstrated deliberate indifference in not protecting her from this risk. It also made clear that prison officials could not escape liability merely by showing that they did not know that a specific inmate posed a risk to the specific plaintiff (see also *Wilson v. Wright*, 1998).

Prison Litigation Reform Act (1996)

A second legal impetus for the PREA legislation emerged in response to the passage of the Prison Litigation Reform Act (PLRA) in 1996. PLRA amended and supplemented the US Code that addressed civil rights litigation and *in forma pauperis* proceedings and was designed to "curtail the ability of prisoners to bring frivolous and malicious lawsuits." The number of prisoners filing civil rights lawsuits annually had risen from 8,235 in 1977 to more than 40,000 in 1996 (Maguire & Pestore, 1997). Advocates of the bill argued that "tying our courts in knots" was unnecessary and that the time and money the state expended defending against these frivolous lawsuits could be used instead to fight crime. Senators Robert Dole and Orrin Hatch were active in this debate and contributed to the publication in the *Congressional Record* that was entitled "Top 10 Frivolous Inmate Lawsuits Nationally." Included in this list were suits brought by prisoners because their ice cream had melted, they were forced to listen to the unit manager's country western music, their dessert cake had arrived "hacked up," they were served chunky instead of smooth peanut butter, they were making $21.00 an hour at work after being promised $29.40, they had to send packages by UPS rather than Federal Express, they were supplied with LA Gear sneakers instead of Converse, and they had been denied sex change operations while in prison (Puplava, 1997).

Critics of the law argued that PLRA made it more difficult for indigent inmates to file reasonable claims and to receive judgment on these claims. Within these parameters, two of the PLRA requirements were seen as particularly antithetical to the rights of individuals who are seeking to litigate allegations of coerced sex and rape. The PLRA (amended 1998) instructed federal district courts to dismiss all actions alleging mental suffering without any showing of prior physical injury (Taylor, 2000). Based upon this instruction, some courts determined that rape constitutes a physical injury (e.g., *Liner v. Goord*, 1999; *Noguera v. Hasty*, 2001; *Nunn v. Michigan Department of Corrections*, 1997), although the holdings provided little useful analysis, stating simply "the alleged sexual assaults qualify as physical injuries as a matter of common sense" (*Liner v. Goord*, 1999). Other courts have refused to find sexual assault a per se physical injury (*Kemner v. Hemphill*, 2002; *Hancock v. Payne*, 2006) (Golden, 2006). A second requirement of the PLRA mandated that all prison avenues for vetting grievances be exhausted by a prisoner before the civil action would be reviewed by the court, even if the prisoner was suing for damages and the grievance system did not provide damages (Columbia Human Rights Law Review, 2009). Criticism of this exhaustion requirement as it pertains to sexual assault in prison underscored the risk that some prisoners might take in documenting sexual assault within a prison environment, particularly when the accused perpetrator might be a correctional officer or member of the prison staff (Ribet, 2010).

The contradictions between these legal mandates, the one arguing for the protection of sexually assaulted prisoners based upon the Eighth Amendment of the US Constitution, and the other limiting inmates' ability to bring suit in federal court, created a legal tension that further contributed to a growing sense that prison rape was a specific and unique hazard of incarceration and one that should be addressed though a unique law and ongoing congressional oversight.

Brief Summary of the Prison Rape Elimination Act

The Prison Rape Reduction Act of 2003 (H.R. 1707) was originally introduced by Representatives Frank Wolf (R-VA10) and Bobby Scott (D-VA3) on April 19, 2003, to the House Committee on the Judiciary. On July 21, 2003, the renamed Prison Rape Elimination Act (S. 1435) passed the Senate with unanimous support after being introduced by Senator Jeff Sessions (R-Ala) and Senator Ted M. Kennedy (D-Mass). On April 22, 2003, H.R. 1765 was referred to the Subcommittee on Crime, Terrorism, and Homeland Security. Six weeks later, on September 4, 2003, the Honorable George W. Bush signed the legislation into law during a White House ceremony. The Act was authorized to spend $302 million over a five-year period to provide for the analysis of the incidence and effects of prison rape in federal, state, and local correctional institutions and to provide information, resources, recommendations, and funding intended to protect individuals from prison rape.

The rationale for the law derived from 13 assertions that were presented in PREA. These assertions included estimates that 13 percent of prison inmates were sexually assaulted in prison, often repeatedly; inmates who are young and who suffer from mental illness were at higher risk for sexual assault; prison rape under-mined the public health by exposing inmates to HIV/AIDS, tuberculosis, and hepatitis C and B; prison rape brutalized inmates and made it more likely that they will be violent when they return to the community; the interracial nature of many prison sexual assaults exacerbated interracial tensions in the prisons and in the community; prison rape contributed to the rate of assaults and homicides against inmates and staff and contributed to the risk of insurrections and riots within institutions; victims of prison rape suffered severe psychological and physical effects that hindered their ability to reintegrate into their communities; the high rate of sexual assault within prisons involved actual and potential violations of the US Constitution as reflected in *Farmer v. Brennan* (1994); and the high incidence of prison rape undermined the effectiveness and efficiency of federal expenditures and the nature of interstate commerce. These assertions were presented in what appears to have been a good faith effort to identify the many ramifications of what was considered an epidemic of sexual violence in prison, although later research demonstrated that some of these assertions were in fact exaggerated and overly simplistic in the definition of the problem and its possible solutions.

Upon first review, the intent and goals of PREA were straightforward. Philosophically, it sought to further define the position of the US Supreme Court in *Farmer v. Brennan* (1994) in which the Court ruled that deliberate indifference to the substantial risk of sexual assault of incarcerated individuals violated the prisoners' rights under the Cruel and Unusual Punishment Clause of the Eighth Amendment of the US Constitution. It required the Bureau of Justice Statistics (BJS) to collect data on the incidence and prevalence of prison rape in a nationally representative manner that included at least a 10 percent random sample of all federal, state, and county prison inmates, mandated all facility administrators to participate in any data collection requests by BJS, and to provide BJS with access to the inmates under their legal custody. Programmatically, PREA sought to create a zero tolerance standard for the incidence of prison rape, to make prison rape prevention a top priority in each prison system, and to create national standards for the detection, prevention, reduc-tion, and punishment of prison rape. These goals were strengthened by a possible reduction in federal subsidies of 5 percent per year if the standards eventually promulgated by the National Prison Rape Reduction Commission were not met and certified by the chief executive of each state. Taken as a whole, PREA suggested a clear-cut commitment to rape reduction and provided financial incentives for research and programming that were robust and convincing in their intent.

PREA has been conceptualized by some as the needed catalyst for changes in societal and institutional attitudes and responses to sexual assault in prison. It required the Attorney General to submit an annual report to Congress and to the Secretary of Health and Human Services on the activities being conducted pursuant to the law and to publish at the end of the study period a final rule adopting national standards for the detection, prevention, reduction, and punishment of prison rape. It appointed a nine member National Prison Rape Reduction Commission (hereafter referred to as the Commission) and provided the Commission full support in collecting information from various agencies and in conducting hearings pertaining to the appropriate means for classifying and assigning prisoners; investigating and resolving complaints of prison sexual assault; preserving physical and testimonial evidence of the investigation of prison rapes; addressing the acute trauma care of rape victims; developing educational and medical testing measures for reducing the incidence of HIV transmission; the training of correctional staff to better understand the significance of prison rape; protecting the confidentiality of prison rape complaints; and creating a system for reporting incidents of prison rape to ensure the impartial resolution of prison rape complaints. Finally, it created a Review Panel of Prison Rape situated within the National Institute of Justice to carry out public hearings each year concerning the operations of the three prisons with the highest incidence of prison rape, and the two prisons with the lowest incidence of prison rape, in each category of facilities to identify the characteristics of prison systems that are associated with different levels of prison rape.

The Contribution of Our Study to PREA Through Three Unique Areas of Inquiry

The purpose of our research, funded by the National Institute of Justice, was to begin the development of a risk classification scheme for use in men's and women's prisons to identify individuals at increased risk for sexual predation or victimization. It was our assumption that with this knowledge, prison officials would be better able to protect inmates from sexual victimization as required under PREA.

To realize this conceptually straightforward but empirically complex goal, we sought to extend the exceedingly small literature on prison rape in three distinct ways. First, as there were no existing sexual violence risk assessment measures, we chose to adapt violence risk assessment measures to study sexual violence in prison. This would also enable us to examine differences between violence and sexual violence risk markers among inmates. Second, we chose a study design that would allow us to directly examine gender differences in sexual behavior among male and female inmates. Finally, we chose to examine the continuum of sexual behavior among incarcerated individuals, thus allowing us to place sexual coercion in the broader context of sexual behavior in prison.

The Adaptation of Clinical Risk Assessment Measures

Clinical violence risk assessment is designed to identify relevant static and dynamic risk factors with interventions being designed to lower the impact of the dynamic factors, contain the static factors, and through these efforts lower the overall level of risk of the individual. We believed that the identification of these dynamic and static risk factors could not only improve classification but also assist in the identification of interventions that prisons might use to lower the level of risk among groups of offenders who were believed early in their prison careers to pose a higher than average risk for either sexual predation or sexual victimization. Our endeavor thus sought to identify the most empirically sound violence risk markers within the clinical violence risk literature, with a particular emphasis on sexual violence, and to explore the combination of factors that would produce risk models intended to inform correctional interventions and classification and management policies.

We believed that this type of study was timely given advances in the clinical assessment of violence risk that had occurred over the past decade and the development of structured clinical assessment instruments that were demonstrating good predictive power and relevance in assessing and managing violence in the community (Borum, Bartel, & Forth, 2002; Monahan et al., 2001; Webster, Douglas, Eaves, & Hart, 1997). We also believed that the field of clinical risk assessment could inform the correctional risk literature which up until this time had focused almost exclusively on the use of demographic, criminal history, and institutional variables to classify offenders and predict physical violence in correctional facilities among male inmates only (Gaes, Wallace, Gilman, Klein-Saffran, & Suppa, 2002; Wooldredge, 1994).

The Inclusion of Males and Females to Assess Gender Differences

As we developed our study design we decided to include an equal number of male and female inmates in our sample, despite this contradicting the significant disparities that exist in the number of males and females currently held in our state and federal prisons. We decided that this was important both to address rather implicit differences in gendered research on prison rape and to allow us to undertake an empirical analysis of the similarities and differences in the risk markers for the various types of sex as they occurred for both men and women.

Our review of the research regarding prison rape led us to the same conclusion as other researchers. Research on male sexual activity in prisons had primarily focused on sexual coercion whereas the research on female sexual activity in prisons had primarily focused on consensual sex (Hensley, Struckman-Johnson, & Eigenberg, 2000). Hensley et al. (2000) noted that as of 2000, only four studies had been conducted on consensual sex in male prisons. In contrast, from the earliest research (Otis, 1913), there has been a focus on consensual sexual activity among female inmates (Koscheski, Hensley, Wright, & Tewksbury, 2002), with studies of sexual coercion among female inmates appearing for the first time in the mid to late 1990s (see Struckman-Johnson, Struckman-Johnson, Rucker, Bumby, & Donaldson, 1996; Struckman-Johnson & Struckman-Johnson, 2002). As noted by

Hensley et al. (2000), it was difficult to determine whether these differences in research orientation reflect reality or whether they reflect researchers' personal attitudes toward sex in prison. Whether males and females experience sex in prisons differently remained an empirical question that to our mind had not been answered.

The Integration of a Full Continuum of Sexual Behavior Observed in Prisons

The PREA legislation identified a forceful mandate to study coerced sexuality in prison. This initial perspective provided us with a clear definition of the illegal acts that we were studying and a pre-existent understanding of the destructive aftermath that could be anticipated particularly in a closed, enduring, and tightly controlled prison environment.

This traditional perspective on sexual assault and victimization, however, began to erode as we left the confines of our university offices and began to visit the many prisons that were to be the site of our data collection. Quickly the wardens and the inmates that were part of our pilot testing began to convey to us a sexual world inside each prison that was far more complex and multifaceted than our initial approach was prepared to handle. We found that there were significant rates of consensual sex occurring in both the male and female prisons, that bartered sex was occurring to obtain various kinds of commodities and psychological benefits, and that there was a small but significant number of rapes that occurred, largely as an expression of dominance and control, and which generally were not reported to the authorities. These were accompanied by a common understanding that retaliation would follow any type of reporting and that there were significant and longstanding effects associated with being labeled a "snitch" in the institution.

As we were encountering this new dimension of prison living, four publications appeared almost simultaneously that helped us appreciate the complexity of the behavior that we were seeking to understand. Smith (2006) published a law review article that explored the motivations that inmates had for being sexual in prison. She observed, "[n]ot withstanding the desire to think otherwise, individuals continue to have an affirmative interest in sexual expression even during institutionalization" (p. 204). Based upon this principle, she identified seven motivational themes that she felt contributed to this continuation of sexual desire including sex for pleasure, trade, freedom, transgression, procreation, safety, and love. Based upon this review, she concluded that sex was a basic drive that did not dissipate upon incarceration but rather reflected an integral but publically unacknowledged part of correctional life commonly recognized by inmates and prison staff alike.

Ristroph (2006) published another law review article in which she argued that distinctions between coerced and consensual sex in prison were sadly artificial and that only a third kind of sex could occur in these surroundings: sex that is "produced by the overwhelmingly coercive environment of prison, sex sought or agreed to under ambiguous circumstances, sex that may constitute prostitution or 'sexual extortion', or just a conflicted quest for a measure of safety in an inherently dangerous environment" (p. 157). Commenting on the prison subculture, she observed that each inmate is by the nature of the institution robbed of any sense of sexual privacy and is contained in an environment in which their body is monitored, restrained, and regulated. The institutional environment is also replete with hierarchical inequalities which spawn opportunities for the "have-nots" to perceive sex as a commodity that can be used to negotiate issues of procurement and safety. From this perspective, Ristroph argued that many inmates consented to sexual encounters not because of a fear of immediate or threatened violence but rather for money, drugs, food, comfort, physical gratification, and love. Acknowledging that some scholars and prison officials insist that no prison sex is fully consensual, she argued that this view was too simplistic and observed that outside the confines of prison, "the law assumes that most adult sex is consensual as long as nobody complains" (p. 6), a perspective not shared by prison officials.

Shortly after the PREA legislation was passed, Mark Fleisher, PhD, an ethnographer with experience in studying criminal behavior from an anthropological perspective, was funded by the National Institute of Justice to explore the culture and language of prison rape. Fleisher and Krienert (2009) conducted 600 semi-structured interviews from both male and female prisons across the country and concluded that while the "idea" of prison rape exerted a powerful influence on inmates' lives, rape "did not frequently occur" (p. 12). Rather, they asserted that these beliefs arose as much from the influence of the family and neighborhood social life, the county jail, and the media, as they did from direct observation or experience in prison. When rape did occur, they were told by inmates that it was often perpetrated against "easy targets" and was frequently associated with getting another inmate's commissary or as retaliation for unpaid debts.

Finally, as we were developing our study design, the BJS published its first in a series of four studies of prison sexual assault. In this first endeavor, the BJS reviewed actual allegations of sexual violence reported to corrections officials throughout the country in male and female prisons during 2004 and 2005 (see Beck & Hughes, 2005; Beck & Harrison, 2006). These data involved 6,241 allegations in 2005, a rate that was up from 5,286 in 2004. The inmate-on-inmate incidents were substantiated in only 15 percent of the allegations made to officials, and these involved primarily younger white male victims, in jail, being assaulted by an older male of a different racial group. Half of these incidents involved the use of force and in the remaining incidents inmates were talked into it, bribed or blackmailed, or offered protection from other inmates. A similar rate of substantiation was found for the staff-on-inmate incidents; however, in two thirds of these incidents the encounters were described by both participants as being romantic in nature. Most substantiated incidents of staff sexual misconduct involved correctional officers, but 16 percent also involved other prison staff including janitors, cooks, and drivers, and 10 percent involved health care staff including counselors, doctors, dentists, and nurses. Two thirds of the perpetrators were female prison staff with male inmates being the presumed "victim."

Based upon the convergence of these early commentaries, combined with our own experience, we decided to include as our primary outcome measures four different types of sexual behavior we had reason to believe occurred in prison either with other inmates, with correctional staff, or with other prison staff or visitors: consensual sex, bartered sex, and coerced sex either as victim or perpetrator. We realized that this approach would provide us with a comparative platform for examining the behavioral interplay between these different types of sexual behaviors in prison. Moreover, given the emergent impression that the rate of authenticated rape would be very low, we concluded that a more inclusive approach would better capture the concerns regarding forced and manipulated sexuality that lay at the heart of the PREA legislation.

Conclusions

Our research emerged in the context of a decade of legal reviews and enactments that positioned the rights of the prisoner in the domains of international human rights and constitutional law, but which simultaneously sought to curtail their access to the federal courts when their attempts at civil litigation were seen as frivolous or malicious. It was within this multifaceted context that we developed a study to identify relevant static and dynamic risk markers recently identified in the clinical risk assessment literature, using samples of both male and female inmates, with the inquiry occurring in the broader context of the continuum of sexual behavior that occurs in the prison environment. Our experiences in the field, combined with the nascent nature of risk research concerning sexual behavior in prison, convinced us that model generation rather than model testing was the appropriate starting place for this type of empirical undertaking.

2

METHODOLOGY

The current chapter includes an overview of our sampling and the data collection process, the demographic characteristics of each of our four samples (male inmates, female inmates, correctional officers, and wardens), and a description of each of our four different types of data collection (interviews, self-report questionnaires, file review measures, and state database measures). We also outline in Appendix A the analyses that we conducted to explore the random nature of our sample and the generalizability of our findings to other prison populations. Appendix B presents state comparisons of correctional officers on key demographic variables. Appendix C presents the training procedures and reliability indices associated with the interview measures.

Prison Selection and Sampling

It was our intention to collect data in three states. We began the process of identifying states by contacting the Commissioners of Criminal Justice Departments in six states. We received interest from two states: Ohio and Texas. A formal proposal was submitted to each state and approved.

Inmate Sample

Within each Department of Criminal Justice, we consulted with members of the justice department staff to identify and gain access to male and female institutions at high, medium, and low security levels. Based upon these efforts we were able to gain access to 164 males and 149 females in Ohio and 124 males and 34 females in Texas across the three security levels. Our overall response rate for inmates in Ohio was 37 percent and varied across sites from a high of 56 percent to a low of 28 percent (see Table 2.1). This rate of response is comparable to other studies

TABLE 2.1 Response Rate of Incarcerated Men (*N*=164) and Women (*N*=149) within Participating Prisons in Ohio

Gender of Prison	Institution	Number of Eligible Inmates	Number Randomly Selected	Number Agreed to Participate	Response Rate
Men's Prisons	A	2783	100	28	28%
	B	980	100	33	33%
	C	955	50	28	56%
	D	116	116	35	30%
	E	1199	100	40	40%
Women's Prisons	F	309	200	74	37%
	G	583	200	75	37%
Total		6925	866	313	37%

of prison sex that have been conducted by academic researchers (Hensley, Tewksbury, & Castle, 2003; Struckman-Johnson & Struckman-Johnson, 2000; Struckman-Johnson & Struckman-Johnson, 2002; Wolff, Blitz, Shi, Bachman, & Siegel, 2006). It is signi-ficantly lower than the response rate obtained by the BJS (39% to 84%) in their study of sexual victimization conducted in 2007. The BJS study was defined by the PREA legislation and carried with it a congressional mandate requiring that all state and federal correctional facilities participate in the study if they were identified through its random sampling procedures.

Although we were able to initially create a list of randomly selected inmates at each Texas institution, we were unable to track refusals due to logistical limitations. For example, using the list of randomly selected inmates, correctional officers, rather than researchers, were first to approach inmates in their quarters and invite them to hear an invitation to participate in the research. However, some of these inmates could not be located, and others declined. Officers did not consistently report these details and were sometimes unavailable to answer questions that might clarify this. Therefore we were unable to calculate a response rate for our Texas sample.

To ensure that the random nature of our sampling was successful in identifying an unbiased pool of participants, we conducted a variety of comparisons between the inmates who participated in the study and those who did not. The comparisons included age, race, minimum aggregate sentence, security level, and gang affiliation. These analyses, described in detail in Appendix A, indicate one signifi-cant difference between the two groups, with inmates who were serving longer sentences being more inclined to participate in the research study.

Demographic Comparisons by State and by Gender

The demographic characteristics of our entire sample are summarized in Table 2.2 and presented separately for Texas and Ohio. Table 2.3 presents the same information, separately for male and female inmates.

TABLE 2.2 Demographic Characteristics of the Entire Sample (N=471), Separately by State

Demographic	Ohio (N=313)		Texas (N=158)		Effect Size	
	N	%	N	%	χ^2	Φ
Sex						
Male	164	52.4	124	78.5	30.07**	−0.25**
Race					39.27**	0.29**
White	153	48.9	65	41.7		
Black	133	42.0	43	27.6		
Hispanic/Other	27	8.6	48	30.8		
Education					1.12	0.05
< High School	64	20.4	26	16.6		
GED/HS Diploma	127	40.6	69	43.9		
> HS Diploma	122	39.0	62	39.5		
Marital Status					4.22	0.10
Never Married	153	48.9	60	39.0		
Separated, Divorced, Widowed	92	29.4	52	33.8		
Married, Common-law	68	21.7	42	27.3		
Employed before Prison?	221	70.6	115	73.2	0.36	0.03
If Yes, Full Time	167	81.5	94	85.5	0.80	−0.05
Longest Period Employed					1.54	0.06
< 6 Months	37	12.5	17	11.3		
6–12 Months	41	13.9	27	18.0		
12–24 Months	71	24.0	32	21.3		
> 24 Months	147	49.7	74	49.3		
Received State Support before Prison	165	53.4	49	31.4	20.17**	−0.21**

Note. **$p < 0.01$.

In later analyses, race is dichotomized into minority and non-minority. Marital status is collapsed into three categories: (1) married/common-law; (2) never married; and (3) divorced/separated/widowed.

These data indicate that the two state samples were the same on all except three variables (see Table 2.7). The Texas sample contained more male inmates, had more Hispanic and fewer black inmates, and contained fewer inmates who had received some type of state support prior to being incarcerated.

Overall, the majority of the inmates had no more than a high school education, with over 60 percent of both samples not progressing beyond a high school diploma. However, four fifths of the inmates did endorse being employed full-time at the time of their arrest and incarceration. Slightly less than half

TABLE 2.3 Demographic Characteristics of Incarcerated Men (*N*=288) and Women (*N*=183) in Sample

Demographic	Male (N=288)		Female (N=183)		Effect Size	
	N	%	N	%	χ^2	Φ
Race					4.43	0.10
White	123	43.0	218	46.5		
Black	111	38.8	65	35.5		
Hispanic/Other	52	18.2	23	12.6		
Education					13.61**	0.17**
< High School	57	19.9	33	18.0		
GED/HS Diploma	136	47.4	60	32.8		
> HS Diploma	94	32.8	90	49.2		
Marital Status					7.51*	0.13*
Never Married	144	50.3	69	38.1		
Separated, Divorced, Widowed	77	26.9	67	37.0		
Married, Common-law	65	22.7	45	24.9		
Employed before Prison?	298	82.2	128	70.3	0.20	−0.02
If Yes, Full Time	161	83.4	100	82.0	0.11	0.02
Longest Period Employed					3.87	0.09
< 6 Months	37	14.0	17	9.3		
6–12 Months	44	16.7	24	13.2		
12–24 Months	57	21.6	46	25.3		
> 24 Months	126	47.7	95	52.2		
Received State Support before Prison	94	33.2	119	66.1	47.93**	0.32**

Note. *p < 0.05, **p < 0.01.

In later analyses, race is dichotomized into minority and non-minority. Marital status is collapsed into three categories: (1) married/common-law; (2) never married; and (3) divorced/separated/widowed.

described themselves as having held a job for more than two years at any time prior to their current incarceration. Reflective of further social instability was the finding that approximately one fifth of the inmates were married at the time of their incarceration, with almost half of the sample never having been married and the rest being either divorced or separated at the time of their incarceration.

Certain gender differences were found in the sample (see Table 2.3). Women tended to have higher levels of education, were more likely to be married at the time of their incarceration, and more often reported receiving some form of state support prior to incarceration. No differences were observed on race and employment history of the inmates.

Correctional Officer Sample: Response Rates and Generalizability

The correctional officers' (CO) survey was completed by a total of 358 COs in Ohio and Texas. Although the response rate was low (43.6% in Ohio), it is not unlike other peer-reviewed research in this field (see Gordon, 2006 [20% response rate]; Tewksbury & Collins, 2006 [22.7% response rate]). To determine whether our sample was comparable to all COs in the Ohio Department of Rehabilitation and Correction (ODRC), comparisons were made on key demographic variables between our participants and the entire population of COs in the ODRC. We found our sample of COs were remarkably similar to all ODRC demographics and thus representative of COs in Ohio. We were unable to obtain comparable data from the Texas Department of Criminal Justice and therefore generalizability was not assessed in Texas. However, Appendix B presents comparisons of COs in Ohio and in Texas on key demographic variables.

Correctional Officer Sample Demographics

Sample demographics for Ohio and Texas COs are presented in Table 2.4, separately by gender. The majority (70%) of COs were White, male (67%), with an average age of 40 years. Over half (56%) of the sample had been to college, although almost a third (32%) had a high school diploma. Two thirds (66%) had been a CO for five years or longer. Nearly three quarters (74%) of the COs had contact with general population inmates. Almost all (92%) COs had contact with inmates on a daily basis, having an average number of contact with 119 inmates per day.

Five gender differences emerged from the CO demographic data. More females were of minority status, $\chi^2(1) = 7.45, p < 0.01$. Males ($M = 41$ years) were significantly older than females ($M = 38$ years), $F(1) = 5.17, p < 0.05$. More females had worked for less than one year at the current facility and fewer females had worked at the current facility for more than ten years, $\chi^2(3) = 8.61, p < 0.05$. Fewer females had contact with segregation/administrative detention inmates, $\chi^2(1) = 4.09, p < 0.05$, and inmates in protective custody, $\chi^2(1) = 3.81, p < 0.05$.

Warden Sample

The participants included nine wardens (one female warden), one from each institution from which data was collected in Ohio and Texas. Wardens had been in their current position between one and ten years, with an average of 2.25 years ($M = 4.68$ years). For four wardens, this was their first time being a warden. All but one became a warden by working up to their current position. Seven of the nine wardens had at least a college degree in one of the following disciplines: criminal justice, sociology, management, or general studies.

TABLE 2.4 Demographic Characteristics of Male (*N*=239) and Female (*N*=119) Correctional Officers in Ohio and Texas

Demographic	Male (N=239)		Female (N=119)		Effect Size	
	N	%	N	%	χ^2	Φ
Race					7.45★★	−0.15★★
White	178	75	71	61		
Minority	61	25	46	39		
Average Age (years)	41	19–67	38	19–64	5.17★	
Education					0.22	0.03
High School Degree	77	32	35	30		
Some college or more	161	68	82	70		
Employment at Facility					3.52★	−0.10
Less than 1 year to 5 years	73	31	48	41		
5 to more than 10 years	165	69	70	59		
Contact with Inmates						
General population	178	75	88	74	0.01	0.01
Medical/psychiatric	28	12	9	8	1.48	0.06
Segregation	70	29	23	19	4.09★	−0.11★
Holdover/transit	2	1	4	3	3.07	−0.09
Pretrial detention	3	1	1	1	0.12	0.02
Protective custody	30	13	7	6	3.81★	−0.10★
Drug therapy	10	4	6	5	0.14	−0.02
Other	14	6	11	9	1.40	−0.06
Contact with Inmates Past 6 Months					1.09	0.06
Never	9	4	3	3		
Once a month	4	1	1	1		
Once a week	9	4	3	3		
Everyday	217	91	110	94		
Average Daily Inmate Contacts	115		128		0.34	

Note. ★*p* < 0.05, ★★*p* < 0.01.

Instrumentation

Inmate Instruments

When we began designing the study, we were aware of the methodological issues associated with collecting data of a very serious nature such as rape. We read, for example, a thorough methodological review completed by Gaes and Goldberg (2004) under the auspices of the National Institute of Justice and provided to the various grantees. In it, the authors reviewed not only prior research on sexual behavior and other risky health behaviors but also studies that sought to query respondents concerning their preferences when being asked about sensitive personal matters (Aquilino, 1994; Catania, 1999; National Research Council, 1979; Tourangeau & Smith, 1998). In this context, they explored the various factors that have been found to influence the self-report of sensitive behaviors including question sensitivity, social undesirability of the response, the intrusiveness of the inquiry, and the perception of disclosure to third parties (Tourangeau, Rips, & Rasinski, 2000). They also summarized the research that had been conducted up until that time on computer–assisted survey instruments (Video CASI and Audio CASI) and concluded these methods appeared to enhance the quality of the data that was obtained in studies of drug use, needle sharing, HIV status, interpersonal violence, and number of sexual partners reported by women (Miller, Gribble, Mazade, & Turner, 1998; Newman et al., 2002; Turner et al., 1998; M. L. Williams et al., 2000).

As we reviewed this summary, we considered the use of CASI technology and consulted with various vendors concerning it. However, we quickly learned that use of this type of computer technology would rob us of all clinical and diagnostic information and eradicate the possibility of coding the various violence risk assessment instruments that lay at the heart of our study. Therefore, we abandoned this approach, concluding that it was relevant to epidemiological studies but not necessarily to clinically based inquiries, and turned our attention to the other factors that had been identified as being relevant to the solicitation of sensitive behaviors.

Questions regarding sexual matters were included in both the interview protocol and in the questionnaires at multiple places in the battery, with different types of questions and probing the same domains of inquiry. The questions that were used to describe sexual behavior were behaviorally and contextually specific and did not use any legal or colloquial terminology (Bachman, 2000; Fisher, Cullen, & Turner, 2000; Lynch, 1996; Williams, Siegel, & Pomeroy, 2000). We arranged to ask the most personal questions about sexual activity in prison after rapport had been established through the first half of the interview and before we embarked on asking each inmate about their criminal history and the offense that led to the current incarceration. We also placed the inquiries about personal behavior after each inmate had been provided with an opportunity to tell us about what he or she believed the other inmates were doing sexually in their prison, in this way hopefully providing some degree of self-justification to any self-reports that were about to follow. Perhaps most importantly, we carefully trained each of our clinical interviewers and ensured that they were not only reliable in their coding of clinical behavior but also actively engaged and non-reactive no matter how provocative and unexpected the information that was provided to them by the various inmates.

Information on inmates was obtained from clinical interviews, standardized and unstandardized measures, file reviews, and state databases. This instrumentation is presented below.

Clinical and Risk Assessment Using Structured Interviews and Actuarial Instruments

Lengthy clinical interviews were conducted by trained clinical faculty and psychology graduate students. The structured interview, termed the Prison Violence Risk Interview (PVRI), required three and a half hours to complete based upon a face-to-face interview with each inmate. The interview and its coding schedule contained 22 sections pertaining to current institutional adjustment, family background, early childhood, adolescence, friendships, interpersonal relationships, marital/romantic relationships, relationships with children, work experience, finances, mental health, alcohol/substance abuse, impulsive behavior, aggression and anger control, emotions and feelings, self-perceptions, criminal behavior, current offenses, manipulation/deceitfulness, career goals, general questions, post-interview observational criteria, and narratives of interest concerning sexual experiences in prison.

The information that was supplied by each inmate during each interview had multiple uses. It was used to quantify certain historical and institutional variables that became independent variables included in the dataset and later analyses. The information was also used to code three structured clinical instruments and one actuarial risk assessment instrument described below.

The Structured Interview for DSM-TV Personality (SIDP-IV; Pfohl, Blum, & Zimmerman, 1995)

The SIDP-IV is a semi-structured interview designed to assess depressive and passive-aggressive personality disorder in addition to the ten DSM-IV personality disorders. It is comprised of 101 questions divided into ten interrelated sections (e.g., Interests & Activities, Work Style, Close Relationships, etc.). The last section of the interview allows interviewers to score criteria based on clinical observation. In contrast to other semi-structured personality disorder interviews, the SIDP-IV questions are organized by clinical topic rather than by disorder, which allows a dialogue to develop between the interviewer and client. In addition, the SIDP-IV questions are posed in a positive way (in contrast to DSM-IV criteria) so that the interview seems less threatening to the client. Individuals being interviewed are asked to respond according to what they are like when they are their "usual self," and they are also instructed that they should think about the last five years when answering the questions.

Psychopathy Checklist-Revised 2 (PCL-R 2 Hare, 2003)

The PCL-R 2 is a 20-item checklist designed to assess the interpersonal, affective, and behavioral traits of psychopathy. It is completed using information gleaned from both a face-to-face clinical interview and a comprehensive file review. The 20 PCL-R 2 items are scored on a three-point Likert scale ranging from 0 to 2 according to the degree to which the examinee matches the trait or behavior described: No (0), Maybe/in some respects (1), or Yes (2). Historically, on the basis of factor analytic research (Harpur, Hare, & Hakstian, 1989), the 20 PCL-R 2 items have been combined to yield a Total score, an Interpersonal/Affective (Factor 1) score, and a Behavioral (Factor 2) score. Based on subsequent research, Cooke and Michie (2001) proposed an alternative, three factor model for the PCL-R 2, which resulted in an Arrogant and Deceitful Interpersonal Style (Factor 1) score, a Deficient Affective Experience (Factor 2) score, and an Impulsive and Irresponsible Behavioral Style (Factor 3) score. Most recently, Hare (2003) developed two Facet scales for the traditional Factor 1 and 2 scales. Accordingly, Factor 1 is comprised of the Interpersonal and Affective Facet scales and Factor 2 is comprised of the Lifestyle and Behavioral Facet scales.

HCR-20 Assessing Risk for Violence Version 2 (Webster, Douglas, Eaves, & Hart, 1997)

The HCR-20 is a structured risk assessment instrument designed to predict violence in civil psychiatric, forensic, and criminal justice populations and is administered and scored by trained clinical raters. The instrument consists of 20 items scored on a Likert scale ranging from 0 (absence of item) to 2 (definite evidence item), including one item that rates a Total PCL-R 2 score. The items on the HCR-20 were selected based on empirical support for logically or analytically derived factors related to risk. They include clinical (e.g., Lack of Insight, Negative Attitudes, Unresponsive to Treatment) and risk management (e.g., Plans Lack Feasibility, Exposures to Destabilizers) items that are dynamic risk factors and, thus, are amenable to change. The instrument can be completed on the basis of file review and interview, however, completion solely on the basis of file review has been supported in some populations (Douglas & Weir, 2003).

Violence Risk Assessment Guide (VRAG; Harris, Rice, & Quinsey, 1993)

The VRAG is an actuarial instrument developed for the prediction of violent recidivism among offenders. The VRAG consists of 12 items. Each item has multiple response options, and each response is assigned a numerical value. For example, the first item inquires whether the individual lived with both biological parents until age 16. A response of "Yes" is assigned −2 points, and a response of "No" is assigned 3 points. Scores on the VRAG can range from −26 to +38, with higher scores indicating a greater risk that the individual will reoffend violently.

Standardized and Study-specific Instrumentation

At three points throughout the interview, the interviewer paused to code certain clinical and risk variables while the inmate completed a number of copyrighted and study generated questionnaires. These self-report questionnaires were color coded to ensure that the most central questionnaires were completed by all inmates in what was often a very time intensive data collection session. The questionnaires included:

Prison Background Information Survey (PBIS; Warren, Loper, & Jackson, 2006)

The PBIS is a 40-item self-report questionnaire that captures demographic characteristics, family background, work history, drug history, prior criminal involvement, and an assortment of violence risk factors identified in the research literature but not measured by any particular standardized instrument (for example, separation from parents before the age of 15 years, at least one head injury with loss of consciousness, parental antisociality, etc.). We also used this instrument to collect information on the inmates' sexual behavior prior to prison and their self-identified sexual orientation in prison and in the community.

Adverse Childhood Experiences Study Questionnaire (ACE SQ; Felitti et al., 1998)

The original ACE SQ was developed for research in the health field and queries the subject about a number of adverse events as a child such as psychological, physical, and sexual abuse; the presence of a household member with substance abuse problems or mental illness; violence toward the individual's mother or step-mother; and criminal behavior in the household. The ACE SQ was modified (ACE SQ-M) for use in the present study. The number of test items was increased from 17 to 38, although two of the original ACE SQ items ("Did a household member attempt suicide?" and "Did a household member go to prison?") were not included as this data was collected elsewhere. Items were also added to the ACE SQ to expand the range of behaviors and events inmates could endorse for each category of adverse childhood events. For example, the ACE SQ sexual abuse items all reflect "hands-on" behaviors such as fondling and penetration. In contrast, the ACE SQ-M sexual abuse items also reflect non-contact behaviors including exposure to pornography and observing others having sex. In addition, items were added to assess witnessing physical violence directed toward one's father or step-father, and the experience of childhood neglect. The scoring of the ACE SQ was also modified so that all ACE SQ-M items are scored exclusively as dichotomous variables.

Prison Violence Inventory (PVI; Warren, 2002)

The PVI was designed to measure the amount of self-reported violence experienced and perpetrated by an inmate since arriving at a correctional institution. This measure was modified from a measure assessing community violence (Monahan et al., 2001). The PVI is coded using a dichotomous response to 34 questions as summed across three dimensions (physical violence, threats, and sexual assault) into an overall perpetration score and an overall victimization score.

Inmate Fear of Victimization (IFV; McCorkle, 1993a, 1993b)

The IFV was initially developed by to investigate inmates' fear of violence in prison and their sense of being protected by the prison staff. In the current study, we expanded the instrument to include nine questions concerning social contact and patterns of affiliation while in prison (such as belonging to a religious group, a gang, having visitors, and having a close relationship with prison staff) and expanded the various items to include fear of a sexual attack and the sense that a report of this type of assault would be taken seriously by prison officials including both correctional staff and the warden.

Paraphilic Interests (PI; Warren, 2006a)

The PI, designed for use in the current study, contained 15 questions that related to the various paraphilic disorders identified by the Diagnostic and Statistical Manual for Mental Disorders–IV-TR (American Psychiatric Association, 2000). The inmates were asked to indicate if they had "no interest in this activity," "fantasized about it but never done it," "done it once," and "done it multiple times." Due to the limited endorsement of these items, responses were coded as dichotomous variables indicating any endorsed interest or not.

Schedule of Imagined Violence (SIV; Grisso, Davis, Vesselinov, Appelbaum, & Monahan, 2000)

The SIV was developed for use in the MacArthur Violence Risk Assessment Study (Monahan et al., 2001; Steadman et al., 1994, 1998) to determine whether imagined violence is correlated with later violent behavior. The SIV consists of eight structured questions with coded response categories including daydreams or thoughts about physically hurting or injuring another person, the recency and frequency of these thoughts, the chronicity of the violent thoughts, the diversity in the type of imagined harm, the specificity of the assumed target, increases in the level of harm imagined, and the respondent's proximity to the target individual.

Relationship Violence in Prison (RVP; Jackson & Warren, 2006)

The RVP was developed for use in the current study based upon the disruptive impact that triangulated love affairs and broken relationships were perceived to have on the prison environment by the warden and other administrative staff. It contains questions about the inmate's experience of intimate relationships while in prison and the behaviors they manifest when this relationship came to an end (e.g., self-injury, violence toward partner, violence toward new lover, rule violations to prompt a move to another area of the prison).

Novaco Anger Scale (NAS; Novaco, 2003)

The NAS is a self-report questionnaire designed to assess anger as a problem of psychological functioning and physical health. It was initially developed in conjunction with the MacArthur Foundation Network on Mental Health and Law (Novaco, 1994). The NAS contains 60 items that focus on how an individual experiences anger. The instrument yields five scale scores: Cognitive, Arousal, Behavioral, and Anger Regulation subscale scores, and a NAS Total score.

Beck Depression Inventory (BDI-II; Beck, Steer, & Brown, 1996)

BDI-II is a 21-item self-report instrument designed to measure the severity of depression in persons aged 13 years or older. It includes questions concerning Sadness, Pessimism, Past Failure, Crying and Irritability. Each item is organized according to severity (lowest to highest) on a 4-point scale ranging from 0–3 although possible responses vary between items. Respondents are asked to endorse the single statement in each item that they feel to be most characteristic "within the past two weeks, including today." The BDI-II is scored by summing the ratings of the 21 items with a maximum score of 63 points.

Conflict Tactics Scale 2 (CTS 2; Straus, Hamby, Boney-McCoy, & Sugarman, 1996)

CTS 2 is a self-report paper-and-pencil measure designed to assess the extent to which partners in a dating, cohabiting, or marital relationship engage in psychological and physical attacks and their use of reasoning or negotiation to deal with these conflicts. It is comprised of 39 pairs of items. One set of items asks about the experiences of the individual completing the CTS 2, and the other set asks about their partner. The 78 CTS 2 items are scored on a 6-point Likert scale, which reflects the frequency of occurrence of the behavior described in each test item ranging from 0 ("This has never happened") to 6 ("More than 20 times in the past year"). The CTS 2 yields scores for five scales: Negotiation, Psychological Aggression, Physical Assault, Sexual Coercion, and Injury. Each of the six parent scales is comprised of two subscales. The Negotiation scale can be divided into Cognitive and Emotional subscales, and the remaining CTS 2 scales are comprised of Minor and Severe subscales.

Self-report Criminal History Questionnaire (SRCHQ; Warren, 2006b)

The SRCHQ was designed for use in the current study to assess each inmate's willingness to report accurately their criminal behavior regardless of whether or not they had been arrested, charged, or convicted of the crime. The instrument queried the inmate about 14 categories of crime, separately as a juvenile and as an adult, and asked if the inmate had participated in that type of illegal behavior, how many times, and if they were arrested for the behavior. The responses were coded as total number of crimes as a juvenile and as an adult.

Sexual Aggression in Prison (SAP; Warren, Jackson, & Loper, 2006)

One single instrument was designed for use as our criterion measures in the study. A thorough review of the research literature indicated that no instrument had been used previously to obtain detailed and gradated information concerning different types of sexual experience in a prison environment.

The SAP was designed specifically for the study from which to derive our criterion variables. The SAP included sections that queried the inmates about consensual sex ("Please mark those sexual experiences that you have had in prison that you and your partner WANTED and ENJOYED and with whom you had them"), bartered sex ("Please mark those sexual experiences you have had in prison as part of TRADING SEX for something you want, e.g. canteen goods, money, protection"), coerced sex as a victim ("Please indicate whether you have been sexually HARASSED, ASSAULTED, or RAPED in prison"), and coerced sex as a perpetrator ("Please mark the sexual behaviors that YOU have done to others WITHOUT THEIR PERMISSION") while incarcerated for their current offense. Sections were presented to inmates in the order described above. The self-report questions used a 16-point continuum to capture information ranging from relatively benign "cat calls" and comments about one's body to anal and vaginal penetration with body parts or objects (see list below). The statements were worded slightly differently for each type of sex under investigation. The instrument allowed the respondent to indicate with whom these incidents occurred (other inmates, groups of inmates, visitors, and/or correctional staff), where the sexual incident occurred, if the sexual behavior caused them any concerns about contracting HIV. They were also asked if they used any type of protection during the reported sexual encounter. For the bartered sex section, we also identified various reasons for participating in bartered sex, including the wish to obtain money or commissary goods, to gain protection, to obtain drugs or alcohol, to get privileges from correctional staff, to repay a debt, to belong to a group or gang, to increase power and standing, and/or to obtain assistance with household activities such as laundry and cleaning. The SAP was scored by indicating the presence or absence of any of the non-contact items ($N = 8$) or any of the contact items ($N = 8$) separately for each type of sex (consensual, bartered, victimization, coerced).

The eight types of non-contact sex included:

- Cat-calls, whistling
- Sexual comments
- Standing close or sitting close
- Looking while naked or partially dressed
- Patting, rubbing, stroking non-sexual body parts
- Asking about sexual experiences
- Telling about sex life
- Sexual letters

The eight types of contact sex included:

- Sexual kissing
- Removing clothes for sexual reasons
- Exposing sexual body parts
- Patting, rubbing sexual body parts
- Watching masturbation
- Oral sex
- Vaginal penetration and inanimate object penetration
- Anal penetration and inanimate object penetration

As derived from the SAP, there were five outcome variables. Bartered sex and consensual sex were created by summing the 16 contact and noncontact items listed above. One additional item was used to measure sexual predation and sexual victimization: Comments about one's sexual orientation. Therefore, sexual predation and sexual victimization are comprised of 17 items. In addition to predatory, victimized, bartered, and consensual sex, we created a variable labeled any-sex, which was defined as any endorsement on any of the previous four variables. This allowed a comparison of those who experienced any form of sex while incarcerated with those who did not.

Onsite Inmate File Review

In addition to the clinical interview and the self-report instrumentation, undergraduate research assistants reviewed each inmate's prison files while the clinical interview was being conducted in another area of the prison. This review was conducted using a specially designed Access database on laptop computers and was designed to collect objective information on the inmate's past criminal history, institutional adjustment, and behavioral observations relevant to the various structured risk instruments (such as the PCL-R 2, HCR-20, and VRAG). It also provided us with information about each inmate's height, weight, and age, three physical characteristics that have been associated with patterns of victimization and predation, particularly in male prisons. As part of the file review, we coded each institutional infraction as violent, non-violent, rule, or sexual, and used these in compiling our composite measures of prison violence and prison sexual activity. Inmate files, which included a presentence report, were rich auxiliary information whereas those lacking this type of summary report were sparse and left us unsure whether we were encountering missing data or the real absence of some behavioral index. We tried to combat this problem by creating composite variables for our most central criterion variables and used multiple sources for coding the presence or absence of some variables. For example, an inmate was coded as having experienced a violent past offense if this was indicated in his prison file, in the prison database, if it was reported during the clinical interview, or if it was included in the self-report criminal history instrument created for use in the study.

Statewide Prison Database

Our data collection was further enriched using data derived directly from the databases maintained statewide by the Ohio Department of Rehabilitation and Correction and the Texas Department of Criminal Justice. These statewide databases were initially used to construct the random sample used in both states, and later became the source of the most accurate information about each inmate's most serious current charge, prior incarcerations, maximum and minimum length of sentence, status as a convicted sex offender, security status, and designation as a gang member.

Correctional Officer Instrument

The Prison Safety and Security Survey was developed to capture the perceptions, thoughts, beliefs, and experiences of individuals who work daily within the prison environment. The instrument was adapted from the Federal Bureau of Prisons Social Climate Survey. Sixty-six questions were selected from the instrument that captured information of interest to this research. The survey instrument is divided into six sections: demographic information, inmate-on-inmate safety, inmate-on-staff safety, staff-on-staff safety, staff-on-inmate safety, facility ideology regarding safety, and facility design and safety. All responses were forced choice. The survey took approximately ten minutes to complete.

Warden Instrument

A semi-structured interview was designed to capture the warden's philosophy regarding their work as a warden, attitudes towards prison sexual behavior, thoughts regarding important issues surrounding prison sex, estimates of prison sex, what consumes the most resources, prevention efforts, risk factors associated with victimization and perpetration, and the most significant aspect of prison sex. Interviews lasted between 30 and 105 minutes, with a mean of 65 minutes.

Interviewers and Data Collectors

Interviewers were two clinical professors and nine graduate students in clinical psychology. The two professors trained the students in administering the PVRI and other instrumentation. The process of establishing reliability and intercoder reliability is presented in Appendix C. Undergraduate students in psychology were hired to conduct file reviews and were trained by one of the PIs. One of the PIs administered the correctional officer surveys and conducted the warden interviews.

Procedure

Inmates

A pilot test was conducted at one Ohio prison prior to data collection. This experience led to revisions of our protocol, namely shortening the interview and interspersing the self-report instruments throughout the clinical interview.

Each state sent the PIs a list of all inmates currently housed at the institution. From this list, a randomly selected group of inmates was identified based on prior agreements with each institution regarding the maximum number of inmates that could be recruited (see Table 2.1). This list was then returned to the institution. The research staff created a notice that was then presented to the inmates by prison staff two weeks prior to our arrival at the institution. On the day of interviewing, those expressing a willingness to participate were escorted (generally one at a time) to where the interviewers were stationed. Interviewing took place in a variety of locations throughout the prison, but attempts were made to find private places for the interviews. Inmates were told briefly about the study and asked if they would like to proceed. If they declined, a correctional officer would escort the inmate back to their cell. If they agreed, four consent forms approved by the University of Virginia's institutional review board (IRB) and each state's IRB were read to the inmates and signed. Once the consent forms were signed, the interviewer would call the file reviewers in the records room and notify them of the inmate's willingness to participate and the file review (described above) would begin. At the same time, the interview would begin. Interviews lasted approximately three and a half hours. The interview began with benign questions that gradually became more personal. Peppered throughout the interview were breaks for completing various paper and pencil instruments.

When conducting our interviews in these settings, we were tied to the prison schedule as tightly as were the inmates and correctional staff. We had to arrive to begin interviews in the early hours of the morning, meet with correctional officers as they changed shift, and adhere to the rigorous nature of cell count every four hours that the institution undertook ensuring that each inmate could be seen and accounted for in the prison. Each member of the research team had to be escorted if they moved from one area of the prison to another. The length of our protocol also required that we complete a three and a half hour interview in a three and a half hour time slot, while establishing rapport, maintaining the proper boundaries, and eliciting very personal information, at times through plexi-glass shields or amidst wire mesh barriers. At the completion of the interview, inmates were thanked for their participation. The correctional officer was notified and the inmate was escorted back to his or her cell.

After conducting two interviews each day, the interviewers would return to their hotel rooms where the file reviewers would print out and deliver the file reviews for the inmates seen that day, allowing each member of the interview team to complete and recalibrate the answers that had been entered earlier based only on the self-report of each inmate.

Correctional Officers

Participants were anonymous and therefore packets were created with an informed consent notice on the front of the Correctional Officer (CO) survey. The entire packet was placed in a manila envelope that could be sealed to ensure confidentiality. COs at each institution in Ohio were invited to participate. To recruit COs, a PI attended each roll call (e.g., 6 am, 2 pm, 10 pm) over a two day period at each institution and invited all COs on duty to complete the survey. Prison officials assured the research team that this approach would capture the largest majority of correctional officers (e.g., some might be out sick, attending training, etc.). COs were handed the survey packet as they left the room. COs were permitted to complete the surveys while on duty in all but one institution. The PI picked up the completed packets throughout the day at the designated depository or at subsequent roll calls.

Only one group of COs in Texas was recruited. Recruitment and administration occurred during one meeting. COs completed the survey during the meeting and packets were returned within 15 minutes.

Wardens

While the research team was onsite collecting data from inmates and correctional officers, an interview was scheduled with the warden. At the designated time, the Warden's Assistant would escort one of the PIs to meet privately with the warden in his/her office. After the consent form was signed, the interview began. Responses to questions were written on the interview form and later transcribed after returning to the university.

Integrating Information from Multiple Sources

As we have described, data was collected on and from inmates, correctional officers, and wardens. The nature of the data that we collected through this procedure was derived from a number of sources and combined eventually into a singular database that contained over 1,000 variables. However, we used these variables in various ways. For example, data collected from the wardens was certainly used to describe their philosophy, but we also used their responses as a measure of the prison environment. Similarly, for correctional officers the survey provided important information about their perceptions, but also was used as a measure of the prison environment.

Data Analysis

Our data analyses are summarized in the following chapters. In each we follow a similar format. We briefly review the research literature pertaining to each of six primary domains of risk factors including child and adolescent violence and victimization, adult violence, victimization and criminal behavior, sexual behavior and offending, affective and perceptual states, personality, and extant risk instruments. We examine the bivariate empirical relationship between each of the individual variables subsumed in these domains as they are statistically associated with our various outcome measures of sexual violence and victimization. At the end, we integrate the various significant risk markers into classification decision trees pertaining to sexual predation and victimization as reported by male and female inmates in the correctional institutions throughout Ohio and Texas. In constructing the classification trees, we use Chi-Square Automated Interaction Detector (CHAID), an analysis technique that is used to create decision trees. CHAID can be conducted on either continuous or categorical data, though it groups continuous data into homogeneous categories. This method of analysis selects the best predictor variables using a statistical test (Chi-square for categorical and F for continuous, $p < 0.05$ with Bonferroni adjustment) to act as the first node in the tree and repeats this process until a full tree is grown.

Conclusions

Our randomized procedures were successful in producing a sample that was consistent on most demographic variables across the prison-wide population and the randomly selected group of inmates who decided not to participate in our study. For those who did participate in our study, they demonstrated an impressive degree of willingness to complete our battery, telling us of crimes and sexual encounters that had never been reported, and at times calling out the last answers to their interview questions as they were being led away in handcuffs and shackles for count. The use of the triangulated data collection strategy created a rich source of data that is described in detail in the ensuing chapters.

Our sample, itself, held few surprises. It was made up of disadvantaged offenders with limited educational success and unstable family and marital lives. There were greater numbers of black inmates in Ohio and Hispanic inmates in Texas with these minority inmates being overrepresented in each of the two prison systems. In both systems, there were racial differences between the correctional officers and the inmates, with the former having a higher representation of non–minority individuals. There were a number of gender differences also identified over the two states with the female inmates having higher levels of education, more likely being married at the time of their incarceration, and more often having received state support prior to incarceration. The correctional officers tended to be of non-minority status, to have completed some college education, and to be on average around 40 years of age. Most of the correctional officers worked with general population inmates and reported an average contact with 119 inmates each day. The wardens were college educated to varying degrees, had generally worked their way up through the ranks to their position of warden, and had often served for less than five years in their current positions.

Our data collection and analyses reflect our effort to apply all of the known clinical risk markers as identified in the research literature to sexual predation and victimization as experienced by male and female inmates. We identify through this review a large array of risk markers that are organized according to six primary risk domains including early adverse life experiences, prior violence in the community, past arrests and behavior in the institution, sexual risk markers including impersonal sex and hyper sexuality, affective and perceptual states associated with violence, the presence of personality disorders including psychopathy, and extant violence risk instruments. We were able to use this process to develop ten CHAID classification models that predicted for each gender five types of sexual behavior: any-sex, predatory sex, victimized sex, bartered sex, and consensual sex. These models successfully classified inmates with a degree of accuracy that was unexpected given the exploratory nature of our research endeavor.

3

THE SEXUAL BEHAVIOR OF INCARCERATED MEN AND WOMEN

We used five outcome measures in our study derived from the Sexual Aggression in Prison (SAP) instrument. Outcomes included: (1) any-sex, which was defined as any of the following four forms of sexual activity while imprisoned (*any-sex*); (2) the experience of perpetrating coerced sexuality against another person while imprisoned (*predatory sex*); (3) the experience of being victimized sexually by another person while imprisoned (*victimized sex*); (4) the experience of engaging in sexual exchanges with another person that were based on the bartering of goods or protection while imprisoned (*bartered sex*); and (5) involvement in consensual sexual behavior with another person while imprisoned (*consensual sex*). Incidents involving sex while incarcerated could have occurred with inmates, visitors/others, or prison staff. We included the incidents in which the inmates reported consensual involvement with prison staff under the rubric of consensual sex. It was our intent to allow inmates to determine the nature of their relationship with correctional staff, fully acknowledging that such acts are illegal (Hensley, 2002; Saum, Surratt, Inciardi, & Bennett, 1995; Solursh, Solursh, & Meyer, 1993). This decision is supported by the research published by the BJS, which identified two thirds of the staff-on-inmate incidents as being romantic in nature (Beck, Harrison, & Adams, 2007).

Predatory Sexual Activity in Prison

The existing research on rape in prisons tends to ignore the larger body of research pertaining to rape in the community, and through this omission, implies that rape in prison is fundamentally different from the rape individuals experience in the community. Eigenberg (2000) has argued for a deconstruction of these distinctions and for a more rigorous use of the community rape research to inform prison rape research. In this regard, she notes that it can be difficult to determine whether the sexual behavior is coercive or consensual. Researchers have identified three methods used by perpetrators to assault their victims in correctional settings: entrapment, intimidation, and physical force (Eigenberg, 2000; Fishman, 1951; Groth, Burgess, & Holmstrom, 1977; Scacco, 1975; Struckman-Johnson & Struckman-Johnson, 2000; Weiss & Friar, 1974). Eigenberg notes that despite the significance of these different forms of coercion in many correctional settings, only incidents involving physical force tend to be investigated and catalogued as *real* incidents of sexual assault or rape.

In attempting to explain the intent of sexual assaults in prison, Groth et al. (1977) reported that sexual gratification is but one reason for a sexual assault. Other motivations include: a need to acquire status and affiliation, to protect oneself from victimization, to take revenge and retaliation, repayment, to dominate (i.e., conquest and control of others), to release pent up emotions, sadism and denigration, and conflict and counteraction (Chonco, 1989; Groth et al., 1977). More recently, Knowles (1999) has offered a review of the prison rape literature and concluded that sexual violence is used primarily as a means to establish or maintain power within the institution.

In 2005, the BJS released their first study of sexual violence identified through a national review of administrative records in adult (and juvenile) correctional facilities (Beck & Hughes, 2005). They defined four different measures of sexual violence as informed by the definition of rape included in the PREA. These included inmate-on-inmate non-consensual sexual acts, inmate-on-inmate abusive sexual contacts, staff-on-inmate sexual misconduct, and staff-on-inmate sexual harassment. Using officially reported allegations of sexual misconduct identified in 2004, Beck and Hughes (2005) determined that there were 8,210 allegations of sexual violence reported nationwide during that year and that 2,100 of these allegations were substantiated, a rate that reflected 30 percent of the completed investigations. Of the reported allegations, 42 percent involved staff misconduct, 37 percent involved inmate-on-inmate non-consensual sexual acts, 11 percent involved staff sexual harassment, and 10 percent involved inmate-on-inmate abusive sexual contact. They found that in state prisons 69 percent of the victims of staff sexual misconduct were male while 67 percent of the perpetrators were female. In jails, the reverse was found to be true, with 70 percent of the victims being female and 65 percent of the perpetrators being male. While not explicitly stated, the data appeared to reflect primarily heterosexual exchanges between staff and inmates.

In 2006, Beck and Harrison reported on a second wave of national survey data. The second study expanded the data collection to include specific information pertaining to each of the substantiated incidents. Physical force or the threat of physical force was used in about half of the incidents of inmate-on-inmate sexual violence and in about one third of the incidents of inmate-on-inmate non-consensual sexual acts. In one sixth of the incidents, the victim was physically injured. Half of the victims of non-consensual sexual acts were placed in protective custody or administrative segregation and most inmate perpetrators received legal sanctions or solitary confinement. Surprising at the time was the finding that two thirds of the incidents of staff misconduct were reported to be romantic in nature, with only 15 percent of these incidents involving physical force, the abuse of power, or pressure by the staff member.

In 2007, a third wave of administrative data submitted to BJS determined that most reported allegations in state and federal prisons were closed as unsubstantiated (55%) or unfounded (29%). Of those incidents that were substantiated, multiple victims were reported in 4 percent to 8 percent of the incidents and multiple perpetrators in 7 percent to 10 percent of the incidents. Both the perpetrators (85%) and victims (92%) of inmate-on-inmate sexual violence were most frequently male. The victims tended to be younger and under the age of 24 years; the majority of perpetrators were older and over the age of 25 years. Correctional authorities reported that physical force or threat of force was used in more than half of the substantiated incidents of inmate-on-inmate sexual violence. The inmates who were victimized reported anal or vaginal tearing, knife or stab wounds, broken bones, chipped or knocked out teeth, internal injuries, black eyes, sprains, cuts, scratches, swelling, and welts (Beck & Harrison, 2008).

Study Results: Sexual Predation

Table 3.1 summarizes the actual predatory behaviors reported by this cohort of male and female inmates. These data indicate, not unexpectedly, that non-contact predatory sexual acts (36.8% of males and 4.3% of females) are more common than contact predatory sexual acts (8.3% of males and 0% of females), a difference that is particularly pronounced among the male inmates. For the male inmates using non-contact predatory sexual acts, they most frequently used cat-calls, sexual comments, and sexual orientation comments, to create a certain type of intrusive form of sexual coercion with others. Exposure was the most frequently reported way of forcing a sexual experience upon another, an experience that is viewed as humiliating and demeaning to the observer. The two male inmates who reported the most aggressive types of sexual behavior describe combinations of oral sex and both forced vaginal intercourse with women, and forced anal intercourse with men, behavior that they recount as having occurred on numerous occasions with multiple victims. The women reported only non-contact sexual predation that most frequently included cat-calls, sexual comments about another's body, sexual orientation comments, and looking at partially clothed or naked inmates. In all eight categories where significant gender differences emerged, more male inmates reported engaging in the sexual behavior than did the female inmates.

Table 3.2 summarizes the rates of sexual predation self-reported by the male and female inmates for each victim category. Male inmates engaged in predatory sex involving other inmates, with 4.5 percent reporting non-contact predatory sex and 0.3 percent reporting contact predatory sex. The female inmates reported

TABLE 3.1 Frequency of Predatory Acts while in Prison Reported by Incarcerated Men (N=288) and Women (N=183) while in Prison

Type of Act	Men		Women		Effect Size	
	N	(%)	N	(%)	χ^2	Φ
Non-Contact Predatory Sexual Acts						
Cat-calls/whistling	28	9.7	3	1.6	11.89★★	−0.16★★
Sexual comments/body	21	7.3	2	1.1	9.26★★	−0.14★★
Sexual orientation comments	19	6.6	2	1.1	7.96★★	−0.13★★
Physical proximity/unwanted	6	2.1	0	0.0	3.86★	−0.09★
Looking at partially clothed/naked	6	2.1	1	0.5	1.81	−0.06
Patting/rubbing/stroking	7	2.4	0	0.0	4.52★	−0.10★
Asking sexual experiences/unwanted	8	2.8	0	0.0	5.17★	−0.11★
Telling sexual experiences/unwanted	6	2.1	0	0.0	3.86★	−0.09
Receiving sexual letters/unwanted	5	1.7	0	0.0	3.21	−0.08
Contact Predatory Sexual Acts						
Sexual kissing/unwanted	4	1.4	0	0.0	2.56	−0.07
Exposing body part/unwanted	11	3.8	0	0.0	7.16★★	−0.12★★
Remove clothes/forced	3	1.0	0	0.0	1.92	−0.06
Sexual patting/rubbing/unwanted	0	0.0	0	0.0	1.92	−0.06
Watching masturbation/unwanted	0	0.0	0	0.0	1.92	−0.06
Oral sex/unwanted	2	0.7	0	0.0	1.28	−0.05
Vaginal penetration/unwanted	2	0.7	0	0.0	1.28	−0.05
Anal penetration/unwanted	2	0.7	0	0.0	1.28	−0.05

Note. ★p < 0.05, ★★p < 0.01.

lower, albeit not significantly lower, levels both of non-contact sexual predation (2.7%) and contact sexual predation (0%) against another inmate.

Male inmates engaged in predatory sex with visitors/others, with 9.7 percent reporting non-contact predatory sex and 4.2 percent reporting contact predatory sex. The female inmates reported significantly lower levels both of non-contact sexual predation (1.1%) and contact sexual predation (0%) against visitors/others.

Male inmates engaged in predatory sex involving staff, with 8.7 percent reporting non-contact predatory sex and 2.8 percent reporting contact predatory sex. The female inmates reported significantly lower levels both of non-contact sexual predation (1.1%) and contact sexual predation (0%) against staff.

Cumulatively, 11.5 percent of male inmates reported having perpetrated non-contact predatory sex and 4.2 percent reported contact predatory sex. Cumulatively, the female inmates reported significantly lower levels both of non-contact sexual predation (2.7%) and contact sexual predation (0%). Extrapolated to a national population, these results suggest that our prison system currently houses 61,225 male inmates who are willing to self-report contact sexual predation.

Inmates who reported sexual predation were asked a number of questions

TABLE 3.2 Frequency of Sexual Predation while in Prison Reported by Incarcerated Men (N=288) and Women (N=183)

	Men		Women		Effect Size	
Against Inmates	N	(%)	N	(%)	χ^2	Φ
Any non-contact sex acts	13	4.5	5	2.7	0.97	−0.05
Any contact sex acts	1	0.3	0	0.0	0.64	−0.04
	M	SD	M	SD	T	
Count of non-contact sex acts	0.13	0.77	0.04	0.29	1.68	
Count of contact sex acts	0.01	0.12	0.00	0.00	0.80	
Against Visitors/Others	N	(%)	N	(%)	χ^2	Φ
Any non-contact sex acts	28	9.7	2	1.1	13.97***	−0.17***
Any contact sex acts	12	4.2	0	0.0	7.82**	−0.13**
	M	SD	M	SD	T	
Count of non-contact sex acts	0.35	1.67	0.01	0.10	3.44***	
Count of contact sex acts	0.10	0.68	0.00	0.00	2.44***	
Against Staff	N	(%)	N	(%)	χ^2	Φ
Any non-contact sex acts	25	8.7	2	1.1	11.92***	−0.16***
Any contact sex acts	8	2.8	0	0.0	5.17*	−0.11*
	M	SD	M	SD	T	
Count of non-contact sex acts	0.22	0.89	0.01	0.10	3.21***	
Count of contact sex acts	0.03	0.19	0.00	0.00	2.74**	
Cumulative Total	N	(%)	N	(%)	χ^2	Φ
Any non-contact sex acts	33	11.5	5	2.7	11.48**	−0.16**
Any contact sex acts	12	4.2	0	0.0	7.82**	−0.13**
Any non-contact or contact sex acts	35	12.2	5	2.7	12.78**	−0.17**
	M	SD	M	SD	T	
Count of non-contact sex acts	0.48	1.92	0.06	0.41	3.66***	
Count of contact sex acts	0.10	0.74	0.00	0.00	2.38*	
Count of any non-contact or contact sex acts	0.58	2.37	0.06	0.34	2.96**	

Note. *$p < 0.05$, **$p < 0.01$, ***$p < 0.001$.

about their predatory sexual behavior (see Table 3.3). Male inmates primarily described bribing other inmates for sexual contact. Their motivation included engaging in a predatory sexual act as a form of sexual release, as an opportunity to gain status, and to get something that they wanted. The one woman who responded to this question reported humiliation as the motivation for predatory sex. Male inmates indicated that they considered the race, age, and size of the person that they chose to victimize and experienced no negative outcome as a result of their predatory actions. Of the twelve male inmates who reported contact predatory

TABLE 3.3 Frequency of Methods and Motives for Coerced Sex in Prison Reported by Predatory Males (*N*=35) and Predatory Females (*N*=5)

Item	Men		Women		Effect Size	
	N	(%)	N	(%)	χ^2	Φ
Techniques Used to Force Sex						
Bribe	3	8.6	0	0.0	0.46	−0.11
Blackmail	0	0.0	0	0.0	—	—
Love withdrawal	0	0.0	0	0.0	—	—
Drunk/stoned	0	0.0	0	0.0	—	—
Threatened harm	0	0.0	0	0.0	—	—
Used size to threaten	0	0.0	0	0.0	—	—
Physically held down	0	0.0	0	0.0	—	—
Physically harmed person	0	0.0	0	0.0	—	—
Used a weapon	0	0.0	0	0.0	—	—
Motivations for Forcing Sex in Prison						
Sexual release	2	5.7	0	0.0	0.30	−0.09
Increase status in group	1	2.9	0	0.0	0.15	−0.06
Force inmates to leave alone	0	0.0	0	0.0	—	—
Punishment	0	0.0	0	0.0	—	—
Anger and rage	0	0.0	0	0.0	—	—
Humiliate another	0	0.0	1	20.0	7.12	0.42
Get something	1	2.9	0	0.0	0.15	−0.06
Gang activity	0	0.0	0	0.0	—	—
Jealously	0	0.0	0	0.0	—	—
Victim Choice Strategies						
Considered race	4	11.4	0	0.0	0.64	−0.13
Considered age	3	8.6	0	0.0	0.46	−0.11
Considered size	2	5.7	0	0.0	0.30	−0.09
Outcome of Coercion						
No bad outcome	3	8.6	0	0.0	0.46	−0.11
Prison infraction	0	0.0	0	0.0	—	—
Prison segregation	0	0.0	0	0.0	—	—
Sexual payback from inmate	0	0.0	0	0.0	—	—
Physical payback from inmate	0	0.0	0	0.0	—	—
Correctional payback	0	0.0	0	0.0	—	—
Concerned about HIV	5	14.3	1	20.0	1.10	−0.30
Used protection	3	8.6	1	20.0	1.14	−0.38

behavior, five reported concerns about HIV infection and three of these five individuals reported using some type of protection. With the exception noted above, none of the five female inmates who reported predatory sexual behavior completed these sections of the SAP, although one did express concerns about HIV infection and indicated that she used protection during her sexual contact.

Sexual Victimization in Prison

Starting in the late 1960s, researchers attempted to estimate the number of inmates who experienced some form of sexual assault in prison. These estimates were found to vary widely over the next 40 years, a fact that may be attributed to evolving prison philosophies and changing inmate and staff characteristics. Eight years ago when the PREA legislation was first passed, Dumond (2003) calculated that there were approximately 20 published epidemiological studies on prison rape reported in the past 35 years, with fewer than four of them including data on women.

The earliest study on the incidence of sexual coercion in prison was conducted by Davis (1968) in the late 1960s. Davis reported that 3 percent of inmates in the Philadelphia jail system had been sexually assaulted by another inmate over a two-year period. Later, Lockwood (1980) concluded from his research in the New York state prison system that 28 percent of inmates had been sexually victimized by another inmate, with about 1.3 percent of inmates experiencing a rape. He reported that the targets of sexual violence tended to be new to the facility, to have a weak public image, and to be considered attractive by other inmates. Three years later, Nacci and Kane (1983) reported that 2 percent of the inmates in their sample experienced unwanted sexual contact (forced or attempted force), with 0.3 percent reporting a completed rape.

Struckman-Johnson, Struckman-Johnson, Rucker, Bumby, and Donaldson (1996) were the first to estimate the number of sexual assaults experienced by female inmates and later reported between 0 percent and 27 percent of women in three Midwestern prisons had been sexually coerced (Struckman-Johnson & Struckman-Johnson, 2002). Rape reportedly ranged from 0 percent to 3 percent among women in these three institutions, differences attributable in part to differences in institutional characteristics. Surprisingly, these estimates are consistent with the estimates for male inmates reported in the previous research.

In 2003, PREA stated that 13 percent of inmates had been sexually victimized while incarcerated. This estimate was the impetus for the National Institute of Justice to conduct an exhaustive review of the incidence and prevalence research concerning sexual violence in prisons. Gaes and Goldberg (2004) concluded that approximately 2 percent of inmates experienced rape while incarcerated. When sexual pressure was included in the definition, the lifetime prevalence rate of sexual assault among inmates rose to 21 percent.

Following this review, Wolff, Blitz, Shi, Bachman, and Siegel (2006) completed a quality of life survey of 6,000 inmates in a single state in the US. As part of the survey, they asked inmates what they thought made another inmate vulnerable to sexual victimization. The majority of the inmates reported that an inmate who was homosexual, weak, small, a pretty boy, or had a prior offense that involved a child or intimate partner placed them at a higher risk for sexual victimization. The following year, Wolff, Blitz, Siegel, and Bachman (2007) reported on a single state, audio computer assisted survey instruments (CASI) survey of 7,785 inmates using questions from the National Violence against Women and Men Survey to query inmates about their experience of sexual assault over the previous six months. They found that 2 percent of inmates reported sexual victimization over a six- to nine-month period. Wolff et al. (2007) contrasted these rates to those in the general population where it is estimated that 0.2 percent to 0.9 percent experience sexual assault over a 12-month period. The risk for sexual victimization in prison was higher among female inmates who had experienced sexual abuse prior to the age of 18 years and who reported believing that gang activity was high in their particular institution.

In 2007 and 2008, the BJS released their study of self-reported sexual victimization in prisons and jails nationwide (Beck & Harrison, 2007, 2008). Both surveys used Audio-CASI technology. The first inmate survey included 23,398 prisoners housed in 46 state and federal prisons. Among the prison sample, Beck and Harrison (2007) found that 1,109 inmates reported one or more incidents of sexual victimization. When estimated totals were calculated, Beck and Harrison concluded that 2.1 percent of inmates reported incidents of sexual victimization involving other inmates and 2.9 percent reported an incident involving staff. For inmates reporting sexual victimization by another inmate, 1.3 percent of the inmates reported non-consensual sex involving giving or receiving oral, anal or vaginal sex, and 0.8 percent reported abusive sexual contact involving unwanted touching of specific body parts in a sexual way. For inmates reporting sexual misconduct by staff, equal proportions of inmates reported unwilling (1.7%) and willing (1.7%) contact with prison staff. Most inmates sexually involved with prison staff reported sexual contacts that were more intimate than simple sexual touching. Again, 58 percent of the staff involved in staff-on-inmate sexual misconduct were female and 65 percent of the inmates involved in staff-on-inmate sexual misconduct were male. Rates of sexual victimization varied across the institutions with three prisons in three different states reporting staff sexual misconduct that exceeded 10 percent.

Study Results: Sexual Victimization

As summarized in Table 3.4, 12.5 percent of male inmates reported non-contact sexual victimization by another inmate and 5.9 percent reported contact sexual victimization by another inmate. The female inmates reported significantly higher levels of non-contact sexual victimization (22.4%), but not significantly higher levels of contact sexual victimization (6.6%) perpetrated by another inmate.

Male inmates were the victims of coerced sexual acts by visitors/others, with 1.4 percent reporting non-contact sexual victimization and 1.0 percent reporting contact sexual victimization. The female inmates reported similarly low levels of non-contact sexual victimization (2.7%) and contact sexual victimization (0.0%) perpetrated by visitors/others.

Male inmates were the victims of coerced sexual behavior by staff, with 6.6 percent reporting non-contact sexual victimization and 2.4 percent reporting contact sexual victimization. The female inmates reported similar levels of non-contact sexual victimization (11.5%) and contact sexual victimization (2.7%)

TABLE 3.4 Frequency of Sexual Victimization while in Prison Reported by Incarcerated Men (*N*=288) and Women (*N*=183)

	Men		Women		Effect Size	
By Inmates	N	(%)	N	(%)	χ^2	Φ
Any non-contact sex acts	36	12.5	41	22.4	8.03**	−0.13**
Any contact sex acts	17	5.9	12	6.6	0.08	0.01
	M	(SD)	M	(SD)	T	
Count of non-contact sex acts	0.57	1.93	0.91	2.07	−1.75	
Count of contact sex acts	0.18	0.89	0.11	0.48	1.02	
By Visitors/Others	N	(%)	N	(%)	χ^2	Φ
Any non-contact sex acts	4	1.4	5	2.7	1.08	0.05
Any contact sex acts	3	1.0	0	0.0	1.92	−0.06
	M	(SD)	M	(SD)	T	
Count of non-contact sex acts	0.07	0.68	0.03	0.17	0.75	
Count of contact sex acts	0.06	0.67	0.00	0.00	1.50	
By Staff	N	(%)	N	(%)	χ^2	Φ
Any non-contact sex acts	19	6.6	21	11.5	3.43	0.09
Any contact sex acts	7	2.4	5	2.7	0.04	0.01
	M	(SD)	M	(SD)	T	
Count of non-contact sex acts	0.20	0.95	0.35	1.09	−1.48	
Count of contact sex acts	0.04	0.34	0.05	0.35	0.23	
Cumulative Total	N	(%)	N	(%)	χ^2	Φ
Any non-contact sex acts	38	13.2	42	23.0	7.55**	0.13**
Any contact sex acts	19	6.6	12	6.6	< 0.01	< 0.01
Any non-contact or contact sex acts	44	15.3	49	26.8	9.34*	0.14*
	M	(SD)	M	(SD)	T	
Count of non-contact sex acts	0.64	2.07	0.94	2.14	−1.49	
Count of contact sex acts	0.23	1.11	0.11	0.48	1.66	
Count of any non-contact or contact sex acts	1.12	3.72	1.45	3.09	−0.98	

Note. * *p* < 0.05, ** *p* < 0.01.

perpetrated by staff. Our data concerning sexual contact that was perceived by the recipient as coercive in nature was higher than that found in the national survey conducted by the BJS (Beck & Harrison, 2007, 2008).

Cumulatively, 13.2 percent of male inmates reported non-contact sexual victimization and 6.6 percent reported contact sexual victimization. Cumulatively, the female inmates reported significantly higher levels of non-contact sexual victimization (23.0%), but not significantly higher levels of contact sexual victimization (6.6%).

The male and female inmates were asked a number of additional questions about their victimization (see Table 3.5). Approximately one quarter of the

TABLE 3.5 Frequency of the Location and Response to Sexual Victimization while in Prison Reported by Incarcerated Men (N=44) and Women (N=49)

Item	Men		Women		χ^2	Φ
	N	(%)	N	(%)		
Victimization in Prison	12	27.3	14	28.6	0.02	0.01
Location of Sexual Victimization						
Cell or dormitory	30	68.2	20	40.8	6.98★★	−0.27★★
Chapel	3	6.8	1	2.0	1.29	−0.10★
Educational area	1	2.3	1	2.0	0.01	−0.01
Counseling/administrative offices	0	0.0	1	2.0	0.91	0.10
Dining hall	0	0.0	3	6.1	2.78	0.17
Recreational area	1	2.3	1	2.0	0.01	−0.01
Showers	15	34.1	19	38.8	0.22	0.05
Workplace	6	13.6	4	8.2	0.72	−0.10
Reporting of Victimization	11	27.5	8	18.6	0.93	0.11
Reported To						
Other inmate	3	6.8	5	10.2	0.34	0.06
Correctional officer	9	20.5	2	4.2	5.96★	−0.25★
Prison official	3	6.8	3	6.1	0.02	−0.01
Outside person	1	2.3	4	8.2	1.58	0.13
Other	3	6.8	1	2.0	1.29	−0.12
Attempts to Avoid Future Victimization						
Report of correctional officer	4	9.1	2	4.1	0.96	−0.10
Assistance from inmate	2	4.5	4	8.2	0.50	0.07
Avoid perpetrator	20	45.5	32	65.3	3.71	0.20
Fight back physically	12	27.3	1	2.0	12.27★★	−0.36★★
Start rumors about perpetrator	1	2.3	0	0.0	1.13	−0.11
Arrange other payback	2	4.5	0	0.0	2.28	−0.16
Join a gang	1	2.3	0	0.0	1.13	−0.11
Join a religious group	3	6.8	2	4.1	0.34	−0.06

Note. ★$p < 0.05$, ★★$p < 0.01$.

male victims and one quarter of the female victims reported a prior sexual victimization in prison, a proportion that suggests that the vulnerability to sexual victimization is cumulative at least for some inmates. For both genders, the most common location for the victimization was in the cell or dormitory where the inmate resided, although this location was significantly higher for male inmates. Showers were the next most common location but did not differ statistically between genders. These two locations highlight the problems with external regulation if the inmate chooses not to report the incident to the prison officials. The residential area is by definition often unsupervised and unmonitored whereas the shower areas can be monitored only by eradicating any sense of privacy for both the male and female inmates involved in these self-care activities.

Our data suggest that most incidents of perceived victimization did go unreported. Only approximately one quarter of the male inmates and one tenth of the female inmates reported their perceived victimization to a correctional officer or a prison official. Male inmates most frequently reported an incident to correctional officers, a prison official, or another inmate, although they were significantly more likely than female inmates to report sexual victimization to correctional officers. Female inmates most frequently reported an incident to another inmate or an outside person, although not significantly more frequently than male inmates. For both sexes the inmates seemed most motivated to try and avoid further victimization through their own efforts. For the male inmates, this involved trying to avoid the perpetrator or fighting back physically. Significantly more male than female inmates reported fighting back physically. For the female inmates this overwhelmingly involved trying to avoid the perpetrator, although not significantly more so than male inmates.

Bartered Sexual Behavior in Prison

We found in conducting our study that bartered sex was frequently mentioned and openly discussed in the various prisons. In both male and female prisons, those inmates who were often referred to as "commissary bunnies" were described as selling sex for money and other commodities that they wanted and could not obtain through other means. The 2006 BJS study reported that in 30 percent of the substantiated inmate-on-inmate incidents, victims were talked into the encounter, and in 7 percent of the incidents the victim was offered protection, bribed, or blackmailed into compliance.

In her writing, Smith (2006) identified trade as one of seven motivations that prompt sexual behavior in prison. She observed that scarce items (potato chips, cigarettes, telephone calls) become extremely valuable and fuel an underground economy for those with limited resources. Ristroph (2006) similarly argues that many prison inmates consent to sex not because of fear but rather due to a wish for money, drugs, food, and comfort. Kunselman, Tewksbury, Dumond, and Dumond (2002), however, underscore the more coercive interpretation of this type of exchange, observing that they are "anything but consensual" and that the majority of these inmates would never consent to such interactions outside the coercive conditions of incarceration (p. 29).

Study Results: Bartered Sex

Table 3.6 summarizes data concerning bartered sex as described by the inmates in our sample. Male inmates participated in bartered sexual behavior with another inmate, with 2.4 percent reporting non-contact bartered sex and 2.4 percent reporting contact bartered sex. The female inmates reported significantly higher levels of non-contact bartered sex (6.0%), but not significantly higher levels of contact bartered sex (3.8%) with another inmate.

Male inmates participated in bartered sexual behavior with visitors/others, with 6.6 percent reporting non-contact bartered sex and 3.5 percent reporting

TABLE 3.6 Frequency of Bartered Sexual Acts while in Prison Reported by Incarcerated Men (N=288) and Women (N=183)

	Men		Women		Effect Size	
With Inmates	N	(%)	N	(%)	χ^2	Φ
Any non-contact sex acts	7	2.4	11	6.0	3.90★	0.09★
Any contact sex acts	7	2.4	7	3.8	0.76	0.04
	M	(SD)	M	(SD)	t	
Count of non-contact sex acts	0.14	0.94	0.16	0.78	−0.35	
Count of contact sex acts	0.10	0.78	0.07	0.45	0.59	
With Visitors/Others	N	(%)	N	(%)	χ^2	Φ
Any non-contact sex acts	19	6.6	3	1.6	6.18★	−0.12★
Any contact sex acts	10	3.5	1	0.5	4.19★	−0.09★
	M	(SD)	M	(SD)	t	
Count of non-contact sex acts	0.24	1.17	0.03	0.31	2.85★★	
Count of contact sex acts	0.15	0.90	0.01	0.07	2.69★★	
With Staff	N	(%)	N	(%)	χ^2	Φ
Any non-contact sex acts	28	9.7	7	3.8	5.66★	−0.11★
Any contact sex acts	23	8.0	2	1.1	10.58★★	−0.15★★
	M	(SD)	M	(SD)	t	
Count of non-contact sex acts	0.34	1.26	0.09	0.56	2.91★★	
Count of contact sex acts	0.26	1.12	0.01	0.10	3.82★★	
Cumulative Total	N	(%)	N	(%)	χ^2	Φ
Any non-contact sex acts	36	12.5	15	8.2	2.15	−0.07
Any contact sex acts	29	10.1	9	4.9	4.00★	−0.09★
Any non-contact or contact sex acts	37	12.8	18	9.8	0.98	−0.05
	M	(SD)	M	(SD)	t	
Count of non-contact sex acts	0.71	2.61	0.29	1.30	2.32★	
Count of contact sex acts	0.52	2.10	0.09	0.47	3.35★★	
Count of any non-contact or contact sex acts	1.24	4.61	0.38	1.69	2.85★★	

Note. ★$p < 0.05$, ★★$p < 0.01$.

contact bartered sex. The female inmates reported significantly lower levels of both non-contact bartered sex (1.6%) and contact bartered sex (0.5%) with visitors/others.

Male inmates participated in bartered sexual behavior with staff, with 9.7 percent reporting non-contact bartered sex and 8.0 percent reporting contact bartered sex. The female inmates reported significantly lower levels both of non-contact bartered sex (3.8%) and contact bartered sex (1.1%) with staff.

Cumulatively, male inmates participated in bartered sexual behavior, with 12.5 percent reporting non-contact bartered sex and 10.1 percent reporting contact

TABLE 3.7 Frequency of Type of Commodity Sought through Bartered Sexual Acts by Men (N=37) and Women (N=18) and Concerns about HIV while in Prison

Commodity	Men		Women		Effect size	
	N	(%)	N	(%)	χ^2	Φ
Money/goods/canteen	12	40.0	2	4.3	2.91	−0.26
Protection	2	7.1	1	7.1	< 0.01	< 0.01
Drugs/alcohol	7	25.0	1	7.1	1.93	−0.21
Privileges from staff	14	50.0	1	7.1	7.47**	−0.42**
Repay debt	3	11.1	0	0.0	1.56	−0.20
Belong to group/gang	2	8.0	1	7.1	0.01	−0.02
Increase power/status	7	26.9	2	14.3	0.83	−0.14
Assistance in tasks/cleaning/laundry	3	12.0	1	7.1	0.23	−0.08
Other	16	5.6	9	4.9	0.10	−0.01
Concerned about HIV	13	52.0	4	33.3	1.14	0.18
Used protection	8	47.4	2	20.0	2.08	0.27

Note. **p < 0.01.

bartered sex. Cumulatively, the female inmates reported similar levels of non-contact bartered sex (8.2%), but significantly lower levels of contact bartered sex (4.9%).

Table 3.7 summarizes data concerning the goals or purpose of the bartered sexual behavior. When asked about the commodity that they sought through the offering of sexual favors, the male inmates most frequently mentioned seeking privileges from staff, money/goods/canteen from inmates, an increase in power and status, and drugs or alcohol. The data concerning the female inmates was limited, but suggested that they most often wanted to enhance their power and status within the social milieu, and, to a lesser extent, were interested in obtaining protection, drugs and alcohol, privileges from staff, group affiliation, and assistance with their cleaning and tasks of daily living. The only gender difference to emerge revealed that male inmates were significantly more likely than female inmates to seek privileges from prison staff (50.0% of males and 7.1% of females). Among these two groups, there were concerns expressed about HIV infection with approximately half of the male inmates and approximately one third of the female inmates reporting concerns about infection. Nearly half of male inmates and one fifth of female inmates reported that they did use some type of protection during the sexual contact that occurred.

Consensual Sexual Behavior in Prison

There has been relatively little research concerning consensual sex in prison, particularly as it pertains to male inmates. Currently, prison regulations define sex between inmates as a higher-tier infraction that is punishable by a variety of sanctions including segregation and movement to another unit or institution. Sex between an inmate and member of the correctional staff is a felony offense in each of the 50 states. This stance of zero tolerance reflects a sustained commitment to maintaining safety and order within this type of institution and the belief that sexual activity, if sanctioned, would contribute to instability, unrest, and a compromised ability of the staff to maintain control over the inmates (Hensley, 2002; Saum et al., 1995; Solursh et al., 1993). Feminist scholars point to the coercive, non-egalitarian, and hierarchical nature of the prison environment, and argue that these elements of its structure erode the ability of any individual situated within it to give consent to a sexual interchange or encounter (Ristroph, 2006).

Koscheski, Hensley, Wright, and Tewskbury (2002) note that prior to 2002 only six studies had addressed consensual sex among male prison inmates despite the awareness of this type of encounter being quite common (Hensley, 2001; Hensley, Tewksbury & Wright, 2001; Nacci & Kane, 1983; Saum et al., 1995; Tewksbury, 1989a; Wooden & Parker, 1982). For example, Tewksbury (1989a) studied 150 inmates in a male Ohio prison and found that between 25 percent and 40 percent of male inmates engaged in consensual sexual activity while incarcerated. Of these inmates, 20 percent had engaged in homosexual behavior during the previous year, with 8.5 percent of these inmates engaging in sexual activity with another person once a week or more. More recently, Hensley (2001) conducted interviews with 174 male inmates in Oklahoma. These inmates reported engaging in a number of behaviors such as kissing another inmate (8%), rubbing their body parts against an inmate (23%), allowing an inmate to touch their penis in a sexual way (24%), and engaging in anal intercourse with another inmate (20%).

Because staff-on-inmate sex is forbidden in the correctional setting, there are no studies directly examining consensual sexual activity between staff and inmates. Beck, Harrison, and Adams (2007) reported that the inmates "appeared to be willing" in 62 percent of the substantiated incidents of staff sexual misconduct and harassment in prisons. In this review, a member of staff was found to be involved with more than one inmate in 18 percent of the incidents and more than one member of staff involved with a single inmate in 2 percent of the incidents. These incidents did not go without consequences. In 2006, three quarters of the staff perpetrators lost their jobs and 56 percent were arrested or referred for prosecution. Half of the inmates involved in staff sexual misconduct were transferred or placed in segregation.

There was an assumption in the early research on incarcerated female sexual behavior that sex between women was consensual (Hensley, Struckman-Johnson, & Eigenberg, 2000). In a sample of females in a juvenile institution, Halleck and Hersko (1962) found that 69 percent of their sample engaged in "girl stuff," behavior ranging from kissing to genital contact. Only 9 percent of these girls reported "girl stuff" prior to incarceration. Similarly, Giallombardo (1966) found that 86 percent of the women in their study had engaged in homosexual activity while incarcerated, although only 5 percent had practiced homosexuality prior to incarceration.

Giallombardo noted that 21 percent of the females described their homosexual relationships as voluntary, explaining that the relationship provided them with love, affection, and companionship.

The most recent research on women (Greer, 2000) suggests that this scenario might be changing. Greer found that only five of the 35 women interviewed were engaging in a sexual relationship, with the majority of women considering themselves to be loners. Hensley, Tewksbury, and Koscheski (2002) sought to explore the predictors of female same-sex encounters and found that being under the age of 34 years and being incarcerated for longer periods of time were the primary factors associated with same-sex encounters.

Study Results: Consensual Sex

As presented in Table 3.8, male inmates engaged in consensual sexual behavior with another inmate, with 14.2 percent reporting non–contact consensual sex and 5.9 percent reporting contact consensual sex. The female inmates reported significantly higher levels both of non–contact consensual sex (39.3%) and contact consensual sex (26.2%) with another inmate.

Male inmates engaged in consensual sexual behavior with visitors/others, with 33.3 percent reporting non–contact consensual sex and 19.4 percent reporting contact consensual sex. The female inmates reported significantly lower levels both of non–contact consensual sex (15.3%) and contact consensual sex (3.8%) with visitors/others.

Male inmates participated in consensual sexual behavior with staff, with 24.3 percent reporting non–contact consensual sex and 17.4 percent reporting contact consensual sex. The female inmates reported significantly lower levels both of non–contact consensual sex (13.7%) and contact consensual sex (2.7%) with staff.

Cumulatively, male inmates participated in consensual sexual behavior with 43.4 percent reporting non–contact consensual sex and 30.6 percent reporting contact consensual sex, rates that did not differ significantly for female inmates who reported similar cumulative levels both of non–contact consensual sex (45.9%) and contact consensual sex (29.5%).

Viewed most broadly, these self-reported endorsements of consensual sexual activity in prison suggest that it is more common than expected given the many rules and laws designed to prevent its occurrence. Conversely, it also indicates that sexual contact can be avoided given the fact that half of inmates reported no contact or non–contact sexual exchanges with others during their current incarceration.

We also queried the inmates about their experience of consensual sex (see Table 3.9). Male inmates cited the cell or dormitory as the most likely location for a consensual sexual encounter, and to a lesser extent showers, the workplace, recreational areas, and the chapel. Female inmates cited cell or dormitory and showers as the most likely location for a consensual sexual encounter. The only two gender differences to emerge indicated that male inmates more often reported

TABLE 3.8 Frequency of Consensual Sexual Acts while in Prison Reported by Incarcerated Men (*N*=288) and Women (*N*=183)

	Men		*Women*		*Effect Size*	
With Inmates	*N*	*(%)*	*N*	*(%)*	χ^2	Φ
Any non-contact sex acts	41	14.2	72	39.3	38.68★★	0.29★★
Any contact sex acts	17	5.9	48	26.2	38.87★★	0.29★★
	M	*SD*	*M*	*SD*	t	
Count of non-contact sex acts	0.42	1.43	1.86	3.04	−5.96★★★	
Count of contact sex acts	0.23	1.10	1.22	2.43	−5.23★★★	
With Visitors/Others	*N*	*(%)*	*N*	*(%)*	χ^2	Φ
Any non-contact sex acts	96	33.3	28	15.3	18.76★★★	−0.20★★★
Any contact sex acts	56	19.4	7	3.8	23.56★★★	−0.22★★★
	M	*SD*	*M*	*SD*	t	
Count of non-contact sex acts	1.28	2.34	0.37	1.10	5.73★★★	
Count of contact sex acts	0.59	1.60	0.12	0.86	4.14★★★	
With Staff	*N*	*(%)*	*N*	*(%)*	χ^2	Φ
Any non-contact sex acts	70	24.3	25	13.7	7.87★★	−0.13★★
Any contact sex acts	50	17.4	5	2.7	23.22★★	−0.22★★
	M	*SD*	*M*	*SD*	t	
Count of non-contact sex acts	0.95	1.96	0.32	1.00	4.60★★★	
Count of contact sex acts	0.56	1.58	0.07	0.48	4.90★★★	
Cumulative Total	*N*	*(%)*	*N*	*(%)*	χ^2	Φ
Any non-contact sex acts	125	43.4	84	45.9	0.28	0.03
Any contact sex acts	88	30.6	54	29.5	0.06	−0.01
Any non-contact or contact sex acts	128	44.4	85	46.4	0.18	0.02
	M	*SD*	*M*	*SD*	t	
Count of non-contact sex acts	2.66	4.16	2.54	3.87	0.30	
Count of contact sex acts	1.38	2.98	1.42	2.71	−0.15	
Count of any non-contact or contact sex acts	4.04	6.87	3.96	6.27	0.12	

Note. ★★*p* < 0.01, ★★★*p* < 0.001.

consensual sexual activity occurring in the chapel, while female inmates more often reported consensual sexual activity occurring in the showers.

Male inmates most frequently indicated their motivation for engaging in consensual sex were feeling sexy and pleasurable, warm and comfortable, and pleasing one's partner. Female inmates most frequently endorsed love and affection, feeling sexy and pleasurable, warm and comfortable, and pleasing one's partner. There were a number of gender differences in the motivations that were

TABLE 3.9 Frequency of Location, Motives, and Timing of Consensual Sex Reported by Men (*N*=128) and Women (*N*=85) while in Prison

Item	Men		Women		Effect Size	
	N	*(%)*	*N*	*(%)*	χ^2	Φ
Location of Sexual Contact						
Cell or dormitory	94	73.4	72	84.7	3.78	0.13
Chapel	15	11.7	2	2.4	6.10★	−0.17★
Educational area	6	4.7	2	2.4	0.77	−0.06
Counseling/administrative offices	4	3.1	1	1.2	0.85	−0.06
Dining hall	12	9.4	4	4.7	1.60	−0.09
Recreational area	16	12.5	13	15.3	0.34	0.04
Showers	49	38.3	71	83.5	42.51★★	0.45★★
Workplace	27	21.1	8	9.4	5.08★	−0.15★
Motivation for Sexual Encounters						
Warm and comfortable	17	13.3	23	27.1	6.36★	0.17★
Sexy and pleasurable	23	18.0	24	28.2	3.13	0.12
Love and affection	12	9.4	34	40.0	28.29★★	0.36★★
Friendship and belonging	10	7.8	12	14.1	2.19	0.10
Status in group	3	2.3	3	3.5	0.26	0.04
Please my partner	13	10.2	22	25.9	9.20★★	0.21★★
Time until Sexual Encounter					22.64★★	0.42★★
with Another Inmate						
No sex (with inmates)	68	81.9	29	34.1		
Less than one month	0	0.0	0	0.0		
One to six months	2	2.4	9	13.8		
Seven months to a year	0	0.0	5	7.7		
More than one year	13	15.7	22	33.8		
Concerned about HIV	29	42.0	30	45.5	0.16	−0.04
Used protection	14	35.0	20	40.0	0.24	−0.05
Led to jealousy	10	23.8	33	65.3	14.72★★	−0.40★★

Note. ★$p < 0.05$, ★★$p < 0.01$.

reported for the consensual sexual activity that occurred. Female inmates were more likely than male inmates to endorse love and affection, warm and comfortable feeling, and for pleasing one's partner. Despite these differences, Table 3.9 illustrates that these were relative discrepancies with some male inmates and some female inmates endorsing all of the six motivations that were offered to them.

The timing of the consensual sexual encounters also varied for the male and female inmates. A higher percentage of the female inmates began to engage in consensual sexual behaviors in prison within one to six months after incarceration (13.8%), with the numbers increasing substantially after one year of incarceration. More typically, the male inmates tended not to become involved in consensual sexual encounters until they had been incarcerated for at least one year. Almost half of the male and female inmates reported initiating these encounters despite concerns about HIV infection (42.0% of males and 45.5% of females) and many of these inmates reported using some type of protection during the encounters that occurred (35% of males and 40% of females). About one quarter (23.8%) of the male inmates, and significantly more of the female inmates (65.3%), reported that these consensual sexual relationships led to feelings of jealously on the part of others, possibly past partners.

Co-occurring Forms of Sexual Activity Among Inmates

Our finding that the rates of sexual activity varied significantly across the different types of sexual behavior prompted us to explore the co-occurring nature of the different types of sexual contact. We were interested in the dynamics that might turn victims into predators and the effect that consensual sex might have on the occurrence of more coerced forms of sexual contact. The correlations between the four different categories of sexual behavior are summarized in Table 3.10, with the data for the female inmates being displayed in the upper diagonal and for the male inmates in the lower diagonal (in bold).

These data reflect gender differences in the pairing of different types of sexual contact. Female inmates that reported sexual victimization were not simultaneously involved in predatory, bartered, or consensual encounters. However, predatory, bartered, and consensual sexual encounters were correlated with one another, suggesting that involvement in one of these three forms of sexual behavior increases the likelihood of engaging in the two other forms of sexual activity. These data indicate that victimization for women is a distinct phenomenon. In contrast, the associations for the male inmates were all-encompassing. Predatory, victimized, bartered, and consensual sexual encounters were correlated with one another, suggesting that involvement in one of these four forms of sex increases the likelihood of engaging in or being the recipient of the other three forms of sexual activity. For both genders, the highest correlations ($r = 0.49$ for males and $r = 0.40$ for females) were between

TABLE 3.10 Correlations between Sexual Victimization, Predation, Bartered, and Consensual Sexual Activity of Men ($N=288$) and Women ($N=183$) while in Prison

Males	Females			
	Victimization	Predation	Bartered	Consensual
Victimization	—	0.14	0.12	0.14
Predation	0.30***	—	0.27***	0.19***
Bartered	0.21***	0.39***	—	0.40***
Consensual	0.25***	0.38***	0.49***	—

Note. ***$p < 0.001$.
Spearman's rho used due to non-normality of variables; Women's coefficients in upper diagonal, Men's coefficients in lower diagonal.

consensual and bartered sex suggesting that conceptually bartered sex may be closer to consensual sex at least in this type of institutional setting.

Inmates' Estimations of Consensual and Bartered Sexual Activity

During the interview with inmates, they were asked to estimate what percentage of inmates in their prison they believed were involved in consensual or bartered sexual relationships with other inmates or with staff. This estimation was obtained to both provide a broader context for the amount of sexual activity that was perceived by inmates as occurring in the prisons while also serving as a proxy measure of a particular inmate's involvement in these types of sexual relationships. We reasoned that while some inmates might be hesitant about acknowledging same-sex encounters while in prison, they would tend, if they were sexually active, to ascribe this behavior to others at a rate that was higher than the mean for the general sample assessed by gender.

The data in Table 3.11 are obviously subjective and involve significant problems with missing data. Nonetheless, they do reflect gender differences that have

TABLE 3.11 Frequency of Inmates Perceptions of the Sexual Activity Occurring within the Prison Environment Reported by Incarcerated Men and Women

	Men		Women		
	N	%	N	%	H
Consensual Sex					0.32**
< 20%	108	46.6	20	15.6	
21–40%	42	18.1	14	10.9	
41–60%	30	12.9	36	28.1	
61–80%	25	10.8	36	28.1	
> 80%	27	11.6	22	17.2	
Bartered Sex					0.26**
< 20%	126	64.6	32	39.0	
21–40%	32	16.4	15	18.3	
41–60%	16	8.2	12	14.6	
61–80%	6	3.1	8	9.8	
> 80%	15	7.7	15	8.3	
Bartered Sex for Protection					0.11*
< 20%	119	70.8	80	89.6	
21–40%	23	13.7	1	1.5	
41–60%	13	7.7	1	1.5	
61–80%	6	3.6	2	3.0	
> 80%	7	4.2	3	4.5	

Note. $*p < 0.05$, $**p < 0.01$.
Consensual sexual activity was missing 111 responses, bartered sex was missing 194 responses, and bartered sex for protection was missing 235 responses.

been given credence by other research (Fleisher & Krienert, 2006). As suggested by these attributions, the inmates perceived or believed that more women are involved in consensual sexual relationships than men while in prison, and that more women barter for sex than do men. However, the inmates reported to the interviewers that more men barter sex for protection than do female inmates.

Conclusions

Our data suggest that inmates in general adopt one of two sexual strategies when they find themselves imprisoned. About one half of the inmates carve out a day-to-day life that does not involve sexual exchanges or encounters with other individuals. The other half of the inmates become involved in non-contact or contact sexual activity with other inmates, visitors/others, or members of the prison staff. The rate of this contact is surprisingly similar across genders, with about 30 percent of the male and female inmates reporting some type of contact sexual experience with another person while in prison. This activity appears to have been initiated after a shorter period of incarceration for the women as compared to the men. Specifically, 13.8 percent of the female inmates reported sexual contact within six months of being incarcerated while the males tended not to become involved in consensual sexual encounters until they had been incarcerated for at least one year.

Significant gender differences were observed in the rates of self-report predation in our male and female samples, with males reporting higher rates of predatory behavior than females in all categories except inmate-on-inmate predatory sexual behavior. Among the male inmates reporting contact predatory sexual behavior, the majority described themselves as being sexually predatory toward staff and visitors/others and fewer described themselves as being sexually predatory toward other inmates. It is not clear if these data reflect an accurate portrayal of the inmates' predatory targets or the wish to retain a heterosexual identity when describing these incidents combined with a possible interest in demonstrating their ability to dominate institutional staff. However, if taken at face value, these data suggest that sexual coercion of prison staff by male inmates is as much a concern as the more widely publicized incidents of inmate coercion by correctional staff (Pecquet, 2006). These data suggest that at least some male inmates view themselves not only able to consent to sexual encounters with correctional staff, but to perpetrate it in a way that implies they are predatory in their efforts and effect.

Rates of self-reported contact victimization were comparable across genders both for encounters involving other inmates (5.9% of males and 6.6% of females), visitors/other (1.0% of males and 0% of females), and members of the prison staff (2.4% of males and 2.7% of females). These rates of victimization were three times higher than the inmate victimization rates reported by Beck and Harrison (2007, 2008), and Wolff et al. (2007). These differences may derive from our smaller sample, our use of a 16-point scale to collect different gradations of sexually coercive behaviors, or our use of face-to-face clinical interviews to collect data on the sexual life of prisoners.

This last possibility would contradict the assumption that greater anonymity promotes higher rates of disclosure and might suggest that intensive interviews conducted by trained clinicians may in fact enhance inmates' willingness to describe to others their sexual lives in prison.

Our data reflected pervasive differences in the amount of homosexual or bisexual behavior reported by the male and female inmates. Within the female sample, 26.2 percent of the women reported contact sexual activity with another inmate and 6.5 percent with visitors/others or staff, with both of these latter categories implying a heterosexual type of sexual contact. In contrast, in the male sample only 5.9 percent of the men reported same-sex sexual activity with other inmates while 19.4 percent reported sexual contact with visitors/others and 17.4 percent with staff, these latter two categories again more generally implying sexual activity of a heterosexual nature. As noted earlier, these data reflected common themes observed during our interviews, with the women appearing more comfortable in acknowledging sexual activity with another woman while the men were more intent upon describing their relationship with visitors and staff of the institution. We were unable to determine if these differences reflected gender differences in sexual behavior, gender differences in levels of comfort in reporting homosexual behavior, or a combination of both. These findings, however, are congruent with emergent research that suggests that sexual arousal is category specific for men but more "erotically plastic" for women with comparable levels of arousal among women to both male and female sexual stimuli (Chivers, Rieger, Latty, & Bailey, 2004).

When inmates did become sexually active, the different types of sexual activities tended to co-occur, particularly with the males. Among the sexually active male inmates, predatory, victimized, bartered, and consensual sex were strongly correlated suggesting that involvement in one sexual activity was a risk marker for sexual activity in another. This was true of the women who engaged in consensual, bartered, and predatory sex, but not for those who reported sexual victimization. Sexual victimization reported by the women was not correlated with any of the other categories of sexual behavior. These findings suggest that for men the best predictive approach might involve trying to identify those who are sexually active in prison from those who are not. Conversely, for female inmates the most relevant categories might involve those who are sexually active, those who are sexually victimized, and those who are interpersonally asexual during incarceration.

We found that both the male and female inmates endorsed the full spectrum of reasons for initiating same-sex relationships while in prison. These included the experience of the contact being warm and comfortable or pleasurable and sexy, while also being an avenue for expressing love and affection, for conveying friendship and belonging, for increasing one's status in a social group, and for pleasing one's partner. The emphasis placed upon these motivations, however, differed between the two genders. Compared to male inmates, female inmates significantly more often endorsed being motivated by feelings of warmth and comfort, love and affection, and pleasing one's partner. Although not significantly different from female inmates, male inmates were most frequently motived by feeling sexy and pleasurable. They also endorsed feeling warm and comfortable and perceived sex as a way to please their partner, but at lower levels than those reported by female inmates. These gender differences seem similar to those that might be found in a community sample of males and females of similar ages, although in many instances they reflect same-sex encounters that may contrast to the individuals' self-reported sexual identity while living in the community.

Sexually active inmates of both genders self-reported a clear differentiation between consensual and coerced sexual encounters and on our instrumentation portrayed themselves as able to consent to some sexual encounters and not to others. This was found to be true both when the sexual activity was occurring with other inmates, visitors/others, and when it was occurring with members of the prison staff. This finding appears relevant to the debate that continues concerning the ability of prison inmates to consent to sexual encounters with correctional staff. Some scholars and prison officials argue that no prison sex can be fully consensual given the power differential intrinsic to the system and the highly coercive nature of the prison environment (Soliman, 2000). However, other legal scholars maintain that such a perspective is overly simplistic while referencing law outside the walls of the prison according to which most adult sex is assumed to be consensual "as long as nobody complains" (Ristroph, 2006, p. 157).

Our data offered some preliminary conceptual support to bartered sex in prison being experientially associated with consensual and predatory sex in the same environment for both male and female inmates. Within both samples, men and women who reported being involved with bartered sexual encounters also tended to report involvement in consensual sexual relationships and at times various forms of sexual predation. Eigenberg (2000) argues that all sex in exchange for goods or services is coercive because of the vulnerable state of the person seeking some type of reimbursement. Conversely, Ristroph (2006) argues that a third kind or sex is generated in the prison environment, one in which "sex [is] sought or agreed to under ambiguous circumstances, sex that may constitute prostitution of 'sexual extortion,' or just a conflicted quest for a measure of safety in an inherently dangerous environment" (p. 157).

Our findings point to the significant medical risks that occur when thousands of inmates participate repeatedly in unprotected sex with others who may have been involved in high risk sexual behavior in the community. As indicated, only 41 percent of our inmates reported any concerns about HIV transmission, and of these, only about one third reported using any type of precaution when they were participating in a sexual encounter. With few exceptions, condoms are considered contraband and forbidden by all local, state, and federal correctional agencies in the US (Hammett, Maruschak, & Harmon, 1999; Spaulding, Lubelczyk, & Flanigan, 2001). As identified by PREA, these same-sex encounters carry the potential of putting community partners at risk when the inmate returns to the community and it is assumed that the incarceration has carried for them no sexual contact and no heightened risk for the transfer of sexually transmitted diseases to others.

4

CHILDHOOD ADVERSE LIFE EXPERIENCES AND ADOLESCENT VIOLENCE AS RISK MARKERS FOR SEXUAL PREDATION AND VICTIMIZATION

Violence risk research has confirmed the substantial association between adverse experiences in early life and aggressive and violent behavior in adulthood (Greenfeld & Snell, 1999; Grella, Stein, & Greenwell, 2005; Widom, 1989a, 1989b). This association has been recognized in clinical practice for many years and now is reflected in most of the major risk assessment schemes or systems (Augimeri, Webster, Koegl, & Levene, 1998; Douglas, Webster, Hart, Eaves, & Ogloff, 2001; Kropp, Hart, Webster, & Eaves, 1995). In this chapter we explore the association of diverse adverse early life experiences, separation from family of origin prior to the age of 15 years, and involvement in different types of juvenile delinquency with five types of sexual behavior of male and female inmates.

Adverse Life Experiences and Brain Development

Research and clinical practice support the proposition that early trauma and exposure to violent behavior predisposes a child to act in a violent manner towards others. This developmental perspective is explained by a wide variety of theories, ranging from the psychodynamic (Bowlby, 1969; Klein, 1935, 1940) to the neuro-biological (Andersen & Teicher, 2009; Raine & Yang, 2006). These theoretical and empirical paradigms underscore the importance of parent–child interactions and exposure to traumatic experiences early in life as they impact the developing mind and brain and hence cognitive and social development throughout later stages of life.

Both cross-sectional and longitudinal research has identified a relationship between childhood sexual and physical abuse and a number of deleterious outcomes. Coid et al. (2001) found that women who experienced less severe forms of sexual abuse in childhood were at greater risk for rape, sexual assault, and other forms of trauma in adulthood, although not domestic violence. In contrast, women who experienced more extreme forms of sexual abuse in childhood, including sexual intercourse and severe beatings, were at higher risk for experiencing both sexual abuse and domestic violence as adults. Further research has found that sexually abused girls are more likely to engage in sexually precocious behavior, to be seductive towards adults, and to exhibit higher levels of sexual activity in adulthood (El-Bassel et al., 1996; Foti, 1995).

Research in primary healthcare settings has examined the relationship between multiple adverse life experiences in childhood and high risk health behaviors associated with elevated levels of mortality among adults. Felitti et al. (1998) developed the Adverse Childhood Experiences (ACE) index to tabulate various types of disruptive early life experiences including sexual abuse, physical abuse, psychological abuse, exposure to substance abuse, exposure to mental illness, observation of violent treatment of a maternal caregiver, and criminal behavior of either parent leading to imprisonment. Using an initial sample of 9,508 health-seeking individuals, they found a relationship between these early adverse experiences and ten adult outcomes including alcoholism, drug abuse, depression, suicide attempts, smoking, sexually transmitted disease, physical inactivity, and severe obesity. Later research extended this list to include relationships with unintended first pregnancy among women (Dietz et al., 1999), smoking in adolescence (Anda et al., 1999), male involvement in teen pregnancy (Anda et al., 2001), sexual risk behavior in women including risk for AIDS (Hillis, Anda, Felitti, & Marchbanks, 2001), attempted suicide throughout the lifespan (Dube et al., 2001), impaired mental health (Edwards, Holden, Felitti, & Anda, 2003), and adolescent pregnancy and fetal death (Hillis et al., 2004).

Recent studies have begun to demonstrate an association between the experience of childhood abuse or neglect and alterations in the brain structure or brain function. These associations have revealed an overall loss in the hippocampus, corpus callosum, and prefrontal cortex, altered cortical symmetry in the frontal lobes and superior temporal gyrus, and reduced neuronal density or neuronal integrity in the anterior cingulate (Bremner et al., 1997; Carrion et al., 2001; De Bellis et al., 1999; De Bellis, Keshavan, Frustaci, et al., 2002; De Bellis, Keshavan, Shifflett, et al., 2002; De Bellis, Keshavan, Spencer, & Hall, 2000; Driessen et al., 2000; Stein, Koverola, Hanna, Torchia, & McClarty, 1997; Teicher et al., 2004; Vythilingam et al., 2002). The nature of correlational research limits the ability of these studies to determine if the experience of abuse led to these neurological irregularities, if children with these pre-existent abnormalities are at increased risk for abuse, or if these morphological differences run in families and give rise to an increased risk for violent behavior by the parents and other family members living in these family units (Teicher, Tomoda, & Andersen, 2006). Teicher et al. (2006), however, explored the effects of trauma using a sensitive period of development perspective and found that repeated episodes of childhood sexual abuse were associated with reduced hippocampal volume if the abuse was reported to occur in early childhood, but with reduced prefrontal cortex volume when the abuse was reported to occur in adolescence. He argues that these findings suggest that there may be distinctly different neuropsychological sequelae of early abuse depending on the timing of the insult, the nature of the insult, the brain region affected, and the maturation period of expression (Teicher et al., 2006).

Adverse Life Experiences and Violent Behavior in Adolescence and Adulthood

Early adverse life experiences have also been associated with violent behavior in adolescence and adulthood. Violence risk research has documented the effects of a disruptive and abusive family environment on physical violence in later life (Bandura, 1973; Earls & Barnes, 1997; Monahan et al., 2001; Widom, 1989a). Parental loss through death or divorce, and disruptions in family life due to parental psychiatric hospitalization or incarceration, have been related to adolescent and adult violence (Convit, Jaeger, Lin, Meisner, & Volavka, 1988; Klassen & O'Connor, 1988; Quinsey, Warneford, Pruesse, & Link, 1975). Bensley, Speiker, van Eenwyck, and Schoder (1999a, 1999b) found higher levels of antisocial behavior, substance abuse, and suicidal behavior among a cohort of high school students who reported being abused in childhood. Widom (1989a, 1999) reported more aggression, violence, depression, suicide, anxiety, substance abuse, and post-traumatic stress disorder among individuals who had experienced abuse as children when compared to a comparable group of controls. The MacArthur Violence Risk Assessment Study found that prior physical abuse as a child, deviant behavior of fathers and mothers including drug and alcohol abuse, and the arrest of a father, were related to violence in adulthood after a period of inpatient psychiatric hospitalization. However, the effects of maternal drug use on violent behavior was found only for the male patients, and the protective impact of living with either parent until the age of 15 years was found only for the White patients (Monahan et al., 2001).

Moreover, early adverse life experiences have been associated with sexual violence in adulthood. Malamuth, Sockloskie, Koss, and Tanaka (1991) explored the effects of early abuse on the sexually coercive attitudes and behavior of community-residing males. They examined the sexual experiences reported by 2,652 college men and found that sexual abuse in childhood, when combined with physical abuse, made a small but significant contribution to the prediction of sexual coercion in adulthood. Langevin, Wright, and Handy (1989) examined a large database of Canadian offenders and found that the men who reported being sexually victimized in youth, particularly by male relatives, were more often involved in rape and other sexually anomalous acts in adulthood. Seghorn, Prentky, and Boucher (1987) studied the background of incarcerated rapists and incarcerated child molesters and found that the child molesters were two times more likely to report childhood sexual abuse when compared to the rapists. However, when the rapists did report early sexual abuse, they were three times more likely to report having been abused by their fathers while living in highly chaotic home environments that involved sexual aggression against female members of the household. Fagan and Wexler (1988) studied violent juvenile offenders and found that the youths charged with sex offenses were more likely to have been the victims of sexual and physical abuse by their parents when compared to other violent juvenile offenders.

Study Analyses

Indicators of the presence of early adverse life experiences were derived from the Adverse Childhood Experiences Study Questionnaire – Modified (ACE SQ-M) and from the Prison Background Information Survey (PBIS). These variables were examined for gender differences and then for their association with the five categories of sexual behavior while in prison.

The data in Table 4.1 reflect the pervasive nature of the adverse life experiences that characterize the early lives of the male and female inmates in our sample. Across

TABLE 4.1 Frequency of Adverse Childhood Events Reported by Incarcerated Men (*N*=288) and Women (*N*=183)

Adverse Event	Men		Women		Effect size	
	N	%	N	%	χ^2	Φ
Any psychological abuse	165	57.9	109	60.2	0.25	0.02
Any physical abuse	141	49.5	89	49.2	< 0.01	< −0.01
Any sexual abuse	185	65.1	109	60.6	1.00	−0.05
Any neglect	152	53.3	76	42.2	5.45★	−0.11★
Away from family <15	105	36.8	60	33.3	0.73	−0.04
Any violence towards mother	124	44.9	87	48.9	0.68	0.04
Any violence towards father	97	35.5	53	29.8	1.61	−0.06
Maternal depression	83	30.0	57	32.4	0.30	0.03
Maternal arrest	72	26.3	37	21.0	1.61	−0.06
Maternal incarceration	55	19.6	29	16.5	0.72	−0.04
Maternal alcohol addiction	69	24.5	55	30.9	2.29	0.07
Maternal drug addiction	40	14.2	39	21.9	4.58★	0.10★
Paternal depression	49	19.5	23	14.4	1.79	−0.07
Paternal arrest	144	55.0	70	42.9	5.81★	−0.12★
Paternal incarceration	116	43.9	57	34.8	3.54	−0.09
Paternal alcohol addiction	122	45.9	81	48.2	0.23	0.02
Paternal drug addiction	70	26.5	36	21.7	1.28	−0.06
Head injury with LOC	133	46.5	66	36.1	4.98★	−0.10★

Note. ★*p* < 0.05.

LOC = Loss of consciousness.

both genders, we found that half or more than half of the inmates had experienced psychological abuse, physical abuse, sexual abuse, neglect, and living away from family prior to age 15. Among these variables, the only significant gender difference involved neglect, with significantly more males reporting the experience of neglect than females. However, the rates of sexual abuse were comparable across genders.

Comparable percentages of male and female inmates had been exposed to violence in their homes as children, with the abuse being perpetrated against both their mothers and their fathers. Maternal indicators of pathology (i.e., depression, arrest, incarceration, alcohol addiction, drug addiction, and overall maternal pathology) ranged from 14.2 percent to 30.0 percent for the male inmates and 16.5 percent to 32.4 percent for the female inmates. Paternal indicators of pathology (i.e., depression, arrest, incarceration, alcohol addiction, drug addiction, and overall paternal pathology) ranged from 19.5 percent to 55.0 percent for the male inmates and 14.4 percent to 48.2 percent for the female inmates. Among this set of variables, the only two significant gender differences involved more female inmates reporting maternal drug addiction, while more male inmates reported paternal arrest. Rates of head injury with a resultant loss of consciousness (LOC) were common among both the male and female inmates, although significantly more frequent among the male inmates.

Table 4.2 (males) and Table 4.3 (females) summarize the association of these 20 early adverse life experiences with the five categories of sexual behavior. The results indicate that the decision to be sexually active or to have experienced sexual victimization in prison were both associated with a number of early adverse life experiences an individual had experienced. Maternal alcohol abuse and paternal alcohol abuse were the only adverse life experiences that exerted no effect on the sexual behavior the individual experienced in prison.

For male inmates, any-sex (i.e., any endorsement of predatory, victimized, bartered, or consensual sex) was associated with psychological abuse, physical abuse, sexual abuse, neglect, living away from family prior to age 15 years, maternal incarceration, paternal drug addiction, and head injury with LOC. Among female inmates, any-sex was associated with psychological abuse, physical abuse, sexual abuse, neglect, any violence observed towards the mother, maternal depression, and maternal arrest.

Among the male inmates, predatory sex was associated with psychological abuse, physical abuse, sexual abuse, and head injury with LOC. Among the female inmates, predatory sex was associated with violence observed towards the father, maternal arrest, maternal drug addiction, paternal depression, and overall maternal pathology as measured by the PBIS.

The sexual victimization of male inmates was associated only with sexual abuse and living away from family prior to age 15 years. The victimization of female inmates was associated with psychological abuse, neglect, and maternal depression.

Bartered sex among the male inmates was associated with psychological abuse, physical abuse, sexual abuse, paternal arrest, paternal incarceration, and overall

TABLE 4.2 Relationship between Adverse Childhood Events Reported by Incarcerated Men (N=288) and Type of Sexual Experience in Prison

Adverse event	Any-sex		Predatory		Victim		Bartered		Consensual	
	No N=143 (%)	Yes N=145 (%)	No N=253 (%)	Yes N=35 (%)	No N=244 (%)	Yes N=44 (%)	No N=251 (%)	Yes N=37 (%)	No N=160 (%)	Yes N=128 (%)
Any psychological abuse	68 (48.2)	97 (67.4)**	140 (55.8)	25 (73.5)*	135 (55.8)	30 (69.8)	137 (55.2)	28 (75.7)*	79 (50.0)	86 (67.7)**
Any physical abuse	58 (41.1)	83 (57.6)**	117 (46.6)	24 (70.6)**	115 (47.5)	26 (60.5)	115 (46.4)	26 (70.3)**	67 (42.4)	74 (58.3)**
Any sexual abuse	78 (55.3)	107 (74.8)**	156 (62.4)	29 (83.5)**	152 (62.8)	33 (78.6)*	154 (62.3)	31 (83.8)*	88 (56.1)	97 (76.4)**
Any neglect	75 (53.2)	77 (53.5)**	130 (51.8)	22 (64.7)	124 (51.2)	28 (65.1)	129 (52.0)	23 (62.2)	85 (53.8)	67 (52.8)
Lived away from family <15	43 (30.7)	62 (42.8)*	87 (34.8)	18 (51.4)	83 (34.4)	22 (50.0)*	86 (34.7)	19 (51.4)	45 (28.7)	60 (46.9)**
Any violence towards mother	55 (41.0)	69 (48.6)	104 (43.0)	20 (58.8)	102 (43.6)	22 (52.4)	102 (42.5)	22 (61.1)	61 (40.4)	63 (50.4)
Any violence towards father	37 (28.2)	60 (42.3)	81 (33.9)	16 (47.1)	79 (34.2)	18 (42.9)	79 (33.3)	18 (50.0)	43 (29.1)	54 (43.2)
Maternal depression	39 (28.1)	44 (31.9)	70 (28.8)	13 (38.2)	69 (29.2)	14 (34.1)	74 (30.5)	9 (26.5)	44 (28.8)	39 (31.5)
Maternal arrest	35 (25.5)	37 (27.0)	65 (27.0)	7 (21.2)	62 (26.3)	10 (26.3)	62 (25.9)	10 (28.6)	38 (25.0)	34 (27.9)
Maternal incarceration	27 (19.3)	28 (20.0)*	51 (20.7)	4 (11.8)	46 (19.2)	9 (22.0)	47 (19.3)	8 (22.2)	29 (18.6)	26 (21.0)
Maternal alcohol addiction	29 (20.9)	40 (28.0)	60 (24.3)	9 (25.7)	56 (23.4)	13 (30.2)	58 (23.7)	11 (29.7)	33 (21.2)	36 (28.6)
Maternal drug addiction	15 (10.8)	25 (17.5)	35 (14.2)	5 (14.3)	32 (13.4)	8 (18.6)	34 (13.9)	6 (16.2)	17 (10.9)	23 (18.3)
Paternal depression	24 (18.6)	25 (20.5)	44 (19.8)	5 (17.2)	43 (19.9)	6 (17.1)	41 (18.5)	8 (27.6)	27 (18.9)	22 (20.4)
Paternal arrest	68 (51.9)	76 (58.0)	124 (54.1)	20 (60.6)	128 (57.1)	16 (42.1)	118 (52.0)	26 (74.3)*	71 (48.6)	73 (62.9)*
Paternal incarceration	54 (40.9)	62 (47.0)	100 (43.5)	16 (47.1)	100 (44.2)	16 (42.1)	92 (40.2)	24 (68.6)**	57 (38.8)	59 (50.4)

TABLE 4.2 Continued

Paternal alcohol addiction	53 (40.2)	69 (51.5)	104 (44.6)	18 (54.5)	99 (44.0)	23 (56.1)	102 (44.2)	20 (57.1)	62 (41.9)	60 (50.8)
Paternal drug addiction	27 (20.5)	43 (32.6)★	60 (26.0)	10 (30.3)	62 (27.6)	8 (20.5)	58 (25.3)	12 (34.3)	28 (18.9)	42 (36.2)★★
Overall maternal pathology (PBIS)	65 (45.5)	72 (49.7)	120 (47.4)	17 (48.6)	115 (47.1)	22 (50.0)	119 (47.4)	18 (48.6)	74 (46.2)	63 (49.2)
Overall paternal pathology (PBIS)	83 (58.0)	98 (67.5)	156 (61.7)	25 (71.4)	149 (61.1)	32 (72.7)	152 (60.6)	29 (78.4)★	95 (59.4)	86 (67.2)
Head injury with LOC	65 (46.1)	68 (46.9)★	111 (44.2)	22 (62.9)★	109 (45.0)	24 (54.5)	114 (45.8)	19 (51.4)	75 (47.5)	58 (45.3)

Note. ★$p < 0.05$, ★★$p < 0.01$.
LOC = Loss of consciousness.

TABLE 4.3 Relationship between Adverse Childhood Events Reported by Incarcerated Women (N=183) and Type of Sexual Experience in Prison

Adverse Event	Any-sex		Predatory		Victim		Bartered		Consensual	
	No N=77 (%)	Yes N=106 (%)	No N=178 (%)	Yes N=5 (%)	No N=134 (%)	Yes N=49 (%)	No N=165 (%)	Yes N=18 (%)	No N=98 (%)	Yes N=85 (%)
Any psychological abuse	38 (49.4)	71 (68.3)**	104 (59.1)	5 (100.0)	73 (55.3)	36 (73.5)*	96 (58.5)	13 (76.5)	53 (54.1)	56 (67.5)
Any physical abuse	31 (40.3)	58 (55.8)*	85 (48.2)	4 (80.0)	60 (45.5)	29 (59.2)	79 (48.2)	10 (58.8)	43 (43.9)	46 (55.4)
Any sexual abuse	37 (48.1)	72 (69.9)**	104 (59.4)	5 (100.0)	75 (57.3)	34 (69.4)	95 (58.3)	14 (82.4)	50 (51.0)	59 (72.0)**
Any neglect	24 (31.2)	52 (50.5)**	73 (41.7)	3 (60.0)	46 (35.1)	30 (61.2)**	64 (39.3)	12 (70.6)*	36 (36.7)	40 (48.8)
Lived away from family <15	22 (28.6)	38 (36.2)	58 (32.8)	2 (40.0)	43 (32.1)	18 (35.4)	55 (33.5)	5 (27.8)	28 (28.6)	32 (38.1)
Any violence towards mother	30 (39.5)	57 (55.9)*	84 (48.6)	3 (60.0)	62 (47.3)	25 (51.0)	77 (47.8)	10 (58.8)	40 (41.2)	47 (58.0)*
Any violence towards father	18 (23.7)	35 (34.3)	49 (28.3)	4 (80.0)*	34 (26.0)	19 (40.4)	45 (28.0)	8 (47.1)	23 (23.7)	30 (37.0)
Maternal depression	16 (21.3)	41 (40.6)**	56 (32.6)	1 (25.0)	36 (27.3)	21 (47.7)*	54 (34.2)	3 (16.7)	27 (28.1)	30 (37.5)
Maternal arrest	10 (13.3)	27 (26.7)*	34 (19.9)	3 (60.0)*	27 (20.6)	10 (22.2)	32 (20.3)	5 (27.8)	12 (12.5)	25 (31.2)**
Maternal incarceration	8 (10.5)	21 (21.0)	29 (16.9)	0 (0.0)	20 (15.2)	9 (20.5)	27 (16.4)	2 (11.1)	10 (10.3)	19 (24.1)*
Maternal alcohol addiction	23 (29.9)	32 (31.7)	52 (30.1)	3 (60.0)	41 (30.8)	14 (31.1)	51 (31.9)	4 (22.2)	26 (25.6)	29 (36.2)
Maternal drug addiction	12 (15.6)	27 (26.7)	36 (20.8)	3 (60.0)*	27 (20.3)	12 (26.7)	34 (21.2)	5 (27.8)	13 (13.3)	26 (32.5)**
Paternal depression	10 (14.5)	13 (14.3)	21 (13.4)	2 (66.7)**	17 (14.3)	6 (14.6)	19 (13.2)	4 (25.0)	12 (13.5)	11 (15.5)
Paternal arrest	26 (36.1)	44 (48.4)	69 (43.1)	1 (33.3)	51 (41.8)	19 (46.3)	63 (42.6)	7 (46.7)	34 (37.0)	36 (50.7)
Paternal incarceration	23 (31.9)	34 (37.0)	56 (34.8)	1 (33.3)	42 (34.1)	15 (36.6)	52 (34.9)	5 (33.3)	30 (32.6)	27 (37.5)
Paternal alcohol addiction	33 (44.6)	48 (51.1)	80 (48.5)	1 (33.3)	61 (48.4)	20 (47.6)	75 (49.3)	6 (37.5)	43 (45.3)	38 (32.1)
Paternal drug addiction	9 (12.3)	27 (29.0)	36 (22.1)	0 (0.0)	27 (21.6)	9 (22.0)	32 (21.3)	4 (25.0)	12 (12.9)	24 (32.9)**
Overall maternal pathology (PBIS)	36 (46.8)	64 (60.4)	95 (53.5)	5 (100.0)*	71 (53.0)	29 (59.2)	89 (53.9)	11 (61.1)	48 (49.0)	52 (61.2)
Overall paternal pathology (PBIS)	43 (55.8)	66 (62.3)	107 (60.1)	2 (40.0)	83 (61.9)	26 (53.1)	99 (60.0)	10 (55.6)	56 (57.1)	53 (62.4)
Head injury with LOC	28 (36.4)	38 (35.8)	65 (36.5)	1 (20.0)	49 (36.6)	17 (34.7)	59 (35.8)	7 (38.9)	34 (34.7)	32 (37.6)

Note. * $p < 0.05$, ** $p < 0.01$.
LOC = Loss of consciousness.

paternal pathology as measured by the PBIS. Bartered sex among the female inmates was associated only with neglect.

Finally, consensual sex among male inmates was associated with psychological abuse, physical abuse, sexual abuse, living away from family prior to age 15 years, paternal arrest, and paternal drug addiction. Consensual sex among female inmates was associated with sexual abuse, observing violence towards the mother, maternal arrest, maternal incarceration, maternal drug addiction, and paternal drug addiction.

Early Violence and Criminality

Developmental research has identified different patterns of offending among juveniles that are associated with different patterns of criminal behavior in adulthood. Two of the dominant paradigms include the identification of a progressively violent subcategory of youth referred to as serious violent juvenile (SVJ) offenders and the classification of delinquent behavior into adolescent-limited (ADL) and life course persistent (LCP) antisocial offending.

Serious Violent Juvenile (SVJ) Offenders

Loeber and Farrington (1998) conducted an extensive review of the research literature concerning juvenile offenders and identified within this larger group a subcategory of particularly violent and chronically delinquent youth they termed *serious violent juvenile* (SVJ) offenders. This group was characterized by an early age of onset, the presence of problematic childhood behavior patterns, relatively high levels of aggression in childhood, and behavior that culminated in serious and violent forms of delinquency in adolescence. As this group reached adolescence they tended to become involved in extensive drug use (Thornberry, Huizinga, & Loeber, 1995), high levels of externalizing and aggressive behavior (Stouthamer-Loeber, Loeber, & Thomas, 1992), truancy and school suspensions (Maguin & Loeber, 1996), involvement with delinquent peers (Farrington, 1989), and familial disruptions that led to separation from family referred to as "early home leaving" (Maguin et al., 1995). Viewed nationally, it was estimated that these SVJ offenders were responsible for more than half of the serious crimes committed by juveniles, with many becoming career criminals in adulthood.

Adolescent-limited and Life Course Persistent Antisocial Offending

Moffitt, Caspi, Rutter, and Silva (2001) studied gender differences in antisocial behavior using data from a longitudinal cohort in Dunedin, New Zealand. They found that both the male and female youth demonstrated one of two patterns of delinquency as they transitioned through adolescence into adulthood. The adolescent-limited (ADL) group was made up of youth who had not shown antisocial behavior in childhood but who took up delinquent behaviors in mid-adolescence, later returning to law abiding behavior as they entered early adulthood. In contrast, the life course persistent (LCP) group tended to manifest earlier problems associated with subtle cognitive deficits, a difficult temperament, and hyperactivity. As adolescents, they were involved in more chronic juvenile offending, which they maintained even as they transitioned into adulthood. Moffitt and her colleagues hypothesized that both the male and female individuals in the LCP group were born with the same risk factors, albeit at higher rates among the boys, and when exposed to a high risk social environment, reached adulthood with a disordered personality characterized by physical aggression and antisocial behavior. Moffitt et al. (2001) found that when these youth reached adulthood, the LCP males demonstrated more psychopathic traits, more mental health problems, a higher rate of substance dependence, a larger number of children, more severe financial and work problems, and more violent crimes committed against women and children. The LCP females were fewer in number, although they demonstrated many of the same problems as the LCP males, although often at sub-threshold levels.

Study Analyses

Information regarding childhood and adolescent life experiences was collected from the Prison Background Information Survey (PBIS), the Self-Report Criminal History Questionnaire (SRCHQ), and the HCR-20 risk instrument. We first assessed these variables for gender differences and then explored their relationship with the five types of sexual behavior in prison.

The results in Table 4.4 illustrate the chronic problems that both the male and female inmates experienced while transitioning through adolescence into adulthood.

TABLE 4.4 Frequency of Juvenile Risk Factors Reported by Incarcerated Men (N=288) and Women (N=183)

Juvenile Risk Factor	Men		Women		Effect Size	
	N	%	N	%	χ^2	Φ
Educational problems	184	65.0	88	48.6	12.24**	−0.16**
Early maladjustment – conduct problems	182	64.1	86	47.3	12.86**	−0.17**
Adolescent failure to establish relationships	87	30.6	74	40.7	4.93*	0.10*
First violent act prior to age 18	196	69.0	70	38.7	41.57**	−0.30**
Self-Report Juvenile Criminal History	171	59.4	87	47.5	6.33*	−0.12*
Juvenile Arrest History	124	43.1	44	24.0	17.63**	−0.19**

Note. *$p < 0.05$, **$p < 0.01$.

Nearly half, or more than half, of both the male and female inmates in our sample experienced educational problems, early conduct problems, first violent act prior to age 18 years, and criminal offending prior to reaching the age of 18 years. In addition, 43.1 percent of the men and 24.0 percent of the women had been arrested as a juvenile and 30.6 percent of the men and 40.7 percent of the women had failed to establish relationships in adolescence. In each of these six categories, the male inmates reported higher levels of impairment except on the relationship measure where the women reported higher levels of relationship distress in adolescence.

As presented in Table 4.5 (males) and Table 4.6 (females), the association between the various adolescent risk markers and sexual behavior in prison was modest, typically with only one risk marker differentiating most of the various categories of sexual behavior in prison, although they varied across the five categories of sex. Among male inmates, any-sex was associated only with early maladjustment with conduct problems, while any-sex among the female inmates was associated only with first violent act before age 18 years. Predatory sex among the male inmates was associated only with first violent act before age 18 years, although no variables correlated with predatory sex for female inmates. Victimized sex was associated with fewer self-reported juvenile arrests among male inmates, but no variables were correlated with sexual victimization among the female inmates. Bartered sex among male inmates was associated only with first violent act before age 18 years, but no variables correlated with bartered sex for the female inmates. And finally, consensual sex among male inmates was associated with educational problems, early maladjustment with conduct problems, and first violent act before age 18 years, while consensual sex among female inmates was associated with higher rates of self-reported criminal offending in adolescence and higher rates of self-reported juvenile arrest history. Failure to establish relationships was the only adolescent variable that was unrelated to all five measures of sexual behavior for both the male and female inmates.

Conclusions

Consistent with prior research, our findings underscore the high rates of early abuse and victimization reported by incarcerated women. However, our comparisons across genders indicate that these rates of early trauma and adverse life experiences are comparable across genders, with the men reporting as much early abuse and neglect as the women. We found this to be true even with self-reported sexual abuse, with 65.1 percent of the male inmates and 60.6 percent of the female inmates reporting exposure to sexually stimulating experiences and/or involvement in sexually intrusive acts in childhood. This finding may derive in part from the broader definition of sexual abuse that we used in our study which included exposure to pornography, being made aware that sex was occurring, being touched or fondled in a sexual manner, touching another in a sexual manner, having another attempt oral, anal, or vaginal intercourse, and/or having experienced

TABLE 4.5 Relationship between Juvenile Risk Factors Reported by Incarcerated Men (N=288) and Type of Sexual Experience in Prison

Juvenile Risk Factor	Any-sex		Predatory		Victim		Bartered		Consensual	
	No N=143 (%)	Yes N=145 (%)	No N=253 (%)	Yes N=35 (%)	No N=244 (%)	Yes N=44 (%)	No N=251 (%)	Yes N=37 (%)	No N=160 (%)	Yes N=128 (%)
Educational problems	86 (61.9)	98 (68.1)	160 (64.5)	24 (68.6)	160 (66.9)	24 (54.5)	156 (63.4)	28 (75.7)	93 (59.6)	91 (71.7)★
Early maladjustment – conduct problems	80 (57.1)	102 (70.8)★	158 (63.5)	24 (68.6)	154 (64.2)	28 (63.6)	154 (62.3)	28 (75.7)	88 (56.1)	94 (74.0)★★
Adolescent failure to establish relationships	38 (27.1)	49 (34.0)	79 (31.7)	8 (22.9)	71 (29.6)	16 (36.4)	72 (29.1)	15 (40.5)	41 (26.1)	46 (36.2)
First violent act prior to age 18	90 (64.3)	106 (73.6)	166 (66.7)	30 (85.7)★	168 (70.0)	28 (63.6)	165 (66.8)	31 (83.8)★	97 (61.8)★★	99 (78.0)★★
Self-Report Juvenile Criminal History	88 (61.5)	83 (57.2)	154 (60.9)	17 (48.6)	150 (61.5)	21 (47.7)	154 (61.4)	17 (45.9)	99 (61.9)	72 (56.2)
Juvenile Arrest History	61 (42.7)	63 (43.4)	109 (43.1)	15 (42.9)	111 (45.5)	13 (29.5)★	109 (43.4)	15 (45.0)	67 (41.9)	57 (44.5)

Note. ★p < 0.05, ★★p < 0.01.

TABLE 4.6 Relationship between Juvenile Risk Factors Reported by Incarcerated Women (N=183) and Type of Sexual Experience in Prison

Juvenile Risk Factor	Any-sex		Predatory		Victim		Bartered		Consensual	
	No N=77(%)	Yes N=106 (%)	No N=178 (%)	Yes N=5(%)	No N=134 (%)	Yes N=49 (%)	No N=165 (%)	Yes N=18(%)	No N=98 (%)	Yes N=85 (%)
Educational problems	39 (52.0)	49 (46.2)	85 (48.3)	3 (60.0)	70 (53.0)	18 (36.7)	80 (49.1)	8 (44.4)	47 (49.0)	41 (48.2)
Early maladjustment – conduct problems	33 (43.4)	53 (50.0)	82 (46.3)	4 (80.0)	64 (48.1)	22 (44.9)	80 (49.1)	6 (33.3)	40 (41.2)	46 (54.1)
Adolescent failure to establish elationships	29 (38.2)	45 (42.5)	70 (39.5)	4 (80.0)	55 (41.4)	19 (38.8)	66 (40.2)	8 (44.4)	37 (38.1)	37 (43.5)
First violent act prior to age 18	22 (28.6)	48 (46.2)*	68 (38.6)	2 (40.0)	48 (36.1)	22 (45.8)	64 (38.7)	7 (38.9)	33 (33.7)	37 (44.6)
Self-Report Juvenile Criminal History	31 (40.3)	56 (52.8)	84 (47.2)	3 (60.0)	64 (47.8)	23 (46.9)	76 (46.1)	11 (61.1)	37 (37.8)	50 (58.8)**
Juvenile Arrest History	13 (16.9)	31 (29.2)	43 (24.2)	1 (20.0)	29 (21.6)	15 (30.6)	38 (230)	6 (33.3)	16 (16.3)	28 (32.9)**

Note. $\star p < 0.05$, $\star\star p < 0.01$.

unwanted oral, anal, or vaginal intercourse. Nonetheless, these data reflect exposure to sexual experiences at an early age for the majority of the male and female inmates at rates far higher than found in community samples (Finkelhor, Turner, Ormrod, & Hamby, 2009).

This early experience of sexual abuse was found to be associated with all five forms of sexual behavior in prison for the male inmates. It was one of many adverse life experiences associated with any-sex, predatory sex, bartered sex, and consensual sex in prison and one of only two risk factors for sexual victimization for the male inmates (sexual abuse and living away from family prior to age 15 years). Early sexual abuse was similarly associated with the sexual behavior of women in prison, but to a lesser extent than found with the men. Within our female sample, early sexual abuse was associated with any-sex and consensual sex in prison, but not with sexual predation, being a victim of sexual coercion, or being involved in bartered sexual exchanges. These findings lend support to the large body of research that examines the effect of adverse experiences in childhood on adult adaptation and, in particular, the impact of these experiences on high risk sexual behavior in adulthood. Moreover, they suggest that the association identified by Coid et al. (2001) between early sexual abuse and sexual victimization in adulthood for community dwelling females might hold equally true, if not even more powerfully, for men given a particular set of living circumstances.

The early adverse experiences associated with any-sex in prison were both similar and different for the male and female inmates, with the common elements reflecting risk markers for antisocial behavior in general. Male inmates involved in any-sex while incarcerated were characterized as having experienced psychological abuse, physical abuse, sexual abuse, neglect, living away from home prior to age 15 years, maternal incarceration, paternal drug addiction, head injury with LOC, and early maladjustment conduct problems. Female inmates involved in any-sex while incarcerated were characterized as having experienced psychological abuse, physical abuse, sexual abuse, neglect, violence observed towards the mother, maternal depression, maternal arrest, and first violent act prior to age 18 years. This wide panoply of adverse and abusive early life experiences has been associated with conduct disorders in adolescence (Loeber & Farrington, 1998; Moffitt et al., 2001; Wiebush, Baird, Krisberg, & Onek, 1995), antisociality in adulthood for both men and women (Johnson, Bromley, & McGeoch, 2005), and rape by men in the community (Lalumière, Harris, Quinsey, & Rice, 2005). The commonality of these early risk markers to adult antisocial behavior in general serves to underscore the complexity of the issues surrounding sex in prison as the life experiences that place individuals at risk for incarceration simultaneously place them at risk for sexual activity in this same environment. The broad array of adverse experiences in childhood that are associated with any-sex in prison also argue against the normalization of this behavior as a natural expression of affection and sexual desire in a restrictive environment and rather points to it being an adaptation that is associated with many other disruptive and traumatic life events.

The gender differences that were superimposed upon these common precursors to any-sex in prison involved the males living away from home prior to the age of 15 years, maternal incarceration, paternal drug addiction, early conduct problems, and the experience of at least one head injury with LOC. For the female inmates, any-sex was uniquely associated with exposure to maternal physical abuse, maternal depression, and first violent act prior to the age of 18 years. These differences may reflect gender differences in sexual promiscuity or sexual appetite, with men being made more open to sexual exchanges in prisons through experiences that neurologically contribute to recklessness, while women are made more open to these same experiences through the disruption of healthy internalizations and non-ambivalent identifications with their mothers.

We discovered not unexpectedly more sexually predatory men than women, but for both genders this behavior was associated with early violence. For the men, predation was manifest by the experience of psychological, physical, and sexual abuse, head injury with LOC, and in the onset of violent behavior before the age of 18 years. For the women, it was associated with a pattern of having observed violence being perpetrated against the father, maternal arrest, maternal drug addiction, paternal depression, and overall maternal pathology, although none of the adolescent variables. These patterns are reflective of the old adage that rape is more about domination and control than sex and that rape is only one of many types of interpersonal violence (Hazelwood & Burgess, 2001; Lalumière et al., 2005).

The male victim of sexual coercion in prison was characterized by sexual abuse in childhood and living away from home prior to the age of 15 years combined with lower rates of arrest in adolescence. The female victim of sexual coercion in prison was characterized by psychological abuse, neglect, and maternal depression, although not with any adolescent variables. These risk factors again support gender differences in the emergence of a victimized stance while incarcerated. Together they suggest that men are made vulnerable to sexual victimization in prison based upon earlier sexual victimization in childhood, while women are made more vulnerable by the absence of active parenting either through maternal depression or overt neglect. Both genders, however, appear to be at higher risk for sexual victimization in adulthood because of a lack of consistent parental support and supervision.

Bartered sex among the male inmates was associated with psychological abuse, physical abuse, sexual abuse, paternal arrest, paternal incarceration, overall paternal pathology as measured by the PBIS, and first violent act prior to age 18 years. Bartered sex among the female inmates was associated only with neglect and no adolescent variables. These patterns suggest that the male inmates who devised ways to barter for goods or safety were familiar with prison life having been involved with fathers who had been arrested, incarcerated, and vulnerable to other forms of psychopathology. The women who bartered sex in prison had been neglected as children suggesting that they could not count on support and assistance from their families during childhood.

Consensual sex for the male inmates was associated with psychological abuse, physical abuse, sexual abuse, living away from family before age 15 years, paternal arrest, paternal drug addiction, educational problems, early conduct problems, and first violent act prior to age 18 years. Consensual sex for the female inmates was associated with sexual abuse in childhood, being exposed to violence perpetrated against the mother, maternal arrest, maternal incarceration, maternal drug addiction, paternal drug addiction, higher rates of self-report offending in adolescence, and higher rates of self-report juvenile arrests. For both the males and females, sexual abuse in childhood increased the probability that these individuals would be sexually active while imprisoned. However, for the male inmates, this sexual abuse was associated with other forms of physical and psychological abuse, while for the women it was associated with higher levels of maternal and paternal psychopathology. These patterns are also consistent with prior research linking early adverse life events to high risk sexual behavior in adulthood (Foti, 1995; Hillis et al., 2001).

The high rates of head injury reported by both the male (45.6%) and female (36.1%) inmates underscore both the chaotic nature of their early lives and the chronicity of the neurological deficits that they carry with them into adulthood. There are few estimates of the prevalence of head injury with LOC in the general population, but estimates in the literature range from 5 percent to 24 percent (McGuire, Burright, Williams, & Donovick, 1998). The rates in this study were two to ten times higher, a finding that is consistent with previous research which has found that the rate of head injury with LOC is substantially higher (25%–87%) among incarcerated populations (Barnfield & Leathem, 1998; Morrell, Merbitz, Jain, & Jain, 1998; Schofield et al., 2006; Slaughter, Fann, & Ehde, 2003). This compromising type of injury was associated with any-sex and sexually predatory behavior among the male inmates, but with none of the categories of sexual behavior among the female inmates.

Finally, for both the male and female inmates, the effects of adverse life events in childhood were more powerfully associated with the different types of prison sexual behavior than were the behavioral disruptions occurring in adolescence. This may reflect normal differences between the early, formative experiences of childhood and the more transitory experiences of adolescence. Nonetheless, in our sample, it clearly demonstrated the significance of these early life traumas and their impact, not only on adult life in the community, but also to adjustment to prison.

When viewed across categories of sexual behavior, our data underscore the gender differences in the impact of early life trauma on sexual behavior in prison. While we found comparable rates of early adverse life experiences among the male and female inmates, and some commonality across categories of sexual behavior in prison, the more persistent finding was that of gender differences in the association of particular types of early adverse experiences with the different types of sexual behavior in prison. Both men and women are placed at higher risk for any type of sexual behavior in prison by chaotic, neglectful, and abusive experiences in childhood. However, as we found, the men are more likely to become sexual victims in prison if they have been previously victimized sexually, while the women are more vulnerable to sexual victimization in prison if they have experienced neglect and parental depression in childhood. Taken most broadly, these differences highlight the importance of gender specific risk paradigms for sexual behavior in prison and the significance of a broad panoply of adverse early life experiences in different types of sexual behavior during incarceration.

5

COMMUNITY AND INSTITUTIONAL VIOLENCE AS RISK MARKERS FOR SEXUAL PREDATION AND VICTIMIZATION

All efforts to predict violent behavior in the community have identified the significance of past violent behavior and criminality. This association has been examined from different theoretical perspectives including criminology, behavioral sciences, forensic psychiatry and psychology, public health, and most recently decision theory and neuroscience (Blumstein, Cohen, Roth, & Visher, 1986; Moffitt et al., 2001; Monahan et al., 2001; Slovic, Finucane, Peters, & MacGregor, 2002; Warren et al., 1998). Intrinsic to each of these domains is the recognition that violent behavior often reflects a patterned behavior that can be predicted if information is collected and assessed concerning past violent behavior. This basic premise was captured in the early history of violence risk assessment research when Monahan reviewed the extant research and concluded, "[p]ast violence is the best predictor of future violence" (Monahan, 1981, p. 76). In this chapter, we examine indices of community and institutional violent behavior and victimization as they are associated with the five categories of sexual behavior in prison.

Community Violence and Victimization

Physical Fights and Violent Crime

All major violence risk instruments include past violence and/or victim injury as a risk factor for future violent behavior (see the HCR-20 and VRAG in Chapter 8). The MacArthur Violence Risk Assessment Study found that arrests for both violent and non-violent crimes were associated with violent behavior after release from a psychiatric institution. The HCR-20 includes past violence as its first historical risk factor and is currently pilot testing additional risk factors that include previous violent and non-violent criminality. The VRAG assesses the degree of victim injury as one of 11 risk factors that predicts violence among forensic patients following release into the community.

Aggregate crime statistics reflect a parallel co-occurrence of violent crime and various types of sexual aggression in the community. Young men under the age of 24 years are responsible for committing both the largest number of reported rapes each year as well as the largest percentage of homicide, assault, and non-violent property offenses (Ellis & Walsh, 2000). Rates of violent crime are also found to co-mingle with rates of rape over different time periods and cultural contexts. America experienced a significant decline in the rate of rape nationwide during the 1990s which mirrored the same decline in rates of homicide, assault, sexual abuse of children, domestic violence, and robbery (Uniform Crime Report, Bureau of Justice Statistics, http://www.ojp. usdoj.gov/bjs).

Intimate Partner Violence

Intimate partner violence perpetrated by males has been associated with dysthymia, adult antisocial behavior, and non-affective psychosis. Recent research has begun to identify the relationship between psychopathic traits and battering specifically as it is associated with deficient affective experiences, heightened impulsivity, and irresponsibility as measured by two of the four facets of the Psychopathy Checklist Revised (PCL-R2) (Swogger, Walsh, & Kosson, 2007). Statistical data maintained by the BJS and the Federal Bureau of Investigation (FBI) indicate that 78 percent of the male inmates incarcerated in jail for domestic violence have a prior conviction and four out of ten male inmates have a criminal status at the time of the incident (Chaiken, 1998; http://www.ojp. usdoj.gov/bjs).

For many women, much of the violence they experience, both as perpetrators and as victims, occurs in the context of their intimate relationships with others. Kessler, Molnar, Feurer, and Appelbaum (2001) analyzed data from the National Co-morbidity Survey and found that 6.5 percent of women and 5.5 percent of men reported having experienced severe domestic violence at some point in their adult lives. The perpetration of severe domestic violence by women has been associated with prior victimization in intimate relationships and patterns of exposure to various high risk behaviors including the use of drugs and having more than ten male sexual partners (Cohen et al., 2000). Research concerning women who are considered generally violent has also found their battering behavior to be more physically assaultive, to involve more instrumental violence, and to entail more emotionally abusive tactics. Battering among this particularly violent group of women was associated with a mean of 7.7 physical fights with a non-partner since the age of 18 years (Babcock, Miller, & Siard, 2003).

Study Analyses

Two primary indices of community violence were used. The number of self-reported physical fights since the age of 18 years was derived from the Prison Background Information Survey (PBIS). The perpetration or victimization of intimate partner violence was obtained from scoring four subscales of the Conflict Tactics Scale (CTS 2). These data were examined for gender differences and then assessed concerning their association with five categories of sexual behavior in prison.

Table 5.1 illustrates the high levels of community violence that characterized the adult lives of both the male and female inmates in our sample prior to incarceration. Over 90 percent of the male inmates reported involvement in at least one physical fight since the age of 18 years and, while significantly lower, over two thirds of the female inmates reported at least one physical fight since reaching adulthood.

Rates of intimate partner violence were also high for both the male and female inmates. Three quarters or more of the male inmates reported using negotiation, psychological, or physical conflict resolution strategies on their partner, and nearly two thirds or more of the female inmates reported using the same strategies. Significantly more male than female inmates used physical strategies with their partner. Yet, significantly more female inmates (43.2%) than male inmates (27.9%) reported inflicting an injury on their partner.

Similar patterns were observed among male and female inmates whose partners used these strategies on them, although significantly more male inmates reported their partner used physical strategies with them. Similar rates of male and

TABLE 5.1 Frequency of Violence and Victimization Prior to Incarceration Reported by Incarcerated Men (N=180) and Women (N=148)

	Men		Women		Effect Size	
	N	$\%$	N	$\%$	χ^2	Φ
Any Fights Since Age 18	263	91.2	125	68.3	40.82★★	−0.29★★
CTS 2 – By Self [a]						
Negotiation	177	98.3	147	99.3	0.66	0.05
Psychological	152	84.9	131	88.5	0.90	0.05
Physical	133	74.3	90	60.8	6.79★★	−0.14★★
Injury	49	27.9	64	43.2	9.02★★	0.17★★
CTS 2 – By Partner [a]						
Negotiation	176	98.3	147	99.3	0.67	0.05
Psychological	157	87.7	128	87.2	0.02	−0.01
Physical	140	78.2	93	62.8	9.35★★	−0.17★★
Injury	49	27.9	51	34.7	2.03	0.08

Note. ★★$p < 0.01$.

[a] N=180 for men and 148 for women due to missing data on CTS 2.

female inmates reported being injured by their partner (27.9% of males and 34.7% of females) during a conflict.

Table 5.2 (males) and Table 5.3 (females) present the correlations of these variables with the five categories of sexual behavior while in prison. Among the male inmates, any-sex was associated with any fights since the age of 18 years and the partner's use of negotiation during a conflict. Opposite patterns were observed among the female inmates, with any-sex being negatively associated with involvement in any fights since the age of 18 years, negatively associated with the physical perpetration of violence, but positively associated with being the victim of psychological and physical violence by a partner prior to incarceration.

Sexual predation and sexual victimization were not associated with any of the community violence or victimization variables for male or female inmates. However, bartered sex was associated with perpetrating physical violence against a partner, a partner's use of negotiation, and experiencing a physical injury in the context of domestic battering. Among female inmates, bartered sex was negatively associated with injuring a partner during a conflict.

Finally, consensual sex among male inmates was associated with any fights since the age of 18 years and a partner's use of negotiation. Consensual sex among female inmates was negatively associated with any fights since the age of 18 years, and negatively associated with the use of negotiation and physical strategies.

Prior Criminal Involvement and Current Prison Status

Correctional Risk Classification Schemes

Correctional risk classification schemes consistently reference prior offending and past violence as part of their security and placement assessment of individuals both while incarcerated and during placement in the community (Gaes et al., 2002; Gendreau, Goggin, & Law, 1997; Gover, Pérez, & Jennings, 2008; Greenfeld & Snell, 1999; Harer & Langan, 2001; Harer & Steffensmeier, 1996; Kury & Smartt, 2002; Skeem & Louden, 2006). Unresolved is the extent to which these risk factors differ between the genders. Some research indicates that these contributory factors to prison violence are the same for males and females, albeit at different levels (Harer & Langan, 2001). Other research suggests that the predictive factors are significantly, and in some instances inversely, predictive of different forms of institutional behavior across genders (Gover et al., 2008).

Study Analyses

Five indices of prior and current criminality and offending were collected from the Prison Background Information Survey (PBIS). Information concerning the inmates' past criminal history was collected from a number of different data sources and cross referenced when determining whether it had occurred. These

TABLE 5.2 Relationship between Violence and Victimization Prior to Incarceration Reported by Incarcerated Men (*N*=180)[a] and Type of Sexual Experience in Prison

Item/Scale	Any-sex		Predatory		Victim		Bartered		Consensual	
	No N=143 (%)	Yes N=145 (%)	No N=253 (%)	Yes N=35 (%)	No N=244 (%)	Yes N=44 (%)	No N=251 (%)	Yes N=37 (%)	No N=160 (%)	Yes N=128 (%)★
Any fights since age 18	125 (87.4)	138 (95.2)★	230 (90.9)	33 (94.3)	223 (91.4)	40 (90.9)	227 (90.4)	36 (97.3)	140 (87.5)	123 (96.1)★
	No N=94 M(SD)	Yes N=86 M(SD)	No N=161 M(SD)	Yes N=19 M(SD)	No N=152 M(SD)	Yes N=28 M(SD)	No N=162 M(SD)	Yes N=18 M(SD)	No N=107 M(SD)	Yes N=72 M(SD)
CTS 2 – By Self[a]										
Negotiation	4.0 (1.6)	4.4 (1.6)	4.2 (1.6)	4.3 (1.8)	4.2 (1.6)	4.0 (1.6)	4.1 (1.6)	4.7 (1.8)	4.0 (1.6)	4.4 (1.6)
Psychological	1.5 (1.4)	1.8 (1.7)	1.6 (1.5)	2.2 (2.0)	1.6 (1.5)	1.6 (1.6)	1.6 (1.5)	1.9 (1.7)	1.5 (1.4)	1.8 (1.7)
Physical	0.8 (1.0)	0.8 (1.0)	0.8 (1.0)	1.1 (1.2)	0.9 (1.1)	0.6 (0.6)	0.8 (1.0)	1.4 (1.4)★	0.8 (1.0)	0.8 (1.0)
Injury	0.2 (0.6)	0.2 (0.4)	0.2 (0.5)	0.3 (0.5)	0.2 (0.5)	0.2 (0.4)	0.2 (0.5)	0.4 (0.6)	0.3 (0.6)	0.2 (0.4)
CTS 2 – By Partner[a]										
Negotiation	4.0 (1.6)	4.5 (1.6)★	4.2 (1.6)	4.2 (2.0)	4.2 (1.6)	4.1 (1.6)	4.1 (1.6)	4.9 (1.6)★	4.0 (1.6)	4.5 (1.6)★
Psychological	1.5 (1.3)	1.9 (1.7)	1.6 (1.5)	2.1 (1.8)	1.7 (1.5)	1.6 (1.5)	1.7 (1.5)	1.9 (1.8)	1.5 (1.4)	1.9 (1.8)
Physical	0.9 (1.1)	0.9 (1.0)	0.9 (1.1)	1.0 (1.0)	0.9 (1.1)	0.7 (0.8)	0.8 (1.0)	1.3 (1.1)	0.9 (1.1)	0.9 (1.0)
Injury	0.3 (0.6)	0.3 (0.7)	0.3 (0.7)	0.5 (0.8)	0.3 (0.7)	0.2 (0.5)	0.3 (0.6)	0.7 (1.1)★★	0.3 (0.6)	0.3 (0.7)

Note. ★*p* < 0.05, ★★*p* < 0.01.

[a]N=180 due to missing CTS 2 data. CTS 2 scaled as 0=never, 7=more than 20 times.

TABLE 5.3 Relationship between Violence and Victimization Prior to Incarceration Reported by Incarcerated Women (N=148)[a] and Type of Sexual Experience in Prison

Item/Scale	Any-sex		Predatory		Victim		Bartered		Consensual	
	No N=77 (%)	Yes N=106 (%)	No N=178 (%)	Yes N=5 (%)	No N=134 (%)	Yes N=49 (%)	No N=165 (%)	Yes N=18 (%)	No N=98 (%)	Yes N=85 (%)
Any fights since age 18	138 (95.2)★	78 (73.6)	33 (94.3)	4 (80.0)	40 (90.9)	38 (77.6)	36 (97.3)	13 (72.2)	123 (96.1)★	63 (74.1)
	No N=63 M(SD)	Yes N=85 M(SD)	No N=144 M(SD)	Yes N=4 M(SD)	No N=110 M(SD)	Yes N=38 M(SD)	No N=134 M(SD)	Yes N=14 M(SD)	No N=78 M(SD)	Yes N=70 M(SD)
CTS 2 – By Self[a]										
Negotiation	4.50 (1.8)	4.65 (1.5)	4.57 (1.6)	5.08 (1.1)	4.65 (1.6)	4.39 (1.4)	4.59 (1.6)	4.55 (1.1)	4.34 (1.7)★	4.86 (1.4)
Psychological	1.96 (1.4)	2.48 (1.8)	2.23 (1.7)	3.29 (2.5)	2.23 (1.7)	2.33 (1.7)	2.28 (1.7)	2.08 (2.0)	2.04 (1.5)	2.51 (1.8)
Physical	0.51 (0.9)★★	1.04 (1.3)	0.79 (1.1)	1.81 (1.5)	0.75 (1.1)	1.02 (1.3)	0.81 (1.2)	0.85 (0.7)	0.62 (1.1)★	1.03 (1.2)
Injury	0.58 (1.1)	0.98 (1.4)	0.80 (1.3)	1.04 (1.3)	0.73 (1.2)	1.02 (1.5)	0.86 (1.3)★	0.27 (0.7)	0.70 (1.2)	0.93 (1.4)
CTS 2 – By Partner[a]										
Negotiation	4.37 (1.8)	4.21 (1.5)	4.27 (1.6)	4.50 (1.4)	4.34 (1.7)	4.08 (1.4)	4.28 (1.7)	4.17 (1.0)	4.21 (1.8)	4.36 (1.4)
Psychological	2.00 (1.6)★	2.67 (2.1)	2.36 (1.9)	3.32 (2.4)	2.27 (1.8)	2.71 (2.1)	2.43 (1.9)	1.92 (2.0)	2.22 (1.8)	2.58 (2.0)
Physical	0.97 (1.6)★	1.70 (1.9)	1.38 (1.8)	1.85 (1.3)	1.27 (1.7)	1.73 (2.0)	1.43 (1.8)	0.95 (0.9)	1.17 (1.8)	1.63 (1.7)
Injury	0.35 (0.7)	0.58 (1.1)	0.47 (0.9)	0.83 (1.3)	0.44 (0.9)	0.60 (1.2)	0.51 (1.0)	0.22 (0.4)	0.45 (1.0)	0.51 (0.9)

Note. ★$p < 0.05$, ★★$p < 0.01$.

[a]N=148 due to missing CTS 2 data.

data were assessed for gender differences and then for their association with the five categories of sexual behavior in prison.

As presented in Table 5.4, both the male and female inmates reported a combination of non-violent, violent, and sexual crimes. The rates of violent crime and sexual crime are significantly higher for the male inmates, although over one half of the female inmates reported involvement in a prior violent crime and 9.9 percent reported involvement in a prior sexual offense. Both male and female inmates were found to be chronic offenders with over half of both genders having served at least three or more (and for some inmates nine or more) prior periods

TABLE 5.4 Frequency of Prior Criminal Involvement and Prison Status by Incarcerated Men (N=288) and Women (N=183)

Item	Men		Women		Effect Size	
	N	%	N	%	χ^2	Φ
Self-Reported Criminal Activity[a]						
Violent	158	76.0	85	52.5	2.96**	−0.24**
Non-violent	185	90.7	139	87.4	0.99	−0.05
Sexual	37	19.0	15	9.9	5.45*	−0.13*
Number of Prior Incarcerations[b]					5.89	0.13
None	68	27.0	42	33.6		
One	27	10.7	12	9.6		
Two	30	11.9	6	4.8		
Three to eight	75	29.8	37	29.6		
Nine or more	52	20.6	28	22.4		
Previous Parole or Probation Violation						
One or more	202	70.1	100	54.6	11.68**	−0.16**
Current Most Serious Offense					69.28**	0.39**
Violent	91	32.3	48	26.2		
Potentially violent	63	22.3	35	19.1		
Other crimes against person	10	3.5	14	7.7		
Sex	56	19.9	1	0.5		
Property	22	7.8	44	24.0		
Drug	27	9.6	36	19.7		
Other	13	4.6	5	2.7		
Current Sentence Length					78.40**	0.41**
<1 year	5	1.8	23	12.8		
1–5 years	51	18.2	77	42.8		
6–10 years	47	16.8	34	18.9		
11–20 years	66	23.6	19	10.6		
>20, but not life	65	23.6	18	10.0		
Life sentence	46	16.4	9	5.0		

Note. *p < 0.01; **p < 0.001.
[a]N=162 due to missing data. [b]N=125 due to missing file data.

of incarceration. Almost three quarters of the male inmates and over one half of the female inmates had experienced a prior supervision failure while on either probation or parole, although significantly more male inmates were in this category. The male inmates were predominately incarcerated for crimes that were classified as violent, potentially violent, or sexual. The female inmates were primarily incarcerated for crimes classified as violent, property, drug related, and potentially violent. Half of the male inmates were serving sentences of 11 years to life as contrasted to the majority of the female inmates who were serving sentences of less than six years.

Most of the criminal history variables commonly used in prison classification schemes were unrelated to sexual behavior in prison among the male inmates (see Table 5.5). Sexual victimization and consensual sex were each associated only with self-report violent criminal activity. Any-sex, predatory sex, and bartered sex were not associated with any of the criminogenic variables included in this study for male inmates.

As with the male inmates, there was little association between the five categories of sexual behavior and most of the criminogenic risk factors among the women in our sample (see Table 5.6). Any-sex was associated with self-report violent criminal activity, "other" instant offense, and a life sentence. Predatory sexual violence was only associated with having nine or more prior incarcerations. Consensual sex was associated with self-report violent criminal activity and serving a life sentence. However, sexual victimization and bartered sex were unrelated to any of the criminogenic risk factor variables for female inmates.

Institutional Violence and Victimization

Male and Female Non-sexual Victimization in Prison

Wolff, Blitz, Siegel, and Bachman (2007) studied victimization in prison across a single state system and found that the 6-month prevalence of inmate-on-inmate physical victimization was 21 percent with this rate being comparable for male and female populations. However, physical assaults on males were more likely to involve the use of a weapon. In addition, although both male and female inmates were victimized by correctional officers, male inmates reported being physically assaulted by a staff member at a rate that was three times higher than for the female inmates (Wolff et al., 2007).

Demographic and personal characteristics have been found to differentiate inmates who are at higher and lower risk for physical victimization while imprisoned. Wolff, Shi, and Bachman (2008) found that Hispanic and Caucasian inmates reported higher rates of inmate physical victimization than did African American inmates. Younger inmates have also been found to be at higher risk for personal and property crime (Kerbs & Jolley, 2007; Wolff & Shi, 2011; Wooldredge, 1998). Kerbs and Jolley (2007) found that 0.8 percent of inmates over the age of 50 years

TABLE 5.5 Relationship between Prior Criminal Involvement and Prison Status by Incarcerated Men ($N = 288$) and Sexual Experience in Prison

Item	Any-sex		Predatory		Victim		Bartered		Consensual	
	No N=143 (%)	Yes N=145 (%)	No N=253 (%)	Yes N=35 (%)	No N=244 (%)	Yes N=44 (%)	No N=251 (%)	Yes N=37 (%)	No N=160 (%)	Yes N=128 (%)
Self-Report Criminal Activity[a]										
Violent	77 (71.8)	81 (81.0)	138 (74.2)	20 (90.9)	143 (79.4)	15(53.6)★★	139 (74.7)	19 (86.4)	83 (68.0)	75 (87.2)★★
Non-violent	97 (91.5)	88 (89.8)	165 (90.2)	20 (95.2)	160 (90.8)	25 (89.3)	166 (90.7)	19 (90.5)	109 (90.8)	76 (90.5)
Sexual	17 (17.2)	20 (20.8)	34 (19.5)	3 (14.3)	29 (17.4)	8 (28.6)	33 (19.0)	4 (19.0)	21 (18.6)	16 (19.5)
Number of Prior Incarcerations[b]										
None	27 (21.6)	41 (32.3)	59 (26.8)	9 (28.1)	57 (26.5)	11 (29.7)	57 (25.8)	11 (35.5)	31 (22.0)	37 (33.3)
One	15 (12.0)	12 (9.4)	24 (10.9)	3 (9.4)	22 (10.2)	5 (13.5)	25 (11.3)	2 (6.5)	17 (12.1)	10 (9.0)
Two	14 (11.2)	16 (12.6)	27 (12.3)	3 (9.4)	25 (11.6)	5 (13.5)	23 (10.4)	7 (22.6)	15 (10.6)	15 (13.5)
Three to eight	40 (32.0)	35 (27.6)	63 (28.6)	12 (37.5)	67 (31.2)	8 (21.6)	68 (30.8)	7 (22.6)	46 (32.6)	29 (26.1)
Nine or more	29 (23.2)	23 (18.1)	47 (21.4)	5 (15.6)	44 (20.5)	8 (21.6)	48 (21.7)	4 (12.9)	32 (22.7)	20 (18.0)
Previous Parole or Probation Violation										
One or more	97 (67.8)	105 (72.4)	175(69.2)	27 (77.1)	166 (68.0)	36 (81.8)	174 (69.3)	28 (75.7)	108 (67.5)	94 (73.4)
Current Most Serious Offense										
Violent	39 (27.9)	52 (36.6)	78 (31.6)	13 (37.1)	81 (33.9)	10 (23.3)	76 (31.0)	15 (40.5)	40 (25.6)	51 (40.5)
Potentially violent	30 (21.4)	33 (23.2)	55 (22.3)	8 (22.9)	57 (23.8)	6 (14.0)	51 (20.8)	12 (32.4)	35 (22.4)	28 (22.2)
Other crimes against person	6 (4.3)	4 (2.8)	9 (3.6)	1 (2.9)	9 (3.8)	1 (2.3)	8 (3.3)	2 (5.4)	6 (3.8)	4 (3.2)
Sex	30 (21.4)	26 (18.3)	52 (21.1)	4 (11.4)	44 (18.4)	12 (27.9)	53 (21.6)	3 (8.1)	37 (23.7)	19 (15.1)
Property	10 (7.1)	12 (8.5)	17 (6.9)	5 (14.3)	14 (5.9)	8 (18.6)	20 (8.2)	2 (5.4)	12 (7.7)	10 (7.9)
Drug	17 (12.1)	10 (7.0)	24 (9.7)	3 (8.6)	23 (9.6)	4 (9.3)	24 (9.8)	3 (8.1)	17 (10.9)	10 (7.9)
Other	8 (5.7)	5 (3.5)	12 (4.9)	1 (2.9)	11 (4.6)	2 (4.7)	13 (5.3)	0 (0.0)	9 (5.8)	4 (3.2)

(Continued overleaf)

TABLE 5.5 Continued

Item	Any-sex		Predatory		Victim		Bartered		Consensual	
	No N=143 (%)	Yes N=145 (%)	No N=253 (%)	Yes N=35 (%)	No N=244 (%)	Yes N=44 (%)	No N=251 (%)	Yes N=37 (%)	No N=160 (%)	Yes N=128 (%)
Current Sentence Length										
<1 year	3 (2.2)	2 (1.4)	5 (2.0)	0 (0.0)	4 (1.7)	1 (2.3)	4 (1.6)	1 (1.7)	4 (2.6)	1 (0.8)
1–5 years	32 (23.5)	19 (13.2)	47 (19.2)	4 (11.4)	45 (19.1)	6 (13.6)	48 (19.8)	3 (8.1)	34 (22.2)	17 (13.4)
6–10 years	24 (17.6)	23 (16.0)	43 (17.6)	4 (11.4)	43 (18.2)	4 (9.1)	39 (16.0)	8 (21.6)	27 (17.6)	20 (15.7)
11–20 years	26 (19.1)	40 (27.8)	54 (22.0)	12 (34.3)	51 (21.6)	15 (34.1)	54 (22.2)	12 (32.4)	30 (19.6)	36 (28.3)
>20, but not life	30 (22.1)	35 (24.3)	57 (23.3)	8 (22.9)	53 (22.5)	12 (27.3)	57 (23.5)	8 (21.6)	34 (22.2)	31 (24.4)
Life sentence	21 (15.4)	25 (17.4)	39 (15.9)	7 (20.0)	40 (16.9)	6 (13.6)	41 (16.9)	5 (13.5)	24 (15.7)	22 (17.3)

Note. **$p < 0.001$.

TABLE 5.6 Relationship between Prior Criminal Involvement and Prison Status by Incarcerated Women (N=183) and Type of Sexual Experience in Prison

Item	Any-sex No N=77 (%)	Any-sex Yes N=106 (%)	Predatory No N=178 (%)	Predatory Yes N=5 (%)	Victim No N=134 (%)	Victim Yes N=49 (%)	Bartered No N=165 (%)	Bartered Yes N=18 (%)	Consensual No N=98 (%)	Consensual Yes N=85 (%)
Self-Report Criminal Activity[a]										
Violent	30 (42.3)	55 (60.4)*	83 (52.9)	2 (40.0)	61 (50.8)	24 (57.1)	73 (50.3)	12 (70.6)	37 (41.6)	48 (65.8)**
Non-violent	57 (82.6)	82 (91.1)	135 (87.7)	4 (80.0)	101 (86.3)	38 (90.5)	123 (86.6)	16 (94.1)	73 (83.9)	66 (91.7)
Sexual	7 (10.8)	8 (9.3)	14 (9.6)	1 (20.0)	12 (10.8)	3 (7.5)	1 (10.4)	1 (6.2)	8 (9.6)	7 (10.3)
Number of Prior Incarcerations[b]										
None	17 (34.7)	25 (32.9)	42 (34.4)	0 (0.0)	30 (33.7)	12 (33.3)	37 (33.6)	5 (33.3)	22 (34.4)	20 (32.8)
One	3 (6.1)	9 (11.8)	12 (9.8)	0 (0.0)	5 (5.6)	7 (19.4)	9 (8.2)	3 (20.0)	6 (9.4)	6 (9.8)
Two	0 (0.0)	6 (7.9)	6 (4.9)	0 (0.0)	4 (4.5)	2 (5.6)	5 (4.5)	1 (6.7)	1 (1.6)	5 (8.2)
Three to eight	16 (32.7)	21 (27.6)	37 (30.3)	0 (0.0)	29 (32.6)	8 (22.2)	34 (30.9)	3 (20.0)	19 (29.7)	18 (29.5)
Nine or more	13 (26.5)	15 (19.7)	25 (20.5)	3 (100.0)*	21 (23.6)	7 (19.4)	25 (22.7)	3 (20.0)	16 (25.0)	12 (19.7)
Previous Parole or Probation Violation										
One or more	41 (53.2)	59 (55.7)	96 (53.9)	4 (80.0)	74 (55.2)	26 (53.1)	92 (55.8)	8 (44.4)	52 (53.1)	48 (56.5)
Current Most Serious Offense										
Violent	18 (23.4)	30 (28.3)	48 (27.0)	0 (0.0)	31 (23.1)	17 (34.7)	42 (25.5)	6 (33.3)	23 (23.5)	25 (29.4)
Potentially violent	10 (13.0)	25 (23.6)	34 (19.1)	1 (20.0)	24 (17.9)	11 (22.4)	29 (17.6)	6 (33.3)	16 (16.3)	19 (22.4)
Other crimes against person	9 (11.7)	5 (4.7)	14 (7.9)	0 (0.0)	14 (10.4)	0 (0.0)	14 (8.5)	0 (0.0)	9 (9.2)	5 (5.9)
Sex	1 (1.3)	0 (0.0)	1 (0.6)	0 (0.0)	1 (0.7)	0 (0.0)	1 (0.6)	0 (0.0)	1 (1.0)	0 (0.0)
Property	25 (32.5)	19 (17.9)	42 (23.6)	2 (40.0)	37 (27.6)	7 (14.3)	42 (25.5)	2 (11.1)	29 (29.6)	15 (17.6)
Drug	11 (14.3)	25 (23.6)	34 (19.1)	2 (40.0)	24 (17.9)	12 (24.5)	32 (19.4)	4 (22.2)	16 (16.3)	20 (23.5)
Other	3 (3.9)	2 (1.9)*	5 (2.8)	0 (0.0)	3 (2.2)	2 (4.1)	5 (3.0)	0 (0.0)	4 (4.1)	1 (1.2)

(Continued overleaf)

TABLE 5.6 Continued

Item	Any-sex		Predatory		Victim		Bartered		Consensual	
	No N=77 (%)	Yes N=106 (%)	No N=178 (%)	Yes N=5 (%)	No N=134 (%)	Yes N=49 (%)	No N=165 (%)	Yes N=18 (%)	No N=98 (%)	Yes N=85 (%)
Current Sentence Length										
<1 year	13 (17.6)	10 (9.4)	21 (12.0)	2 (40.0)	20 (15.3)	3 (6.1)	20 (12.3)	3 (16.7)	14 (14.7)	9 (10.6)
1–5 years	43 (58.1)	34 (32.1)	76 (43.4)	1 (20.0)	58 (44.3)	19 (38.8)	71 (43.8)	6 (33.3)	52 (54.7)	25 (29.4)
6–10 years	7 (9.5)	27 (27.5)	33 (18.9)	1 (20.0)	25 (19.1)	9 (18.4)	32 (19.8)	2 (11.1)	11 (11.6)	23 (27.1)
11–20 years	3 (4.1)	16 (15.1)	18 (10.3)	1 (20.0)	10 (7.6)	9 (18.4)	14 (8.6)	5 (27.8)	8 (8.4)	11 (12.9)
>20, but not life	5 (6.8)	13 (12.3)	18 (10.3)	0 (0.0)	14 (10.7)	4 (8.2)	17 (10.5)	1 (5.6)	6 (6.3)	12 (14.1)
Life sentence	3 (4.1)	6 (5.7)★★	9 (5.1)	0 (0.0)	4 (3.1)	5 (10.2)	8 (4.9)	1 (5.6)	4 (4.2)	5 (5.9)★★

Note. ★$p < 0.01$; ★★$p < 0.001$.

reported having been punched, kicked, pushed, or attacked without a weapon in the past year, primarily by younger inmates.

Recently, Wolff and Shi (2009) identified seven distinct types of physical victimization encountered in prison environments. They found that theft (24.3%), being threatened or harmed with a knife or shank (12.4%), and being slapped, hit, kicked, or bit (10.2%) were the most common forms of physical victimization reported by the male inmates. The majority of the male inmates reported experiencing one of two types of physical victimization over the past six months, with most stating that they did not report the incident to the authorities unless they were seriously injured. Wolff and Shi (2009) also found that the majority of the physical assaults occurred during the day in the yard and in recreational areas and were likely to involve gang-affiliated inmates who were acquainted with the victim. Only a minority of the victims reported knowing why they were assaulted, but of those who offered a reason, one third stated that the assault was motivated by racial or ethnic factors. Most victims reported protecting themselves by avoiding certain people and areas and generally isolating themselves from others.

Male and Female Sexual Victimization in Prison

Prior research has indicated that Caucasian inmates (Austin, Fabelo, Gunter, & McGinnis, 2006; Chonco, 1989; Hensley, Castle, & Tewksbury, 2003; Struckman-Johnson & Struckman-Johnson, 2000, 2006; Tewksbury, 1989a, 1989b), who are diminutive in size (Chonco, 1989; Lockwood, 1980), and who are physically attractive (Chonco, 1989; Lockwood, 1980) are at greater risk for being sexually assaulted while imprisoned. Sexual orientation has also been found to be associated with risk for sexual victimization. Non-heterosexual inmates report higher rates of sexual assault in prison (Bowker, 1980; Hensley, Tewksbury, & Castle, 2003; Nacci & Kane, 1983; Struckman-Johnson & Struckman-Johnson, 2006; Wooden & Parker, 1982), with transgendered inmates reporting a 41 percent rate of sexual assault while incarcerated. This rate is 20 times higher than the 2 percent rate found among a random sample of inmates in the same prison system (Jenness, Maxson, Matsuda, & Sumner, 2007).

BJS reported that sexual victimization was largely unrelated to facility characteristics and more strongly related to inmate characteristics (Beck, Harrison, & Adams, 2007; Beck & Harrison, 2008). These inmate characteristics included gender (women higher), race (multiple race higher), age (younger inmates higher), education (college education higher), sexual orientation (non-heterosexual higher), number of prior sexual partners (more than 21 previous sexual partners higher), sexual assault in the community (prior sexual assault higher), and victimization experience in prison (prior prison assault higher).

Wolff et al. (2007) reported similar results. Inmates who suffered from a mental disorder, who had attained higher levels of education, and who had experienced sexual victimization in the past were at significantly higher risk for sexual victimization while incarcerated. Male inmates who were involved in staff-on-inmate sexual victimization tended to be younger, African American, and to have experienced prior treatment for depression, anxiety, and post-traumatic stress disorder. They were also found to have been convicted of a prior violent crime, to believe that gang activity was high in their particular institution, and to have experienced sexual victimization prior to the age of 18 years. Wolff et al. (2008) later studied the context and aftermath of the incidents of sexual assault reported in their study. They found that the risk for sexual victimization between inmates was greatest between 6 p.m. and midnight, and for sexual victimization involving staff between noon and 6 p.m. The perceived homosexuality of the victim and the presence of a mental illness were identified as the motivating factor in over one quarter of the incidents. Reactions of fear, nightmares, and flashbacks were reported by a majority of the victims.

Gang Affiliation in Prison

The impact of gang affiliation on prison violence was first observed in the 1970s when Texas, California, and Ohio had a series of prison homicides, each of which were found to be gang related (Crouch & Marquart, 1989; Irwin, 1980; Jacobs, 1977). Shelden (1991) conducted one of the first studies of gang members in prison. Compared to non-gang-affiliated inmates, gang-affiliated inmates had more total arrests, more juvenile court referrals, more felony arrests, and were more likely to have used a weapon during their last offense. These gang members were also found to be involved in more disciplinary actions including drug infractions and fighting than non-gang members. More recently, Gaes et al. (2002) used three-tiered data from the FBI to evaluate both gang membership and gang embeddedness (i.e., core vs peripheral role in the gang) as it impacted rule infractions and violence throughout the federal prison system. As with street gang membership, they found that prison gang affiliation increased violent and almost all other forms of prison misconduct. This association was found to exist even when they controlled for individual risk factors including previous history of violence and current security–custody classification. Gaes et al. (2002) also found that gang embeddedness was associated with violence levels in prison. Core members were more likely than peripheral members, and peripheral members were more likely than non-members, to commit violent acts while incarcerated.

Study Analyses

The risk markers for violence and victimization in prison were collected from three sources. Self-report sexual orientation was obtained from the Prison Background Information Survey (PBIS). The perpetration and victimization of threatened physical, actual physical, sexual, and relational violence while imprisoned were obtained from the Prison Violence Inventory (PVI). Physical attributes, gang affiliation, and status as a sex offender were collected from prison databases maintained by both state (Ohio and Texas) Departments of Corrections. These behavioral domains were assessed first by gender and then in terms of their relationship with the five categories of sexual behavior in prison.

As presented in Table 5.7, male and female inmates did not differ in terms of race or age. Approximately one half the male and female inmates were Caucasian

TABLE 5.7 Frequency of Physical Attributes, Sexual Orientation, and Institutional Misconduct Reported by Incarcerated Men (N=288) and Women (N=183)

Item	Men		Women		Effect Size	
	N	$\%$	N	$\%$	χ^2	Φ
Race						
White	123	43.0	95	51.9	*4.43*	*0.10*
Other	52	18.2	23	12.6		
Black	111	38.8	65	35.3		
	M	SD	M	SD	t	
Age	37.0	10.5	37.8	10.7	-0.80	
Weight (lbs)	186.7	37.8	168.4	40.2	*4.63★★*	
Height (inches)	67.1	9.7	64.2	3.1	*4.51★★*	
BMI	30.2	7.7	28.8	6.8	*1.89*	
	N	$\%$	N	$\%$	χ^2	Φ
Self-Reported Sexual Orientation						
Heterosexual	266	96.7	122	71.3	60.06★★	0.37★★
Bisexual	6	2.2	34	19.9		
Homosexual	3	1.1	15	8.8		
Perpetration–Self-Report						
Threatened prison violence (PVI)	162	57.2	39	21.5	57.29★★	-0.35★★
Physical prison violence (PVI)	199	70.3	43	23.8	95.10★★	-0.46★★
Sexual violence/harassment in prison (SAP)	35	12.2	5	2.7	12.78★★	-0.17★★
Relational violence in prison (PVI)	151	53.5	70	38.7	9.77★★	-0.15★★
Victimization–Self-Report						
Threatened prison violence (PVI)	187	66.1	66	36.5	39.05★★	-0.29★★
Physical prison violence (PVI)	191	67.5	60	33.1	52.43★★	-0.34★★
Sexual violence/harassment in prison (SAP)	44	15.3	49	26.8	9.34★★	0.14★★
Relational violence in prison (PVI)	238	84.4	135	74.6	6.78★★	-0.12★★
Sexual Offending						
Current sex offense	56	19.4	1	0.5	37.57★★	-0.28★★
Any history of sex offense (self or file report)	75	26.0	15	8.2	23.05★★	-0.22★★
Gang Member	28	9.9	5	2.8	8.36★★	-0.13★★

Note. ★★p < 0.001.

with an average age of 37 years. Not surprisingly, the male inmates were significantly heavier and taller than female inmates. However, our sample was characterized by an overrepresentation of females who self-identified as either bisexual or homosexual. In our female sample, 8.8 percent of the women self-identified as homosexual and 19.9 percent as bisexual compared to 2.2 percent and 1.1 percent of the male inmates, respectively.

The male inmates reported significantly higher rates of institutional violence as perpetrators of all four categories of behavior, i.e., threatened violence, physical violence, sexual violence, and relational violence, and as victims in three of the four categories. The one exception concerned sexual victimization, of which significantly more female inmates reported being in this category. The most commonly referenced form of violence was physical assault followed by threatened physical violence and relational violence. Significantly more male than female inmates reported a current or past incarceration for a sex offense. In addition, significantly more male inmates reported gang affiliation when compared to the female inmates, although a small percentage of the female inmates did report gang affiliation during their current incarceration.

The correlations of these variables with the five categories of sexual behavior are presented in Table 5.8 (males) and Table 5.9 (females). Among the male inmates, any-sex was associated with being African American, younger age, the perpetration of threatened physical, actual physical, and relational violence, and being the victim of threatened physical, actual physical, and relational violence. Among the female inmates, any-sex was associated with being African American, younger age, homosexual orientation, the perpetration of threatened physical, actual physical, and relational violence, being the victim of threatened physical, actual physical, and relational violence, and gang affiliation.

Predatory sex initiated by male inmates was associated with self-identifying as being heterosexual, perpetrating threatened physical, actual physical, and relational violence, and being the victim of threatened physical, actual physical, sexual, and relational violence. Predatory sex initiated by female inmates was associated with homosexual orientation, perpetrating threatened physical, actual physical, and relational violence, and being the victim of threatened and actual physical violence.

Sexual victimization among male inmates was associated with lighter weight, shorter height, a smaller body mass index (BMI), homosexual orientation, perpetrating sexual violence and relational violence, and being the victim of relational violence. Sexual victimization experienced by female inmates was associated with perpetrating threatened physical violence and relational violence, and also being the victim of threatened physical, actual physical, and relational violence.

Bartered sex among male inmates was associated with being African American, younger age, non-homosexual orientation, perpetrating threatened physical, actual physical, sexual, and relational violence, being the victim of threatened physical, actual physical, sexual, and relational violence, and gang affiliation. Bartered sex engaged in by female inmates was related to homosexual orientation,

TABLE 5.8 Relationship between Physical Attributes, Sexual Orientation, and Institutional Misconduct Reported by Incarcerated Men (N=288) and Type of Sexual Experiences in Prison

Item	Any-sex		Predatory		Victim		Bartered		Consensual	
	No N=143 (%)	Yes N=145 (%)	No N=253 (%)	Yes N=35 (%)	No N=244 (%)	Yes N=44 (%)	No N=251 (%)	Yes N=37 (%)	No N=160 (%)	Yes N=128 (%)
Race										
White	63 (44.4)	60 (41.7)	114 (45.2)	9 (26.5)	98 (40.3)	25 (58.1)	115 (46.2)	8 (21.6)	76 (47.8)	47 (37.0)
Other	33 (23.2)	19 (13.2)	44 (17.5)	8 (23.5)	46 (18.9)	6 (14.0)	43 (17.3)	9 (24.3)	34 (21.4)	18 (14.2)
Black	46 (32.4)	65 (45.1)★	94 (37.3)	17 (50.0)	99 (40.7)	12 (27.9)	91 (36.5)	20 (54.1)★	49 (30.8)	62 (48.8)★★
	M (SD)	M (SD)	M (SD)	M (SD)	M (SD)	M (SD)	M (SD)	M (SD)	M (SD)	M (SD)
Age	38.7 (11.1)	35.3 (9.6)★★	37.2 (10.7)	36.0 (8.9)	36.8 (10.8)	37.9 (8.5)	37.6 (10.7)	32.6 (7.4)★★	39.0 (11.0)	34.5 (9.2)★★
Weight	189.3 (33.1)	184.1 (41.9)	188.1 (36.8)	177.3 (43.2)	189.2 (37.2)	172.1 (38.4)★★	186.9 (37.5)	184.6 (40.0)	189.2 (32.9)	183.4 (43.0)
Height	66.4 (5.8)	67.9 (12.4)	66.8 (7.4)	69.4 (18.8)	66.6 (7.6)	70.1 (17.4)★	66.9 (7.4)	68.5 (19.4)	66.6 (5.7)	67.8 (13.1)
BMI	30.7 (7.1)	29.6 (8.1)	30.4 (7.5)	28.5 (8.3)	30.8 (7.6)	26.8 (7.0)★★	30.1 (7.5)	30.8 (9.1)	30.6 (7.1)	29.7 (8.3)
	N (%)	N (%)	N (%)	N (%)	N (%)	N (%)	N (%)	N (%)	N (%)	N (%)
Self-Reported Sexual Orientation										
Heterosexual	136 (98.6)	130 (94.9)	237 (97.9)	29 (87.9)	228 (97.9)	38 (90.5)	233 (97.5)	33 (91.7)	151 (98.1)	115 (95.0)
Bisexual	1 (0.7)	5 (3.6)	2 (0.8)	4 (12.1)	4 (1.7)	2 (4.8)	3 (1.3)	3 (1.3)	1 (0.6)	5 (4.1)
Homosexual	1 (0.7)	2 (1.5)	3 (1.2)	0 (0.0)★★	1 (0.4)	2 (4.8)★★	3 (1.3)	0 (0.0)★★	2 (1.3)	1 (0.8)
Perpetration–Self-Report										
Threatened prison violence (PVI)	61 (43.0)	101 (71.6)★★	134 (53.6)	28 (84.8)★★	134 (55.6)	28 (66.7)	129 (52.2)	33 (91.7)★★	69 (43.4)	93 (75.0)★★

(Continued overleaf)

TABLE 5.8 Continued

Item	Any-sex		Predatory		Victim		Bartered		Consensual	
	No N=143 (%)	Yes N=145 (%)	No N=253 (%)	Yes N=35 (%)	No N=244 (%)	Yes N=44 (%)	No N=251 (%)	Yes N=37 (%)	No N=160 (%)	Yes N=128 (%)
Physical prison violence (PVI)	83 (58.5)	116 (82.3)**	169 (67.6)	30 (90.9)**	167 (69.3)	32 (76.2)	166 (67.2)	33 (91.7)**	95 (59.7)	104 (83.9)**
Sexual violence/ harassment in prison (SAP)	—	—	—	—	20 (8.2)	15 (34.1)**	19 (7.6)	16 (43.2)**	3 (1.9)	32 (25.0)**
Relational violence in prison (PVI)	59 (41.5)	92 (65.7)**	128 (51.2)	23 (71.9)*	120 (50.0)	31 (73.8)**	124 (50.4)	27 (75.0)**	68 (42.8)	83 (67.5)**
Victimization-Self-Report										
Threatened prison violence (PVI)	77 (54.2)	110 (78.0)**	156 (62.4)	31 (93.9)**	154 (63.9)	33 (78.6)	152 (61.5)	35 (97.2)**	89 (56.0)	98 (79.0)**
Physical prison violence (PVI)	79 (55.6)	112 (79.4)**	162 (64.8)	29 (87.9)**	158 (65.7)	33 (78.6)	157 (63.6)	34 (94.4)**	91 (57.2)	100 (80.6)**
Sexual violence/ harassment in prison (SAP)	—	—	29 (11.5)	15 (42.9)**	—	—	32 (12.7)	12 (32.4)**	14 (8.8)	3 (23.4)**

Relational violence in prison (PVI)	106 (74.6)	132 (94.3)**	206 (82.4)	32 (100.0)**	198 (82.5)	40 (95.2)*	202 (82.1)	36 (100.0)**	121 (76.1)	117 (95.1)**
Sexual Offending										
Current sex offense	30 (21.0)	26 (17.9)	52 (20.6)	4 (11.4)	44 (18.0)	12 (27.3)	53 (21.1)	3 (8.1)	37 (23.1)	19 (14.8)
Any history of sex offense (self or file report)	40 (28.0)	35 (24.1)	69 (27.3)	6 (17.1)	62 (25.4)	13 (29.5)	69 (27.5)	6 (16.2)	47 (29.4)	28 (21.9)
Gang Member	10 (7.0)	18 (12.7)	23 (9.2)	5 (14.7)	23 (9.5)	5 (11.6)	18 (7.3)	10 (27.0)**	10 (6.3)	18 (14.4)*

Note. $\star p < 0.01$, $\star\star p < 0.001$.

TABLE 5.9 Relationship between Physical Attributes, Sexual Orientation, and Institutional Misconduct Reported by Incarcerated Women (N=183) and Type of Sexual Experience in Prison

Item	Any-sex No N=77 (%)	Any-sex Yes N=106 (%)	Predatory No N=178 (%)	Predatory Yes N=5 (%)	Victim No N=134 (%)	Victim Yes N=49 (%)	Bartered No N=165 (%)	Bartered Yes N=18 (%)	Consensual No N=98 (%)	Consensual Yes N=85 (%)
Race										
White	44 (57.1)	51 (48.1)	92 (51.7)	3 (60.0)	70 (52.2)	25 (51.0)	87 (52.7)	8 (44.4)	57 (58.2)	38 (44.7)
Other	4 (5.2)	19 (17.9)	23 (12.9)	0 (0.0)	14 (10.4)	9 (18.4)	20 (12.1)	3 (16.7)	8 (8.2)	15 (17.6)
Black	29 (37.7)	36 (34.0)*	63 (35.4)	2 (40.0)	50 (37.3)	15 (30.6)	58 (35.2)	7 (38.9)	33 (33.7)	32 (37.6)
	M(SD)	M(SD)	M(SD)	M(SD)	M(SD)	M(SD)	M(SD)	M(SD)	M(SD)	M(SD)
Age	40.2 (11.3)	36.1 (0.0)**	37.9 (10.7)	36.2 (12.9)	38.3 (11.0)	36.6 (10.1)	38.2 (10.8)	34.4 (9.9)	39.9 (11.1)	35.5 (9.8)**
Weight	165.9 (6.7)	170.2 (42.7)	167.3 (39.1)	206.5 (67.5)	170.2 (41.5)	164.5 (36.5)	168.2 (39.1)	169.5 (49.1)	166.3 (36.9)	170.8 (43.9)
Height	64.0 (2.8)	64.3 (3.2)	64.2 (3.1)	64.3 (2.2)	64.2 (3.2)	64.1 (2.8)	64.1 (3.0)	65.1 (3.3)	63.9 (2.8)	64.5 (3.4)
BMI	28.5 (6.4)	30.0 (7.1)	28.6 (6.5)	35.3 (12.6)	29.1 (6.9)	28.0 (6.3)	28.8 (6.5)	28.3 (8.8)	28.7 (6.5)	28.8 (7.1)
	N(%)	N(%)	N(%)	N(%)	N(%)	N(%)	N(%)	N(%)	N(%)	N(%)
Self-Reported Sexual Orientation										
Heterosexual	65 (91.5)	57 (57.0)	121 (72.0)	1 (20.0)	92 (71.9)	30 (69.8)	117 (76.0)	5 (29.4)	85 (92.4)	37 (46.8)
Bisexual	3 (4.2)	31 (31.0)	32 (19.3)	2 (40.0)	23 (18.0)	2 (4.7)	26 (16.9)	8 (47.1)	4 (4.3)	30 (38.0)
Homosexual	3 (4.2)	12 (12.0)**	13 (7.8)	2 (40.0)*	13 (10.2)	11 (25.6)	11 (7.1)	4 (23.5)**	3 (3.3)	12 (15.2)**
Perpetration–Self-Report										
Threatened prison violence (PVI)	5 (6.5)	34 (32.7)**	36 (20.5)	3 (60.0)*	22 (16.7)	17 (34.7)**	31 (18.9)	8 (47.1)**	7 (7.1)	32 (38.6)**
Physical prison violence (PVI)	8 (10.4)	35 (33.7)**	39 (22.2)	4 (80.0)**	28 (21.2)	15 (30.6)	33 (20.2)	10 (58.8)**	9 (9.2)	34 (41.0)**

Sexual violence/harassment in prison (SAP)	—	—	—	—	2 (1.5)	3 (6.1)	2 (1.2)	3 (16.7)★★	0 (0.0)	5 (5.9)★
Relational violence in prison (PVI)	17 (22.1)	53 (51.0)★★	65 (36.9)	5 (100.0)★★	40 (30.3)	30 (61.2)★★	56 (34.1)	14 (82.4)★★	28 (28.6)	42 (50.6)★★
Victimization–Self-Report										
Threatened prison violence (PVI)	13 (16.9)	52 (51.0)★★	61 (34.7)	5 (100.0)★★	34 (25.8)	32 (65.3)★★	55 (33.5)	11 (64.7)★★	20 (20.4)	46 (55.4)★★
Physical prison violence (PVI)	13 (16.9)	47 (45.2)★★	56 (31.8)	4 (80.0)★	34 (25.8)	26 (53.1)★★	49 (29.9)	11 (64.7)★★	17 (17.3)	43 (51.8)★★
Sexual violence/harassment in prison (SAP)	—	—	46 (25.8)	3 (60.0)	—	—	41 (24.8)	8 (44.4)	21 (21.4)	28 (32.9)
Relational violence in prison (PVI)	48 (62.3)	87 (83.7)★★	130 (73.9)	5 (100.0)	92 (69.7)	43 (87.8)★	119 (72.6)	16 (94.1)	64 (65.3)	71 (85.5)★★
Sexual Offending										
Current sex offense	1 (1.3)	0 (0.0)	1 (1.6)	0 (0.0)	1 (0.7)	0 (0.0)	1 (0.6)	0 (0.0)	1 (1.0)	0 (0.0)
Any history of sex offense (self or file report)	7 (9.1)	8 (7.5)	14 (7.9)	1 (20.0)	12 (9.0)	3 (6.1)	14 (8.5)	1 (5.6)	8 (8.2)	7 (8.2)
Gang Member	0 (0.0)	5 (4.9)★	5 (2.9)	0 (0.0)	3 (2.3)	2 (4.1)	4 (2.5)	1 (5.9)	0 (0.0)	5 (6.1)★

Note. ★ $p < 0.01$, ★★ $p < 0.001$.

perpetrating threatened physical, actual physical, sexual, and relational violence, and being the victim of threatened and actual physical violence.

Consensual sexual activity engaged in by male inmates was related to being African American, younger age, perpetrating threatened physical, actual physical, sexual, and relational violence, being the victim of threatened physical, actual physical, sexual, and relational violence, and gang affiliation. Consensual sexual activity engaged in by female inmates was related to younger age, homosexual orientation, perpetrating threatened physical, actual physical, sexual, and relational violence, being the victim of threatened physical, actual physical, and relational violence, and gang affiliation.

Overall, male and female inmates exhibited remarkably similar patterns of paired aggressive and sexual behaviors. All five categories of sexual behavior were related to the perpetration and victimization of threatened physical, actual physical, and relational violence, and sometimes sexual violence. While race, age, and sexual orientation played a prominent role across these forms of sexual behavior, the physical attribute of size was more closely associated with the victimization of male inmates and played no role in the victimization of women. The five forms of sexual behavior while incarcerated were not associated with prior or current sexual offending for either male or female inmates.

Conclusions

Sexual behavior in prison, whether consensual or not, was found to be highly correlated with physical and interpersonal violence in the institutional setting. The male and female inmates who reported being sexually active in prison simultaneously reported being involved in the perpetration of threatened physical, actual physical, and relational violence against other inmates and being victimized by these same forms of violent behavior. These associations between forms of sexual behavior and physical and relational violence for both male and female inmates suggest that sexual activity in prison is a correlate of interpersonally violent behavior and that these behaviors serve as risk factors for each other in this type of institutional setting. They also point to the amalgamation of sexual aggression and sexual victimization in the experience of a single individual and suggest that any type of sexual behavior in prison serves as a risk factor for other types of sexual behavior. Interestingly, the relational forms of violence often attributed in the literature to women were endorsed by significantly more male than female inmates in our sample.

Physical attributes, demographic factors, and sexual orientation were also of central importance in explaining aspects of inmates' sexual behavior during incarceration, although they impacted male and female inmates differently. Younger, African American men were more likely to engage in bartered and consensual sex while in prison. However, men who were shorter (66.6 inches or less in height) and lighter (weighing 172 pounds or less) were more likely to be sexually victimized while incarcerated in comparison to those men who were heavier and taller. Homosexual males were also at heightened risk for sexual victimization.

Among female inmates, generally age and race played little role in their sexual behavior. Younger age was only related to consensual sex and race was only related to any-sex. Size was not important and played no role in their predatory sexual behavior or victimization. A self-reported homosexual orientation, however, was associated with any-sex, predatory, bartered, and consensual sex in prison, although not with sexual victimization as was observed among the male inmates.

Few elements of the inmates' past criminal history impacted their sexual behavior in prison. Self-reported past violent crime, however, was associated with sexual behavior in prison for both the male and female inmates, and prior drug offenses and a life sentence for female inmates only. However, sexual activity for both male and female inmates was not associated with the number of prior incarcerations, nature of the instant offense, past supervision failures, and/or length of the current sentence (with the exception of a life sentence for the female inmates). These findings suggest that sexual activity in prison is not a simple and straightforward attempt to release pent up sexual feelings, nor a personal assimilation of the same-sex encounters being observed over time. Rather, it seems to represent one particular form of prison adaptation that is further characterized by the commingling of other forms of physical violence and interpersonal aggression.

Our analyses documented an association between intimate partner violence in the community and sexual activity in prison. For the male inmates, having a partner who used negotiation to resolve conflicts, the use of physical conflicts resolution strategies against a partner, and experiencing physical injury in the context of battering were all associated with the various types of sexual behavior experienced while incarcerated. Similarly for the female inmates, being involved in domestic violence as either a victim or perpetrator was associated with the any-sex, bartered, and consensual categories of sexual behavior in prison. These findings suggest that the potentially disruptive nature of the sexual behavior that occurs in prison might be a replication and continuation of the unstable and mutually violent relationships that occurred in the community.

Of possible conceptual significance was our finding that bartered sex in prison was correlated with various forms of predatory behavior. Among our two samples, bartered sex was associated with perpetrating physical abuse against a domestic partner (male inmates), evoking greater injury to a domestic partner (female inmates), gang membership (male inmates), and most domains of threatened physical, actual physical, sexual, and relational violence (for both male and female inmates). These associations argue against the definition of bartering as a purely coerced activity that is forced upon the individual through the exertion of power and/or need. Rather it appears to be another form of prison adaptation which is more common among both male and female inmates who are aggressive in their behavior both in the community and during incarceration.

Our data support both the gender threshold and gender effect outcomes observed in other prison research. Clearly, the male inmates report higher rates of institutional violence both as perpetrators and victims across all four categories of prison violence, with the exception of sexual victimization. They also had more significant correlations between their violent and sexual behavior in prison. However, this same pattern of associations between community and prison violence and various types of sexual behavior in prison were also observed among the female inmates, albeit at reduced levels. However, unlike with their male counterparts, women who self-reported prior violent offending were more likely to be involved in consensual sex in prison. These findings suggest that while community and prison violence is associated with sexual behavior in prison for male and female inmates, self-reported violent crime in the community appears to serve as a protective factor against sexual victimization in prison for women.

6

PATTERNS OF SEXUAL ADAPTATION AS RISK MARKERS FOR SEXUAL PREDATION AND VICTIMIZATION

Sexually coercive behavior has been associated with a particular pattern of impersonal sexuality that has been observed among non-offending promiscuous males and females, delinquent youth, incarcerated adults, and individuals who have been charged specifically with sexual assault or rape. The name given to this behavioral construct has varied over time with some research referencing the sexual promiscuity path to sexual aggression (Malamuth, Heavey, & Linz, 1993), the predominance of a mating effort over parental investment in sexual behavior (Lalumière, Harris, Quinsey, & Rice, 2005), and the relative and situational correlates of hypersexual desire (Kafka, 1997). Unrelated to the issue of sexual arousal during a rape, these behavioral descriptors refer to the general pattern of sexual adaptation which characterizes the sexual behavior of an individual generally and which are hypothesized to be associated with precocious and sexually coercive behavior. In this chapter we explore the association of these different patterns of sexual behavior with the five categories of sexual behavior in prison.

Precocious and Impersonal Sex

As one of the first cohesive theories of rape behavior, Malamuth et al. (1993) proposed a three-dimensional theory of rape made up of six measurable risk factors each of which was distinct but interactive in their effect upon behavior. One of these risk factors sought to capture the individual's prior sexual experience as it might reflect a propensity for coercive sexual behavior. Initially, this risk factor was operationalized using the Sexual Behavior Inventory (Bentler, 1968), a self-report measure which quantified conventional sexual experiences such as fondling, oral sex, and sexual intercourse. Over time, Malamuth and his colleagues began to broaden this risk domain and position it more centrally in their theory as one of three primary pathways to sexual aggression. Within this context, it came to encompass the individual's age at first intercourse and the total number of lifetime sexual partners. Originally conceptualized as a proxy measure for the amount of opportunity an individual had to rape, it later came to represent a pattern of sexual adaptation that defined the manner or style through which an individual sought out sexual contact. Based upon motivational theory, the authors posited that it was not sex drive per se that was significant in predicting future sexual coercion but rather the individual's attraction to impersonal sex. This preference for impersonal sex was seen as a factor that motivated sexual involvement with more partners, usually devoid of true intimacy, and which inevitably was characterized by a "strong connection between sex and power" (Malamuth et al., 1993, p. 89).

Using latent variable structural equation modeling, Malamuth et al. (1993) explored their theory using data collected from a large national sample of male college students. They found that individuals who were above the mean on both sexual promiscuity and hostile masculinity were also significantly higher on sexual aggression as self-reported on the Sexual Experiences Survey. When they applied the theory to longitudinal data, they found that earlier self-reports of sexual aggression were predictive of adult sexual and non-sexual aggression toward women and correlated with maladaptive narcissism and an inability to experience or express feelings of empathy.

Knight and his colleagues later sought to replicate Malamuth's model using the Multidimensional Assessment of Sex and Aggression, a measure designed to quantify the various behaviors used in classifying rapists according to the MTC:3R rape classification system (Knight & Cerce, 1999). They found across studies that hypersexuality paired differentially with other behaviors in forming the motivational nexus for their primary typology of adult rapists (Johnson & Knight, 1998; Knight & Guay, 2006; Knight & Sims-Knight, 1999, 2003, 2004). Specifically, non-sadistic sexual rapists were characterized primarily by a hypersexual motivation for rape with few other intervening factors, opportunistic rapists were found to reflect a combination of impulsive and antisocial motivations, and angry and vindictive rapists were characterized by both hypersexuality and impulsivity with a significantly higher level of offense-related violence and victim injury.

Mating Effort and Parental Investment

Lalumière et al. (2005) developed a construct they refer to as mating effort to explain individual differences in a male's propensity toward sexual aggression. In developing their theory, the authors explore the sexual behavior associated with various aspects of delinquency and antisocial behavior. They reference the research that underscores the relationship between aggressive antisocial behavior and early sexual intercourse (Bingham & Crockett, 1996), childhood aggression and early pregnancy (Serbin et al., 1998), and the association between fathering children in adolescence and involvement in serious crime (Stouthamer-Loeber & Wei, 1998). Citing the Oregon Youth Study sample, they observed that the boys who became fathers before the age of 20 years were characterized by lower socioeconomic status, parental antisocial behavior, poor parental discipline, deviant peer involvement, academic failure, and antisocial behavior (Fagot, Pears, Capaldi, Crosby, & Leve, 1998). They also reference the links found between the early onset of sexual behavior, number of sexual partners, criminality, and drug use compounded by the association found between gang membership and total number of lifetime sexual partners (Ellis & Walsh, 2000; Palmer & Tilley, 1995). Concerning rape behavior specifically, Lalumière and Quinsey (1998) examined the attitudes and behavior of convicted rapists and found that rapists, when compared to non-sex offenders, self-reported an earlier age of first intercourse, more lifetime sexual partners, and a higher degree of involvement in uncommitted and short-term sexual relationships.

Research on sexual promiscuity and delinquency among women has been more limited, although clinical practice and social welfare programming underscores the relationship between early pregnancy and involvement in drug use and other antisocial behavior with delinquent peers. The Dunedin study (Moffitt et al., 2001) found that conduct disordered females were more likely to physically develop earlier, to enter menses at a younger age, to become precociously sexually active with older male youth, to have more children while still in adolescence, and to more often become involved with and conceive children with males who were also antisocial in attitudes and behaviors.

Hypersexual Desire

Kafka was the first to coin the term hypersexual desire and to associate it with men who reported life difficulties associated with particularly high rates of sexual interest and activity (Kafka, 1991, 1994, 1997; Kafka & Prentky, 1992a, 1992b, 1994). Referencing earlier research by Krafft-Ebing (1886/1965), Kinsey, Pomeroy, and Martin (1948), Janus and Janus (1993), and Laumann, Gagnon, Michael, and Michaels (1994), Kafka argued that sexual response among men is best reflected by a continuous frequency distribution with some degree of overrepresentation at the upper end of the distribution.

Based upon a survey of 5,300 males, Kinsey, Pomeroy, and Martin (1948) found that the mean number of total sexual outlets (TSO) reported by males aged 14 through 30 years was 2.14 per week. For males aged 30 through 85 years, TSOs declined only slightly to 1.99 per week. In their study of 1,860 males, Janus and Janus (1993) found that 15 percent of males aged 18 through 50 years reported daily sexual activity. Kinsey, Pomeroy, Martin, and Gebhard (1953), reporting on a sample of 5,940 females, found the TSO of married women was 2.2 per week for females ages 16 to 20 years, declining to 1.0 for females ages 41 to 45 years, and 0.5 by the age of 60 years.

Based upon the convergence of behaviors identified in these large samples, Kafka identified a pattern of sexual behavior that he encountered in his treatment activities. Defined as a pattern of sexual behavior that reflected a minimum of seven TSO per week over a six-month period since age 15 years, he began a series of studies to explore the relationship of this condition to various paraphilic and non-paraphilic sexual disorders. When applying this definition to treatment seeking men, he observed that a TSO of seven or more per week was often associated with compulsive masturbation, protracted promiscuity, and dependence on pornography. When he compared the TSO of this group of men to men who presented with a diagnosable paraphilic disorder, he found that there was no difference between the two groups in terms of the amount of preferred sexual activity. Both groups reported a modal maximum frequency of two orgasms per day and a mean TSO of seven or eight orgasms each week over the previous six-month period.

Based upon his research, Kafka (1997) recommended further research into the relationship between high TSOs and impulsivity and aggression. He referenced the documented co-occurrence of heightened sexual desire and aggression with the dysregulation of the monoaminergic activity of the brain and the powerful use of serotonin reuptake inhibitors in the treatment of compulsive sexual disorders. Further supporting this hypothesis, Kafka referenced the earlier Kinsey study which found that almost half of the men involved in the arguably highly aggressive "underworld occupations" reported a persistent TSO of seven or more orgasms a week (Kinsey, Pomeroy, & Martin, 1948).

Study Analyses

In our study, we used five indices of maladaptive sexual behavior and hypersexual desire. These included promiscuity as reflected in the PCL-R2 coding of impersonal, casual, and trivial sexual encounters and self-reported sexual history on the Prison Background Information Survey (PBIS) including age at first sexual encounter, number of lifetime sexual partners, and average number of orgasms while living in the community and while in prison. These variables were assessed for gender differences and for their association with the five categories of sexual behavior while in prison.

Significant gender differences were observed across all five variables (see Table 6.1). Both our male and female samples reported becoming sexually active at early ages, although male inmates were significantly younger at age of first sexual experience than female inmates. Over a third of the male inmates (35.4%) reported having had their first sexual experience by the age of 12 years and 69.8 percent by the time they reached 14 years of age. Age at first sexual experience was older for

TABLE 6.1 Frequency of Precocious Sexuality and Hypersexuality Reported by Incarcerated Men (N=288) and Women (N=183)

Item	Men			Women			Effect size	
	N	%		N	%		χ^2	Φ
Age at First Experience								
<10 years	38	13.2		13	7.1		54.32★★	0.34★★
11–12 years	64	22.2		10	5.5			
13–14 years	99	34.4		48	26.2			
15–16 years	46	16.0		62	33.9			
17–18 years	24	8.3		37	20.2			
>18 years	17	5.9		13	7.1			
Promiscuity on PCL-R 2	121	42.5		55	30.2		7.08★★	−0.12★★
	N	%	M Rank	N	%	M Rank	Z[a]	
# Partners			257.93			190.46	−5.48★★	
0–5	41	14.6		61	33.7			
6–14	63	22.4		55	30.4			
15–35	84	29.9		28	15.5			
>35	93	33.1		37	20.4			
On Outside								
# Orgasms/week			260.65			173.05	−7.17★★	
0	6	2.2		25	14.4			
1–3	61	21.9		75	43.1			
4–8	98	35.1		44	25.3			
9–12	70	25.1		13	7.5			
+12	44	15.8		17	9.8			
On Inside								
# Orgasms/week			265.67			169.91	−8.35★★	
0	104	37.3		135	76.3			
1–3	113	40.5		35	19.8			
4–8	40	14.3		6	3.4			
9–12	9	3.2		1	0.6			
+12	13	4.7		0	0.0			

Note. ★$p < 0.05$, ★★$p < 0.001$.
[a]For Mann-Whitney U test, Z represents standard score of difference between ranks.

the female inmates, with 38.8 percent having had their first sexual experience by the time they reached the age of 14 years. However, by age 16, 72.7 percent of the women had their first sexual experience. The number of lifetime sexual partners self-reported by the inmates also varied by gender. The modal number of lifetime sexual partners for the male inmates was more than 35, whereas the modal number of lifetime partners for the female inmates was 0 to 5. However, many of the female inmates reported having at least 15 sexual partners with 20.4 percent reportedly having over 35 partners prior to their incarceration.

Significantly more male (42.5%) than female (30.2%) inmates were coded as promiscuous on the PCL-R2 reflecting more trivial and casual sexual encounters, the indiscriminate selection of sexual partners, and participation in frequent sexual infidelities. There also were differences in TSO reported by the male and female inmates. The modal number of orgasms in the community for the male inmates was four to eight per week and one to three per week for the female inmates. With hypersexual desire being defined by Kafka as seven or more orgasms per week, 40.9 percent of the male inmates would be classified as manifesting this behavioral pattern prior to prison and 17.3 percent of the female inmates. While in prison, the majority of male inmates remained orgasmic on at least a weekly basis (62.7%) while the majority of female inmates did not (76.3%).

Correlations of maladaptive sexual behavior and hypersexual desire with the five categories of sexual behavior are presented in Table 6.2 (males) and Table 6.3 (females). Among male inmates, any-sex was associated inversely both with being over age 18 years at first sexual experience and having 12 or more orgasms per week while incarcerated. Among female inmates, any-sex was associated with having more than 35 lifetime partners, promiscuity as coded on the PCL-R2, and having 12 or more orgasms per week while living in the community.

Predatory sex initiated by male inmates was not associated with any of these variables. However, predatory sex initiated by female inmates was associated with having more than 35 lifetime partners and promiscuity as coded on the PCL-R2.

The sexual victimization of male inmates was inversely associated with having more than 35 lifetime partners, and no variables were associated with the sexual victimization of female inmates.

Bartered sex participated in by male inmates was inversely associated both with being over the age of 18 years at first sexual experience and having 12 or more orgasms per week while incarcerated. Among female inmates, bartered sex was associated with 12 or more orgasms per week while residing in the community and 12 or more orgasms per week while incarcerated.

Consensual sex among male inmates was associated inversely with being over the age of 18 years at the time of first sexual experience and with having 12 or more orgasms per week while incarcerated. Among female inmates, consensual sex was negatively associated with being over the age of 18 years at the time of first sexual experience, having more than 35 lifetime partners, promiscuity, and experiencing on average 12 or more orgasms per week while residing in the community.

TABLE 6.2 Relationship between Precocious Sexuality and Hypersexuality Reported by Incarcerated Men (N=288) and Type of Sexual Experience in Prison

Item	Any-sex No N=143 (%)	Yes N=145 (%)	Predatory No N=253 (%)	Yes N=35 (%)	Victim No N=244 (%)	Yes N=44 (%)	Bartered No N=251 (%)	Yes N=37 (%)	Consensual No N=160 (%)	Yes N=128 (%)
Age at First Experience										
<10 years	14 (9.8)	24 (16.6)	34 (13.4)	4 (11.4)	31 (12.7)	7 (15.9)	32 (12.7)	6 (16.2)	16 (10.0)	22 (17.2)
11–12 years	26 (18.2)	38 (26.2)	53 (20.9)	11 (31.4)	52 (21.3)	12 (27.3)	50 (19.9)	14 (37.8)	28 (17.5)	36 (28.1)
13–14 years	48 (33.6)	51 (35.2)	87 (34.4)	12 (34.3)	89 (36.5)	10 (2.7)	85 (33.9)	14 (37.8)	53 (33.1)	46 (35.9)
15–16 years	28 (19.6)	18 (12.4)	40 (15.8)	6 (17.1)	37 (15.2)	9 (20.5)	45 (17.9)	1 (2.7)	32 (20.0)	14 (10.9)
17–18 years	18 (12.6)	6 (4.1)	23 (9.1)	1 (2.9)	21 (8.6)	3 (6.8)	22 (8.8)	2 (5.4)	19 (11.9)	5 (3.9)
>18 years	9 (6.3)	8 (5.5)★★	16 (6.3)	1 (2.9)	14 (5.7)	3 (6.8)	17 (6.8)	0 (0.0)★	12 (7.5)	5 (3.9)★★
# Partners										
0–5	22 (15.8)	19 (13.4)	36 (14.6)	5 (14.3)	29 (12.2)	12 (27.9)	39 (16.0)	2 (5.4)	29 (18.6)	12 (9.6)
6–14	29 (20.9)	34 (23.9)	53 (21.5)	10 (28.6)	53 (22.3)	10 (23.3)	48 (19.7)	15 (40.5)	29 (18.6)	34 (27.2)
15–35	43 (30.9)	41 (28.9)	74 (30.1)	10 (28.6)	75 (31.5)	9 (20.9)	75 (30.7)	9 (24.3)	46 (29.5)	38 (30.4)
>35	45 (32.4)	48 (33.8)	83 (33.7)	10 (28.6)	81 (34.0)	12 (27.9)★	82 (33.6)	11 (29.7)	52 (33.3)	41 (32.8)
Promiscuity on PCL-R 2	58 (41.1)	63 (43.8)	109 (43.6)	12 (34.3)	105 (43.6)	16 (36.4)	109 (44.0)	12 (32.4)	66 (41.8)	55 (43.3)

(Continued overleaf)

TABLE 6.2 Continued

Item	Any-sex		Predatory		Victim		Bartered		Consensual	
	No N=143 (%)	*Yes* N=145 (%)	*No* N=253 (%)	*Yes* N=35 (%)	*No* N=244 (%)	*Yes* N=44 (%)	*No* N=251 (%)	*Yes* N=37 (%)	*No* N=160 (%)	*Yes* N=128 (%)
On Outside										
# Orgasms/week										
0	4 (2.9)	2 (1.4)	6 (2.5)	0 (0.0)	6 (2.5)	0 (0.0)	5 (2.1)	1 (2.7)	4 (2.6)	2 (1.6)
1–3	38 (27.5)	23 (16.3)	52 (21.3)	9 (25.7)	52 (22.0)	9 (20.9)	56 (23.1)	5 (13.5)	43 (27.7)	18 (14.5)
4–8	52 (37.7)	46 (32.6)	90 (36.9)	8 (22.9)	81 (34.3)	17 (39.5)	90 (37.2)	8 (21.6)	59 (38.1)	39 (31.5)
9–12	25 (18.1)	45 (31.9)	62 (25.4)	8 (22.9)	60 (25.4)	10 (23.3)	58 (24.0)	12 (32.4)	29 (18.7)	41 (33.1)
+12	19 (13.8)	25 (17.7)	34 (13.9)	10 (28.6)	37 (15.7)	7 (16.3)	33 (13.6)	11 (29.7)	20 (12.9)	24 (19.4)
On Inside										
# Orgasms/week										
0	65 (47.4)	39 (27.5)	97 (39.8)	7 (20.0)	88 (37.4)	16 (36.4)	95 (39.3)	9 (24.3)	74 (48.1)	30 (24.0)
1–3	54 (39.4)	59 (41.5)	96 (39.3)	17 (48.6)	95 (40.4)	18 (40.9)	96 (39.7)	17 (45.9)	61 (39.6)	52 (41.6)
4–8	12 (8.8)	28 (19.7)	35 (14.3)	5 (14.3)	35 (14.9)	5 (11.4)	36 (14.9)	4 (10.8)	13 (8.4)	27 (21.6)
9–12	1 (0.7)	8 (5.6)	7 (2.9)	2 (5.7)	6 (2.6)	3 (6.8)	5 (2.1)	4 (10.8)	1 (0.6)	8 (6.4)
+12	5 (3.6)	8 (5.6)★★	9 (3.7)	4 (11.4)	11 (4.7)	2 (4.5)	10 (4.1)	3 (8.1)★★	5 (3.2)	8 (6.4)★★

Note. ★*p* < 0.05 ★★*p* < 0.001.

TABLE 6.3 Relationship between Precocious Sexuality and Hypersexuality Reported by Incarcerated Women (N=183) and Type of Sexual Experience in Prison

Item	Any-sex		Predatory		Victim		Bartered		Consensual	
	No N=77 (%)	*Yes* N=106 (%)	*No* N=178 (%)	*Yes* N=5 (%)	*No* N=134 (%)	*Yes* N=49 (%)	*No* N=165 (%)	*Yes* N=18 (%)	*No* N=98 (%)	*Yes* N=85 (%)
Age at First Experience										
<10 years	4 (5.2)	9 (8.5)	12 (6.7)	1 (20.0)	7 (5.2)	5 (12.2)	12 (7.3)	1 (5.6)	6 (6.1)	7 (8.2)
11–12 years	3 (3.9)	7 (6.6)	9 (5.1)	1 (20.0)	5 (3.7)	5 (10.2)	10 (6.1)	0 (0.0)	5 (5.1)	5 (5.9)
13–14 years	18 (23.4)	30 (28.3)	47 (26.4)	1 (20.0)	39 (29.1)	9 (18.4)	41 (24.8)	7 (38.9)	22 (22.4)	26 (30.6)
15–16 years	27 (35.1)	35 (33.0)	61 (34.3)	1 (20.0)	45 (33.6)	17 (34.7)	58 (35.2)	4 (22.2)	32 (32.7)	30 (35.3)
17–18 years	17 (22.1)	20 (18.9)	37 (20.8)	0 (0.0)	26 (19.4)	11 (22.4)	32 (19.4)	5 (27.8)	24 (24.5)	13 (15.3)
>18 years	8 (10.4)	5 (4.7)	12 (6.7)	1 (20.0)	12 (9.0)	1 (2.0)	12 (7.3)	1 (5.6)	9 (9.2)	4 (4.7)★
# Partners										
0–5	33 (42.9)	28 (26.9)	61 (34.7)	0 (0.0)	48 (36.4)	13 (26.5)	56 (36.2)	2 (11.1)	40 (40.8)	21 (25.3)
6–14	23 (29.9)	32 (30.8)	54 (30.7)	1 (20.0)	43 (32.6)	12 (24.5)	48 (29.4)	7 (38.9)	30 (30.6)	25 (30.1)
15–35	7 (9.1)	21 (20.2)	26 (24.8)	2 (40.0)	15 (11.4)	14 (26.5)	24 (14.7)	4 (22.2)	13 (13.3)	15 (18.1)
>35	14 (18.2)	23 (22.1)★	35 (19.9)	2 (40.0)★	26 (19.7)	11 (22.4)	32 (19.6)	5 (27.8)	15 (15.3)	22 (26.2)★
Promiscuity on PCL-R 2	16 (20.8)	39 (37.1)★	51 (28.8)	4 (80.0)★	36 (26.9)	19 (39.6)	49 (29.7)	5 (35.3)	21 (21.4)	34 (40.5)★★

(Continued overleaf)

TABLE 6.3 Continued

Item	Any-sex		Predatory		Victim		Bartered		Consensual	
	No N=77 (%)	Yes N=106 (%)	No N=178 (%)	Yes N=5 (%)	No N=134 (%)	Yes N=49 (%)	No N=165 (%)	Yes N=18 (%)	No N=98 (%)	Yes N=85 (%)
On Outside										
# Orgasms/week										
0	13 (18.3)	12 (11.7)	25 (14.8)	0 (0.0)	20 (15.7)	5 (10.6)	23 (14.7)	2 (11.1)	16 (17.4)	9 (11.0)
1–3	33 (46.5)	42 (40.8)	73 (43.2)	2 (40.0)	51 (40.2)	24 (24.1)	67 (42.9)	8 (44.4)	40 (43.5)	35 (42.7)
4–8	17 (23.9)	27 (26.2)	43 (25.4)	1 (20.0)	35 (27.6)	9 (19.1)	39 (25.0)	5 (27.8)	23 (25.0)	21 (25.6)
9–12	3 (4.2)	10 (9.7)	12 (7.1)	1 (20.0)	10 (7.9)	3 (6.4)	11 (7.1)	2 (11.1)	6 (6.5)	7 (8.5)
+12	5 (7.0)	12 (11.7)★	16 (9.5)	1 (20.0)	11 (8.7)	6 (12.8)	16 (10.3)	1 (5.6)★	7 (7.6)	10 (12.2)★★
On Inside										
# Orgasms/week										
0	68 (93.2)	67 (64.4)	135 (78.5)	0 (0.0)	100 (76.9)	35 (74.5)	125 (78.6)	10 (55.6)	88 (93.6)	45 (56.6)
1–3	3 (4.1)	32 (30.8)	31 (18.0)	4 (80.0)	24 (18.5)	11 (23.4)	28 (17.6)	7 (38.9)	4 (4.3)	31 (37.3)
4–8	2 (2.7)	4 (3.8)	5 (2.9)	1 (20.0)	5 (3.8)	1 (2.1)	5 (3.1)	1 (5.6)	2 (2.1)	4 (4.8)
9–12	0 (0.0)	1 (1.0)	1 (0.6)	0 (0.0)	1 (0.8)	0 (0.0)	1 (0.6)	0 (0.0)	0 (0.0)	1 (1.2)
+12	0 (0.0)	0 (0.0)★	1 (0.6)	0 (0.0)★★	0 (0.0)	0 (0.0)	0 (0.0)	0 (0.0)★★	0 (0.0)	0 (0.0)★★

Note. ★ $p < 0.05$ ★★ $p < 0.001$.

Conclusions

Among the men, young age at first sexual experience was unrelated to the various indices of sexual behavior in prison. However, being over the age of 18 years at the time of first sexual intercourse was found to serve a protective function concerning three of the five categories of sexual activity in prison. Males who became sexually active at an age older than expected according to social norms self-reported less any-sex, consensual sexual activity, and bartered sexual behavior while incarcerated. In the female sample, younger age at first sexual experience was also not associated with any of the sexual behaviors in prison. However, as with the male inmates, having been over the age of 18 years at the time of first intercourse was associated with a significantly lower level of consensual sex in prison.

In our male sample, sexual promiscuity as coded on the PCL-R2 was found to be uncorrelated with any of the sexual behaviors in prison. In contrast, in the female sample sexual promiscuity as coded on the PCL-R2 was associated with the any-sex, predatory, and consensual categories of sexual behavior. Women who scored higher on this item were more likely to be identified in the any-sex category and to self-report higher rates of bartered sex and higher rates of consensual sex during their incarceration.

For the men, number of lifetime sexual partners prior to the current incarceration was unrelated to all five subcategories of sexual behavior in prison. For the women, number of lifetime sexual partners was associated with three of the five categories of prison sexual behavior. Specifically, having more than 35 sexual partners was associated with inclusion in the any-sex category and with self-reported predatory sex and higher rates of consensual sex during incarceration. Forty percent of the women who reported more than 35 lifetime sexual partners also self-reported as being predatory in their sexual behavior in prison.

In the male sample, number of orgasms experienced while living in the community was unrelated to all five subcategories of sexual activity while imprisoned. However, having more than 12 orgasms per week during incarceration was associated with the any-sex, bartered and consensual sex categories, with each of these being associated with greater degrees of hypersexuality. For the women, number of experienced orgasms while living in the community was associated with higher rates of consensual sex in prison but with none of the other subcategories of sexual behavior. There was only one woman who reported having 12 or more orgasms per week in prison and she self-identified herself as being predatory in her prison sexual behavior.

In line with the research conducted by Kinsey over 60 years ago, our data support the finding that almost half of the men involved in the criminal "underworld occupations" reported a persistent TSO of seven or more orgasms a week prior to prison. In our study, 40.9 percent of the men self-reported an interest in more than eight orgasms per week while living in the community. As an extension to this earlier research, we found that 17.3 percent of the women in our sample also reported a level of preferred sexual activity which meets Kafka's definition of hypersexuality. These findings suggest that hypersexuality represents a type of sexual adjustment that can be found in both genders albeit at lower levels among women. The impact of this sexual behavior on prison adjustment, however, varied across genders with hypersexuality being unrelated to all five sexual behaviors in prison for men, but being related to higher levels of consensual sex for women. These findings underscore the complex interplay that contributes to sexual behavior in prison, particularly for the male inmates, and argues against a simplistic explanation describing these encounters as alternative outlets for strong sexual feelings during incarceration.

Our data offered no support for Malamuth's theory of rape behavior which posited that sexual aggression in men was associated with impersonal sex reflected by an early age at first intercourse and total number of lifetime sexual partners. For the men, young age at first intercourse and total number of lifetime sexual partners were unrelated to all five categories of sexual behavior in prison. However, for the female inmates, total number of lifetime sexual partners was associated with higher levels of consensual and predatory sexual behavior in prison. These findings suggest that the theory of rape developed to explain rape behavior by men in the community might in fact be more appropriate for explaining promiscuous and predatory sexual behavior by women while living in the prison environment. Similarly, we found no support for the mating effort thesis developed by Lalumière and Quinsey (1998) and their finding that male rapists self-reported an earlier age of first intercourse, more lifetime sexual partners, and higher degrees of involvement in uncommitted and short-term sexual relationships. Coding on the PCL-R2 designed to capture the impersonal sexual activity implied by these findings was found to be unrelated to all five categories of sexual behavior in prison for the male inmates, but as with Malamuth's research, was associated with predatory sexual behavior among the female inmates.

7

AFFECTIVE AND PERCEPTUAL STATES AS RISK MARKERS FOR SEXUAL PREDATION AND VICTIMIZATION

The identification of risk markers for violence and sexual aggression in the community has come to include a constellation of negative affective states and cognitive or perceptual beliefs that predispose the individual to various forms of interpersonal violence. The affective states tend to include anger, impulsivity, and fear and are believed to be relevant to understanding some violent behavior both legally and psychologically as being more reactive than instrumental in nature (Cornell et al., 1996; Heilbrun et al., 1998; Eaves, Douglas, Webster, Ogloff, & Hart, 2000). A second body of research identifies certain thought processes and distortions of reality that are associated with different types of community violence perpetrated by delinquent and gang associated youth and adults who are diagnosed with a significant mental illness (Dodge, Price, Coie, & Christopoulos, 1990; Monahan et al., 2001). The social cognitive deficits identified in delinquent youth tend to include the attribution of hostility when it was not intended, and among psychiatric patients, the perception of others trying to do them harm combined with retaliatory thoughts of wanting to do harm to others. In the current chapter, we examine the affective states of anger, impulsivity, and fear of victimization, along with repetitive thoughts of harming another and threat control override symptoms as they are associated with the five categories of sexual behavior while in prison.

Anger Associated with Violence and Sexual Violence

Anger and Violence

The role of anger as an affective state that precedes or precipitates aggressive behavior has historically been linked to the power of the human passions to overcome normal behavior. This association was addressed by Plato, Aristotle, and the philosophers of the Renaissance and the Enlightenment, all of whom commented on the power of anger to overcome civilized behavior and lead to mental disorder and violence. In modern times, anger has become one of the primary risk markers that has been identified in violence risk research and quantified using multiple domains as it pertains to interpersonal and sexual violence against others.

As part of violence risk research, Novaco (1994) developed a theory of anger which posited an association between anger as a subjective emotional state and the condition of physiological arousal with behavior expressed through different forms of aggressive behavior. The Novaco Anger Scale (NAS), which was designed to capture these components of anger, includes cognitive items reflecting attentional focus, suspicion, rumination, and hostile attitude; arousal items that quantify the intensity, duration, somatic tension, and irritability of the experience; and behavioral items that capture the nature of the ensuing impulsive reactions, verbally aggressive acts, physical confrontations, and other indirect expressions of the mental and physical state being experienced by the individual. The NAS was used in the MacArthur Violence Risk Assessment Study (Monahan et al., 2001), which found that the highest levels of anger were among individuals who were younger, of minority status, and who suffered from co-morbid major mental illnesses and substance abuse disorders. When exploring the relationship of anger to violence, Monahan et al. (2001) found that individuals with higher anger scores at hospitalization were twice as likely to engage in violent acts post-discharge throughout the 12-month period following their discharge.

Anger and Sexual Violence

Lalumière and Quinsey (1996) factor analyzed the many behavioral indices that they found had correlated with sexually coercive behavior perpetrated by males living in the community. The first factor included a mix of antisocial behaviors and an impersonal mating strategy. The second factor was made up of different experiences and attitudes that reflected hostility and aggression toward others. Zamble and Quinsey (1997) found that negative moods were noted among released offenders, including rapists, prior to their relapse. Oliver, Beech, Fisher, and Beckett (2007) examined the role of different emotional and behavioral precursors in the lives of murderers and rapists. They compared 58 sexual murderers and 112 rapists and found that rapists had more prior violent non-deviant offenses and scored higher on measures of paranoid suspicion and resentment.

Various rape paradigms developed either by law enforcement or in the context of criminological research have further emphasized the role of anger in rape behavior. The widely referenced crime scene taxonomy developed by Hazelwood (1987) identified four primary rapist types including the power reassurance, the power assertive, the anger retaliatory, and the anger excitation rapist. Hazelwood (2008) described the anger retaliatory rapist as an offender who is angry with women for a variety of real or imagined wrongdoings and who uses the sexual acts as a means of humiliating and degrading the victim. The MTC:3 taxonomy developed by Prentky, Knight, and Rosenberg (1988) identified seven rapist types including the opportunistic (low and high competence), pervasively angry, sexual seeking (sadistic and non-sadistic), and vindictive (low and moderate social competence) rapist types. These different types were found to cluster according to eight behavioral dimensions including juvenile and adult antisocial behavior, social competence, expressive aggression in the offense, offense planning, global or pervasive anger, overt or muted sadism, sexualized thoughts, paraphilic fantasies, and hostility toward women (Knight, 1999).

Study Analyses

Five indices of anger were derived from the Novaco Anger Scale (NAS) and two diagnostic criteria were identified based upon the Structured Interview for DSM-IV Personality (SIDP-IV) coding of Antisocial personality disorder (PD)–irritability and aggression and Borderline PD–inappropriate anger. These measures were explored for gender differences and as they impacted the various categories of sexual behavior in prison.

The results in Table 7.1 reflect gender differences on two of the three NAS domains and on both of the Borderline PD and the Antisocial PD diagnostic criteria. On both the NAS cognitive and NAS behavioral regulation domains, the male inmates reported significantly higher levels of agitation and distress, although there were no significant gender differences in the NAS arousal, NAS anger regulation, and NAS Total score. The males were also clinically assessed as demonstrating higher levels of anger on the Borderline criteria of inappropriate anger and the Antisocial criteria of irritability and aggressiveness.

The correlations of the seven anger variables with the five categories of sexual behavior are presented in Table 7.2 (males) and Table 7.3 (females). Among male

TABLE 7.1 Descriptive Statistics for Anger Measures Reported by Incarcerated Men (N=288) and Women (N=183)

Anger Item	Men		Women		
	M	SD	M	SD	t
NAS cognitive	28.75	5.29	27.24	4.85	2.88**
NAS arousal	26.35	5.74	26.67	5.48	−0.57
NAS behavioral regulation	26.10	5.50	24.80	5.05	2.37*
NAS anger regulation	26.06	3.80	26.63	3.34	−1.55
NAS Total	81.19	15.45	78.72	13.48	1.68
	N	%	N	%	χ^2
Borderline-inappropriate anger	166	59.3	84	46.4	7.34**
Antisocial-irritability and aggressiveness	187	68.8	62	34.8	50.08**

Note. $*p < 0.05$, $**p < 0.01$.

For Borderline and Antisocial items, numbers reflect those in which criteria is endorsed.

TABLE 7.2 Relationship between Measures of Anger Reported by Incarcerated Men (N=288) and Type of Sexual Experience in Prison

Anger Item	Any-sex		Predatory		Victim		Bartered		Consensual	
	No N=143 (%)	Yes N=145 (%)	No N=253 (%)	Yes N=35 (%)	No N=244 (%)	Yes N=44 (%)	No N=251 (%)	Yes N=37 (%)	No N=160 (%)	Yes N=128 (%)
	M(SD)	M(SD)	M(SD)	M(SD)	M(SD)	M(SD)	M(SD)	M(SD)	M(SD)	M(SD)
NAS cognitive	27.5 (5.2)	30.2 (5.1)★★	28.5 (5.3)	30.6 (4.6)	28.6 (5.2)	30.0 (5.5)	28.6 (5.2)	30.6 (5.7)	27.5 (5.1)	30.5 (5.1)★★
NAS arousal	25.4 (5.7)	27.4 (5.6) ★★	26.2 (5.8)	27.6 (5.2)	26.3 (5.7)	26.8 (6.1)	26.2 (5.7)	27.6 (6.1)★★	25.3 (5.6)	27.8 (5.6)★★
NAS behavioral regulation	24.8 (5.2)	27.5 (5.5)★★	25.8 (5.5)	28.7 (4.6)★	25.9 (5.3)	27.2 (6.5)★	25.8 (5.3)	29.1 (6.6)	24.8 (5.0)	28.0 (5.6)★★
NAS anger regulation	25.7 (4.2)	26.4 (3.3)	26.1 (3.9)	26.0 (2.9)	25.8 (3.8)	27.4 (3.6)★	26.1 (3.9)	25.8 (2.9)	25.9 (4.1)	26.3 (3.3)
NAS Total	77.6 (15.0)	85.1 (15.0)★★	80.5 (15.6)	86.9 (13.1)	80.8 (15.2)	83.9 (17.1)	80.5 (15.1)	87.3 (17.6)	77.6 (14.8)	86.2 (15.1)★★
	N(%)	N(%)	N(%)	N(%)	N(%)	N(%)	N(%)	N(%)	N(%)	N(%)
Borderline-inappropriate anger	72 (52.2)	94 (66.2)★	141 (57.6)	25 (71.4)	144 (61.0)	22 (50.0)	138 (56.6)	28 (77.8)★	80 (51.6)	86 (68.8)★★
Antisocial-irritability and aggressiveness	90 (65.2)	97 (72.4)	162 (68.4)	25 (71.4)	165 (71.7)	22 (52.4)★	159 (67.4)	28 (77.8)	96 (62.7)	91 (76.5)★

Note. ★ $p < 0.05$, ★★ $p < 0.01$.

TABLE 7.3 Relationship between Measures of Anger Reported by Incarcerated Women (*N*=183) and Type of Sexual Experience in Prison

Anger Item	Any-sex		Predatory		Victim		Bartered		Consensual	
	No N=77 (%)	Yes N=106 (%)	No N=178 (%)	Yes N=5 (%)	No N=134 (%)	Yes N=49 (%)	No N=165 (%)	Yes N=18 (%)	No N=98 (%)	Yes N=85 (%)
	M(SD)	M(SD)	M(SD)	M(SD)	M(SD)	M(SD)	M(SD)	M(SD)	M(SD)	M(SD)
NAS cognitive	26.2 (4.2)	28.1 (5.2)★★	27.2 (4.9)	28.6 (5.2)	26.8 (4.8)	28.5 (4.9)	27.0 (4.9)	29.4 (3.5)	26.4 (4.4)	28.3 (5.3)★
NAS arousal	25.8 (5.4)	27.4 (5.5)	26.6 (5.5)	27.8 (5.8)	26.5 (5.6)	27.1 (5.3)	26.4 (5.5)	28.9 (4.6)	25.9 (5.4)	27.7 (5.5)★
NAS behavioral regulation	24.3 (4.5)	25.2 (5.4)	24.6 (4.9)	30.2 (6.9)★	24.8 (5.2)	25.0 (4.7)	24.6 (4.9)	26.8 (6.3)	24.2 (4.6)	25.6 (5.5)
NAS anger regulation	26.7 (3.6)	26.5 (3.1)	26.7 (3.3)	25.6 (4.2)	26.6 (3.4)	26.7 (3.1)	26.8 (3.4)	25.1 (1.7)★★	26.6 (3.5)	26.7 (3.1)
NAS total	76.2 (12.6)	80.9 (13.9)★	78.5 (13.3)	86.6 (16.9)	78.1 (13.7)	80.5 (12.8)	78.0 (13.4)	85.1 (13.0)★	76.5 (12.7)	81.6 (14.0)★
	N(%)	N(%)	N(%)	N(%)	N(%)	N(%)	N(%)	N(%)	N(%)	N(%)
Borderline-inappropriate anger	33 (43.4)	51 (48.6)	89 (45.50)	4 (80.0)	62 (46.6)	22 (45.8)	73 (44.5)	11 (64.7)	41 (42.3)	43 (51.2)
Antisocial-irritability and aggressiveness	21 (27.3)	41 (40.6)	60 (34.5)	2 (50.0)	42 (32.6)	19 (41.3)	54 (33.3)	8 (50.0)	27 (27.8)	35 (43.2)★

Note. ★*p* < 0.05, ★★*p* < 0.01.

inmates, any-sex was associated with all indicators of anger with the exception of NAS anger regulation and Antisocial-irritability and aggressiveness. Among the female inmates, any-sex was only associated with NAS cognitive and NAS Total score.

Among both male and female inmates, predatory sex was associated only with NAS behavioral regulation.

Male sexual victimization was associated with NAS behavioral regulation, NAS anger regulation, and lower levels of Antisocial – irritability and aggressiveness. Among female inmates, sexual victimization was not associated with any of these variables.

Bartered sex among male inmates was associated with NAS arousal and Borderline-inappropriate anger. Bartered sex among female inmates was associated with NAS anger regulation and NAS Total score.

Consensual sex among male inmates was associated with all measures of anger except NAS anger regulation. Among the female inmates, consensual sex was related to NAS cognitive, NAS arousal, NAS Total score, and Antisocial – irritability and aggressiveness.

Impulsivity Associated with Violence and Sexual Violence

Impulsivity and Violence

Research has demonstrated a consistent relationship between impulsivity and antisocial behavior (Barratt, Stanford, Kent, & Felthous, 1997). Wang and Diamond (1999) used structural equation modeling to predict institutional aggression among mentally disordered offenders and found that anger, antisocial personality style, and impulsivity were more robust predictors of institutional aggression than ethnicity or incarceration for a violent crime. Blackburn and Coid (1998) examined the association between psychopathy and the various personality disorders (PD) and found that impulsivity was the primary factor identified in a factor analytic analysis of DSM-III data. It was also found to be the factor that correlated most robustly with psychopathy and other measures of violent and non-violent criminality. Barratt (1991) studied the relationship between impulsivity and violence among violent male offenders. He found that aggressive inmates were characterized by higher levels of anger, more impulsivity, poorer performance on neuropsychological tests, and reduced neural involvement in frontal cortical areas when compared to non-inmate controls.

Research on female offenders similarly reflects higher rates of impulsivity among personality disordered offenders and more violent institutional infractions among women with higher scores on any of the three domains of the Barratt Impulsivity Scale (cognitive impulsivity, motor impulsivity, and non-planning impulsivity). Komarovskaya, Loper, and Warren (2007) found in a study of 802 female inmates that the predictive power of impulsivity and institutional violence eradicated the earlier association between age and institutional violence. Using a structured research design, Cherek and Lane (1999) found that female parolees who had been charged with a violent offense tended more often to make impulsive behavioral choices over self-controlled behavioral choices while living in the community. Hochhausen, Lorenz, and Newman (2002) examined the relationship of Borderline PD to criminality and found that incarcerated women who had been diagnosed with Borderline PD committed more passive avoidance errors and reported more impulsivity compared to a control group of non-incarcerated women.

Moffitt et al. (2001) studied antisocial behavior in a large birth cohort of males and females over a 20-year period. They found that impulsivity was a consistent predictor of delinquency for both their male and female respondents throughout their adolescence and into early adulthood.

Impulsivity and Sexual Violence

Impulsivity reflects a form of behavioral and affective instability that results in erratic behavior, frequent mood changes, and a tendency to respond without reflection to both real and imagined insults and perceived sources of provocation. Moeller, Barratt, Dougherty, Schmitz, and Swann (2001) examined the concept of impulsivity as it was used diagnostically in DSM-IV-TR and concluded that impulsivity is a significant symptom of disturbance within both Axis I and Axis II disorders, although it is not defined explicitly or differentially in the multiple disorders in which it appears.

The MTC:3R rape typology examined lifestyle impulsivity as it captured patterns of poor impulse control beginning in preadolescence and continuing in various forms throughout adulthood. It was found to correlate robustly with other indices of antisocial behavior and to differentiate rates and timing of re-offense among a large sample of rapists following release (Prentky, Knight, & Lee, 1989). The commonality of this behavior across all rapist types, however, diminished its usefulness as a classification dimension and necessitated it being replaced with the construct of social competence which was more powerful in differentiating between the opportunistic, sexual, and vindictive rapist types. Within the revised taxonomy, the opportunistic rapist was described as being the most impulsive in his behavior. Knight (1999) described this type of rapist as tending to rape when encountering a woman during the commission of some other crime or when a woman became accessible through an impersonal social encounter (Knight & Prentky, 1990; Knight, 1999).

Study Analyses

In our study we used clinical assessments of impulsivity as defined and collected in four different domains. These included the Structured Interview for DSM-IV

Personality (SIDP-IV) coding of criteria 4 of the Borderline PD, a SIDP-IV coding of criteria 3 of the Antisocial PD, item 14 of the Psychopathy Checklist Revised-2 (PCL-R2) coding form, and coding of item C4 on the HCR-20 violence risk assessment. These variables were assessed for gender differences and for their correlation with five categories of sexual behavior in prison.

Our data indicated only one gender difference in levels of impulsivity as clinically assessed in the male and female samples (see Table 7.4). The male inmates were coded as manifesting more impulsive behavior on the Borderline – impulsivity criteria. There were no gender differences in Antisocial – impulsivity or the impulsivity items contained in either the PCL-R2 or the HCR-20.

Table 7.5 (males) and Table 7.6 (females) present the correlations of the impulsivity measures with inmates' sexual behavior while incarcerated. Among the male inmates, any-sex was associated with endorsement of the Antisocial PD diagnostic criteria concerning an inability to plan ahead. Among the female inmates, any-sex was associated with higher levels of endorsement on the Borderline PD impulsivity diagnostic criteria.

Predatory sex and sexual victimization were not associated with any indicators of impulsivity for male or female inmates.

Bartered sex among both the male and female inmates was associated with the clinical endorsement of the impulsivity clinical risk factor on the HCR-20.

Consensual sex among male inmates was associated with the Borderline PD diagnostic criteria concerning impulsive behavior, the Antisocial PD diagnostic criteria of failing to plan ahead, and the impulsivity item on the clinical dimension of the HCR-20. Among female inmates, consensual sex was associated with higher endorsement on the Borderline PD impulsivity diagnostic criteria.

TABLE 7.4 Frequency of Impulsivity Measures for Incarcerated Men (N=288) and Women (N=183)

Impulsivity Item	Men		Women		Effect Size	
	N	$\%$	N	$\%$	χ^2	Φ
Borderline-impulsivity	236	84.3	133	73.1	8.62	−0.14**
Antisocial-impulsivity	145	51.4	78	42.9	3.25	0.07
PCL-R2-impulsivity	127	44.6	77	42.1	0.28	−0.02
HCR-20 instability					4.37	0.10
No	39	13.5	38	20.8		
Possible	113	39.2	62	33.9		
Yes	130	45.1	83	45.4		

Note. * $p < 0.05$, ** $p < 0.01$.

TABLE 7.5 Relationship between Impulsivity Measures for Incarcerated Men (N=288) and Type of Sexual Experience in Prison

Impulsivity Item	Any-sex		Predatory		Victim		Bartered		Consensual	
	No N=143 (%)	Yes N=145 (%)	No N=253 (%)	Yes N=35 (%)	No N=244 (%)	Yes N=44 (%)	No N=251 (%)	Yes N=37 (%)	No N=160 (%)	Yes N=128 (%)
Borderline-impulsivity	114 (82.0)	122 (86.5)	203 (82.9)	44 (94.3)	202 (85.6)	34 (77.3)	205 (83.7)	31 (88.6)	125 (80.1)	111 (89.5)★
Antisocial-impulsivity	63 (45.0)	82 (57.7)★	123 (49.8)	22 (62.9)	124 (51.9)	21 (48.8)	123 (50.0)	22 (61.1)	71 (45.2)	74 (59.2)★
PCL-R2-impulsivity	57 (40.7)	70 (48.3)	111 (44.4)	16 (45.7)	107 (44.4)	20 (45.5)	107 (43.1)	20 (54.1)	63 (40.1)	64 (50.0)
HCR-20-instability										
No	26 (18.8)	13 (9.0)	37 (15.0)	2 (5.7)	33 (13.9)	5 (13.6)	38 (15.5)	1 (2.7)	29 (18.7)	10 (7.9)
Possible	53 (38.4)	60 (41.7)	99 (40.1)	14 (40.0)	92 (38.7)	21 (47.7)	101 (41.2)	12 (32.4)	61 (39.4)	52 (40.9)
Yes	59 (42.8)	71 (49.3)	111 (44.9)	19 (54.3)	113 (47.5)	17 (38.6)	106 (13.3)	24 (64.9)★	65 (41.9)	65 (51.2)★

Note. ★ $p < 0.05$.

TABLE 7.6 Relationship between Impulsivity Measures for Incarcerated Women (N=183) and Type of Sexual Experience in Prison

Impulsivity Item	Any-sex		Predatory		Victim		Bartered		Consensual	
	No N=77 (%)	Yes N=106 (%)	No N=178 (%)	Yes N=5 (%)	No N=134 (%)	Yes N=49 (%)	No N=165 (%)	Yes N=18 (%)	No N=98 (%)	Yes N=85 (%)
Borderline-impulsivity	47 (61)	86 (81.9)**	128 (72.3)	5 (100.0)	94 (70.1)	39 (81.2)	119 (72.1)	14 (82.4)	64 (65.3)	69 (82.1)*
Antisocial-impulsivity	33 (42.9)	45 (42.9)	74 (41.8)	4 (80.0)	56 (42.1)	22 (44.9)	70 (42.7)	8 (44.4)	41 (41.8)	37 (44.0)
PCL–R2-impulsivity	28 (36.4)	49 (46.2)	74 (41.0)	4 (80.0)	54 (40.3)	23 (46.9)	68 (41.2)	9 (50.0)	36 (36.7)	41 (48.2)
HCR–20-instability										
No	20 (26.0)	18 (17.0)	38 (21.3)	0 (0.0)	32 (23.9)	6 (12.2)	33 (20.0)	5 (27.8)	20 (20.4)	18 (21.2)
Possible	28 (36.4)	34 (32.1)	61 (34.3)	1 (20.0)	42 (31.3)	20 (40.8)	61 (37.0)	1 (5.6)	40 (40.8)	22 (25.9)
Yes	29 (37.7)	54 (50.9)	79 (44.4)	4 (80.0)	60 (44.8)	23 (46.9)	71 (43.0)	12 (66.7)*	38 (38.8)	45 (52.9)

Note. $* p < 0.05$, $** p < 0.01$.

Fear of Victimization, Associated with Violence and Sexual Violence

Studies of fear of crime in the community became a topic of interest to researchers beginning in the 1960s following the death of John F. Kennedy when President Lyndon Johnson signed into law the Commission on Law Enforcement. Using a sample of 10,000 households, researchers contracted by the Commission sought to identify levels of fear of crime and the factors influencing perceived and real vulnerability for individuals living in different communities across the country (US President's Commission on Law Enforcement and the Administration of Justice, 1967). This interest was transferred to institutionalized and incarcerated populations beginning in the 1990s when the incidence of violent and sexual crime in jails and prisons began to be more fully documented and with it a growing recognition of the impact of these experiences on the re-entry of inmates to the community (McCorkle, 1993a).

Fear of Victimization in Prison

In studying inmates' fear of victimization in prison, McCorkle (1993a, 1993b) found that most prison inmates had been the subject of a serious threat and a quarter had been approached for sexual favors. Although the largest proportion of inmates (49%) reported feeling reasonably safe, almost an equal number of inmates reported feeling "somewhat" or "very" unsafe in the institutional setting in which they resided.

In a study of one adult and two juvenile facilities in England, O'Donnell and Edgar (1999) found that almost a third of the juvenile inmates had been assaulted over the past month and yet the majority reported feeling relatively safe in their current environments. In contrast, the adult inmates reported feeling much more unsafe, particularly after experiencing any type of assault or incivility. Both the younger and older inmates reported feeling the most unsafe in the segregation unit, the showers, during their reception to the facility, and during movement to and from their residential units. In a study of inmates being released from the Texas prison system, Hemmens and Marquart (1999) found that age was the most relevant factor in perceptions of one's experience while in prison. Younger inmates, both at the time of first arrest and at the time they completed the survey, were more likely to report having problems with other inmates, feeling that there were not enough guards to guarantee safety and security, and tending to endorse the observation that "inmates attack other inmates very often." Race was significant in one of the logistic models, with Caucasian inmates more often than African American inmates reporting that they were worried "a lot" about being beaten up or attacked while incarcerated.

Fear has been associated with various psychological and behavioral outcomes among both juvenile and adult offenders. Maitland and Sluder (1996) found that the fear of victimization was significant in predicting general well-being among youthful inmates and associated not only with various psychological symptoms, but also different types of physical pain and illnesses. In a sample of 300 inmates in the Tennessee State Prison (a maximum security prison), McCorkle (1993a) found that fear was significantly related to victimization, even after controlling for physical and social vulnerabilities.

There are currently no studies of fear of victimization among incarcerated women. However, Warren, Hurt, Loper, and Chauhan (2004) found in a study of 802 women incarcerated in a maximum security prison that the majority of women felt safer in prison than in the community. Only 23 percent of the women reported being more afraid of being attacked in prison than in the community. Similarly, 90 percent of the women reported being more concerned about fights while living in the community than while incarcerated.

Study Analyses

Nine items used to assess inmates' self-report levels of fear of victimization while incarcerated were derived from a modified version of the Inmate Fear of Victimization (IFV). These variables were assessed for gender differences and for their association with the five categories of sexual behavior while in prison.

Table 7.7 reflects significant gender differences on six of the nine measures of fear of physical and sexual victimization in prison. Significantly more female than male inmates reported feeling safe in prison, while significantly more male than female inmates reported worrying about being attacked by prison staff. Similarly, significantly more female inmates reported that the prison system protects them from sexual contact, that correctional officers monitor them and keep them safe, and that both correctional officers and wardens take sexual assault seriously.

No significant gender differences emerged concerning the level of worry experienced by inmates of being physically or sexually attacked by another inmate or being sexually attacked by prison staff. Across these three variables, less than 4 percent of male or female inmates reported being "significantly" concerned about being attacked by another inmate or about being sexually attacked by another inmate or by prison staff.

The correlations among these variables and the five categories of sexual behavior in prison are presented in Table 7.8 (males) and Table 7.9 (females). Among the male inmates, any-sex was associated with inmates who felt minimally concerned about being attacked by other inmates, minimally concerned about being attacked by prison staff, and minimally concerned about being sexually assaulted by other inmates. Among female inmates, any-sex was associated only with minimal monitoring by correctional staff to keep inmates safe.

Male inmates who reported being sexually predatory reported feeling significantly more unsafe in prison yet reported feeling only minimally concerned about being attacked by other inmates or being sexually attacked by prison staff.

TABLE 7.7 Frequency of Fear of Victimization in Prison Reported by Incarcerated Men (*N*=288) and Women (*N*=183)

Fear Item	Men		Women		Effect Size	
	N	%	N	%	χ^2	Φ
How safe do you feel in prison?					21.08	0.21**
Safe	151	53.5	134	74.9		
Neutral	93	33.0	32	17.9		
Unsafe	38	13.5	13	7.3		
How much worry about attack by inmate?					0.34	0.03
Significantly	7	2.5	6	3.4		
Neutral	15	5.3	10	5.6		
Minimally	260	92.2	162	91.0		
How much worry about attack by prison staff?					38.8	0.29**
Significantly	38	13.5	3	1.7		
Neutral	58	20.6	13	7.3		
Minimally	185	65.8	162	91.0		
How much worry about sexual assault by inmate?					0.34	0.03
Significantly	7	2.5	6	3.4		
Neutral	15	5.3	10	5.6		
Minimally	260	92.2	163	91.0		
How much worry about sexual assault by prison staff?					1.13	0.05
Significantly	5	1.8	3	1.7		
Neutral	10	3.5	10	5.6		
Minimally	267	94.7	165	92.7		

(*Continued overleaf*)

TABLE 7.7 Continued

Fear Item	Men		Women		Effect Size	
	N	%	N	%	χ^2	Φ
How much does prison system protect you from sexual contact?					16.56	0.19**
Significantly	80	28.9	80	45.3		
Neutral	65	23.5	44	24.9		
Minimally	132	47.7	53	29.9		
How much do correctional officers monitor to keep you safe?					9.80	0.15**
Significantly	84	30.1	77	43.5		
Neutral	74	26.5	45	25.4		
Minimally	121	23.4	55	31.3		
How much do correctional officers take sexual assault seriously?					10.52	0.15**
Significantly	131	47.3	110	62.5		
Neutral	67	24.2	34	19.3		
Minimally	79	28.5	32	18.2		
How much does warden take sexual assault seriously?					22.41	0.22**
Significantly	168	60.4	143	81.2		
Neutral	61	21.9	15	8.5		
Minimally	49	17.6	18	10.2		

Note. ** $p < 0.01$.

TABLE 7.8 Relationship between Fear of Victimization Reported by Incarcerated Men (N=288) and Type of Sexual Experience in Prison

Fear Item	Any-sex		Predatory		Victim		Bartered		Consensual	
	No N=143 (%)	Yes N=145 (%)	No N=253 (%)	Yes N=35 (%)	No N=244 (%)	Yes N=44 (%)	No N=251 (%)	Yes N=37 (%)	No N=160 (%)	Yes N=128 (%)
How safe do you feel in prison?										
Safe	80 (56.7)	71 (50.4)	133 (53.6)	18 (52.9)	133 (55.4)	18 (42.9)	134 (54.7)	17 (45.9)	87 (55.1)	64 (51.6)
Neutral	47 (33.3)	46 (32.6)	86 (34.7)	7 (20.6)	79 (32.9)	14 (33.3)	81 (33.1)	12 (32.4)	54 (34.2)	39 (31.5)
Unsafe	14 (9.9)	24 (17.0)	29 (11.7)	9 (26.5)★	28 (11.7)	10 (23.8)	30 (12.22)	8 (21.6)	17 (10.8)	21 (16.9)
How much worry about attack by inmate?										
Significantly	0 (0.0)	7 (5.0)	4 (1.6)	3 (8.8)	2 (0.8)	5 (11.9)	3 (1.2)	4 (10.8)	1 (0.6)	6 (4.8)
Neutral	8 (5.7)	7 (5.0)	15 (6.0)	0 (0.0)	10 (4.2)	5 (11.9)	14 (5.7)	1 (2.7)	12 (7.6)	3 (2.4)
Minimally	133 (94.3)	127 (90.1)★	229 (92.3)	31 (91.2)★	228 (95.0)	32 (76.2)★★	228 (93.1)	32 (86.5)★★	145 (91.8)	115 (92.7)★
How much worry about attack by prison staff?										
Significantly	13 (9.3)	25 (17.7)	30 (12.1)	8 (23.5)	31 (13.0)	7 (16.7)	29 (11.9)	9 (24.3)	14 (8.9)	24 (19.4)
Neutral	25 (17.9)	33 (23.4)	52 (21.1)	6 (17.6)	46 (19.2)	12 (28.6)	49 (20.1)	9 (24.3)	30 (19.1)	28 (22.6)
Minimally	102 (72.9)	83 (58.9)★	165 (66.8)	20 (58.8)	162 (67.8)	23 (54.8)	166 (68.0)	19 (51.4)	113 (72.0)	72 (58.1)★
How much worry about sexual assault by inmate?										
Significantly	0 (0.0)	7 (5.0)	4 (1.6)	3 (8.8)	2 (0.8)	5 (11.9)	3 (1.2)	4 (10.8)	1 (0.6)	6 (4.8)
Neutral	8 (5.7)	7 (5.0)	15 (6.0)	0 (0.0)	10 (4.2)	5 (11.9)	14 (5.7)	1 (2.7)	12 (7.6)	3 (2.4)
Minimally	133 (94.3)	127 (90.1)★	229 (92.3)	31 (91.2)★	228 (95.0)	32 (76.2)★★	228 (93.1)	32 (86.5)★★	145 (91.8)	115 (92.7)★
How much worry about sexual assault by prison staff?										
Significantly	0 (0.0)	5 (3.5)	3 (1.2)	2 (5.9)	4 (1.7)	1 (2.4)	3 (1.2)	2 (5.4)	0 (0.0)	5 (4.0)
Neutral	5 (3.5)	5 (3.5)	10 (4.0)	0 (0.0)	7 (2.9)	3 (7.1)	10 (4.1)	0 (0.0)	7 (4.4)	3 (2.4)
Minimally	136 (96.5)	131 (92.9)	235 (94.8)	32 (94.1)	229 (95.4)	38 (90.5)	232 (94.7)	35 (94.6)	151 (95.6)★	115 (93.5)★

(Continued overleaf)

TABLE 7.8 Continued

Fear Item	Any-sex		Predatory		Victim		Bartered		Consensual	
	No N=143 (%)	Yes N=145 (%)	No N=253 (%)	Yes N=35 (%)	No N=244 (%)	Yes N=44 (%)	No N=251 (%)	Yes N=37 (%)	No N=160 (%)	Yes N=128 (%)
How much does the prison system protect you from sexual contact?										
Significantly	46 (33.1)	34 (24.6)	71 (29.2)	9 (26.5)	70 (29.7)	10 (24.4)	69 (28.6)	11 (30.6)	48 (31.0)	32 (26.2)
Neutral	35 (25.2)	30 (21.7)	61 (25.1)	4 (11.8)	60 (25.4)	5 (12.2)	59 (24.5)	6 (16.7)	36 (23.2)	29 (23.8)
Minimally	58 (41.7)	74 (53.6)	111 (45.7)	21 (61.8)	106 (44.9)	26 (63.4)	113 (46.9)	19 (52.8)	71 (45.8)	61 (50.0)
How much do correctional officers monitor to keep you safe										
Significantly	50 (36.0)	34 (24.3)	77 (31.4)	7 (20.6)	78 (32.8)	6 (14.6)	76 (31.4)	8 (21.6)	53 (34.0)	31 (25.2)
Neutral	37 (26.6)	37 (26.4)	64 (26.1)	10 (29.4)	65 (27.3)	9 (22.0)	64 (26.4)	10 (27.0)	39 (25.0)	35 (28.5)
Minimally	52 (37.4)	69 (49.2)	104 (42.4)	17 (50.0)	95 (39.9)	26 (63.4)★	102 (42.1)	19 (51.4)	64 (41.0)	57 (46.3)
How much do correctional officers take sexual assault seriously?										
Significantly	67 (48.6)	64 (46.0)	115 (47.3)	16 (47.1)	112 (47.5)	19 (46.3)	112 (46.7)	19 (51.4)	72 (46.5)	59 (48.4)
Neutral	35 (25.4)	32 (23.0)	63 (25.9)	4 (11.8)	59 (25.0)	8 (19.5)	62 (25.8)	5 (13.5)	40 (25.8)	27 (22.1)
Minimally	36 (26.1)	43 (30.9)	65 (26.7)	14 (41.2)	65 (27.5)	14 (34.1)	66 (25.7)	13 (35.1)	43 (27.7)	36 (29.5)
How much does the warden take sexual assault seriously?										
Significantly	78 (56.5)	90 (64.3)	146 (59.8)	22 (64.7)	142 (59.9)	26 (63.4)	140 (58.1)	28 (75.7)	86 (55.5)	82 (66.7)
Neutral	33 (23.9)	28 (20.0)	57 (23.4)	4 (11.8)	54 (22.8)	7 (17.1)	59 (24.5)	2 (5.4)	38 (24.5)	23 (18.7)
Minimally	27 (19.6)	22 (15.7)	41 (16.8)	8 (23.5)	41 (17.3)	8 (19.5)	42 (17.2)	7 (18.9)★	31 (20.0)	18 (14.6)

Note. ★ $p < 0.05$, ★★ $p < 0.01$.

TABLE 7.9 Relationship between Fear of Victimization Reported by Incarcerated Women (N=183) and Type of Sexual Experience in Prison

Fear Item	Any-sex		Predatory		Victim		Bartered		Consensual	
	No N=77 (%)	Yes N=106 (%)	No N=178 (%)	Yes N=5 (%)	No N=134 (%)	Yes N=49 (%)	No N=165 (%)	Yes N=18 (%)	No N=98 (%)	Yes N=85 (%)
How safe do you feel in prison?										
Safe	61 (80.3)	73 (70.9)	132 (75.9)	2 (40.0)	103 (79.2)	31 (63.3)	123 (75.9)	11 (64.7)	73 (75.3)	61 (74.4)
Neutral	11 (14.9)	21 (20.4)	29 (16.7)	3 (60.0)	19 (14.6)	13 (26.5)	27 (16.7)	5 (29.4)	18 (18.6)	14 (17.1)
Unsafe	4 (5.3)	9 (8.7)	13 (7.5)	0 (0.0)★	8 (6.2)	5 (10.2)	12 (7.4)	1 (5.9)	6 (6.2)	7 (8.5)
How much worry about attack by inmate?										
Significantly	2 (2.6)	4 (4.0)	6 (3.5)	0 (0.0)	3 (2.3)	3 (6.4)	6 (3.7)	0 (0.0)	4 (4.1)	2 (2.5)
Neutral	1 (1.3)	9 (8.9)	10 (5.8)	0 (0.0)	3 (2.3)	7 (14.9)	10 (6.2)	0 (0.0)	7 (7.1)	3 (3.8)
Minimally	74 (96.1)	88 (87.1)	157 (90.8)	5 (100.0)	125 (95.4)	37 (78.7)★★	145 (90.1)	17 (100.0)	87 (88.8)	75 (93.8)
How much worry about attack by prison staff?										
Significantly	1 (1.3)	2 (2.0)	3 (1.7)	0 (0.0)	2 (1.5)	1 (2.1)	3 (1.9)	0 (0.0)	1 (1.0)	2 (2.5)
Neutral	2 (2.6)	11 (10.9)	13 (7.5)	0 (0.0)	5 (3.8)	8 (17.0)	13 (8.1)	0 (0.0)	7 (7.1)	6 (7.5)
Minimally	74 (96.1)	88 (87.1)	157 (90.8)	5 (100.0)	124 (94.7)	40 (80.9)★	145 (90.1)	17 (100.0)	90 (91.8)	72 (90.0)
How much worry about sexual assault by inmate?										
Significantly	2 (2.6)	4 (4.0)	6 (3.5)	0 (0.0)	3 (2.3)	3 (6.4)	6 (3.7)	0 (0.0)	4 (4.1)	2 (2.5)
Neutral	1 (1.3)	9 (8.9)	10 (5.8)	0 (0.0)	3 (2.3)	7 (14.9)	10 (6.2)	0 (0.0)	7 (7.1)	3 (3.8)
Minimally	74 (96.1)	88 (87.1)	157 (90.8)	5 (100.0)	125 (95.4)	37 (78.7)★★	145 (90.1)	1 (100.0)	87 (88.8)	75 (93.8)
How much worry about sexual assault by prison staff?										
Significantly	1 (1.3)	2 (2.0)	3 (1.7)	0 (0.0)	2 (1.5)	1 (2.1)	3 (1.9)	0 (0.0)	2 (2.0)	1 (1.2)
Neutral	2 (2.6)	8 (7.9)	10 (5.8)	0 (0.0)	3 (2.3)	7 (14.9)	10 (6.2)	0 (0.0)	6 (6.1)	4 (5.0)
Minimally	74 (96.1)	91 (90.1)	160 (92.5)	5 (100.0)	126 (96.2)	39 (83.0)★★	148 (91.9)	17 (100.0)	90 (91.8)	75 (93.8)

(Continued overleaf)

TABLE 7.9 Continued

Fear Item	Any-sex		Predatory		Victim		Bartered		Consensual	
	No N=77 (%)	Yes N=106 (%)	No N=178 (%)	Yes N=5 (%)	No N=134 (%)	Yes N=49 (%)	No N=165 (%)	Yes N=18 (%)	No N=98 (%)	Yes N=85 (%)
How much does prison system protect you from sexual contact?										
Significantly	41 (53.2)	39 (39.0)	80 (46.5)	0 (0.0)	63 (48.1)	17 (37.0)	74 (46.2)	6 (35.3)	48 (49.0)	32 (40.5)
Neutral	15 (19.5)	29 (29.0)	42 (24.4)	2 (40.0)	34 (26.0)	10 (21.7)	38 (23.8)	6 (35.3)	19 (19.4)	25 (31.6)
Minimally	21 (27.3)	32 (32.0)	50 (29.1)	3 (60.0)	34 (26.0)	19 (41.3)	48 (30.0)	5 (29.4)	31 (31.6)	22 (27.8)
How much do correctional officers monitor to keep you safe?										
Significantly	40 (51.9)	37 (37.0)	76 (44.2)	1 (20.0)	61 (46.6)	16 (34.8)	71 (44.4)	6 (35.3)	46 (46.9)	31 (39.2)
Neutral	22 (28.6)	23 (23.0)	44 (25.6)	1 (20.0)	36 (27.5)	9 (19.6)	39 (24.4)	6 (35.3)	26 (26.5)	19 (24.1)
Minimally	15 (19.5)	40 (40.0)★	52 (30.2)	4 (60.0)	34 (26.0)	21 (45.7)★	50 (31.2)	5 (29.4)	26 (26.5)	29 (36.7)
How much do correctional officers take sexual assault seriously?										
Significantly	51 (67.1)	59 (59.0)	108 (63.2)	2 (40.0)	86 (66.2)	24 (52.2)	102 (64.2)	8 (47.1)	64 (66.0)	46 (58.2)
Neutral	13 (17.1)	21 (21.0)	32 (18.7)	2 (40.0)	25 (19.2)	9 (19.6)	29 (18.2)	5 (29.4)	15 (15.5)	19 (24.1)
Minimally	12 (15.8)	20 (20.0)	31 (18.1)	1 (20.0)	19 (14.6)	13 (28.3)	28 (17.6)	4 (23.5)	18 (18.6)	14 (17.7)
How much does warden take sexual assault seriously?										
Significantly	62 (81.6)	81 (81.0)	139 (81.3)	4 (80.0)	108 (83.1)	35 (76.1)	130 (81.8)	13 (76.5)	81 (83.5)	62 (78.5)
Neutral	7 (9.2)	8 (8.0)	14 (8.2)	1 (20.0)	9 (6.9)	6 (13.0)	13 (8.2)	2 (11.8)	7 (7.2)	8 (10.1)
Minimally	7 (9.2)	11 (11.0)	18 (10.5)	0 (0.0)	13 (10.0)	5 (10.9)	16 (10.1)	2 (11.8)	9 (9.3)	9 (11.4)

Note. ★ $p < 0.05$, ★★ $p < 0.01$.

Female inmates reporting sexual predation were less likely to feel unsafe while in prison.

Male inmates who reported being sexually victimized in prison reported a low level of concern of physical and sexual attack by other inmates, yet reported feeling correctional officers were only minimally involved in monitoring inmates to keep them safe. Female inmates who reported being sexually victimized reported being more worried about being attacked by another inmate, more worried about being attacked by prison staff, more worried about being sexually attacked by another inmate, more worried about being sexually attacked by prison staff, and more likely to report that correctional officers engage in only minimal monitoring to keep inmates safe.

The male inmates who endorsed involvement in sexual bartering were more worried about physical and sexual assault by other inmates, and were less likely to believe that wardens take sexual assault seriously. Bartered sex was unrelated to any of these fear measures among the female inmates.

Male inmates who reported being involved in consensual sexual encounters reported feeling only minimally worried about being physically or sexually attacked by another inmate, but more likely to worry about being physically or sexually attacked by prison staff. Consensual sex was unrelated to any of these fear measures reported by female inmates.

Social Cognitions Associated with Violence and Sexual Violence

Thoughts of Harm and Sexual Violence

While all psychiatric evaluations include questions concerning homicidal ideation, the process of thinking about violence before perpetrating violence has seldom been studied empirically. This possible risk factor was included in the MacArthur Violence Risk Assessment Study using the Schedule of Imagined Violence (SIV; Grisso, Davis, Vesselinov Appelbaum, & Monahan, 2000). The SIV quickly divides respondents according to a SIV positive (+) or SIV negative (−) status, and among the endorsing SIV+ group, explores the frequency, chronicity, and target focus of violent thoughts over the previous two months.

The SIV was administered to all participants in the MacArthur study at baseline and during each follow-up assessment. Within the sample, 339 patients (30%) self-reported thoughts of harming others during their inpatient hospitalization, with this frequency increasing to 57 percent by the end of the one-year follow-up. The rate of violent behavior was also found to vary with the presence or absence of violent thoughts, with 24 percent of the SIV− patients being violent as contrasted to 36 percent of the SIV+ patients over the course of the study. In particular, racial minority males and females who were SIV+ were found to be two to three times more likely than those who were SIV- to engage in some form of community violence. The effect of this variable remained significant when entered into the multiple regression analyses and was the most significant factor in the third iteration of the classification tree development (Monahan et al., 2001). No studies have used the SIV to study sexual violence in the community or within institutions.

Threat Control Override Symptoms

The MacArthur Violence Risk Assessment Study also sought to parse out the effects of specific psychotic symptoms on the manifestation of violent behavior. Link and Stueve (1994) examined 13 common psychotic symptoms and found that three of these symptoms, which they labeled threat control override (TCO) symptoms, explained most of the association between psychotic thinking and violent behavior. The TCO constellation included the perception that one's mind was being controlled by some external force, that thoughts were being inserted into one's mind, and/or that there were others around who wished to do harm to the person having this experience. Link and Stueve found no association between other odd perceptions, ideas of thought broadcasting, possession, special powers, or audio and visual hallucinations and violent behavior.

Swanson, Borum, Swartz, and Monahan (1996) found that individuals with TCO symptoms were twice as likely to be assaultive as those with other delusions and hallucinations and five times more likely to be assaultive than those with no mental disorder. This relationship was compounded when associated with substance abuse and intoxication, with the rates of violent behavior increasing to 86 percent when both constellations of behaviors were combined in the experience of a single individual.

Final analyses of the MacArthur data, however, failed to confirm the relationship between TCO symptoms and violent behavior in the community. Subsequent analyses of these data suggest that they may contain significant gender differences, with men being more likely to be violent when they experience perceptions of being controlled or harmed by others, while women are less likely to be violent when having these same internal perceptions (Teasdale, Silver, & Monahan, 2006). No studies have used TCO symptoms to study sexual violence in the community or within institutions.

Study Analyses

The SIV was used to code each participant as SIV+ or SIV−. The four threat control override (TCO) symptoms were assessed through self-report queries embedded in the Prison Background Information Survey (PBIS). We chose in our analyses to include TCO symptoms in our social cognitions category of risk factors as our analyses suggested that most respondents interpreted the three TCO questions as reflecting reality-based perceptions of others rather than internal stimuli associated with a psychotic illness. These social cognition variables were assessed for gender differences and for their association with the five categories of sexual behavior in prison.

The results in Table 7.10 underscore the violent perceptions that characterize the experiences of the male and female inmates in our sample. Significantly more male than female inmates reported having thoughts of harming others (i.e., SIV+). However, no gender differences emerged in terms of TCO symptoms. Overall, over one third of the male (42.4%) and female (39.9%) inmates reported at least one of the three TCO symptoms, most often the perception that others were intending harm toward the individual.

The correlations of the social cognition variables with types of sex are presented in Table 7.11 (males) and Table 7.12 (females). For both the male and female inmates, any-sex was associated with thoughts of harming others (SIV+), thoughts that others wanted to harm the individual, and endorsement of at least one TCO symptom.

Predatory sex among the male inmates was associated with thoughts of harming others (SIV+), thoughts that others wanted to harm the individual, and endorsement of at least one TCO symptom. None of these social cognition variables were associated with predatory sex among the female inmates.

Male sexual victimization was associated only with thoughts that others wanted to hurt the individual. Among the female inmates, sexual victimization was associated with both thoughts that others wanted to harm the individual and with the endorsement of at least one TCO symptom.

Bartered sex engaged in by male inmates was more likely to be associated with thoughts of harming others (SIV+), less likely to be associated with thoughts of others wanting to cause harm to the individual, and less likely to be associated with at least one TCO symptom. No social cognition variables were associated with bartered sex among the female inmates.

Male inmates engaging in consensual sex were less likely to experience thoughts of harming others (SIV+), were less likely to experience thoughts of others wanting to harm the individual, and were less likely to have endorsed any

TABLE 7.10 Frequency of SIV and TCO Endorsement Reported by Incarcerated Men (N=288) and Women (N=183)

Item	Men		Women		Effect Size	
	N	%	N	%	χ^2	Φ
Thoughts of harming others (SIV+)	89	31.9	20	11.3	25.27**	0.24**
Others controlling thoughts (TCO)	35	12.3	29	16.2	1.39	−0.06
Others want to hurt you (TCO)	110	39.0	67	37.2	0.15	0.02
Inserting thoughts (TCO)	19	6.7	6	3.3	2.44	0.07
Any TCO symptom	122	42.4	73	39.9	0.28	−0.02

Note. ** $p < 0.01$.

TABLE 7.11 Relationship between SIV and TCO Measures Reported by Incarcerated Men (*N*=288) and Type of Sexual Experience in Prison

Item	Any-sex		Predatory		Victim		Bartered		Consensual	
	No N=143 (%)	*Yes* N=145 (%)	*No* N=253 (%)	*Yes* N=35 (%)	*No* N=244 (%)	*Yes* N=44 (%)	*No* N=251 (%)	*Yes* N=37 (%)	*No* N=160 (%)	*Yes* N=128 (%)
Thoughts of harming others (SIV+)	35 (24.8)	54 (39.1)★	70 (28.5)	19 (57.6)★★	73 (30.5)	16 (40.0)	71 (29.2)	18 (50.0)★	40 (25.3)	49 (0.5)★★
Others controlling thoughts (TCO)	16 (11.3)	19 (13.4)	28 (11.2)	7 (20.0)	28 (11.6)	7 (16.7)	30 (12.1)	5 (13.5)	142 (89.3)	107 (85.6)
Others want to hurt you (TCO)	41 (29.1)	69 (48.9)★★	89 (36.0)	21 (60.0)★★	87 (36.4)	23 (53.5)★	88 (35.9)	22 (9.5)★★	47 (29.7)	63 (0.8)★★
Inserting thoughts (TCO)	11 (7.7)	8 (5.6)	16 (6.4)	3 (8.6)	16 (6.6)	3 (7.0)	17 (6.9)	2 (5.4)	11 (6.9)	8 (6.4)
Any TCO symptom	47 (32.9)	75 (51.7)★★	99 (39.1)	23 (65.7)★★	98 (40.2)	24 (54.5)	99 (39.4)	37 (2.2)★★	54 (33.8)	68 (3.1)★★

Note. ★ $p < 0.05$, ★★ $p < 0.01$.

TABLE 7.12 Relationship between SIV and TCO Measures Reported by Incarcerated Women (N=183) and Type of Sexual Experience in Prison

Item	Any-sex		Predatory		Victim		Bartered		Consensual	
	No N=77 (%)	Yes N=106 (%)	No N=178 (%)	Yes N=5 (%)	No N=134 (%)	Yes N=49 (%)	No N=165 (%)	Yes N=18 (%)	No N=98 (%)	Yes N=85 (%)
Thoughts of harming others (SIV+)	4 (5.3)	16 (16.0)★	19 (11.0)	1 (20.0)	13 (9.9)	7 (15.2)	16 (10.0)	4 (23.5)	5 (5.1)	15 (19.0)★★
Others controlling thoughts (TCO)	9 (11.8)	20 (19.4)	27 (15.5)	2 (40.0)	21 (16.0)	9 (16.7)	24 (14.9)	5 (27.8)	11 (11.5)	18 (21.7)
Others want to hurt you (TCO)	20 (26.3)	47 (45.2)★	64 (36.6)	3 (60.0)	41 (31.3)	26 (53.1)★★	58 (35.8)	9 (50.0)	31 (32.0)	36 (43.4)
Inserting thoughts (TCO)	2 (2.6)	4 (3.8)	6 (3.4)	0 (0.0)	4 (3.1)	2 (4.1)	5 (3.1)	1 (5.6)	2 (2.1)	4 (4.8)
Any TCO symptom	23 (29.9)	50 (47.2)★	69 (38.8)	4 (80.0)	46 (34.3)	27 (55.1)★	63 (38.2)	10 (55.6)	34 (34.7)	39 (45.9)

Note. ★p < 0.05, ★★p < 0.01.

of the TCO symptoms. Female inmates engaging in consensual sex were more likely to have thoughts of harming others (SIV+).

Conclusions

Our results suggested that the majority of the male and female inmates experienced themselves as being relatively safe while living in the prison environment. They reported minimal concerns about being sexually assaulted by either other inmates or the correctional staff, and minimal concerns about being physically attacked by other inmates, although male inmates endorsed significant concerns about being physically attacked by prison staff. Despite this experience of relative safety, both the male and female inmates reported reservations concerning the commitment of the prison system to protecting them from sexual assault. They reflected reservations about the interest or ability of correctional officers to keep them safe, and of correctional officers taking sexual assault seriously. However, the majority of the male inmates (60%) and most of the female inmates (81%) believed that the wardens of their prisons did take sexual assault seriously.

States of affective arousal were high as reported and observed with both the male and female inmates in our sample. Over half of the male inmates were coded positive on the Borderline PD criteria of inappropriate anger and two thirds on the Antisocial PD criteria of irritable and aggressive behavior. The rates were lower among the women but similarly reflected relatively high levels of inappropriate anger (46.4%) and irritability and aggressiveness (34.8%). Superimposed on these high levels of anger was a tendency toward impulsive behavior as coded across multiple measures. These included a high level of endorsement on the Borderline PD impulsivity criteria (84.3% of males and 73.1% of females) associated with self-damaging acts such as spending, sex, substance abuse, and reckless driving; on the Antisocial PD impulsivity criteria (51.4% of males and 42.9% of females) associated with impulsive life style and a failure to plan ahead; on the PCL-R2 coding on impulsivity (44.6% of males and 42.1% of females), which is coded to reflect a tendency to act on the "spur of the moment" and to break off relationships, quit jobs, change plans suddenly, or move from place to place on little more than a whim; and on the HCR-20 item of impulsivity (45.1% of males and 45.4% of females), which seeks to capture behavior that is unpremeditated and lacking in reflection or forethought. These measures of impulsivity derived from the clinical coding of the research interviewers and reflected high levels of impulsive behavior reflected in different aspects of life, both while living in prison and while living in the community.

The social cognition of thinking about harming another person or experiencing at least one of the three TCO symptoms were also common among the male and female inmates. Almost one third of the males self-reported thinking about physically hurting or injuring some other person while approximately one in ten of the female inmates similarly endorsed these kinds of aggressive thoughts towards others. Forty-two percent of the male inmates and 40 percent of the female inmates also self-reported experiencing one or more of the TCO symptoms. These perceptions were often interpreted literally in terms of others wishing to do one harm. However, it was not possible to assess how accurate or distorted these experiences of others might be for these individuals during incarceration. However, as summarized above, most of the inmates reported feeling relatively safe in prison suggesting that some of these attributions of harm might reflect a perceptual stance that was not entirely a reflection of immediate harm in the environment.

When we examined the association between these different affective and cognitive states and sexual behavior in prison, significant gender differences emerged in the analyses. For any-sex, male inmates reported no concerns of being victimized by other inmates or members of the prison staff. In contrast, female inmates expressed the sense that correctional staff were doing little to keep them safe in the prison environment. Predatory sex for the male inmates was associated with a single scale on the Novaco Anger Scale (NAS), the NAS behavioral regulation subscale, which is designed to capture impulsive reactions, verbal aggression, physical confrontation, and indirect expression of anger toward others. Men who reported sexual predation against other inmates while incarcerated scored significantly higher on this behavioral dimension of anger suggesting a tendency toward the outward expression of angry feelings. For the male inmates, this association between high levels of anger and sexual aggression may be capturing some of the covariance identified in the rape typologies which seek to describe sexual aggression against women in the community. For the male inmates, predatory sexual behavior was also associated with perceptions of being unsafe in the prison environment, having thoughts of harming others (SIV+), and experiencing at least one of the TCO symptoms. These perceptual experiences underscore the dangerous and aggressive perceptions associated with sexual predation in prison and combine to support the interpretation of sexual aggression in the community as an act of violence and control rather than of sexual arousal and need. Female inmates' predatory sexual behavior was associated similarly with the NAS behavioral regulation subscale and feeling less unsafe in prison, but not with thoughts of harming others or of being threatened by them.

Bartered sex was associated with a different constellation of self-report and clinical coding of emotional states and social cognitions. Male inmates who self-reported bartering sex for various goods and for protection described themselves as being more aroused by feelings of anger and fear and were clinically observed to manifest the inappropriate anger associated with Borderline PD along with the dimension of impulsivity coded on the HCR-20. These male inmates also endorsed thoughts of causing harm to others, being worried about being attacked sexually by inmates, and believing that wardens did not take their plight seriously. The pattern was similar with the female inmates: Female inmates who self-reported bartering sex reported elevated levels of anger and problems with anger regulation as captured on the NAS and impulsive behavior as coded on the HCR-20, but not elevated fears about their living conditions in prison. These patterns across genders suggest that bartering sex in prison may reflect a continuation of unstable and impulsive behavior that is observed in the inmates' patterns of community living as well as in the inmates' adaptation to life in prison. Moreover, it appears to reflect a personal experience of emotional arousal and aggressive and fearful cognitions that are not solely based upon the financial and safety needs of the individual inmate.

The sexual victimization reported by the male inmates was associated with higher levels of anger as measured by the NAS but lower levels of Antisocial-irritability and aggression. As a group, these men also reported more fears of being sexually victimized by other inmates, having thoughts of harming others, and believing that correctional staff inadequately monitored the inmates to keep them safe. The female inmates who self-reported being the victims of sexual aggression did not demonstrate elevated anger on the NAS or through clinical coding on the symptoms of Borderline PD, Antisocial PD, or on the coding of the HCR-20. They did, however, endorse believing that others wanted to do them harm and reported more fear of being victimized by other inmates and staff. These patterns are again similar across genders and combine to describe individuals who are innately less angry and aggressive when compared to the perpetrators of sexual aggression and who report higher levels of fear, less trust in the correctional staff to keep them safe, and greater fear of others combined with the perception of others intending to do the individual harm.

Male inmates who self-reported consensual sexual involvement with other inmates or with correctional staff reported higher levels of anger on the cognitive and arousal domains of the NAS and elevated clinical coding on the Borderline PD criteria of inappropriate anger and the Antisocial PD criteria of irritability and aggressiveness. They were also coded higher on the impulsivity clinical item on the HCR-20 reflecting elevated levels of behavioral and affective instability. They reported minimal worries about being sexually attacked by other inmates or correctional staff and lower levels of endorsement of wishing to do harm to others (SIV+) or believing that others wanted to do harm to the individual (TCO). The women who self-reported engaging in consensual sex similarly reported higher levels of cognitive and emotional arousal on the NAS, more thoughts of wanting to do harm to others (SIV+), and clinical elevations on the Antisocial PD criteria of irritability and aggressiveness. These women were also coded clinically as being more impulsive on the Borderline PD criteria of impulsive behavior associated with self-damaging behavior, the Antisocial PD criteria of impulsivity associated with a failure to plan ahead, and impulsivity as coded on the HCR-20 and reflective of persistent behavioral and affective instability. These patterns suggest that across genders, consensual sex in prison is associated with heightened levels of affective arousal and a pervasive pattern of impulsive behavior that appears from the clinical codings to have followed most inmates from the community into their adaption to living in prison.

These varied associations when viewed in isolation suggest that predatory, bartered, and consensual sex in prison for both genders is associated with behavior that to some extent predates incarceration and which is associated with impulsive behavior that is observed over many domains of a person's life both in prison and in the community. This is less true with inmates who report sexual victimization as they are characterized by the emotions and cognitions often associated with all kinds of victimization, specifically the sense of being vulnerable to others, less safe in their environment, and angry but less aggressive in the stance they adopt to others. Inversely, these findings further suggest that individuals who are not sexually active in prison are less impulsive and less preoccupied with angry feelings and the wish to harm others.

8

DIMENSIONS OF PERSONALITY AS RISK MARKERS FOR SEXUAL PREDATION AND VICTIMIZATION

In the following chapter, we assess the influence of the more static, personality-based risk markers as they impact sexual behavior in prison. We examine two constructs with a pivotal history in the assessment of violence and aggressive sexuality, antisociality and psychopathy. These two personality-based constructs have a significant amount of overlap, although psychopathy is encountered less frequently in both community and prison samples, it appears to be more biologically determined across all populations, and is viewed by many as representing the more malignant end of the antisocial continuum (Patrick, 2006). We also explore the remaining nine personality disorders (PDs) identified in the Diagnostic and Statistical Manual of Mental Disorders-IV–Text Revision (DSM-IV-TR; American Psychiatric Association, 2000). These variables are assessed for gender differences and for their influence on the inmate's sexual behavior in prison.

The Role of Antisociality and Criminal History in the Prediction of Sexual Aggression

Sixty years of developmental and risk research has documented the relationship between general antisociality and violent crime including rape across a wide range of samples. Whether explored through patterns of violent crime, the behavior of sexually coercive offenders, or the assessment of psychopathy as it predicts future behavior, the research underscores the relationship between personality and lifestyle and the perpetration of interpersonal violence. Longitudinal research has also begun to broaden this inquiry by describing the evolution of these patterns of behavior from childhood through adolescence into adulthood (Moffitt et al., 2001).

Antisociality and Sexual Coercion in Community Samples

Community studies of rape have demonstrated a relationship between attitudes that reflect antisocial values and sexually coercive behavior in non-incarcerated males. Using the Sexual Experiences Survey, Koss and Dinero (1988) studied the self-report behavior of a national sample of 2,972 male college students. They found that 4 percent of the sample reported having raped a woman, 3 percent having attempted to rape a woman, 7 percent having used sexually coercive tactics to obtain sexual contact, and 10 percent having used a position of authority or threats to obtain sexual gratification. The sexually coercive men were found to be characterized by psychopathic-like traits such as callousness, a lack of empathy, aggression, and non-sexual antisocial behaviors (Kosson, Kelly, & White, 1997; Walker, Rowe, & Quinsey, 1993; Wheeler, George, & Dahl, 2002). Malamuth, Linz, Heavy, Barnes, and Acker (1995) later conducted a follow-up study of men who had been assessed while attending college and were able to locate 132 of these individuals along with their current romantic partner some years later. They found that the men who had self-reported sexually coercive acts while in college were more likely to self-report sexual coercion in adulthood ($r = 0.41$). Their partners also reported a higher incidence of non-sexual aggression being directed toward them in the context of their current relationship ($r = 0.55$).

Research on sexual coercion among women in the community is limited. Fromuth and Conn (1997) surveyed college women and found that 22 percent acknowledged having had sexual contact with younger children, usually when they themselves were children or adolescents. However, none of these young women had ever come to the attention of the police or a mental health counselor, although many reported prior sexual abuse as children.

Criminal History and Sexual Coercion

Bard et al. (1987) studied the criminal history of 100 rapists using information contained in their treatment files. They found that 93 percent of their sample had committed various forms of property crime including breaking and entering, and another 45 percent had committed a non-sexual violent crime such as assault. Barbaree and Seto (1998) examined the official criminal histories of 200 rapists and found that they had perpetrated a mean of 13 non-violent, non-sexual crimes and a mean of two non-sexual violent crimes. Weinrott and Saylor (1991) used a computerized self-report measure of criminal behavior with 37 convicted rapists. This group self-reported 19,000 non-sexual crimes in the 12 months preceding their arrest. This reflected a mean of 136 offenses per offender including public drunkenness, stealing, the use of hard drugs, and physically assaulting a woman. Hagan and Gust-Brey (1999) conducted a ten-year follow-up of 50 youths who had been committed to a secure treatment facility after having been determined to be sexually aggressive youth. Following release from the intensive treatment milieu, 90 percent of the youth were involved in one or more non-sexual crimes, with many of them being incarcerated for their adult crimes. Only 16 percent of the sample perpetrated another sexual assault by the end of the ten-year follow-up.

Research on sexually coercive behavior among women has been expanded recently, based upon data obtained from sexual offender registries in Texas and New York. In Texas, Vandiver and Kercher (2004) identified six groups that were differentiated by their sexual orientation, victim choice, and motivations for the crimes. One of the six groups involved the *female sexual predators* who were found to behave in a manner that suggested a sexual preference for male victims slightly under the age of puberty and who had a fairly high rate of re-arrest for crimes that were similar in nature to the one that led to their registration. Another group involved the *homosexual criminals* who were in their mid-thirties and who targeted females who were similar to them in age. They had multiple arrest histories, displayed a variety of antisocial behaviors, and often forced their female victims into prostitution which they used as a source of support.

Sandler and Freeman (2007) replicated this research using 390 women registered in New York, a group that constituted 2 percent of the sex offenders registered statewide. They also identified six offender groups, but differentiated them based upon their choice of victim and their perceived level of risk for re-offense. The *criminally-prone hebephile* group tended to choose male and female victims around the age of 14 years and had high rates of prior arrests, re-arrests, more periods of incarcerations, and more frequent supervision failures. The *high risk chronic offenders* group abused children who were on average five years of age. They tended to have a mean of 15 prior convictions, high rates of re-arrest, numerous prior incarcerations, and the highest rate of supervision failures.

Recently, Wijkman, Bijleveld, and Hendricks (2011) used a sample from the Netherlands to classify female sex offenders according to their criminal careers. They identified three groups which included the once-only offender, the generalist, and the specialist. The generalist group was the most diverse of the three groups with broader criminal histories that included both sexual and violent crime. Muskens, Bogaerts, van Casteren, & Labrijn (2011) conducted a follow-up of the same sample and found that the mean number of DSM-IV PDs were higher among co-offenders as compared to solo female sex offenders.

Study Analyses

We used the Structured Interview for DSM-IV Personality (SIDP-IV) to assess for the presence of symptoms of Antisocial personality disorders (PD). We assessed these Antisocial PD symptoms for gender differences and then for their association with the five categories of sex.

The results in Table 8.1 reflect the commonly observed gender differences in antisociality symptoms, with 60 percent of the male inmates meeting diagnostic criteria for Antisocial PD and 36 percent of the female inmates. These gender differences, while substantial, are smaller than those found in the community where five to seven times more men than women are found to meet diagnostic criteria for Antisocial PD (Torgersen, 2007). We also found gender differences in symptom patterns that resulted in this diagnosis, with the males reporting more aggressive/irritable behavior (38.9%) and women reporting higher rates of irresponsibility (25.6%).

By definition, individuals must meet criteria for a conduct disorder before the age of 15 years to be diagnosed with Antisocial PD in adulthood. In the current data, the majority of males (74%) who met criteria for conduct disorder did go on to meet criteria for Antisocial PD as adults. In contrast, only 50 percent of the females who met diagnostic criteria for conduct disorder by the age of 15 years met criteria for Antisocial PD as adults. These data may reflect a different trajectory of personality development in girls, with these adolescent behaviors more often being associated among women with the development of other Cluster B diagnoses, severe levels of post-traumatic stress disorder, and depression in women.

Table 8.2 (males) and Table 8.3 (females) present the correlations of the Antisocial PD symptoms with the five categories of sex. Among male inmates, any-sex was associated with a diagnosis of conduct disorder prior to age 15 years, failure to conform to social norms, and impulsivity. Among the female inmates, any-sex was associated with a diagnosis of conduct disorder prior to age 15 years, failure to conform to social norms, and recklessness.

Predatory sex initiated by male inmates was associated only with a diagnosis of conduct disorder prior to age 15 years, and no variables correlated with predatory sex among the female inmates.

Sexual victimization among male inmates was related only to lower levels of irritability/aggressiveness, although no variables correlated with sexual victimization among the female inmates.

Bartered sex among the male inmates was associated with both a diagnosis of conduct disorder prior to age 15 years and lack of remorse, although no variables correlated with bartered sex among the female inmates.

Finally, consensual sex among the male inmates was related to a diagnosis of conduct disorder prior to age 15 years, failure to conform to social norms, impulsivity, irritability/aggressiveness, and recklessness. Among the female inmates, consensual sex was associated with a diagnosis of conduct disorder prior to age 15 years, failure to conform to social norms, and symptom criteria of both irritability/aggressiveness and reckless disregard for the safety of self and others.

TABLE 8.1 Frequency of Antisocial PD Symptoms by Antisocial PD (APD), Stratified by and Across Gender for Incarcerated Men (N=288) and Women (N=183)

Antisocial Symptom	Men						Women					
	Non (N=116)		APD (N=165)		Non v. APD (N=281)		Non (N=115)		APD (N=65)		Non v. APD (N=180)	
	N	%	N	%	χ^2	Φ	N	%	N	%	χ^2	Φ
Conduct disorder < age 15	43	37.1	165	100.0	140.28**	0.71**	26	22.6	65	100.0	99.50**	0.74**
Fail to conform to norms	55	50.5	149	92.0	60.35**	0.47**	53	46.1	61	93.8	40.79**	0.48**
Deceitfulness	24	21.6	96	58.5	35.68**	0.37**	29	24.8	39	60.0	22.14**	0.35**
Impulsivity	31	27.2	114	69.1	47.41**	0.41**	37	31.9	40	61.5	14.97**	0.29**
Irritability/aggressiveness	42	38.9	142	88.2	72.72**	0.52**	29	25.2	33	52.4	13.23**	0.27**
Recklessness	21	18.4	75	46.3	22.92**	0.29**	19	16.4	24	36.9	9.71**	0.23**
Irresponsibility	21	18.4	70	42.9	18.29**	0.26**	30	25.6	40	61.5	22.75**	0.35**
Lack of remorse	36	32.1	112	68.7	35.71**	0.36**	38	32.5	30	46.2	3.34	0.14

Note. **$p < 0.01$.
Frequencies reflect number who met DSM-IV criteria for symptom.

TABLE 8.2 Relationship between Antisocial PD Symptoms for Incarcerated Men (N=288) and Type of Sexual Experience in Prison

Antisocial Symptom	Any-sex		Predatory		Victim		Bartered		Consensual	
	No N=143 (%)	Yes N=145 (%)	No N=253 (%)	Yes N=35 (%)	No N=244 (%)	Yes N=44 (%)	No N=251 (%)	Yes N=37 (%)	No N=160 (%)	Yes N=128 (%)
Conduct disorder < age 15	93 (66.5)	115 (81.0)**	178 (72.1)	30 (88.2)*	176 (73.9)	32 (74.4)	175 (71.7)	33 (89.2)*	101 (64.8)	107 (85.6)**
Fail to conform to norms	95 (68.8)	112 (82.4)**	180 (74.7)	27 (81.8)	178 (76.7)	29 (69.0)	180 (74.7)	27 (81.8)	107 (69.0)	100 (84.0)**
Deceitfulness	60 (43.2)	62 (44.6)	106 (43.3)	16 (48.5)	107 (45.7)	15 (34.1)	106 (43.6)	16 (45.7)	64 (41.0)	58 (47.5)
Impulsivity	65 (45.0)	82 (57.7)*	123 (49.8)	22 (62.9)	124 (51.9)	21 (48.8)	123 (50.0)	22 (61.1)	71 (45.2)	74 (59.2)*
Irritability/ aggressiveness	90 (65.2)	97 (72.4)	162 (68.4)	25 (71.4)	165 (71.7)	22 (52.4)*	159 (7.4)	28 (77.8)	96 (62.7)	91 (76.5)*
Recklessness	41 (29.5)	56 (40.0)	80 (32.8)	17 (48.6)	82 (34.9)	15 (34.1)	82 (33.6)	15 (42.9)	46 (29.5)	51 (41.5)*
Irresponsibility	49 (35.5)	43 (30.3)	78 (31.8)	14 (40.0)	77 (32.6)	15 (34.1)	81 (33.2)	11 (30.6)	53 (34.2)	39 (31.2)
Lack of remorse	71 (51.1)	89 (57.6)	129 (52.7)	22 (66.7)	133 (56.6)	18 (41.9)	126 (51.9)	25 (71.4)*	79 (50.6)	72 (59.0)

Note. *p < 0.05, **p < 0.01.

TABLE 8.3 Relationship between Antisocial PD Symptoms for Incarcerated Women (N=183) and Type of Sexual Experience in Prison

Antisocial Symptom	Any-sex		Predatory		Victim		Bartered		Consensual	
	No N=77 (%)	Yes N=106 (%)	No N=178 (%)	Yes N=5 (%)	No N=134 (%)	Yes N=49 (%)	No N=165 (%)	Yes N=18 (%)	No N=98 (%)	Yes N=85 (%)
Conduct disorder < age 15	31 (40.3)	60 (58.3)★	88 (50.3)	3 (60.0)	69 (51.9)	22 (46.8)	85 (52.1)	6 (35.3)	39 (39.8)	52 (63.4)★★
Fail to conform to norms	38 (49.4)	77 (74.0)★★	111 (63.1)	4 (80.0)	82 (61.2)	33 (70.2)	101 (61.6)	14 (82.4)	50 (51.5)	65 (77.4)★★
Deceitfulness	25 (32.5)	43 (40.6)	65 (36.5)	3 (60.0)	50 (37.3)	18 (36.7)	60 (36.4)	8 (44.4)	33 (33.7)	35 (41.2)
Impulsivity	33 (42.9)	45 (42.9)	74 (41.8)	4 (80.0)	56 (42.1)	22 (44.9)	70 (42.7)	8 (44.4)	41 (41.8)	37 (44.0)
Irritability/ aggressiveness	21 (27.3)	41 (40.6)	60 (34.5)	2 (50.0)	43 (32.6)	19 (41.3)	54 (33.3)	8 (50.0)	27 (27.8)	35 (43.2)★
Recklessness	12 (15.6)	32 (30.5)★	41 (23.2)	3 (60.0)	28 (20.9)	16 (33.3)	38 (23.0)	6 (35.3)	17 (17.3)	27 (32.1)★
Irresponsibility	26 (33.8)	44 (41.5)	68 (38.2)	2 (40.0)	55 (41.0)	15 (30.6)	63 (38.2)	7 (38.9)	32 (32.7)	38 (44.7)
Lack of remorse	33 (42.9)	36 (34.0)	66 (37.1)	3 (60.0)	50 (37.3)	19 (38.8)	59 (35.8)	10 (55.6)	40 (40.8)	29 (34.1)

Note. ★ $p < 0.05$, ★★ $p < 0.01$.

The Role of Psychopathy in the Prediction of Sexual Coercion

The relationship between personality and violence has been rigorously studied using the construct of psychopathy developed by Hare (1978) and operationalized by him using the Psychopathy Checklist (PCL). Hare attributes the development of his powerful instrument to the early writings of Hervey Cleckley who in 1941 published his book, *The Mask of Sanity: An Attempt to Clarify Some Issues about the So-called Psychopathic Personality and Psychopathy*. As reflected in his title, Cleckley was interested in trying to describe systematically a group of patients who were by nature unsuited for the dominant mode of treatment at that time, psycho-analysis. He structured his description using 15 case studies which included both men and women and identified 16 common features of their personalities which included unstable lifestyles, chronic patterns of lying, stealing, truancy, and sexual promiscuity.

Since its inception, the PCL has undergone three revisions that reflect both changes in the item number and the factor structure that is used to interpret and score the instrument (Hare, 1991, 2003). For many years, a two-factor model (*Interpersonal/Affective Factor* and *Social Deviance Factor*) dominated the research literature (Harpur, Hakstian, & Hare, 1988). Meta-analyses of composite datasets, however, led Cooke and Michie (2001) to propose a three-factor model made up of an *Arrogant and Deceitful Interpersonal Style; Deficient Affective Experience*; with the addition of *Impulsive and Irresponsible Behavior*. In the revised PCL-R 2nd (PCL-R2) Edition Manual, Hare (2003) advocates a four-factor model that includes *Interpersonal, Affective, Lifestyle*, and *Antisocial* structural components.

Psychopathy and Criminal Offending in Men

Research conducted since the inception of the PCL suggests that the psychopathy construct has an ability to predict violent behavior among male inmates and forensic patients with predictive capabilities that exceeds most, if not all, other risk markers (Chase, O'Leary, & Heyman, 2001; Edens, Buffington-Vollum, Keilen, Roskamp, & Anthony, 2005; Hare, Clark, Grann, & Thornton, 2000; Hart, Kropp, & Hare,1988; Hart, Cox, & Hare, 1995; Harris et al., 2003; Hemphill, Hare, & Wong, 1998; Hicks, Rogers, & Cashel, 2000; Quinsey, Harris, Rice, & Cormier, 1998). General research comparing male psychopathic offenders with non-psychopathic offenders has found that the psychopaths have more extensive and varied criminal histories, manifest higher levels of instrumental violence, more frequently use weapons, and cause more significant injuries to their victims (Gacono, 2000). One of the first meta-analyses conducted by Hemphill et al. (1998) using only prospective data from offenders released into the community found a weighted correlation of 0.27 for general recidivism ($N = 1,275$), 0.27 for violent recidivism ($N = 1,374$), and 0.23 for sexual recidivism ($N = 178$). Later meta-analyses conducted by Gendreau,

Goggin, and Smith (2002) and Walters (2003) reported weighted effect sizes of 0.23 to 0.26 for general recidivism and 0.21 for violent recidivism.

Psychopathy and Sexual Offending in Men

When the psychopathy construct is explored in the context of sex offending, the role of psychopathy again appears to be appreciable, at least among those who are involved in forcible rapes against others. Psychopathy serves as a dominant risk marker for high levels of recidivism among institutionalized rapists following release (Hanson & Morton-Bourgon, 2004; Harris et al., 2003) and sexual recidivism among sex offenders even when controlling for age, criminal history, and psychiatric history (Rice, Harris, & Quinsey, 1990). When compared to other types of sex offenders, rapists were found by Rice and Harris (1997) to have higher scores on the PCL-R than other offenders held in the same federal prison system. Brown and Forth (1997) studied psychopathy in the context of the MTC:3R (Massachusetts Treatment Center Revised) Rapist Typology and found that the psychopathic rapists tended to fall within the opportunistic and pervasively angry categories. They demonstrated more extensive criminal histories beginning at an earlier age, but inflicted similar amounts of victim injury as non-psychopathic rapists. Prentky and Knight (2000) reviewed base rate data from the MTC:3R treatment sample and concluded that the opportunistic, pervasively angry, and overtly sadistic rapists were the most psychopathic in their behavior and attitudes. Within these groups, higher levels of psychopathy were associated with more violence and a more sexualized fantasy underlying the assault.

Psychopathy and Criminal Offending in Incarcerated Women

Studies of female inmates suggest slightly lower rates of psychopathy compared to male inmates when the score of 30 is used to diagnose or identify the condition. Research in Canada and the US suggest base rates ranging from 9 percent to 31 percent depending on the sample size and the security level of the female inmates being studied (Loucks & Zamble, 2000; Salekin, Rogers, & Sewell, 1997; Strachan, 1993; Vitale, Smith, Brinkley, & Newman, 2002). These reduced rates have led to speculations of a possible gender bias in some PCL-R items such as criminal versatility, juvenile delinquency, and the revocation of conditional release. Jackson, Rogers, Neumann, and Lambert (2002) reviewed the various studies and their samples and concluded that PCL-R scores among female samples average about four to six points lower than among male samples, but that the construct remains consistent in its ability to identify a continuum of similar behavior among women.

However, research suggests that psychopathy might have a different relationship to violent crime when encountered in women. Warren and her colleagues (Warren et al., 2005) found that PCL-R scores demonstrated an inverse ability to predict convictions for murder, a close to chance ability to predict violent crime, and a shared ability to predict property and minor crime among a group of incarcerated female felons. Salekin et al. (1997) found in their follow-up of 78 female inmates that scores on the PCL-R were unrelated to violent behavior, verbal aggression, noncompliant behavior, and estimated overall dangerousness while incarcerated. They also found that psychopathy scores were modest to poor predictors of recidivism when the women returned to the community. Strachan (1993), in her dissertation research, found that psychopathic women were more involved in prostitution and more likely to surrender their children for adoption when compared to non-psychopathic female inmates.

Study Analyses

We used the Psychopathy Checklist Revised-2 (PCL-R2) to assess psychopathy among both the male and female inmates. These variables were assessed for gender differences and then for their association with the five categories of sexual behavior.

Frequencies and factor scores are presented in Table 8.4. The scores on the PCL-R2 ranged from a low of 4 to a high of 36, with a mean total score of 18.95 for the males and 15.51 for the females. As summarized below, 10.5 percent of the males and 3.3 percent of the females scored above a cut-off score of 30, and 23.5 percent of the males and 12.1 percent of the females scored above a cut-off score of 25. In both cases, significantly more male than female inmates were above the

TABLE 8.4 Frequency of Psychopathy Checklist Items and Factor Scores for Incarcerated Men (N=288) and Women (N=183)

PCL-R2 Item	Men		Women		Effect Size	
	N	$\%$	N	$\%$	χ^2	Φ
1. Glibness					10.88***	0.15***
No	130	45.5	112	61.2		
Possible	94	33.0	44	24.0		
Yes	61	21.4	27	14.6		
2. Grandiose					0.01	0.01
No	118	41.3	76	41.6		
Possible	90	31.5	57	31.3		
Yes	78	27.3	49	26.9		
3. Needs Stimulation					0.67	0.04
No	65	22.8	40	21.9		
Possible	103	36.1	61	33.3		
Yes	117	41.1	82	44.8		
4. Pathological Lying					9.62**	0.14**
No	144	50.7	117	64.3		
Possible	96	33.8	39	21.4		
Yes	44	15.5	26	14.3		

TABLE 8.4 Continued

PCL-R2 Item	Men		Women		Effect Size	
	N	*%*	*N*	*%*	χ^2	Φ
5. Manipulative					4.84	0.10
No	116	40.8	56	30.8		
Possible	85	29.9	64	35.2		
Yes	83	29.2	62	34.1		
6. Lacks Remorse					13.96★★	0.17★★★
No	63	22.1	69	37.9		
Possible	107	37.5	58	31.9		
Yes	115	40.4	55	30.2		
7. Shallow Affect					16.91★★	0.19★★★
No	148	51.9	116	63.7		
Possible	79	27.7	54	29.7		
Yes	58	20.4	12	6.6		
8. Callous					11.07★★	0.15★★★
No	95	33.3	86	47.3		
Possible	118	41.4	68	37.4		
Yes	72	25.3	28	15.4		
9. Parasitic Lifestyle					4.96	0.10
No	121	44.2	64	35.4		
Possible	96	35.0	65	35.9		
Yes	57	20.8	52	28.7		
10. Poor Behavioral Control					24.37★★	0.23★★
No	50	17.5	67	36.6		
Possible	94	32.9	57	31.1		
Yes	142	49.7	59	32.2		
11. Promiscuous					21.19★★	0.21★★
No	94	33.0	99	54.4		
Possible	70	24.6	28	15.4		
Yes	121	42.5	55	30.2		
12. Early Behavior Problems					18.02★★	0.20★★
No	94	32.9	94	51.4		
Possible	68	23.8	40	21.9		
Yes	124	43.4	49	26.8		
13. Lacks Goals					7.20★	0.13★
No	116	41.1	96	52.7		
Possible	96	34.0	56	30.8		
Yes	70	24.8	30	16.5		
14. Impulsivity					5.37	0.11
No	34	11.9	36	19.7		
Possible	124	43.5	70	38.3		
Yes	127	44.6	77	42.1		

(*Continued overleaf*)

TABLE 8.4 Continued

PCL-R2 Item	Men		Women		Effect Size	
	N	%	N	%	χ^2	Φ
15. Irresponsibility					1.36	0.05
No	96	33.7	53	29.1		
Possible	110	38.6	79	43.4		
Yes	79	27.7	50	27.5		
16. Fails to Accept Responsibility					11.78★★	0.16★★
No	86	30.2	80	44.0		
Possible	103	36.1	63	34.6		
Yes	96	33.7	39	21.4		
17. Many Marital Relationships					7.88★	0.14★
No	185	73.1	106	60.6		
Possible	27	10.7	31	17.7		
Yes	41	16.2	38	21.7		
18. Juvenile Delinquency					65.38★★	0.37★★
No	104	36.4	125	68.3		
Possible	39	13.6	31	16.9		
Yes	143	50.0	27	14.8		
19. Revocation of Conditional Release					0.49	0.03
No	111	41.9	74	45.1		
Possible	18	6.8	11	5.7		
Yes	136	51.3	79	48.2		
20. Criminal Versatility					37.70★★	0.28★★
No	155	54.0	147	80.8		
Possible	77	26.8	27	14.8		
Yes	55	19.2	8	4.4		
PCL-R 2 > 30	30	10.5	6	3.3	8.16★★	−0.13★★
PCL-R 2 > 25	67	23.5	22	12.1	9.36★★	−0.14★★

	M	SD	M	SD	t	
Factor 1: Interpersonal (1,2,4,5)	3.16	2.31	2.91	2.10	1.18	
Factor 2: Affective (6,7,8,16)	3.82	2.33	2.81	2.24	4.69★★	
Factor 3: Behavioral (3,9,13,14)	4.13	2.07	4.03	2.02	0.50	
Factor 4: Antisocial (10,12,18,19,20)	5.31	2.64	3.39	2.42	8.09★★	
PCL-R2 Total score (all items)	18.95	7.77	15.51	7.21	4.80★★	

Note. ★$p < 0.05$, ★★$p < 0.01$, ★★★$p < 0.001$.

respective cut-off scores. Gender differences were found on 13 of the 20 item scores. All of these involved the male inmates scoring higher on the item when compared to the female inmates except for the multiple marital relationships, an item on which more females than males received a score of 2 (16.2% for males and 21.7% for females). Seven items did not reflect gender differences: grandiosity (item 2), the need for stimulation (item 3), manipulativeness (item 5), parasitic lifestyle (item 9), impulsivity (item 14), irresponsibility (item 15), and the revocation of conditional release (item 19). Gender differences were found on two of the factor scores—the Affective (Factor 2) and Antisocial (Factor 4) facets, again with the male inmates scoring higher. However, no gender differences were found on the Interpersonal (Factor 1) and Behavioral (Factor 3) scores.

Table 8.5 (males) and Table 8.6 (females) present the correlations of the psychopathy variables with the five categories of sex. Any-sex among both the male and female inmates was associated only with Factor 4 (Antisocial).

Predatory sex was not associated with any of the psychopathy variables among the male inmates, although it was associated with a PCL-R2 score of 30 or greater, Factor 2 (Affective), Factor 3 (Behavioral), and PCL-R2 Total score among the female inmates.

Sexual victimization experienced by both the male and female inmates was not associated with any of the psychopathy variables.

Bartered sex was associated with an elevated PCL-R2 score for both the male and female inmates. For the male inmates this involved a score of 25 or higher on the PCL-R2 and for the females a score of 30 or higher on the PCL-R2.

Consensual sex was associated with similar patterns of elevation on the PCL-R2 for both the male and female inmates. For both genders, consensual sex was associated with higher scores on Factor 4 (Antisocial) and a higher PCL-R2 Total score.

The Role of Personality Disorders in the Prediction of Sexual Coercion

Only recently has research begun to methodically study the high prevalence of DSM personality disorders (PD) among criminal populations (Casey, 2000; Davison, Leese, & Taylor, 2001; Singleton, Meltzer, Gatward, Coid, & Deasy, 1998). This high prevalence is particularly pronounced for the four disorders identified as the Cluster B disorders—Antisocial, Borderline, Histrionic, and Narcissistic—all of which have been found to be overrepresented in both forensic and criminal justice settings (Daniel, Robins, Reid, & Wilfley, 1988; Fazel & Danesh, 2002; Hiscoke, Langstrom, Ottosson, & Grann, 2003; Maden, Curie, Meux, Burrow, & Gunn, 1995).

Taylor et al. (1998) conducted a study of 1,740 male and female patients committed to two British hospitals for dangerous, violent, or criminal behavior over a six-month period. They found that 58 percent of the patients were suffering from some type of psychotic illness, with one-quarter of these individuals also meeting criteria for an independent PD. Another 26 percent of the sample was suffering from

TABLE 8.5 Relationship between Psychopathy Checklist Total and Factor Scores for Incarcerated Men (N=288) and Type of Sexual Experience in Prison

PCL-R2	Any-sex		Predatory		Victim		Bartered		Consensual	
	No N=143 (%)	Yes N=145 (%)	No N=253 (%)	Yes N=35 (%)	No N=244 (%)	Yes N=44 (%)	No N=251 (%)	Yes N=37 (%)	No N=160 (%)	Yes N=12 (%)
PCL-R 2 > 30	15 (10.7)	15 (10.3)	24 (9.6)	6 (17.1)	25 (10.4)	5 (11.4)	23 (9.3)	7 (18.9)	15 (9.6)	15 (11.7)
PCL-R 2 > 25	29 (20.7)	38 (26.2)	57 (22.8)	10 (28.6)	57 (23.7)	10 (22.7)	53 (21.4)	14 (37.8)★	32 (20.4)	35 (27.3)
	M(SD)	M(SD)	M(SD)	M(SD)	M(SD)	M(SD)	M(SD)	M(SD)	M(SD)	M(SD)
Factor 1: Interpersonal (1,2,4,5)	3.0 (2.4)	3.3 (2.2)	3.2 (2.3)	3.2 (2.1)	3.2 (2.4)	3.0 (2.0)	3.1 (2.3)	3.7 (2.3)	2.9 (2.4)	3.5 (2.2)
Factor 2: Affective (6,7,8,16)	3.8 (2.4)	3.8 (2.3)	3.8 (2.3)	4.2 (2.3)	3.9 (2.3)	3.5 (2.4)	3.8 (2.3)	4.1 (2.3)	3.8 (2.4)	3.8 (2.3)
Factor 3: Behavioral (3,9,13,14)	4.1 (2.1)	4.2 (2.1)	4.1 (2.1)	4.2 (2.0)	4.2 (2.1)	3.7 (1.9)	4.0 (2.1)	4.8 (2.0)★	4.0 (2.1)	4.3 (2.0)
Factor 4: Antisocial (10,12,18,19,20)	4.9 (2.6)	5.7 (2.6)★★	5.2 (2.7)	5.9 (2.5)	5.4 (2.6)	5.1 (2.9)	5.2 (2.6)	6.2 (2.6)★	4.8 (2.7)	6.0 (2.4)★★
PCL-R2 Total score (all items)	18.2 (8.0)	19.6 (7.5)	18.7 (7.7)	20.4 (8.0)	19.1 (7.7)	18.1 (8.2)	18.6 (7.8)	21.4 (7.5)★	17.9 (8.0)	20.2 (7.3)★

Note. ★$p < 0.05$, ★★$p < 0.01$.

TABLE 8.6 Relationship between Psychopathy Checklist Total and Factor Scores for Incarcerated Women (N=183) and Type of Sexual Experience in Prison

PCL-R2	Any-sex		Predatory		Victim		Bartered		Consensual	
	No N=77 (%)	Yes N=106 (%)	No N=178 (%)	Yes N=5 (%)	No N=134 (%)	Yes N=49 (%)	No N=165 (%)	Yes N=18 (%)	No N=98 (%)	Yes N=85 (%)
PCL-R2 > 30	2 (2.6)	4 (3.8)	5 (2.8)	1 (20.0)★	6 (4.5)	0 (0.0)	4 (2.4)	2 (11.8)★	2 (2.0)	4 (4.8)
PCL-R2 > 25	9 (11.7)	13 (12.4)	20 (11.3)	2 (40.0)	16 (11.9)	6 (12.5)	20 (12.1)	2 (11.8)	10 (10.2)	12 (14.3)
	M(SD)	M(SD)	M(SD)	M(SD)	M(SD)	M(SD)	M(SD)	M(SD)	M(SD)	M(SD)
Factor 1: Interpersonal (1,2,4,5)	2.6 (2.2)	3.1 (2.0)	2.9 (2.1)	4.2 (3.1)	2.8 (2.1)	3.3 (2.1)	2.9 (2.1)	3.2 (2.2)	2.7 (2.2)	3.1 (2.0)
Factor 2: Affective (6,7,8,16)	3.1 (2.3)	2.6 (2.2)	2.8 (2.2)	4.8 (2.9)★	2.8 (2.3)	2.8 (2.2)	2.8 (2.2)	3.2 (2.7)	3.0 (2.3)	2.6 (2.2)
Factor 3: Behavioral (3,9,13,14)	3.7 (2.0)	4.3 (2.0)	4.0 (2.0)	5.8 (2.9)★	4.0 (2.1)	4.3 (1.9)	4.0 (2.0)	4.6 (2.5)	3.8 (2.0)	4.3 (2.1)
Factor 4: Antisocial (10,12,18,19,20)	3.0 (2.4)	3.7 (2.4)★	3.4 (2.4)	4.4 (2.3)	3.4 (2.4)	3.4 (2.4)	3.4 (2.4)	3.5 (2.5)	2.9 (2.4)	4.0 (2.4)★
PCL-R2 Total score (all items)	14.6 (7.4)	16.2 (7.0)	15.3 (7.0)	22.9 (10.0)★	15.4 (7.2)	15.9 (7.2)	15.4 (7.1)	16.5 (8.7)	14.5 (7.1)	16.7 (7.2)★

Note. ★p < 0.05.

a PD without any psychotic complications. Of the 119 individuals who were diagnosed with a PD only, 26 percent had been committed for a homicide, 40 percent for other violent acts, 15 percent for sex offenses, and 18 percent for arson.

In a longitudinal study of 717 American youth, Johnson et al. (2000) found that community-living adolescents with symptoms of DSM-IV Cluster A and B PDs were more likely than other community-living adolescents to commit violent acts during adolescence. These results remained significant even after controlling for the youths' age, gender, socioeconomic status, degree of parental pathology, and co-occurring psychiatric disorder.

Using a combination of structured clinical interviews and a battery of instruments, Coid (1992) studied PDs among 243 male and female violent offenders detained under either psychopathic civil law or highly dangerous criminal law in England. Only 10 percent of the sample did not meet criteria for at least one Axis II diagnosis. Within this sample, the most common diagnoses were Borderline (69%) and Antisocial PD (53%), with a high degree of co-morbidity reflected in a mean of 3.6 Axis II diagnoses per offender. Blackburn (2007) obtained similar results with a sample of 168 mentally disordered male offenders. He found a strong association between a factor-analytically derived Antisocial dimension of behavior and Narcissistic–Histrionic personality traits and violence. However, he found no relationship between the various personality diagnoses and a conviction for sexual offending.

Warren, Hurt, Loper, and Chauhan (2004) examined Cluster B PDs among a group of 261 female inmates incarcerated at a maximum security prison. As a group, the four Cluster B disorders did not predict incarceration for a violent crime or violent institutional infractions, although they were associated with self-reported violent behavior within the institution. Narcissistic PD alone was found to predict current incarceration for both any violent crime including murder and any violent crime excluding murder.

Lynam and Derefinko (2006) recently identified eight published studies that examined the relationship between the ten PDs and scores on the PCL-R. They found the strongest association was Antisocial PD combined with Paranoid PD, Histrionic PD, and Narcissistic PD. Warren et al. (2003) examined independent assessments of Axis II disorders and scores on the PCL-R among female inmates and found a strong inter-correlation of PCL-R scores with Antisocial, Narcissistic, Histrionic, and Paranoid PDs. Widiger (2006) explored the relationship between psychopathy and the various DSM-IV diagnoses conceptually and emphasized the link between psychopathy and Narcissistic PD as reflected in earlier empirical studies (Blackburn, Logan, Donnelly, & Renwick, 2003; Salekin, Trobst, & Krioukova, 2001).

Study Analyses

The diagnoses of the ten PDs were determined using the Structured Interview for DSM-IV Personality (SIDP-IV). PDs were assessed for gender differences and then for their association with the five categories of sex.

TABLE 8.7 Frequency of Personality Disorders (PD) for Incarcerated Men (N=288) and Women (N=183)

Diagnosis	Men		Women		Effect Size	
	N	%	N	%	χ^2	Φ
Cluster A						
Paranoid PD	86	30.0	66	36.1	1.90	0.06
Schizoid PD	10	3.5	4	2.2	0.65	−0.04
Schizotypal PD	10	3.5	8	4.4	0.24	0.02
Cluster B						
Antisocial PD	165	58.1	65	35.7	22.23	−0.22**
Borderline PD	36	12.5	55	30.1	21.95	0.22**
Histrionic PD	7	2.4	12	6.6	4.89	0.10*
Narcissistic PD	53	18.5	38	20.8	0.38	0.03
Cluster C						
Avoidant PD	26	9.1	34	18.6	9.09	0.14**
Dependent PD	6	2.1	13	7.1	7.24	0.12**
Obsessive-compulsive PD	45	15.7	65	35.5	24.53	0.23**
Continuous Score	M	SD	M	SD	t	
Cluster A						
Paranoid PD	2.37	2.03	2.75	1.99	−1.97*	
Schizoid PD	0.87	1.14	0.85	1.09	0.17	
Schizotypal PD	1.27	1.45	1.24	1.34	0.28	
Cluster B						
Antisocial PD	4.21	2.11	3.26	2.03	4.83**	
Borderline PD	2.57	1.81	3.18	2.30	−3.06**	
Histrionic PD	1.22	1.30	1.68	1.70	−3.13**	
Narcissistic PD	2.48	2.25	2.61	2.28	−0.63	
Cluster C						
Avoidant PD	0.94	1.50	1.56	2.02	−3.52**	
Dependent PD	0.65	1.07	1.32	1.67	−4.80**	
Obsessive-compulsive PD	1.86	1.62	2.62	1.94	−4.38**	

Note. *$p < 0.05$, **$p < 0.01$.

The data presented in Table 8.7 underscore the high rates of PDs found among these inmates. Among Cluster A diagnoses, there were no significant gender differences. However, while approximately one third of male and female inmates had a Paranoid diagnosis, 5 percent of either gender had a diagnosis of Schizoid or Schizotypal PD. Three of the four diagnoses in Cluster B exhibited gender differences. Male inmates were significantly more likely than female inmates to have an Antisocial PD diagnosis, whereas more female than male inmates had a Borderline and a Histrionic PD diagnosis. Almost one in five of the inmates met diagnostic criteria for Narcissistic PD with no gender difference on this particular Cluster B diagnosis. All diagnoses in Cluster C were significantly different, with more female than male inmates receiving a diagnosis of Avoidant, Dependent, and Obsessive-Compulsive PD.

As reflected in Table 8.8, there were high rates of co-morbidity between the various PD diagnoses for both the male and female inmates. Only 28.2 percent of the male inmates and 26.2 percent of the female inmates did not meet criteria for at least one PD diagnosis. This reflects a rate that is 10 to 20 times higher than found in the general population for both genders (Torgersen, 2007). Although there were no gender differences in any diagnosis in Cluster A or in Cluster B, significantly more females than males received a Cluster C diagnosis. We found that the Cluster B constellation was overrepresented among both samples with over half of both the male and female inmates meeting diagnostic criteria for at least one of these Cluster B diagnoses. Female inmates also reflected a higher degree of co-morbidity across the various PD diagnoses with the mean number of PD diagnoses being 1.97 compared to 1.55 for the male inmates.

Table 8.9 (males) and Table 8.10 (females) present the correlations of the ten PD diagnoses and continuous scores with the five categories of sex. Among the male inmates, any-sex was associated with a Cluster B diagnosis of Antisocial PD, and among female inmates, with a Cluster B diagnosis of Narcissistic PD.

Predatory sex among the male inmates was associated with a Cluster B diagnosis of Antisocial PD, and among female inmates, with a Cluster B diagnosis of Narcissistic PD.

TABLE 8.8 Frequency Count of all Personality Disorder (PD) Diagnoses among Incarcerated Men (N=288) and Women (N=183)

	Men		Women		Effect Size	
	N	%	N	%	χ^2	Φ
Number of PDs					17.07*	0.19*
0	81	28.2	48	26.2		
1	80	27.9	41	22.4		
2	53	18.5	31	16.9		
3	45	15.7	24	13.1		
4	20	7.0	19	10.4		
5	5	1.7	13	7.1		
6	3	1.0	5	2.7		
7	0	0.0	2	1.1		
Any Cluster A	90	31.4	67	36.6	1.39	0.05
Any Cluster B	181	63.1	100	54.6	3.30	−0.08
Any Cluster C	64	22.3	82	44.8	26.44**	0.24**
Any PD	206	71.8	135	73.8	0.22	0.02
Mean # of PD diagnoses (SD)	1.55	1.40	1.97	1.78	t = −2.70**	

Note. $*p < 0.05$, $**p < 0.01$.

TABLE 8.9 Relationship between Personality Disorders (PD) for Incarcerated Men (N=288) and Type of Sexual Experience in Prison

Personality Disorder	Any-sex		Predatory		Victim		Bartered		Consensual	
	No N=143 (%)	Yes N=145 (%)	No N=253 (%)	Yes N=35 (%)	No N=244 (%)	Yes N=44 (%)	No N=251 (%)	Yes N=37 (%)	No N=160 (%)	Yes N=128 (%)
Diagnosis										
Cluster A										
Paranoid	41 (28.9)	45 (31.0)	74 (29.4)	12 (34.3)	72 (29.6)	14 (31.8)	74 (29.6)	12 (32.4)	47 (29.6)	39 (30.5)
Schizoid	6 (4.2)	4 (2.8)	8 (3.2)	2 (5.7)	8 (3.3)	2 (4.5)	10 (4.0)	0 (0.0)	7 (4.4)	3 (2.3)
Schizotypal	4 (2.8)	6 (4.1)	8 (3.2)	2 (5.7)	6 (2.5)	4 (9.1)★	10 (4.0)	0 (0.0)	5 (3.1)	5 (3.9)
Cluster B										
Antisocial	72 (51.4)	93 (64.6)★	139 (55.8)	26 (74.3)★	142 (59.2)	23 (52.3)	136 (55.1)	29 (78.4)★★	77 (49.0)	88 (69.3)★★
Borderline	20 (14.1)	16 (11.0)	32 (12.7)	4 (11.4)	32 (13.2)	4 (9.1)	30 (12.0)	6 (16.2)	21 (13.5)	15 (11.7)
Histrionic	1 (0.7)	6 (4.1)	6 (2.4)	1 (2.9)	7 (2.9)	0 (0.0)	6 (2.4)	1 (2.7)	1 (0.6)	6 (4.7)★
Narcissistic	23 (16.2)	30 (20.7)	44 (17.5)	9 (25.7)	44 (18.1)	9 (20.5)	44 (17.6)	9 (24.3)	24 (15.1)	29 (22.7)
Cluster C										
Avoidant	13 (9.2)	13 (9.0)	24 (9.5)	2 (5.7)	19 (7.8)	7 (15.9)	26 (10.4)	0 (0.0)★	18 (11.3)	8 (6.2)
Dependent	3 (2.1)	3 (2.1)	5 (2.0)	1 (2.9)	5 (2.1)	1 (2.3)	5 (2.0)	1 (2.7)	4 (2.5)	2 (1.6)
Obsessive-compulsive	23 (16.2)	22 (15.2)	40 (25.9)	5 (14.3)	36 (14.8)	9 (20.5)	42 (16.8)	3 (8.1)	29 (18.2)	16 (12.5)
Continuous Score										
Cluster A										
Paranoid	2.2 (2.1)	2.6 (2.0)	2.3 (2.0)	2.7 (2.0)	2.3 (2.0)	2.7 (2.0)	2.3 (2.1)	2.8 (1.8)	2.3 (2.1)	2.5 (2.0)
Schizoid	0.8 (1.2)	0.9 (1.1)	0.8 (1.1)	1.2 (1.3)★	0.8 (1.2)	1.0 (1.1)	0.9 (1.2)	0.7 (0.9)	0.9 (1.2)	0.9 (1.1)
Schizotypal	1.2 (1.3)	1.4 (1.6)	1.2 (1.4)	1.7 (1.9)	1.2 (1.3)	1.7 (2.0)	1.3 (1.5)	1.3 (1.2)	1.2 (1.4)	1.3 (1.6)

(Continued overleaf)

TABLE 8.9 Continued

Personality Disorder	Any-sex		Predatory		Victim		Bartered		Consensual	
	No N=143 (%)	Yes N=145 (%)	No N=253 (%)	Yes N=35 (%)	No N=244 (%)	Yes N=44 (%)	No N=251 (%)	Yes N=37 (%)	No N=160 (%)	Yes N=128 (%)
Cluster B										
Antisocial	4.0 (2.2)	4.5 (1.9)★	4.1 (2.1)	5.0 (1.8)★	4.3 (2.1)	3.8 (2.0)	4.1 (2.1)	4.8 (2.0)	3.9 (2.2)	4.6 (1.9)★★
Borderline	2.5 (2.0)	2.7 (1.7)	2.5 (1.9)	2.9 (1.4)	2.6 (1.8)	2.5 (1.8)	2.5 (1.8)	2.9 (1.9)	2.4 (1.9)	2.8 (1.6)
Histrionic	1.0 (1.1)	1.4 (1.4)★	1.2 (1.3)	1.3 (1.4)	1.2 (1.3)	1.2 (1.1)	1.2 (1.3)	1.5 (1.4)	1.0 (1.1)	1.5 (1.4)★★
Narcissistic	2.3 (2.2)	2.7 (2.3)	2.4 (2.2)	2.8 (2.5)	2.5 (2.2)	2.5 (2.4)	2.4 (2.2)	2.8 (2.4)	2.2 (2.2)	2.8 (2.3)★
Cluster C										
Avoidant	0.9 (1.5)	1.0 (1.5)	0.9 (1.5)	0.9 (1.4)	0.9 (1.4)	1.4 (1.9)	1.0 (1.6)	0.6 (0.9)	1.0 (1.6)	0.9 (1.4)
Dependent	0.7 (1.1)	0.6 (1.0)	0.6 (1.1)	0.8 (1.2)	0.6 (1.1)	0.8 (1.1)	0.6 (1.1)	0.8 (1.1)	0.7 (1.1)	0.6 (1.0)
Obsessive-compulsive	2.0 (1.7)	1.8 (1.6)	1.9 (1.6)	1.6 (1.6)	1.8 (1.6)	2.1 (1.7)	1.9 (1.6)	1.4 (1.6)	2.0 (1.7)	1.7 (1.5)

Note. ★p < 0.05, ★★p < 0.01.

TABLE 8.10 Relationship between Personality Disorders (PDF) for Incarcerated Women (N=183) and Type of Sexual Experience in Prison

Personality Disorder	Any-sex		Predatory		Victim		Bartered		Consensual	
	No N=77 (%)	Yes N=106 (%)	No N=178 (%)	Yes N=5 (%)	No N=134 (%)	Yes N=49 (%)	No N=165 (%)	Yes N=18 (%)	No N=98 (%)	Yes N=85 (%)
Diagnosis										
Cluster A										
Paranoid	26 (33.8)	40 (37.7)	64 (36.0)	2 (40.0)	43 (32.1)	23 (46.9)	58 (35.2)	8 (44.4)	35 (35.7)	31 (36.5)
Schizoid	3 (3.9)	1 (0.9)	4 (2.2)	0 (0.0)	4 (3.0)	0 (0.0)	4 (2.4)	0 (0.0)	3 (3.1)	1 (1.2)
Schizotypal	4 (5.2)	4 (3.8)	8 (4.5)	0 (0.0)	5 (3.7)	3 (6.1)	8 (4.8)	0 (0.0)	6 (6.1)	2 (2.4)
Cluster B										
Antisocial	24 (31.2)	41 (39.0)	63 (35.6)	2 (40.0)	51 (38.1)	14 (29.2)	60 (36.4)	5 (29.4)	27 (27.6)	38 (45.2)★
Borderline	20 (26.0)	35 (33.0)	53 (29.8)	2 (40.0)	37 (27.6)	18 (36.7)	49 (29.7)	6 (33.3)	30 (30.6)	25 (29.4)
Histrionic	3 (3.9)	9 (8.5)	11 (6.2)	1 (20.0)	9 (6.7)	3 (6.1)	11 (6.7)	1 (5.6)	5 (5.1)	7 (8.2)
Narcissistic	9 (11.7)	29 (27.4)★	35 (18.7)	3 (60.0)★	25 (18.7)	13 (26.5)	31 (18.8)	7 (38.9)★	14 (14.3)	24 (28.2)★
Cluster C										
Avoidant	16 (20.8)	18 (17.0)	32 (18.0)	2 (40.0)	21 (15.7)	13 (26.5)	33 (20.0)	1 (5.6)	23 (23.5)	11 (12.9)
Dependent	3 (3.9)	10 (9.4)	12 (6.7)	1 (20.0)	6 (4.5)	7 (14.3)★	12 (7.3)	1 (5.6)	8 (8.2)	5 (5.9)
Obsessive-compulsive	32 (41.6)	33 (31.1)	64 (36.0)	1 (20.0)	48 (35.8)	17 (34.7)	60 (36.4)	5 (27.8)	41 (41.8)	24 (28.2)
Continuous Score										
Cluster A										
Paranoid	2.6 (2.1)	2.8 (1.9)	2.7 (2.0)	2.8 (1.9)	2.5 (2.0)	3.3 (1.9)★	2.7 (2.0)	3.4 (2.1)	2.8 (2.1)	2.7 (1.9)
Schizoid	1.0 (1.2)	0.7 (1.0)	0.9 (1.1)	0.6 (0.5)	0.9 (1.1)	0.7 (1.0)	0.8 (1.1)	0.9 (0.9)	1.0 (1.2)	0.7 (1.0)
Schizotypal	1.4 (1.4)	1.1 (1.3)	1.3 (1.4)	0.6 (0.5)	1.2 (1.3)	1.4 (1.5)	1.3 (1.4)	1.0 (1.0)	1.5 (1.4)	0.9 (1.2)★★

(Continued overleaf)

TABLE 8.10 Continued

Personality Disorder	Any-sex		Predatory		Victim		Bartered		Consensual	
	No N=77 (%)	Yes N=106 (%)	No N=178 (%)	Yes N=5 (%)	No N=134 (%)	Yes N=49 (%)	No N=165 (%)	Yes N=18 (%)	No N=98 (%)	Yes N=85 (%)
Cluster B										
Antisocial	2.8 (2.0)	3.6 (2.0)*	3.2 (2.0)	4.8 (2.4)	3.2 (2.0)	3.3 (2.1)	3.2 (2.0)	3.7 (2.1)	2.8 (2.0)	3.7 (2.0)**
Borderline	2.8 (2.1)	3.4 (2.4)	3.2 (2.3)	4.2 (2.2)	3.0 (2.2)	3.6 (2.5)	3.2 (2.3)	3.3 (1.9)	3.2 (2.3)	3.2 (2.3)
Histrionic	1.2 (1.4)	2.0 (1.8)**	1.7 (1.7)	2.4 (2.2)	1.5 (1.7)	2.1 (1.7)*	1.6 (1.7)	1.9 (1.6)	1.4 (1.6)	2.0 (1.8)*
Narcissistic	2.2 (2.0)	3.0 (2.4)*	2.6 (2.3)	4.6 (2.1)*	2.5 (2.3)	3.0 (2.2)	2.5 (2.2)	4.0 (2.6)**	2.2 (2.1)	3.1 (2.4)**
Cluster C										
Avoidant	1.6 (2.2)	1.6 (1.9)	1.5 (2.0)	2.4 (2.9)	1.4 (2.0)	2.0 (2.1)	1.6 (2.1)	0.9 (1.3)	1.8 (2.2)	1.3 (1.8)
Dependent	1.1 (1.4)	1.5 (1.8)	1.3 (1.6)	1.8 (2.5)	1.2 (1.5)	1.7 (2.0)	1.3 (1.7)	1.1 (1.5)	1.4 (1.7)	1.3 (1.6)
Obsessive-compulsive	2.7 (1.9)	2.6 (2.0)	2.6 (1.9)	1.8 (1.3)	2.6 (1.9)	2.7 (2.1)	2.6 (2.0)	2.4 (1.7)	2.8 (2.0)	2.4 (1.9)

Note. $*p < 0.05$, $**p < 0.01$.

Sexual victimization among male inmates was associated with a Cluster A diagnosis of Schizotypal, and among female inmates, with a Cluster C diagnosis of Dependent PD.

Bartered sex among male inmates was associated with a Cluster B diagnosis of Antisocial PD and with the absence of a Cluster C diagnosis of Avoidant PD. Among the female inmates, bartered sex was associated only with a Cluster B diagnosis of Narcissistic PD.

Consensual sexual behavior among male inmates was associated with a Cluster B diagnosis of Antisocial and Histrionic PD. Among female inmates, consensual sexual behavior was associated with a Cluster B diagnosis of Antisocial and Narcissistic PD.

Conclusions

Our data confirm the earlier research that underscores the high rates of PDs found among prison inmates. Within our two samples, three quarters of the inmates met diagnostic criteria for at least one of the ten PDs identified in DSM-IV-TR with many of these individuals meeting criteria for two or more Axis II diagnoses. Rates of PDs in the community range from 5 percent to 15 percent across studies (Torgersen, 2007; Grant et al., 2004), further highlighting the significant role that these chronic patterns of maladjustment play in the behavior that leads to incarceration for many of these individuals.

The nature of these PD diagnoses, however, differed across genders with more males meeting diagnostic criteria for Antisocial PD and more females meeting diagnostic criteria for Borderline PD. Rates of Narcissistic PD were found to occur at similar rates across the two genders with about one in five of the inmates meeting criteria for this particular Cluster B diagnosis. More of the female inmates met criteria for the various Cluster C diagnoses including Avoidant, Dependent, and Obsessive-Compulsive PDs. Such high rates of endorsement raise complex questions concerning rehabilitation and the role that these Axis II psychiatric diagnoses can play in mitigating and exacerbating culpability and the assessment of future risk.

Antisocial PD and Narcissistic PD were the two PDs that exerted the greatest effect on the sexual behavior of the male and female inmates. For the male inmates, irritability/aggressiveness and recklessness, two criteria embedded in the diagnosis of Antisocial PD, contributed not only to higher rates of predatory sex but also to involvement in bartered and consensual sexual encounters. For the women, Antisocial PD had an effect on their consensual sexual behavior in prison but not to the extent of a Narcissistic PD. Specifically, female inmates who meet diagnostic criteria for Narcissistic PD, using either diagnostic cut-offs or continuous scores, reported higher rates of any-sex, predatory sex, bartered sex, and consensual sex during their incarceration. These differences across the two genders suggest that the motivations for sexual encounters in prison vary between them, with male sexual activity being associated with chronic patterns of aggressive, reckless, and impulsive behavior, and for women with a grandiose sense of self, fantasies of being special, arrogance and entitlement, and feelings of envy toward others.

The presence of a PD also served as a risk factor for sexual victimization in prison. Males who met diagnostic criteria for Schizotypal PD and females who met diagnostic criteria for Dependent PD were both at higher risk for sexual victimization during incarceration. These findings suggest some degree of gendered difference in perceived vulnerability. Male inmates who were odd and eccentric in their behavior appeared to be at higher risk for sexual victimization. Women who were anxious, unsure, and dependent in their relationships appeared to be at higher risk for sexual victimization. Both diagnoses suggest less autonomy and a more vulnerable personality style, which appears to heighten the risk for being coerced into sexual contact. This finding is in line with previous research that suggests that inmates with a mental illness are at higher risk for all types of victimization during incarceration (Wolff, Blitz, & Shi, 2007).

Psychopathy as measured by the PCL-R2 played a relatively minor role in predicting sexual behavior among the male inmates. It demonstrated no role in elevating the risk for predatory sexual behavior. It did, however, increase the likelihood that the inmates would be involved in bartering sex. In particular, total scores over 25 on the PCL-R2 and elevated scores on Factor 3, *Behavioral*, and Factor 4, *Antisocial*, of the PCL-R2 were associated with more self-reported bartering behavior that involved sex among the male inmates. With the female inmates, PCL-R2 scores were more robust in predicting predatory, bartered, and consensual sex during incarceration. PCL-R2 Total score over 30 was associated with elevated rates of predatory and bartered sex and a score of at least 16 was Associated with consensual sex. These gender differences suggest that psychopathic males are not sexually violent but sexually manipulative in their behavior while incarcerated. In contrast, psychopathic females are more predatory, more manipulative, and more likely to get involved in consensual sexual relationships while living in the confines of a prison environment.

The robust nature of the relationship between PDs and incarceration and between PDs and sex in prison illustrate that the maladaptive patterns of behavior that contribute to the trajectory that leads to imprisonment similarly contribute to the sexual activity that occurs in this environment. These associations are compelling and suggest that sexual violence and victimization is not exclusively situationally determined within this particular type of living situation.

9

STRUCTURED AND ACTUARIAL VIOLENCE RISK INSTRUMENTS AS RISK MARKERS FOR SEXUAL PREDATION AND VICTIMIZATION

The third generation of violence risk research was launched when the MacArthur Violence Risk Assessment Study sought to identify the various problems that had plagued previous efforts to study and predict violent behavior. After a review of the extant literature, they concluded that research needed to identify more powerful predictor variables, to more clearly define relevant criterion variables, to identify and use broader sampling groups, and to synchronize and coordinate research over different research initiatives and studies (Monahan & Steadman, 1994). Monahan and Steadman concluded that this kind of integrated effort could rejuvenate the field of risk assessment and provide clinicians with factors that they could reliably use in their practice, thereby helping to obviate the ethical concerns and social policy quandaries that were being identified based upon the poor accuracy of violence risk assessment in many significant policy domains (Monahan, 1981).

These conclusions gave impetus to the MacArthur Violence Risk Assessment Study (Monahan et al., 2001) and prompted the creation of an assortment of actuarial and semi-structured clinical assessments for violence risk for use with forensic populations, delinquent youth, cohabitating couples, conduct disordered children, and parolees charged with both violent and sexual crimes (Augimeri, Koegl, Webster, & Levene, 2001; Borum, Bartel, & Forth, 2002; Kropp, Hart, Webster, & Eaves, 1995; Quinsey et al., 1998; Webster, Douglas, Eaves, & Hart, 1997). In the current study, we used two of these instruments, the *HCR-20 Assessing Risk for Violence* (Webster et al., 1997), a semi-structured clinical assessment, and the *Violence Risk Assessment Guide* (Quinsey et al., 1998), an actuarial instrument. These instruments were assessed for gender differences and their association with the five categories of sexual behavior experienced by male and female inmates during incarceration.

HCR-20 Assessing Risk for Violence (Version 2)

The HCR-20 is a structured clinical risk assessment protocol that integrates a clinical interview and file review with the coding of 20 risk factors associated with threatened, attempted, or physical harm to another person (Webster, Douglas, Eaves, & Hart, 1997; Douglas, Guy, Reeves, & Weir, 2008). The development of the HCR-20 was based upon a thorough review of the risk factors identified in the empirical literature for violent behavior and was designed to reflect a professional standard of clinical assessment across different clinical and forensic contexts. The instrument was designed to illustrate and encompass a consistent, well-validated set of risk factors, the use of third party verification of the relevant information, and the integration of clinical judgment pertaining to certain exceptional circumstances which are integrated into the assessment process.

Nicholls, Douglas, and Ogloff (1997) utilized a retrospective file review to investigate the predictive validity of the historical and clinical items (HC-15), as well as the screening version of the Psychopathy Checklist (PCL:SV) and the Violence Screening Checklist (VSC; McNiel & Binder, 1994). Results from psychometric reliability investigations conducted by Douglas and Webster (1999) indicated that inmates with scores above the median on the HCR-20 had on average four times the odds of past violence and antisocial behavior. In addition, total scores, clinical scores, and risk scores were found to be predictive of institutional violence by psychopaths in prison (Belfrage, Fransson, & Strand, 2000). Douglas and Webster (1999) found that the AUC ranged from 0.68 (any physical violence) to 0.80 (violent crime), depending on the offense. Later, Douglas, Ogloff, and Hart (2003) obtained AUCs for the HCR-20 total score ranging from moderate to good (0.67, any violence; 0.70, physical violence; 0.67, non-physical violence).

Since its development, research nationally and internationally has demonstrated the instrument's predictive accuracy with different court-involved populations including psychiatric patients (Nicholls, Ogloff, & Douglas, 2004), forensic patients (Strand, Belfrage, Fransson, & Levander, 1999; Urheim, Jakobsen, & Rasmussen, 2003), incarcerated males (Dahle, 2006; de Vogel & de Ruiter, 2005), incarcerated females (Logan & Blackburn, 2009; Warren et al., 2005); juvenile offenders (Lusignan & Marleau, 2007), and offenders with intellectual disabilities (Gray, Fitzgerald, Taylor, MacCulloch, & Snowden, 2007; Morrissey, Mooney, Hougue, Lindsay, & Taylor, 2007). This research has found AUC values ranging from .16 to .39 for violence upon return to the community and from 0.77 to 0.81 for violence perpetrated while hospitalized psychiatrically or forensically. Additional studies have found that the HCR-20 is correlated with minor ($r = 0.32$) and major ($r = 0.11$) institutional misconduct (Kroner & Mills, 2001) and previous violence ($r = 0.50$) (Douglas & Webster, 1999).

Study Analyses

The HCR-20 was used to obtain scores on three domains: the individual's past (historical items), present (clinical items), and future (risk management items) risk for violence, and a total score, a three-point rating scale indicting low, moderate, and high levels of risk. These variables were assessed for gender differences and for their association with five categories of sexual behavior in prison.

The data in Table 9.1 confirm the violence that characterizes the history of both the male and female inmates, although frequently at significantly different rates. Gender differences were observed on six of the ten historical risk factors, two of the five clinical risk factors, and one of the five risk management risk factors. Among the historical risk factors, significantly more males had been

TABLE 9.1 Frequency of HCR-20 Items for Incarcerated Men (N=288) and Women (N=183)

HCR-20 Item	Men		Women		Effect Size	
	N	%	N	%	χ^2	Φ
Historical						
H1. Previous Violence						
None	16	6	47	26		
1–2 moderate	45	16	43	24		
>2 or any severe	222	78	93	51	48.92***	0.32***
H2. Young Age at First Violent Act						
≥40 years	23	8	60	33		
20–39 years	65	23	51	28		
<20 years	196	69	70	39	57.89***	0.35***
H3. Relationship Instability						
Stable/conflict free	52	19	16	9		
Possible/less serious instability	118	42	54	30		
Definite/serious instability	108	39	112	62	23.95***	0.23***
H4. Employment Problems						
None	54	20	32	18		
Possible/less serious	43	16	23	13		
Definite/serious	169	64	124	69	1.65	0.06
H5. Substance Use Problems						
None	52	18	44	24		
Possible/less serious	64	23	24	13		
Definite/serious	166	59	114	63	7.29*	0.13*
H6. Major Mental Illness						
None	247	87	146	80		
Possible/less serious	13	5	13	5		
Definite/serious	23	8	24	13	4.74	0.10
H7. Psychopathy						
PCL-R2 < 20	154	54	126	69		
PCL-R2 2–29	101	35	50	28		
PCL-R2 3–40	30	11	6	3	13.99**	0.17**

(Continued overleaf)

TABLE 9.1 Continued

HCR-20 Item	Men		Women		Effect Size	
	N	%	N	%	χ^2	Φ
H8. Early Maladjustment						
None	78	28	53	29		
Possible/less serious	77	27	37	20		
Definite/serious	128	28	93	51	3.03	0.08
H9. Personality Disorder						
None	81	28	48	26		
Definite/serious	206	72	135	74	0.22	0.02
H10. Supervision Failure						
None	102	36	89	49		
Possible/less serious	27	10	13	7		
Definite/serious	151	54	80	44	7.14★	0.12★
Clinical						
C1. Lack of Insight						
None	101	36	67	37		
Possible/less serious	110	39	80	44		
Definite/serious	72	25	36	20	2.26	0.07
C2. Negative Attitudes						
None	82	29	72	40		
Possible/less serious	109	38	81	45		
Definite/serious	93	33	29	16	16.83★★	0.19★★★
C3. Active Symptoms of Major Mental Illness						
None	267	94	162	89		
Possible/less serious	8	3	10	6		
Definite/serious	9	3	11	6	4.49	0.10
C4. Impulsivity						
None	39	14	38	21		
Possible/less serious	113	40	62	34		
Definite/serious	130	46	83	45	4.37	0.10
C5. Unresponsive to Treatment						
None	134	48	109	60		
Possible/less serious	85	30	56	31		
Definite/serious	63	22	16	9	15.19★★	0.18★★
Risk Management						
R1. Plans Lack Feasibility						
Low probability	98	35	77	42		
Moderate probability	115	41	75	41		
High probability	69	25	31	17	4.51	0.10
R2. Exposure to Destabilizers						
None	94	33	71	39		
Possible/less serious	118	42	73	40		
Definite/serious	71	25	39	21	1.74	0.06

TABLE 9.1 Continued

HCR-20 Item	Men		Women		Effect Size	
	N	%	N	%	χ^2	Φ
R3. Lack of Personal Support						
Low probability	117	41	96	53		
Moderate probability	112	40	58	32		
High probability	54	19	29	16	5.50	0.11
R4. Noncompliance with Remediation						
Low probability	135	48	106	58		
Moderate probability	81	29	56	31		
High probability	66	23	21	12	10.74**	0.15**
R5. Stress						
Low probability	59	21	24	13		
Moderate probability	140	50	103	56		
High probability	83	29	56	31	4.78	0.10
	M	SD	M	SD	T	
Total Historical	12.19	4.02	11.74	4.21	1.15	
Total Clinical	4.30	2.35	3.94	2.34	1.64	
Total Risk Management	4.43	2.67	3.92	2.38	2.18*	
Total HCR-20	20.94	7.63	19.60	7.33	1.89	

Notes. *$p < 0.05$, **$p < 0.01$, ***$p < 0.001$.
Eleven experimental items identified by Douglas were included in the data analyses but not summarized above. These included previous non-violent criminal conduct, previous violent criminality, substance abuse associated with criminality, early maladjustment: victim of child abuse, early maladjustment: conduct problems, relationship problems in adolescence, educational problems in adolescence, homicidal ideation, suicidal ideation, major non-psychotic mental illness, and non-psychotic symptoms of major mental illness.

violent previously, were under the age of 20 years at the time of their first violent act, met criteria for a coding of psychopathy, and had experienced some type of supervision failure in the past. The female inmates were more likely to have experienced significant relationship instability and to have a substance abuse problem. No gender differences were observed for employment problems, major mental illness, early maladjustment, and the presence of a personality disorder.

Among the clinical risk factors, significantly more male inmates had negative attitudes and were unresponsive to treatment. No gender differences were observed for lack of insight, active symptoms of major mental illness, and impulsivity.

Among the risk management risk factors, only one gender difference was identified, with the male inmates reporting more prior noncompliance with remediation. Variables that were not significantly different across gender included future plans lacking feasibility, exposure to destabilizers, lack of personal support, and stress.

Table 9.2 (males) illustrates that any-sex among male inmates was associated only with a lower Total Risk management score. Table 9.3 (females) illustrates that

TABLE 9.2 Relationship between HCR-20 Items for Incarcerated Men (N=288) and Type of Sexual Experience in Prison

HCR-20 Item	Any-sex		Predation		Victim		Bartered		Consensual	
	No N=143 (%)	Yes N=145 (%)	No N=253 (%)	Yes N=35 (%)	No N=244 (%)	Yes N=44 (%)	No N=251 (%)	Yes N=37 (%)	No N=160 (%)	Yes N=128 (%)
Historical										
H1. Previous Violence										
None	9 (6.5)	7 (4.5)	15 (6.0)	1 (2.9)	12 (5.0)	4 (9.1)	16 (16.5)	0 (0.0)	11 (7.1)	5 (3.9)
1–2 moderate	24 (17.3)	21 (14.6)	39 (15.7)	6 (17.1)	36 (15.2)	9 (20.5)	39 (15.9)	6 (16.2)	29 (17.9)	17 (13.4)
>2 or any severe	106 (76.3)	116 (80.6)	194 (78.2)	28 (80.0)	191 (79.9)	31 (70.5)	191 (77.6)	31 (83.8)	117 (75.0)	105 (82.7)
H2. Young Age at First Violent Act										
≥ 40 years	11 (7.9)	12 (8.3)	21 (8.4)	2 (5.7)	14 (5.8)	9 (20.5)	22 (8.9)	1 (2.7)	16 (10.2)	7 (5.5)
20–39 years	39 (27.9)	26 (18.1)	62 (24.9)	3 (8.6)	58 (24.2)	7 (15.9)	60 (24.3)	5 (13.5)	44 (28.0)	21 (16.5)
< 20 years	90 (64.3)	106 (73.6)	166 (66.7)	30 (85.7)★	168 (70.0)	28 (63.6)★★	165 (66.8)	31 (82.8)	97 (61.8)	99 (78.0)★
H3. Relationship Instability										
Stable/conflict free	24 (17.6)	28 (19.7)	50 (20.5)	2 (5.9)	46 (19.6)	6 (14.0)	48 (19.6)	4 (11.1)	26 (17.0)	26 (20.8)
Possible/less serious instability	59 (43.4)	59 (41.5)	100 (41.0)	18 (52.9)	99 (42.1)	19 (44.2)	104 (43.0)	14 (38.9)	70 (45.8)	48 (38.4)
Definite/serious instability	53 (39.0)	55 (38.7)	94 (38.5)	14 (41.2)	90 (38.3)	18 (41.9)	90 (37.2)	18 (50.0)	57 (37.3)	51 (40.8)
H4. Employment Problems										
None	29 (21.6)	25 (18.9)	49 (21.0)	5 (15.2)	44 (19.5)	10 (25.0)	50 (21.6)	4 (11.8)	34 (22.7)	20 (17.2)
Possible/less serious	23 (17.2)	20 (15.2)	37 (15.9)	6 (18.2)	34 (15.0)	9 (22.5)	36 (15.5)	7 (20.6)	26 (17.3)	17 (14.7)
Definite/serious	82 (61.2)	87 (65.9)	147 (63.1)	22 (66.7)	148 (65.5)	21 (52.5)	146 (62.9)	23 (67.6)	90 (60.0)	79 (68.1)

H5. Substance Use Problems

None	26 (18.8)	26 (18.1)	49 (19.8)	3 (8.6)	43 (18.1)	9 (20.5)	44 (18.0)	8 (21.6)	30 (19.4)	22 (17.3)
Possible/less serious	27 (19.6)	37 (25.7)	52 (21.1)	12 (34.3)	52 (21.8)	12 (27.3)	52 (21.2)	12 (32.4)	30 (19.4)	34 (26.8)
Definite/serious	85 (61.6)	81 (56.2)	146 (56.1)	20 (57.1)	142 (60.1)	23 (52.3)	149 (60.8)	17 (45.9)	95 (61.3)	71 (55.9)

H6. Major Mental Illness

None	121 (87.1)	126 (87.5)	213 (85.9)	34 (97.1)	208 (87.0)	39 (88.6)	213 (86.6)	34 (91.9)	136 (87.2)	111 (87.4)
Possible/less serious	5 (3.6)	8 (5.6)	13 (5.2)	0 (0.0)	13 (5.6)	0 (0.0)	11 (4.5)	2 (5.4)	5 (3.2)	8 (6.3)
Definite/serious	13 (9.4)	10 (6.9)	22 (8.9)	1 (2.9)	18 (7.5)	5 (11.4)	22 (8.9)	1 (2.7)	15 (9.6)	8 (6.3)

H7. Psychopathy

PCL-R2 < 20	81 (57.9)	73 (50.3)	139 (55.6)	15 (42.9)	127 (52.7)	27 (61.4)	138 (55.6)	16 (43.2)	92 (58.6)	62 (48.4)
PCL-R2 20–29	44 (31.4)	57 (39.3)	87 (34.8)	14 (40.0)	89 (36.4)	12 (27.3)	87 (35.1)	14 (37.8)	50 (31.8)	51 (39.8)
PCL-R2 30–40	15 (10.7)	15 (10.3)	24 (9.6)	6 (17.1)	25 (10.4)	5 (11.4)	23 (9.3)	7 (18.9)	15 (9.6)	15 (11.7)

H8. Early Maladjustment

None	44 (31.7)	34 (23.6)	73 (29.4)	5 (14.3)	7 (29.3)	8 (19.2)	73 (29.7)	5 (13.5)	50 (32.1)	28 (22.0)
Possible/less serious	34 (24.5)	43 (29.9)	66 (26.6)	11 (31.4)	67 (28.0)	10 (22.7)	64 (26.0)	13 (35.1)	40 (25.6)	37 (29.1)
Definite/serious	61 (43.9)	67 (46.5)	109 (44.0)	19 (54.3)	102 (42.7)	26 (59.1)	109 (44.3)	19 (51.4)	66 (42.3)	62 (48.8)

H9. Personality Disorder

None	46 (32.6)	35 (24.1)	74 (29.4)	7 (20.0)	70 (28.8)	11 (25.0)	74 (29.6)	7 (18.9)	50 (31.4)	31 (24.2)
Definite/serious	96 (67.6)	110 (75.9)	178 (70.6)	28 (80.0)	173 (71.2)	33 (75.0)	176 (70.4)	30 (81.1)	109 (68.6)	97 (75.8)

H10. Supervision Failure

None	52 (37.1)	50 (35.7)	92 (37.4)	10 (29.4)	89 (37.6)	13 (30.2)	89 (39.3)	13 (37.1)	61 (38.9)	41 (33.3)
Possible/less serious	12 (8.6)	15 (10.7)	21 (8.5)	6 (17.6)	22 (9.3)	5 (11.6)	23 (9.4)	4 (11.4)	13 (8.3)	14 (11.4)
Definite/serious	76 (54.6)	75 (53.6)	133 (54.1)	18 (52.9)	126 (53.2)	25 (58.1)	133 (54.3)	18 (51.4)	83 (52.9)	68 (55.3)

Clinical

C1. Lack of Insight

None	57 (41.0)	44 (30.6)	91 (36.7)	10 (28.6)	89 (37.2)	12 (27.3)	91 (37.0)	10 (27.0)	60 (38.5)	41 (32.3)
Possible/less serious	51 (36.7)	59 (41.0)	93 (37.5)	17 (48.6)	90 (37.7)	20 (45.5)	92 (37.4)	18 (48.6)	60 (38.5)	50 (39.4)
Definite/serious	31 (22.3)	41 (28.5)	64 (25.8)	8 (22.9)	60 (25.1)	12 (27.3)	63 (25.6)	9 (24.3)	36 (23.1)	36 (28.3)

(Continued overleaf)

TABLE 9.2 Continued

HCR-20 Item	Any-sex		Predation		Victim		Bartered		Consensual	
	No N=143 (%)	Yes N=145 (%)	No N=253 (%)	Yes N=35 (%)	No N=244 (%)	Yes N=44 (%)	No N=251 (%)	Yes N=37 (%)	No N=160 (%)	Yes N=128 (%)
C2. Negative Attitudes										
None	47 (33.6)	35 (24.3)	71 (28.5)	11 (31.4)	67 (27.9)	15 (34.1)	73 (29.6)	9 (24.3)	51 (32.5)	31 (24.4)
Possible/less serious	48 (34.3)	61 (42.4)	95 (38.2)	14 (40.0)	92 (38.3)	17 (38.6)	96 (38.9)	13 (35.1)	53 (33.8)	56 (44.1)
Definite/serious	45 (32.1)	48 (33.3)	83 (33.3)	10 (28.6)	81 (33.6)	12 (27.3)	78 (31.6)	15 (40.5)	53 (33.8)	40 (31.5)
C3. Active Symptoms of Major Mental Illness										
None	130 (92.9)	137 (95.1)	233 (93.6)	34 (97.1)	227 (94.6)	40 (90.6)	231 (93.5)	36 (97.3)	146 (93.0)	121 (95.3)
Possible/less serious	5 (3.6)	3 (2.1)	8 (3.2)	0 (0.0)	7 (2.9)	1 (2.3)	7 (2.8)	1 (2.7)	6 (3.8)	2 (1.6)
Definite/serious	5 (3.6)	4 (2.8)	8 (3.2)	1 (2.9)	6 (2.5)	3 (6.8)	9 (3.6)	0 (0.0)	5 (3.2)	4 (3.1)
C4. Impulsivity										
None	26 (18.8)	13 (9.0)	37 (15.0)	2 (5.7)	33 (13.9)	6 (13.6)	38 (15.5)	1 (2.7)	29 (18.7)	10 (7.9)
Possible/less serious	53 (38.4)	60 (41.7)	99 (40.1)	14 (40.0)	92 (38.7)	21 (47.7)	101 (41.2)	12 (32.4)	61 (39.4)	52 (40.9)
Definite/serious	59 (42.8)	71 (49.3)	111 (44.9)	19 (54.3)	113 (47.5)	17 (38.6)	106 (43.3)	24 (64.9)★	65 (41.9)	65 (51.2)★
C5. Unresponsive to Treatment										
None	75 (54.0)	59 (41.3)	120 (48.4)	14 (41.2)	116 (48.7)	18 (40.9)	120 (48.8)	14 (38.9)	81 (51.9)	53 (42.1)
Possible/less serious	36 (25.9)	49 (34.3)	72 (29.0)	13 (38.2)	72 (30.3)	13 (29.5)	76 (30.9)	9 (25.0)	42 (26.9)	43 (34.1)
Definite/serious	28 (20.1)	35 (24.5)	56 (22.6)	7 (20.6)	50 (21.0)	13 (29.5)	50 (20.3)	13 (36.1)	33 (21.2)	30 (23.8)

Risk Management

R1. Plans Lack Feasibility

	M(SD)	M(SD)	M(SD)	M(SD)	M(SD)	M(SD)	M(SD)	M(SD)	M(SD)	M(SD)
Low probability	56 (40.3)	42 (29.4)	88 (35.6)	10 (28.6)	84 (35.3)	14 (31.8)	93 (38.0)	5 (13.5)	64 (41.0)	34 (27.0)
Moderate probability	51 (36.7)	64 (44.8)	97 (39.3)	18 (51.4)	96 (40.3)	19 (43.2)	97 (39.6)	18 (48.6)	57 (36.5)	58 (46.0)
High probability	32 (23.0)	37 (25.9)	62 (25.1)	7 (20.0)	58 (24.2)	11 (25.0)	55 (22.4)	14 (37.8)★	35 (22.5)	34 (27.0)★

R2. Exposure to Destabilizers

	M(SD)	M(SD)	M(SD)	M(SD)	M(SD)	M(SD)	M(SD)	M(SD)	M(SD)	M(SD)
None	54 (38.6)	40 (28.0)	85 (34.3)	9 (25.7)	79 (33.1)	15 (34.1)	86 (35.0)	8 (21.6)	62 (35.9)	32 (25.4)
Possible/less serious	57 (40.1)	61 (42.7)	104 (41.9)	14 (40.0)	103 (43.1)	15 (34.1)	104 (42.3)	14 (37.8)	63 (40.1)	55 (43.7)
Definite/serious	29 (20.7)	42 (29.4)	59 (23.8)	12 (34.3)	57 (23.8)	14 (31.8)	56 (22.8)	15 (40.5)	32 (20.4)	39 (31.0)★

R3. Lack of Personal Support

	M(SD)	M(SD)	M(SD)	M(SD)	M(SD)	M(SD)	M(SD)	M(SD)	M(SD)	M(SD)
Low probability	65 (46.4)	52 (36.4)	102 (41.1)	15 (42.9)	104 (43.5)	13 (29.5)	104 (42.3)	13 (35.1)	72 (45.9)	45 (35.7)
Moderate probability	50 (35.7)	62 (43.4)	99 (39.9)	13 (37.1)	91 (38.0)	21 (47.7)	96 (39.0)	15 (43.2)	54 (34.4)	58 (46.0)
High probability	25 (17.9)	29 (20.3)	47 (19.0)	7 (20.0)	44 (18.4)	10 (22.7)	46 (18.7)	8 (21.6)	31 (19.7)	23 (18.3)

R4. Noncompliance with Remediation

	M(SD)	M(SD)	M(SD)	M(SD)	M(SD)	M(SD)	M(SD)	M(SD)	M(SD)	M(SD)
Low probability	72 (51.8)	63 (44.1)	115 (46.6)	20 (57.1)	110 (46.2)	25 (56.8)	122 (49.8)	13 (35.1)	80 (51.3)	55 (43.7)
Moderate probability	40 (28.8)	41 (28.7)	74 (30.0)	7 (20.0)	73 (30.7)	8 (18.2)	69 (28.2)	12 (32.4)	45 (28.8)	36 (28.6)
High probability	27 (19.4)	39 (27.3)	58 (23.5)	8 (22.9)	55 (23.1)	11 (25.0)	54 (22.0)	12 (32.4)	31 (19.9)	35 (27.8)

R5. Stress

	M(SD)	M(SD)	M(SD)	M(SD)	M(SD)	M(SD)	M(SD)	M(SD)	M(SD)	M(SD)
Low probability	34 (24.5)	25 (17.5)	50 (20.2)	9 (25.7)	53 (22.3)	6 (13.6)	50 (20.4)	9 (24.3)	36 (23.1)	23 (18.3)
Moderate probability	66 (47.5)	74 (51.7)	123 (49.8)	17 (48.6)	121 (50.8)	19 (43.2)	123 (50.2)	17 (45.9)	73 (46.8)	67 (53.2)
High probability	39 (28.1)	44 (30.8)	74 (30.0)	9 (25.7)	64 (29.6)	19 (43.2)	72 (29.4)	11 (29.7)	47 (30.1)	36 (28.6)

	M(SD)	M(SD)	M(SD)	M(SD)	M(SD)	M(SD)	M(SD)	M(SD)	M(SD)	M(SD)
Total Historical	11.9 (4.2)	12.4 (3.8)	12.0 (4.1)	13.4 (3.4)	12.2 (4.0)	12.2 (4.1)	12.1 (4.0)	13.1 (3.8)	11.8 (4.1)	12.7 (3.8)
Total Clinical	4.0 (2.5)	4.6 (2.2)	4.3 (2.4)	4.4 (2.2)	4.3 (2.4)	4.6 (2.3)	4.2 (2.4)	5.0 (2.2)	4.2 (2.5)	4.5 (2.2)
Total Risk Management	4.1 (2.7)	4.8 (2.6)★	4.4 (2.7)	4.4 (2.7)	4.4 (2.7)	4.8 (2.7)	4.3 (2.6)	5.3 (2.8)★	4.1 (2.7)	4.8 (2.6)★
Total HCR-20	20.1 (7.9)	21.8 (7.2)	20.8 (7.7)	22.2 (7.3)	20.8 (7.7)	21.6 (7.5)	20.6 (7.5)	23.4 (7.9)★	20.1 (7.7)	22.0 (7.4)★

Note. ★p < 0.05, ★★p < 0.01.

TABLE 9.3 Relationship between HCR-20 Items for Incarcerated Women (N=183) and Type of Sexual Experience in Prison

HCR-20 Item	Any-sex		Predatory		Victim		Bartered		Consensual	
	No N=77 (%)	Yes N=106 (%)	No N=178 (%)	Yes N=5 (%)	No N=134 (%)	Yes N=49 (%)	No N=165 (%)	Yes N=18 (%)	No N=98 (%)	Yes N=85 (%)
Historical										
H1. Previous Violence										
None	24 (31.2)	23 (21.7)	47 (26.4)	0 (0.0)	36 (26.9)	11 (22.4)	44 (26.7)	3 (16.7)	32 (32.7)	15 (17.6)
1–2 moderate	19 (24.7)	24 (22.6)	41 (23.0)	2 (40.0)	30 (22.4)	13 (26.5)	40 (24.2)	3 (16.7)	23 (23.5)	20 (23.5)
>2 or any severe	34 (44.2)	59 (55.7)	90 (50.6)	3 (60.0)	68 (50.7)	25 (51.0)	81 (49.1)	12 (66.7)	43 (43.9)	50 (58.8)★
H2. Young Age at First Violent Act										
≥ 40 years	35 (45.5)	25 (24.0)	60 (34.1)	0 (0.0)	49 (36.8)	11 (22.9)	57 (35.0)	3 (16.7)	42 (42.9)	18 (21.7)
20–39 years	20 (26.0)	31 (29.8)	48 (27.3)	3 (60.0)	36 (27.1)	15 (31.2)	43 (26.4)	8 (44.4)	23 (23.5)	28 (33.7)
< 20 years	22 (28.6)	48 (46.2)★★	6 (38.6)	2 (40.0)	48 (36.1)	22 (45.8)	63 (38.7)	7 (38.9)	33 (33.7)	37 (44.6)★★
H3. Relationship Instability										
Stable/conflict free	10 (13.0)	6 (5.7)	16 (9.0)	0 (0.0)	13 (9.8)	3 (6.1)	14 (8.5)	2 (11.1)	11 (11.2)	5 (6.0)
Possible/less serious instability	21 (27.3)	33 (31.4)	54 (30.5)	0 (0.0)	39 (29.3)	15 (30.6)	49 (29.3)	6 (33.3)	26 (26.5)	28 (33.3)
Definite/serious instability	46 (59.7)	66 (62.9)	107 (60.5)	5 (100.0)	81 (60.9)	31 (63.3)	102 (62.2)	10 (55.6)	61 (62.2)	51 (60.7)
H4. Employment Problems										
None	14 (18.4)	18 (17.5)	32 (18.4)	0 (0.0)	21 (15.9)	11 (23.4)	26 (16.0)	6 (35.3)	19 (19.6)	13 (15.9)
Possible/less serious	5 (6.6)	18 (17.5)	22 (12.6)	1 (20.0)	14 (10.6)	9 (19.1)	22 (13.6)	1 (5.9)	10 (10.3)	13 (15.9)
Definite/serious	57 (75.0)	67 (65.0)	120 (69.0)	4 (80.0)	97 (73.5)	27 (57.4)	114 (70.4)	10 (58.8)	68 (70.1)	56 (68.3)

H5. Substance Use Problems

None	21 (27.3)	23 (21.9)	44 (24.9)	0 (0.0)	33 (24.6)	11 (22.9)	40 (24.2)	4 (23.5)	26 (26.5)	18 (21.4)
Possible/less serious	9 (11.7)	15 (14.3)	24 (13.6)	0 (0.0)	19 (14.2)	5 (10.4)	23 (13.9)	1 (5.9)	12 (12.2)	12 (14.3)
Definite/serious	47 (61.0)	67 (63.8)	109 (61.6)	5 (100.0)	82 (61.2)	32 (66.7)	102 (61.8)	12 (70.6)	60 (61.2)	54 (64.3)

H6. Major Mental Illness

None	61 (79.2)	85 (80.2)	142 (79.8)	4 (80.0)	110 (82.1)	36 (73.5)	130 (78.8)	16 (88.9)	75 (76.5)	71 (83.5)
Possible/less serious	5 (6.5)	8 (7.5)	12 (6.7)	1 (20.0)	7 (5.2)	6 (12.2)	11 (6.7)	2 (11.1)	7 (7.1)	6 (7.1)
Definite/serious	11 (14.3)	13 (12.3)	24 (13.5)	0 (0.0)	17 (12.7)	7 (14.3)	24 (14.5)	0 (0.0)	16 (16.3)	8 (9.4)

H7. Psychopathy

PCL-R2 < 20	57 (74.0)	69 (65.7)	125 (70.6)	1 (20.0)	94 (70.1)	32 (66.7)	116 (70.3)	10 (58.8)	73 (74.5)	53 (63.1)
PCL-R2 20-29	18 (23.4)	32 (30.5)	47 (26.6)	3 (60.0)	34 (25.4)	15 (33.3)	45 (27.3)	5 (29.4)	23 (23.5)	27 (32.1)
PCL-R2 30-40	2 (2.6)	4 (3.8)	5 (2.8)	1 (20.0)*	6 (4.5)	0 (0.0)	4 (2.4)	2 (11.8)	2 (2.0)	4 (4.8)

H8. Early Maladjustment

None	28 (36.4)	25 (23.6)	53 (29.8)	0 (0.0)	38 (28.4)	15 (30.6)	48 (29.1)	5 (27.8)	35 (35.7)	18 (21.2)
Possible/less serious	13 (16.9)	23 (22.6)	35 (19.7)	2 (40.0)	23 (17.2)	14 (28.6)	32 (19.4)	5 (27.8)	18 (18.4)	19 (22.4)
Definite/serious	36 (46.8)	57 (53.8)	90 (50.6)	3 (60.0)	73 (54.5)	20 (40.8)	85 (51.5)	8 (44.4)	45 (45.9)	48 (56.5)

H9. Personality Disorder

None	21 (27.3)	27 (25.5)	48 (27.0)	0 (0.0)	37 (27.6)	11 (22.4)	44 (26.7)	4 (22.2)	26 (26.5)	22 (25.9)
Definite/serious	56 (72.6)	79 (74.5)	130 (73.0)	5 (100.0)	97 (72.4)	38 (77.6)	121 (73.3)	14 (77.8)	72 (73.5)	63 (74.1)

H10. Supervision Failure

None	41 (53.2)	48 (45.7)	88 (49.7)	1 (20.0)	67 (50.0)	22 (45.8)	80 (48.5)	9 (52.9)	51 (52.0)	38 (45.2)
Possible/less serious	6 (7.8)	7 (6.7)	13 (7.3)	0 (0.0)	10 (7.5)	3 (6.2)	13 (7.9)	0 (0.0)	7 (7.1)	6 (7.1)
Definite/serious	30 (39.0)	50 (47.6)	76 (42.9)	4 (80.0)	57 (42.5)	23 (47.9)	72 (43.6)	8 (47.1)	40 (40.8)	40 (47.6)

(Continued overleaf)

TABLE 9.3 Continued

HCR-20 Item	Any-sex		Predatory		Victim		Bartered		Consensual	
	No N=77 (%)	Yes N=106 (%)	No N=178 (%)	Yes N=5 (%)	No N=134 (%)	Yes N=49 (%)	No N=165 (%)	Yes N=18 (%)	No N=98 (%)	Yes N=85 (%)
Clinical										
C1. Lack of Insight										
None	25 (32.5)	42 (39.6)	66 (37.1)	1 (20.0)	51 (38.1)	16 (32.7)	58 (35.2)	9 (50.0)	32 (32.7)	35 (41.2)
Possible/less serious	35 (45.5)	45 (42.5)	79 (44.4)	1 (20.0)	59 (44.0)	21 (42.9)	74 (44.8)	6 (33.3)	43 (43.9)	37 (43.5)
Definite/serious	17 (22.1)	19 (17.9)	33 (18.5)	3 (60.0)	24 (17.9)	12 (24.5)	33 (20.0)	3 (16.7)	23 (23.5)	13 (15.3)
C2. Negative Attitudes										
None	26 (33.8)	46 (43.8)	70 (39.5)	2 (40.0)	50 (37.3)	22 (45.8)	64 (38.8)	8 (47.1)	38 (38.8)	34 (40.5)
Possible/less serious	40 (51.9)	41 (39.0)	80 (45.2)	1 (20.0)	63 (47.0)	18 (37.5)	77 (46.7)	4 (23.5)	47 (48.0)	34 (40.5)
Definite/serious	11 (14.3)	18 (17.1)	27 (15.3)	2 (40.0)	21 (15.7)	8 (16.7)	24 (14.5)	5 (29.4)	13 (13.3)	16 (19.0)
C3. Active Symptoms of Major Mental Illness										
None	69 (89.6)	93 (87.7)	158 (88.8)	4 (80.0)	120 (89.6)	42 (85.7)	146 (88.5)	16 (88.9)	85 (86.7)	77 (90.6)
Possible/less serious	3 (3.9)	7 (6.6)	9 (5.1)	1 (20.0)	6 (4.5)	4 (8.2)	8 (4.8)	2 (11.1)	5 (5.1)	5 (5.9)
Definite/serious	5 (6.5)	6 (5.7)	11 (6.2)	0 (0.0)	8 (6.0)	3 (6.1)	11 (6.7)	0 (0.0)	8 (8.2)	3 (3.5)
C4. Impulsivity										
None	20 (20.6)	18 (17.0)	38 (21.3)	0 (0.0)	32 (23.9)	6 (12.2)	33 (20.0)	5 (27.8)	20 (20.4)	18 (21.2)
Possible/less serious	28 (36.4)	34 (32.1)	61 (34.3)	1 (20.0)	42 (31.3)	20 (40.8)	61 (37.0)	1 (5.6)	40 (40.8)	22 (25.9)
Definite/serious	29 (37.7)	54 (50.9)	79 (44.4)	4 (80.0)	60 (44.8)	23 (46.9)	71 (43.0)	12 (66.7)*	38 (38.8)	45 (52.9)

C5. Unresponsive to Treatment

None	47 (61.8)	62 (59.0)	108 (61.4)	1 (20.0)	79 (59.4)	30 (62.5)	102(62.2)	7 (41.2)	61 (62.9)	48 (57.1)
Possible/less serious	22 (28.9)	34 (32.4)	55 (31.2)	1 (20.0)	43 (32.3)	13 (27.1)	50 (30.5)	6 (35.3)	29 (29.9)	27 (32.1)
Definite/serious	7 (9.2)	9 (8.6)	13 (7.4)	3 (60.0)★★	11 (8.3)	5 (10.4)	12 (7.3)	4 (23.5)	7 (7.2)	9 (10.7)

Risk Management
R1. Plans Lack Feasibility

Low probability	36 (46.8)	41 (38.7)	76 (42.1)	1 (20.0)	60 (44.8)	17 (34.7)	71 (43.0)	6 (33.3)	46 (46.9)	31 (36.5)
Moderate probability	25 (33.8)	49 (46.2)	74 (41.6)	1 (20.0)	49 (36.6)	26 (53.1)	66 (40.0)	9 (50.0)	36 (36.7)	39 (45.9)
High probability	15 (19.5)	16 (15.1)	28 (15.7)	3 (60.0)★	25 (18.1)	6 (12.2)	28 (17.0)	3 (16.7)	16 (16.3)	15 (17.6)

R2. Exposure to Destabilizers

None	30 (39.0)	41 (38.7)	70 (39.3)	1 (20.0)	53 (39.6)	18 (36.7)	66 (40.0)	5 (27.8)	38 (38.8)	33 (38.8)
Possible/less serious	31 (40.3)	42 (39.6)	72 (40.4)	1 (20.0)	52 (38.8)	21 (42.9)	64 (38.8)	9 (50.0)	40 (40.8)	33 (38.8)
Definite/serious	16 (20.8)	23 (21.7)	36 (20.2)	3 (60.0)	29 (21.6)	10 (20.4)	35 (21.2)	3 (22.2)	20 (20.4)	19 (22.4)

R3. Lack of Personal Support

Low probability	39 (50.6)	57 (53.8)	95 (53.5)	1 (20.0)	70 (52.2)	26 (53.1)	84 (50.9)	12 (66.7)	49 (50.0)	47 (55.3)
Moderate probability	24 (31.2)	34 (32.1)	56 (31.5)	2 (40.0)	42 (31.3)	16 (32.7)	54 (32.7)	4 (22.2)	32 (32.7)	26 (30.6)
High probability	14 (18.2)	15 (14.2)	27 (15.2)	2 (40.0)	22 (16.4)	7 (14.3)	27 (16.4)	2 (11.1)	17 (17.3)	12 (14.1)

R4. Noncompliance with Remediation

Low probability	47 (61.0)	59 (55.7)	105 (59.0)	1 (20.0)	78 (58.2)	28 (57.1)	97 (58.8)	9 (50.0)	60 (61.2)	46 (54.1)
Moderate probability	22 (28.6)	34 (32.1)	55 (30.9)	1 (20.0)	40 (29.9)	16 (32.7)	50 (30.3)	6 (33.3)	30 (30.6)	26 (30.6)
High probability	8 (10.4)	13 (12.3)	18 (10.1)	3 (60.0)★★	16 (11.9)	5 (10.2)	18 (10.9)	3 (16.7)	8 (8.2)	13 (15.3)

(Continued overleaf)

TABLE 9.3 Continued

HCR-20 Item	Any-sex		Predatory		Victim		Bartered		Consensual	
	No N=77 (%)	Yes N=106 (%)	No N=178 (%)	Yes N=5 (%)	No N=134 (%)	Yes N=49 (%)	No N=165 (%)	Yes N=18 (%)	No N=98 (%)	Yes N=85 (%)
R5. Stress										
Low probability	7 (9.1)	17 (16.0)	24 (13.5)	0 (0.0)	16 (11.9)	8 (16.3)	22 (13.3)	2 (11.1)	11 (11.2)	13 (15.3)
Moderate probability	47 (61.0)	56 (52.8)	102 (57.3)	1 (20.0)	77 (57.5)	26 (53.1)	94 (57.0)	9 (54.0)	58 (59.2)	45 (52.9)
High probability	23 (29.9)	33 (31.1)	52 (29.2)	4 (80.0)★	41 (30.6)	15 (30.6)	49 (29.7)	7 (38.9)	29 (29.6)	27 (31.8)
	M(SD)	M(SD)	M(SD)	M(SD)	M(SD)	M(SD)	M(SD)	M(SD)	M(SD)	M(SD)
Total Historical	11.1 (4.3)	12.2 (4.1)	11.6 (4.2)	16.4 (1.8)★	11.6 (4.2)	12.1 (4.3)	11.7 (4.1)	12.1 (5.4)	11.2 (4.3)	4.0 (4.0)
Total Clinical	4.0 (2.3)	3.9 (2.4)	3.9 (2.3)	6.4 (2.4)★	3.9 (2.3)	4.2 (2.4)	3.9 (2.3)	4.1 (2.9)	4.0 (2.2)	3.9 (2.5)
Total Risk Management	3.9 (2.4)	3.9 (2.3)	3.8 (2.3)	7.2 (3.6)★★	3.9 (2.4)	3.9 (2.5)	3.9 (2.3)	4.2 (2.9)	3.8 (2.3)	4.0 (2.4)
Total HCR-20	18.9 (7.6)	20.1 (7.1)	19.3 (7.1)	30.0(7.0)★★	19.4 (7.3)	20.1 (7.4)	19.5 (7.0)	20.3 (10.0)	19.0 (7.2)	20.3 (7.5)

Note. ★ $p < 0.05$, ★★ $p < 0.01$.

among female inmates, any-sex was associated only with being under age 20 years at first violent act.

Predatory sex initiated by male inmates was not associated with any of the HCR-20 items. In contrast, predatory sex committed by female inmates was associated with a psychopathy score over 30, being unresponsive to treatment, having future plans that lack feasibility, noncompliance with remediation, high levels of stress, and higher Total Clinical and Total Risk Management scores, but lower Total Historical and Total HCR-20 scores.

Sexual victimization of male inmates was associated only with lower rates of committing a first violent act before the age of 20 years. There were no significant associations between sexual victimization among the female inmates and any of the HCR-20 items.

Bartered sex engaged in by male inmates was associated with impulsivity, plans that lacked feasibility, and lower Total Risk Management and Total HCR-20 scores. Bartered sex engaged in by the female inmates was associated only with impulsivity.

Consensual sex among male inmates was associated with being under the age of 20 years at first violent act, impulsivity, plans that lack feasibility, exposure to destabilizers, and a lower Total Risk Management and Total HCR-20 score. Consensual sex among female inmates was associated with previous violence and being under the age of 20 years at first violent act.

Violence Risk Appraisal Guide (VRAG)

In 1998, Quinsey, Harris, Rice, and Cormier published two actuarial instruments, one designed to predict violent recidivism of any type (VRAG), including sex crimes, and the other to predict sexual recidivism exclusively (SORAG). We chose to use the VRAG in the current study as it was more encompassing in the factors utilized and because it did not require a phallometric sexual deviance assessment as did the SORAG.

Research using the VRAG demonstrates a strong relationship between VRAG Total score and violent recidivism among males (Quinsey et al., 1998). Using 618 male offenders, Quinsey et al. (1998) found a classification accuracy of 74 percent over a seven-year period. Later inclusion of an additional 150 inmates, including some juveniles and some offenders with developmental delays, did not diminish the predictive power of the assessment instrument. Subsequent studies have yielded AUC estimates of 0.80 in predicting violent recidivism in a forensic sample (Harris, Rice, & Cormier, 2002) and 0.72 in predicting violent recidivism in a non-forensic sample (Harris, Rice, & Camilleri, 2004). The VRAG has also demonstrated reliable prediction of sexual recidivism, although the effect size for the prediction of sexual recidivism was more modest (AUC = 0.60; Rice & Harris, 1997). No research has been conducted using the VRAG with female offenders.

Study Analyses

Twelve items from the VRAG were used to assess risk in the male and female samples of our study. These items were assessed for gender differences and for their association with the five categories of sexual behavior in prison.

As seen in Table 9.4, there were significant gender differences on 7 of the 12 VRAG items (including VRAG Total score). Male inmates were more likely to endorse elementary school maladjustment, criminal history for a non-violent offense, younger age at index offense, having had a female victim, and a score of 25 or higher on the Psychopathy Checklist (PCL-R2). In contrast, female inmates were more likely to have married. No gender differences were observed for having lived with biological parents to age 16 years, having a history of alcohol problems, failure while on conditional release, or having met criteria for a personality disorder or for Schizophrenia. On the VRAG Total score, the male inmates obtained a mean score of 8.70, placing them as a group within the midsection of violence risk category with a cumulative risk of 0.44 over the next seven years and 0.58 over the next 10 years. The female inmates obtained a significantly different mean score of 5.38, placing them as a group in the fifth level with an associated group recidivism rate of 0.35 over the next seven years and 0.48 over the next ten years.

As presented in Table 9.5 (males) and Table 9.6 (females), any-sex for male inmates was associated with elementary school maladjustment, being under age 26 years at time of index offense, being less likely to meet criteria for DSM Schizophrenia, and a lower VRAG Total score. Any-sex among female inmates was associated with being under the age of 26 years at time of index offense and a lower VRAG Total score.

Predatory sex committed by male inmates was associated with being less likely to have had a female victim. No VRAG variables correlated with predatory sex among female inmates. Similarly, no VRAG variables correlated with sexual victimization for either the male or female inmates.

Bartered sex among male inmates was associated with elementary school maladjustment, being under age 26 years at time of index offense, and a lower VRAG Total score. No VRAG variables correlated with bartered sex among the female inmates.

Consensual sex among male inmates was associated with elementary school maladjustment, never being married, a higher criminal history for non-violent offenses, being under age 26 years at time of index offense, and a lower VRAG Total score. Consensual sex among female inmates was associated with being under the age of 26 years at time of index offense and a lower VRAG Total score.

Conclusions

Our data underscore the many risk factors for violence that characterize the prior life experience and current adjustment of the men and women in our sample. Among the male inmates, the majority received a score of 2 on the HCR-20 items of previous violence, young age at first violence, substance abuse problems,

TABLE 9.4 Frequency of VRAG Item Scores for Incarcerated Men (N=288) and Women (N=183)

VRAG Item	Men		Women		Effect Size	
	N	(%)	N	(%)	χ^2	Φ
Lived with a Biological Parent to Age 16 Years (except for death of parent) (−2, +3)	88	31.0	49	26.8	0.95	0.05
Elementary School Maladjustment (−1, +2, +5)					20.68	0.21★★
No problems	111	38.9	110	60.4		
Slight	91	31.9	36	19.8		
Severe	83	29.1	36	19.8		
History of Alcohol Problems (−1, 0, +1, +2)					3.32	0.09
0	67	23.7	44	24.3		
1 or 2	124	43.8	86	47.5		
3	41	14.5	16	8.8		
4 or 5	51	18.0	36	19.3		
Ever Married	219	76.8	157	85.8	5.65	−0.11★
Criminal History Score for Non-violent Offenses (−2, 0, +3)					10.59★★	0.15★★
0	29	10.2	34	18.6		
1 or 2	74	26.1	58	31.7		
>3	180	63.6	91	49.7		
Failure on Conditional Release (0, +3)	165	58.1	91	49.7	3.15	−0.08
Age at Index Offense (−5, −2, −1, 0, +2)					36.48	0.28★★
>39	43	15.1	45	24.6		
34–38	36	12.6	40	21.9		
28–33	40	14.0	43	23.5		
27	13	4.6	2	1.1		
<26	153	53.7	53	29.0		

(*Continued overleaf*)

TABLE 9.4 Continued

VRAG Item	Men		Women		Effect Size	
	N	(%)	N	(%)	χ^2	Φ
Victim Injury (−2, 0, +1, +2)					5.67	0.11
Death	68	24.1	32	17.5		
Hospitalized	38	13.5	19	10.4		
Treated and released	37	13.1	22	12.0		
None or slight	139	49.3	110	60.1		
Any female victims (−1, +1)	108	38.3	53	29.0	4.27	0.10*
Meets DSM for a PD (−2, +3)	8	2.8	7	3.8	0.37	−0.03
Meets DSM Criteria for Schizophrenia (−3, +1)	206	71.8	135	73.8	0.22	0.02
Psychopathy Checklist Score (−5, −3, −1, 0, +4, +12)					22.28	0.22**
< 4	2	0.7	9	4.9		
5–9	36	12.6	34	18.7		
10–14	14	16.5	39	21.4		
15–25	133	46.7	78	42.9		
25–34	61	21.4	22	12.1		
> 35	6	2.1	0	0.0		
	M	SD	M	SD	T	
VRAG Total score	8.70	9.07	5.38	8.23	4.01**	

Note. * $p < 0.05$, ** $p < 0.01$, *** $p < 0.001$.

TABLE 9.5 Relationship between VRAG Item Scores for Incarcerated Men (N=288) and Type of Sexual Experience in Prison

VRAG Item	Any-sex		Predation		Victim		Bartered		Consensual	
	No N=143 (%)	Yes N=145 (%)	No N=253 (%)	Yes N=35 (%)	No N=244 (%)	Yes N=44 (%)	No N=251 (%)	Yes N=37 (%)	No N=160 (%)	Yes N=128 (%)
Lived with a Biological Parent to Age 16 Years (−2, +3)										
	46 (32.9)	42 (29.2)	78 (31.2)	10 (29.4)	77 (32.1)	11 (25.0)	81 (32.7)	9 (19.4)	53 (33.8)	35 (27.6)
Elementary School Maladjustment (−1, +2, +5)										
None	64 (45.4)	47 (32.6)	99 (39.4)	12 (35.3)	90 (37.3)	21 (47.7)	102 (41.0)	9 (25.0)	76 (48.1)	35 (27.6)
Slight	44 (31.2)	47 (32.6)	81 (32.3)	10 (29.4)	83 (34.4)	8 (18.2)	83 (33.3)	8 (22.2)	45 (28.5)	46 (36.2)
Severe	33 (23.4)	50 (34.7)★	71 (28.3)	12 (35.3)	68 (28.2)	15 (34.1)	65 (25.7)	19 (52.8)★★	37 (23.4)	46 (36.2)★★
History of Alcohol Problems (−1, 0, +1, +2)										
0	33 (23.6)	34 (23.8)	60 (24.1)	7 (20.6)	54 (22.6)	13 (29.5)	54 (22.6)	13 (29.5)	55 (22.3)	12 (33.3)
1 or 2	60 (42.9)	64 (44.8)	107 (43.0)	17 (50.0)	103 (43.1)	21 (47.7)	103 (43.1)	21 (47.7)	107 (43.3)	17 (47.2)
3	20 (14.3)	21 (14.7)	37 (14.9)	4 (11.8)	38 (15.9)	3 (6.8)	38 (15.9)	3 (6.8)	38 (15.4)	3 (8.3)
4 or 5	27 (19.3)	24 (16.8)	45 (18.1)	6 (17.6)	44 (18.4)	7 (15.9)	44 (18.4)	7 (15.9)	47 (19.0)	4 (11.1)
Ever Married	115 (81.6)	104 (72.2)	193 (76.9)	26 (76.5)	183 (75.9)	36 (81.8)	193 (77.5)	26 (72.2)	131 (82.9)	88 (69.3)★★
Criminal History Score for Non-Violent Offenses (−2, 0, +3)										
0	16 (11.4)	13 (9.1)	26 (10.4)	3 (8.8)	23 (9.6)	6 (13.6)	24 (9.7)	5 (13.9)	19 (12.1)	10 (7.9)
1 or 2	41 (29.3)	33 (23.1)	66 (26.5)	8 (23.5)	60 (25.1)	14 (31.8)	64 (25.9)	10 (27.8)	49 (31.2)	25 (19.8)
>3	83 (59.3)	97 (67.8)	157 (63.1)	23 (67.6)	156 (65.3)	24 (54.5)	159 (64.4)	21 (58.3)	89 (56.7)	91 (72.2)★
Failure on Conditional Release (0, +3)										
	85 (60.3)	80 (55.9)	144 (57.6)	21 (61.8)	137 (56.8)	28 (65.1)	144 (57.8)	21 (60.0)	92 (58.2)	73 (57.9)
Age at Index Offense (−5, −2, −1, 0, +2)										
>39	27 (19.2)	16 (11.1)	39 (15.5)	3 (11.8)	36 (14.9)	7 (15.9)	42 (16.9)	1 (2.8)	31 (19.6)	12 (9.4)
34–38	23 (16.3)	13 (9.0)	34 (13.5)	2 (5.9)	30 (12.4)	6 (13.6)	34 (13.7)	2 (5.6)	27 (17.1)	9 (7.1)
28–33	25 (17.7)	15 (10.4)	39 (15.5)	1 (2.9)	35 (14.5	5 (11.4)	38 (15.3)	2 (5.6)	26 (15.6)	14 (11.0)

(Continued overleaf)

TABLE 9.5 Continued

VRAG Item	Any-sex		Predation		Victim		Bartered		Consensual	
	No N=143 (%)	Yes N=145 (%)	No N=253 (%)	Yes N=35 (%)	No N=244 (%)	Yes N=44 (%)	No N=251 (%)	Yes N=37 (%)	No N=160 (%)	Yes N=128 (%)
27	6 (4.3)	7 (4.9)	10 (4.0)	3 (8.8)	12 (5.0)	1 (2.3)	12 (4.8)	1 (2.8)	6 (3.8)	7 (5.5)
<26	60 (42.6)	93 (64.6)**	129 (51.4)	24 (70.6)	128 (53.1)	25 (26.8)	123 (49.4)	30 (83.3)**	68 (43.0)	85 (66.9)***
Victim Injury (−2, 0, +1, +2)										
Death	29 (20.7)	39 (27.5)	58 (23.4)	10 (29.4)	58 (24.4)	10 (22.7)	59 (24.0)	9 (25.0)	31 (19.7)	37 (29.6)
Hospitalized	21 (15.0)	17 (12.0)	36 (14.5)	2 (5.9)	34 (14.3)	4 (9.1)	32 (13.0)	6 (16.7)	22 (14.0)	16 (12.8)
Treated and released	17 (12.1)	20 (14.1)	32 (12.9)	5 (14.7)	31 (13.0)	6 (13.6)	32 (13.0)	5 (13.9)	21 (13.4)	16 (12.8)
None or slight	73 (52.1)	66 (46.5)	122 (49.2)	17 (50.0)	115 (48.3)	24 (54.5)	123 (50.0)	16 (44.4)	83 (52.9)	56 (44.8)
Any female victims (−1, +1)	57 (41.0)	51 (35.7)	101 (40.7)	7 (20.6)*	94 (39.5)	14 (31.8)	96 (39.0)	12 (33.3)	64 (41.0)	44 (34.9)
Meets DSM for a PD (−2, +3)	96 (67.6)	110 (75.9)	178 (70.6)	28 (80.0)	173 (71.2)	33 (75.0)	176 (70.4)	30 (81.1)	109 (68.6)	97 (75.8)
Meets DSM Criteria for Schizophrenia (−3, +1)	7 (5.0)	1 (0.7)*	7 (2.8)	1 (2.9)	7 (2.9)	1 (2.3)	8 (3.2)	0 (0.0)	7 (4.4)	1 (0.8)
Psychopathy Checklist Score (−5, −3, −1, 0 +4, +12)										
<4	1 (0.7)	1 (0.7)	2 (0.8)	0 (0.0)	1 (0.4)	1 (2.3)	2 (0.8)	0 (0.0)	2 (1.3)	0 (0.0)
5–9	22 (15.7)	14 (9.7)	32 (12.8)	4 (11.4)	31 (12.9)	5 (11.5)	33 (13.3)	3 (8.1)	25 (15.9)	11 (8.6)
10–14	23 (16.4)	24 (16.6)	40 (16.0)	7 (20.0)	36 (14.9)	11 (25.0)	42 (16.9)	5 (13.5)	26 (16.6)	21 (16.4)
15–25	65 (45.4)	68 (46.9)	119 (47.6)	14 (40.0)	116 (48.1)	17 (38.6)	118 (47.6)	15 (40.5)	72 (45.9)	61 (47.7)
25–34	27 (19.3)	34 (23.4)	53 (21.2)	8 (22.9)	52 (21.6)	9 (20.5)	49 (19.4)	13 (35.1)	30 (19.1)	31 (24.2)
>35	2 (1.4)	4 (2.8)	4 (1.6)	2 (5.7)	5 (2.1)	1 (2.3)	5 (2.0)	1 (2.7)	2 (1.3)	4 (3.1)
	M(SD)	M(SD)	M(SD)	M(SD)	M(SD)	M(SD)	M(SD)	M(SD)	M(SD)	M(SD)
VRAG Total score	7.1 (9.6)	10.2 (8.2)**	8.4 (9.1)	11.0 (8.5)	8.7 (9.1)	8.7 (9.1)	8.2 (9.1)	12.2 (8.3)*	6.8 (9.5)	11.0 (8.0)**

Note: $*p < 0.05$, $**p < 0.01$, $***p < 0.001$.

TABLE 9.6 Relationship between VRAG Item Scores for Incarcerated Women (N=183) and Type of Sexual Experience in Prison

VRAG Item	Any-sex No N=77 (%)	Any-sex Yes N=106 (%)	Predatory No N=178 (%)	Predatory Yes N=5 (%)	Victim No N=134 (%)	Victim Yes N=49 (%)	Bartered No N=165 (%)	Bartered Yes N=18 (%)	Consensual No N=98 (%)	Consensual Yes N=85 (%)
Lived with a Biological Parent to Age 16 years (−2, +3)										
	22 (28.6)	27 (25.5)	48 (27.0)	1 (20.0)	32 (23.9)	17 (34.7)	46 (27.9)	3 (16.7)	31 (31.6)	18 (21.2)
Elementary School Maladjustment (−1, +2, +5)										
None	46 (59.7)	64 (61.0)	107 (60.5)	3 (60.0)	78 (58.6)	32 (65.3)	99 (60.4)	11 (61.1)	62 (63.3)	48 (57.1)
Slight	18 (23.4)	18 (17.1)	35 (19.8)	1 (20.0)	30 (22.6)	6 (12.2)	32 (19.5)	4 (22.2)	19 (19.4)	17 (20.7)
Severe	13 (16.9)	23 (21.9)	35 (19.8)	1 (20.0)	25 (18.8)	11 (22.4)	33 (20.1)	3 (16.7)	17 (17.3)	19 (22.6)
History of Alcohol Problems (−1, 0, +1, +2)										
0	22 (28.6)	22 (21.2)	42 (23.9)	2 (40.0)	32 (23.9)	12 (25.5)	38 (23.2)	6 (35.3)	25 (25.5)	19 (22.9)
1 or 2	32 (41.6)	54 (51.9)	85 (48.3)	1 (20.0)	64 (47.8)	22 (46.8)	78 (47.6)	8 (47.1)	43 (43.9)	43 (51.8)
3	8 (10.4)	8 (7.7)	15 (8.5)	1 (20.0)	12 (9.0)	4 (8.5)	15 (9.1)	1 (5.9)	9 (9.2)	7 (8.4)
4 or 5	15 (19.5)	20 (19.2)	34 (19.3)	1 (20.0)	26 (19.4)	9 (19.1)	33 (20.1)	2 (11.8)	21 (21.4)	14 (16.9)
Ever Married										
	67 (87.0)	90 (84.9)	154 (86.5)	3 (60.0)	115 (85.8)	42 (85.7)	142 (86.1)	15 (83.3)	86 (87.7)	71 (83.5)
Criminal History Score for Non-Violent Offenses (−2, 0, +3)										
0	16 (20.8)	18 (17.0)	33 (18.5)	1 (20.0)	26 (19.4)	8 (16.3)	30 (18.2)	4 (22.2)	19 (19.4)	15 (17.6)
1 or 2	23 (29.9)	35 (33.0)	57 (32.0)	1 (20.0)	38 (28.4)	20 (40.8)	55 (33.3)	3 (16.7)	29 (29.6)	19 (34.1)
3>	38 (49.4)	53 (50.0)	88 (49.4)	3 (60.0)	70 (52.2)	21 (42.9)	80 (48.5)	11 (61.1)	50 (51.0)	41 (48.2)
Failure on Conditional Release (0, +3)										
	35 (45.5)	56 (52.8)	88 (49.4)	3 (60.0)	66 (49.3)	25 (51.0)	83 (50.3)	8 (44.4)	46 (46.9)	45 (52.9)
Age at Index Offense (−5, −2, −1, 0, +2)										
>39	29 (37.7)	16 (15.1)	44 (24.7)	1 (20.0)	37 (27.6)	8 (16.3)	42 (25.5)	3 (16.7)	34 (34.7)	11 (12.9)
34–38	13 (16.9)	27 (25.5)	39 (21.9)	1 (20.0)	25 (18.7)	15 (30.6)	38 (23.0)	2 (11.1)	21 (21.4)	19 (22.4)
28–33	20 (26.0)	23 (21.7)	41 (23.0)	2 (40.0)	34 (25.4)	9 (18.4)	36 (21.8)	7 (38.9)	23 (23.5)	20 (23.5)

(Continued overleaf)

TABLE 9.6 Continued

VRAG Item	Any-sex		Predatory		Victim		Bartered		Consensual	
	No N=77 (%)	Yes N=106 (%)	No N=178 (%)	Yes N=5 (%)	No N=134 (%)	Yes N=49 (%)	No N=165 (%)	Yes N=18 (%)	No N=98 (%)	Yes N=85 (%)
27	1 (1.3)	1 (0.9)	2 (1.1)	0 (0.0)	2 (1.5)	0 (0.0)	2 (1.2)	0 (0.0)	1 (1.0)	1 (1.2)
<26	14 (18.2)	39 (36.8)**	52 (29.2)	1 (20.0)	36 (26.9)	17 (34.7)	47 (28.5)	6 (33.3)	19 (19.4)	34 (40.0)**
Victim Injury (−2, 0, +1, +2)										
Death	13 (16.9)	19 (17.9)	32 (18.0)	0 (0.0)	25 (18.7)	7 (14.3)	30 (18.2)	2 (11.1)	14 (14.3)	18 (21.2)
Hospitalized	5 (6.5)	14 (13.2)	18 (10.1)	1 (20.0)	12 (9.0)	7 (14.3)	15 (9.1)	4 (22.2)	8 (8.2)	11 (12.9)
Treated and released	11 (14.3)	11 (10.4)	22 (12.4)	0 (0.0)	16 (11.9)	6 (12.2)	21 (12.7)	1 (5.6)	15 (15.3)	7 (8.2)
None or slight	48 (62.3)	62 (58.5)	106 (59.6)	4 (80.0)	81 (60.4)	29 (59.2)	99 (60.0)	11 (61.1)	61 (62.2)	49 (57.6)
Any female victims (−1, +1)	24 (31.2)	29 (27.4)	52 (29.2)	1 (20.0)	43 (32.1)	10 (20.4)	47 (28.5)	6 (33.3)	26 (26.5)	27 (31.8)
Meets DSM for a PD (−2, +3)	56 (72.7)	79 (74.5)	130 (73.0)	5 (100.0)	97 (72.4)	38 (77.6)	121 (73.3)	14 (77.8)	72 (73.5)	63 (74.1)
Meets DSM Criteria for Schizophrenia (−3, +1)	4 (5.2)	3 (2.8)	6 (3.4)	1 (20.0)	6 (4.5)	1 (2.0)	5 (3.0)	2 (11.1)	4 (4.1)	3 (3.5)
Psychopathy Checklist Score (−5, −3, −1, 0, +4, +12)										
< 4	5 (6.5)	4 (3.8)	9 (4.1)	0 (0.0)	6 (4.5)	3 (6.2)	8 (4.8)	1 (5.9)	6 (6.1)	3 (3.6)
5–9	20 (26.0)	14 (13.3)	33 (18.6)	1 (20.0)	28 (20.9)	6 (12.5)	31 (18.8)	3 (17.6)	23 (23.5)	11 (13.1)
10–14	12 (15.6)	27 (25.7)	39 (22.0)	0 (0.0)	29 (21.6)	10 (20.8)	36 (21.8)	3 (17.6)	20 (20.4)	19 (22.6)
15–25	31 (40.3)	47 (44.8)	76 (42.9)	2 (40.0)	55 (41.0)	23 (47.9)	70 (42.4)	8 (47.1)	39 (39.8)	39 (46.4)
25–34	9 (11.7)	13 (12.4)	20 (11.3)	2 (40.0)	16 (11.9)	6 (12.5)	20 (21.1)	2 (11.8)	10 (10.2)	12 (14.3)
> 35	0 (0.0)	0 (0.0)	0 (0.0)	0 (0.0)	0 (0.0)	0 (0.0)	0 (0.0)	0 (0.0)	0 (0.0)	0 (0.0)
	M(SD)	M(SD)	M(SD)	M(SD)	M(SD)	M(SD)	M(SD)	M(SD)	M(SD)	M(SD)
VRAG Total score	3.9 (8.6)	6.4 (7.8)*	5.3 (8.2)	10.0 (10.1)	5.2 (8.5)	5.8 (7.6)	5.3 (8.2)	6.2 (8.5)	4.2 (8.4)	6.8 (7.9)*

Note. $*p < 0.05$, $**p < 0.01$.

early maladjustment, the presence of a personality disorder, prior supervision failures, and impulsivity. A majority of the female inmates were scored at the highest 2 level on previous violence, young age at first violence, relationship instability, employment problems, substance abuse problems, presence of a personality disorder, and impulsivity. Embedded in these clusters were gender differences with the male inmates having experienced more prior violence and behavior associated with psychopathy, and the women more relationship instability and higher rates of substance abuse.

On the HCR-20, the Total scores for both genders tended to cluster around 20 to 22, suggesting that as a group the inmates were at moderate levels of risk for future violent behavior. The one exception was the predatory females who obtained an average score of 30 out of 40 on the HCR-20, placing them at significant risk for future violent behavior. On the VRAG Total score, the male inmates obtained a mean score of 8.70, placing them as a group within the sixth of nine risk categories with a cumulative risk of violent recidivism of 0.44 over the next seven years and 0.58 over the next ten years. The female inmates obtained a mean score of 5.38, placing them as a group in the fifth level with an associated violent recidivism rate of 0.35 over the next seven years and 0.48 over the next ten years.

For both the male and female inmates, the association between the two risk instruments and sexual behavior in prison varied by the type of sexual behavior being studied. For the male inmates, any-sex was associated with a lower Total Risk Management score on the HCR-20; although on the VRAG, any-sex was associated with elementary school maladjustment, being under age 26 years at time of index offense, being less likely to meet diagnostic criteria for DSM Schizophrenia, and a lower VRAG Total score. Any-sex among female inmates was associated with being under age 20 years at first violent act on the HCR-20 combined with being under the age of 26 years at time of index offense and a lower VRAG Total score. Together these patterns suggest that sexual behavior in prison for both men and women tends to be associated with early and chronic forms of maladjustment and involvement in violent and criminal behavior from a relatively early age.

Predatory sex initiated by male inmates was not associated with any of the HCR-20 items. On the VRAG, however, it was associated with only a single risk variable, being less likely to have had a female victim. In contrast, predatory sex by female inmates was associated with multiple risk factors on the HCR-20, including a psychopathy score over 30, being unresponsive to treatment, having future plans that lack feasibility, noncompliance with remediation, high levels of stress, and higher mean Total Clinical and Total Risk Management scores but lower Total Historical and HCR-20 Total scores. Predatory sex by women was unrelated to any of the risk factors on the VRAG. These gender differences were substantial and suggest that the patterns of sexual predation for men and women differ widely and poorly predicted male inmates using either the HCR-20 or the VRAG.

Being sexually victimized was an experience that lay outside the cluster of other types of sexual behavior in prison. Among the male inmates, sexual victimization was associated only with lower rates of committing a first violent act before the age of 20 years and none of the risk factors identified on the VRAG. There were no significant associations between sexual victimization among the female inmates and any of the HCR-20 or VRAG risk variables. This absence of significant associations for both the male and female inmates suggests that the victims of sexual aggression in prison are in general less violent and have experienced histories that are less plagued with instability, maladjustment, and the perpetration of violent and criminal crime.

Bartered sex among male inmates was associated with multiple HCR-20 risk factors including impulsivity, plans that lack feasibility, and a lower Total Risk Management and Total HCR-20 scores. On the VRAG bartered sex was associated with elementary school maladjustment, being under age 26 years at the time of index offense, and a lower VRAG Total score. Bartered sex among the female inmates was associated with impulsivity on the HCR-20, although none of the risk items on the VRAG. As with earlier analyses, these findings suggest that bartered sex derives as much from impulsivity and instability as it does from an exaggerated state of need among those who chose to participate.

Consensual sex among male inmates was associated with being under the age of 20 years at first violent act, impulsivity, plans that lack feasibility, exposure to destabilizers, and a lower Total Risk Management and Total HCR-20 scores. On the VRAG, consensual sex was associated with elementary school maladjustment, never having been married, higher rates of a criminal history for non-violent offenses, being under the age of 26 at the time of the index offense, and a lower VRAG Total score. Consensual sex among female inmates was associated with previous violence and being under the age of 20 years at first violent act. On the VRAG, it was associated with being under the age of 26 years at the time of the index offense and a lower VRAG Total score. The extent of these associations across two risk instruments suggest that consensual sex in prison for both genders is associated with chronically maladjusted and violent behavior.

The clustering of the various types of sexual behavior in prison, excluding sexual victimization, again points toward the association of the different types of sexual behavior in prison and the relationship of these behaviors with criminal and violent behavior in general. It further suggests that there is a sub-group in prison that is most likely to be sexually active and to be involved in other violent behavior, both during incarceration and following release from prison.

10

CHAID CLASSIFICATION FOR SEXUAL BEHAVIOR IN PRISON

To create ten risk models (five types of sex derived from the Sexual Aggression in Prison (SAP), separately for male and female inmates), we used exploratory exhaustive Chi-Square Automated Interaction Detector (CHAID). Due to our relatively small sample size, analyses were considered exploratory. We therefore used a cross-validation method which divides the sample into ten folds and verifies the original risk model. This method produces a risk estimate as well as a cross-validated risk estimate that represents the average of all risk estimates across the ten sub-samples. We allowed as few as five cases per cell.

The method of selecting which variables to include in each CHAID model was to use the bivariate variables that correlated significantly with a type of sex. For example, if child maltreatment only correlated with consensual sex for the female inmates, then child maltreatment was included as a predictor variable in the consensual sex CHAID model for the female inmates only, but not the other CHAID models. The Self-Report Criminal History Questionnaire and the Conflict Tactics Scale were not included in the analyses because of missing data limitations. The psychometrics for each CHAID model is presented in Table 10.1.

Model Predicting Any-sex in Prison for Male Inmates

The model correctly classified roughly 71 percent of all cases and had a sensitivity of 83 percent and a specificity of 58 percent. As observed in Figure 10.1, of the overall sample, 145 men (50.4%) reported having any-sex in prison. Perpetration of threatened physical violence in prison was the best predictor of any-sex in prison ($\chi^2 = 24.95$, df $= 1$, $p < 0.0001$). Of those who self-reported perpetrating threatened physical violence, 62.9 percent reported any-sex in prison as compared

TABLE 10.1 Psychometrics for Each CHAID Model

Psychometric	Any-Sex– Male	Any-Sex– Female	Predatory – Male	Predatory – Female	Victim – Male	Victim – Female	Bartered – Male	Bartered – Female	Consensual – Male	Consensual – Female
N	288	183	288	183	288	183	288	183	288	183
Risk estimate for model (% of misclassified cases)	0.295 (SE=0.027)	0.224 (SE=0.031)	0.108 (SE=0.018)	0.011 (SE=0.001)	0.111 (SE=0.019)	0.175 (SE=0.028)	0.090 (SE=0.017)	0.093 (SE=0.021)	0.285 (SE=0.027)	0.163 (SE=0.027)
Cross validation risk estimated	0.392 (SE=0.029)	0.371 (SE=0.036)	0.132 (SE=0.020)	0.038 (SE=0.015)	0.160 (SE=0.022)	0.235 (SE=0.031)	0.118 (SE=0.019)	0.120 (SE=0.024)	0.378 (SE=0.029)	0.345 (SE=0.035)
False Positives	61	61	26	1	28	22	0	15	45	11
False Negatives	24	24	5	1	4	10	26	2	37	19
True Positives	121	121	248	177	240	39	11	163	91	66
True Negatives	82	82	9	4	16	112	251	3	115	87
Sensitivity	0.834	0.783	0.980	0.994	0.984	0.800	0.300	0.988	0.711	0.776
Specificity	0.573	0.767	0.257	0.800	0.363	0.836	1.00	0.167	0.719	0.888
PPV	0.665	0.822	0.905	0.994	0.900	0.640	1.00	0.916	0.670	0.857
NPV	0.774	0.720	0.642	0.800	0.800	0.918	0.906	0.600	0.757	0.820
False + rate	0.427	0.234	0.743	0.200	0.636	0.164	<0.01	0.833	0.281	0.112
False – rate	0.166	0.217	0.020	0.006	0.016	0.204	0.703	0.012	0.289	0.224
Accuracy	0.705	0.776	0.892	0.990	0.889	0.825	0.910	0.907	0.715	0.836

Note. PPV = Positive predictive value; NPV = negative predictive value; Accuracy = correctly classified.

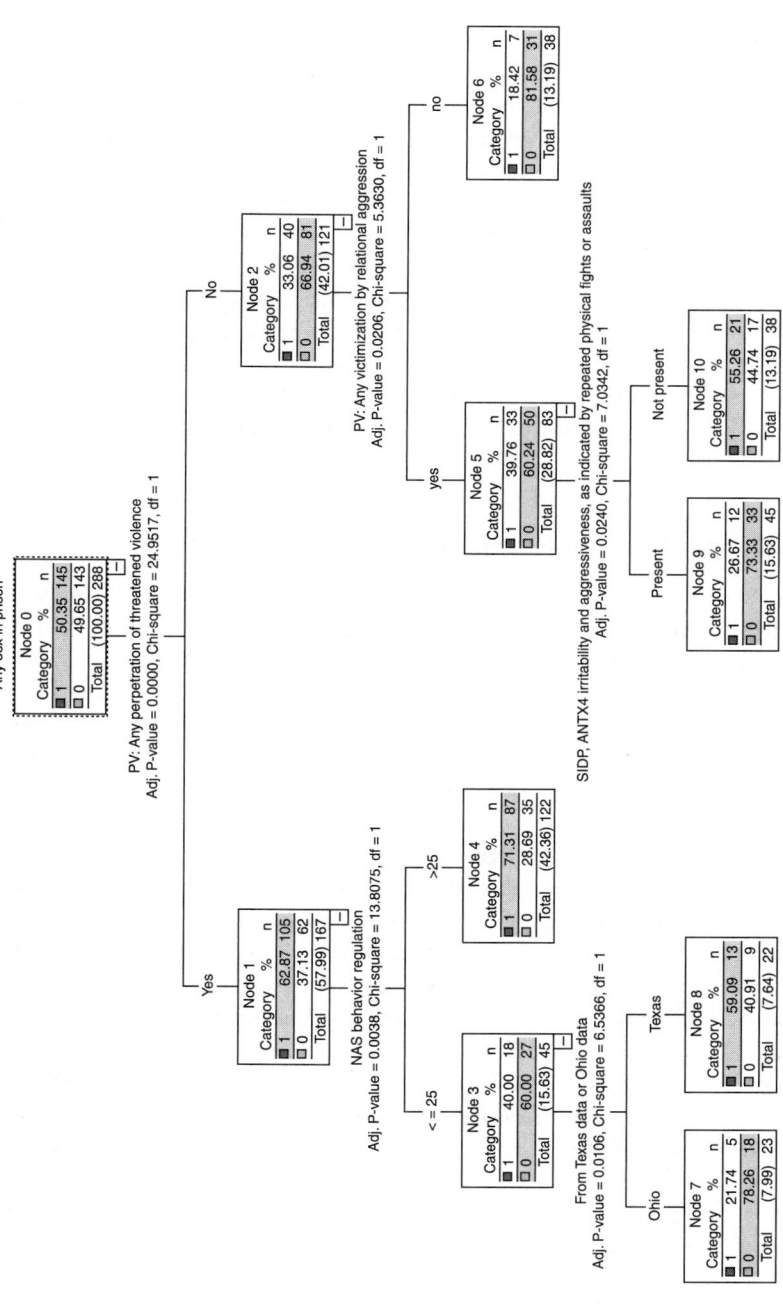

FIGURE 10.1 CHAID analyses for any-sex behavior for male inmates

to 33.1 percent of those who self-reported not perpetrating threatening physical violence.

Among those reporting the perpetration of threatened physical violence, NAS behavior regulation scores were the next best predictor of any-sex in prison ($\chi^2 = 13.81$, df = 1, $p < 0.001$), with those having scores under 25 more likely to report any-sex in prison (71.3%) than those having scores equal to or more than 25 (40.0%). Among those with scores above 25, inmates from Texas were more likely to self-report any-sex than inmates from Ohio (59.1% vs 21.7%, respectively; $\chi^2 = 6.54$, df = 1, $p < 0.01$).

Among those who did not perpetrate threatened physical violence, those who were a victim of relational violence were more likely to report any-sex (39.8%) than those who had not been a victim of relational violence (18.4%) ($\chi^2 = 5.36$, df = 1, $p < 0.05$). Finally, among those reporting victimization by relational violence, those endorsing the Antisocial PD symptom of irritability/aggressiveness were less likely to report any-sex than those without this symptom (26.7% vs 55.3%; $\chi^2 = 7.03$, df = 1, $p < 0.05$).

Model Predicting Any-sex in Prison for Female Inmates

The model correctly classified roughly 77 percent of all cases and had a sensitivity of 78 percent and a specificity of 77 percent. As observed in Figure 10.2, of the overall sample, 106 women (57.9%) reported to having any-sex in prison. Being the victim of threats of physical violence was the best predictor of any-sex in prison ($\chi^2 = 23.41$, df = 1, $p < 0.0001$). Of those who reported being threatened with physical violence, 80.9 percent admitted to any-sex in prison as compared to 44.4 percent of those who reported not being threatened with physical violence.

Among those reporting victimization by threats of physical violence, those who endorsed the Borderline PD symptom of impulsivity were more likely to report any-sex in prison than women who did not endorse this symptom (89.1% vs 46.2%) ($\chi^2 = 12.54$, df = 1, $p < 0.05$). Among those without this symptom, those who were younger than 39 years at the time of their current offense were more likely to report any-sex in prison than those who were 39 years and older (75% vs 0%) ($\chi^2 = 6.96$, df = 1, $p < 0.05$).

Among those who did not experience victimization by threats of physical violence, women who self-identified as homosexual or bisexual were more likely to report any-sex in prison than women who self-identified as heterosexual (80% vs 36.8%) ($\chi^2 = 12.47$, df = 1, $p < 0.01$). Among heterosexual women, those who met criteria for Narcissistic PD were more likely to report any-sex in prison than women not meeting diagnostic criteria for the disorder (66.7% vs 29.9%) ($\chi^2 = 8.49$, df = 1, $p < 0.05$).

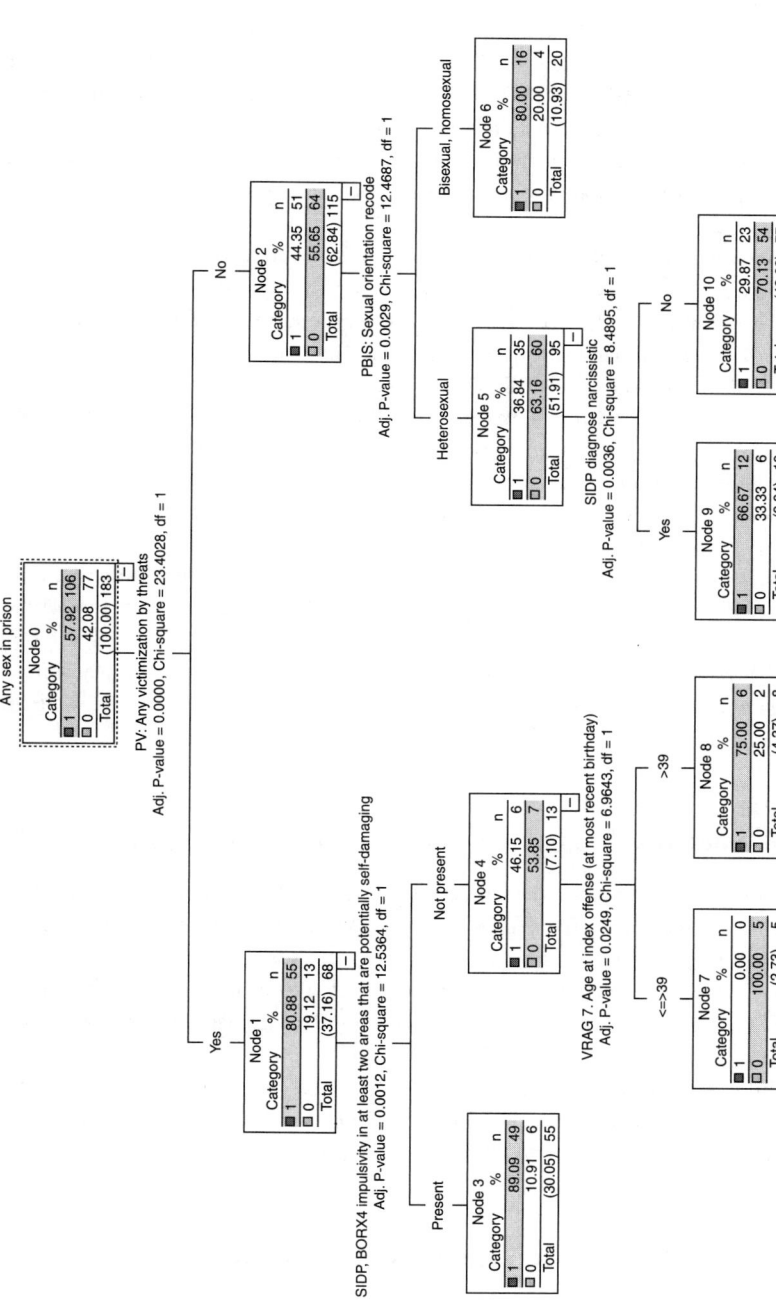

FIGURE 10.2 CHAID analyses for any-sex behavior for female inmates

Model Predicting Sexual Predation for Male Inmates

The model correctly classified roughly 89 percent of all cases and had a sensitivity of 98 percent and a specificity of 26 percent. As observed in Figure 10.3, of the overall sample, 35 men (12.2%) reported sexual predation in prison. Sexual victimization was the best predictor of sexual perpetration ($\chi^2 = 23.42$, df = 1, $p < 0.0001$). Men who reported sexual victimization were far more likely to be sexually predatory than those who did not experience sexual victimization (34.1% vs 8.2%).

Among those who did not self-report sexual victimization, perpetration of threatened physical violence was the next best predictor of sexual predation ($\chi^2 = 14.14$, df = 1, $p < 0.001$), with those reporting the perpetration of threatened physical violence being more likely to report sexual predation (14% vs 1%). Among those reporting the perpetration of threatened physical violence, inmates from Texas (24.0%) were more likely than inmates from Ohio (8.3%) to report sexual predation ($\chi^2 = 6.32$, df = 1, $p < 0.05$). Among those who did not perpetrate threatened physical violence, those with continuous scores on the SIDP-IV Antisocial scale less than or equal to 6 (0%) were less likely than those with higher scores (14.3%) to be sexually predatory ($\chi^2 = 14.85$, df = 1, $p < 0.01$).

Among those reporting sexual victimization, those who were diagnosed with an Antisocial PD were more likely to report sexual predation (47.8%) than those who were not diagnosed with an Antisocial PD (19.1%) ($\chi^2 = 4.04$, df = 1, $p < 0.05$). Among those with an Antisocial PD diagnosis, those with a history of head injury with loss of consciousness were more likely to report sexual predation (64.3%) than those without such an injury (22.2%) ($\chi^2 = 3.89$, df = 1, $p < 0.05$).

Model Predicting Sexual Predation for Female Inmates

The model correctly classified roughly 99 percent of all cases and had a sensitivity of 99 percent and a specificity of 80 percent. As observed in Figure 10.4, of the overall sample, five women (2.7%) admitted to sexual predation in prison. HCR-20 Total score was the best predictor of sexual predation among the female inmates. Higher scores tended to be associated with increased reporting of sexual predation (94.4% vs 5.6 %) ($\chi^2 = 30.4$, df =3, $p < 0.001$).

Among women with HCR-20 Total scores higher than 29, women who reported having had an orgasm with a partner in prison were more likely to report sexual predation (80% vs 0%) ($\chi^2 = 13.37$, df = 1, $p < 0.05$).

Model Predicting Sexual Victimization for Male Inmates

The model correctly classified roughly 89 percent of all cases and had a sensitivity of 98 percent and a specificity of 36 percent. As observed in Figure 10.5, of the

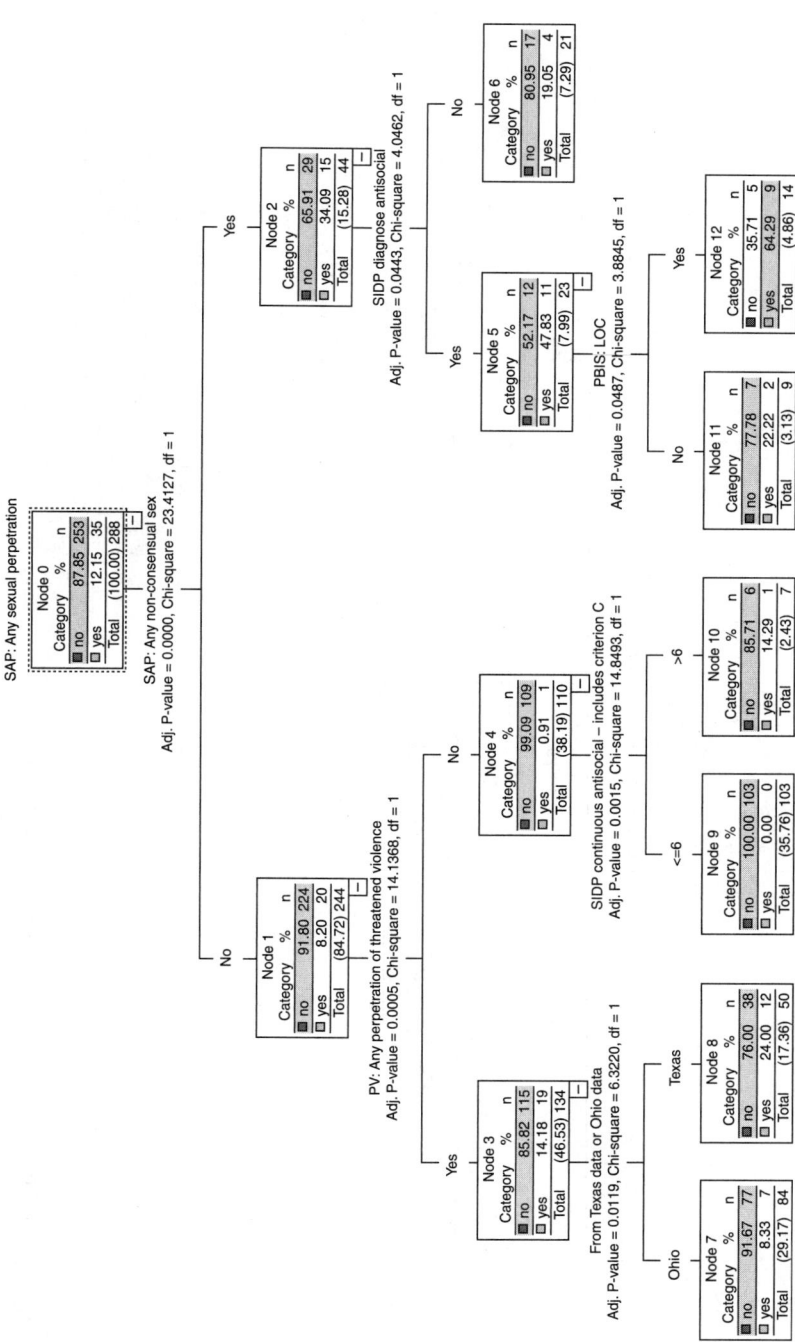

FIGURE 10.3 CHAID analyses for sexual predation for male inmates

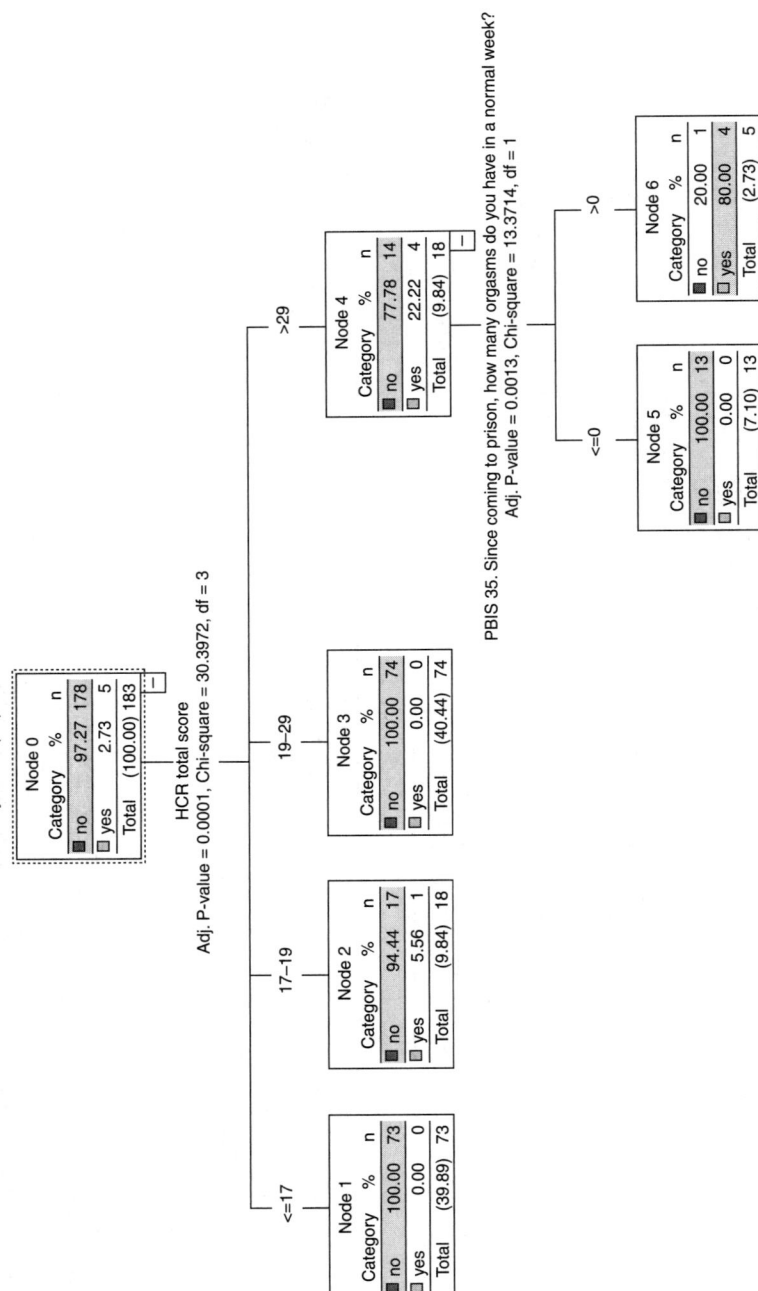

FIGURE 10.4 CHAID analyses for sexual predation for female inmates

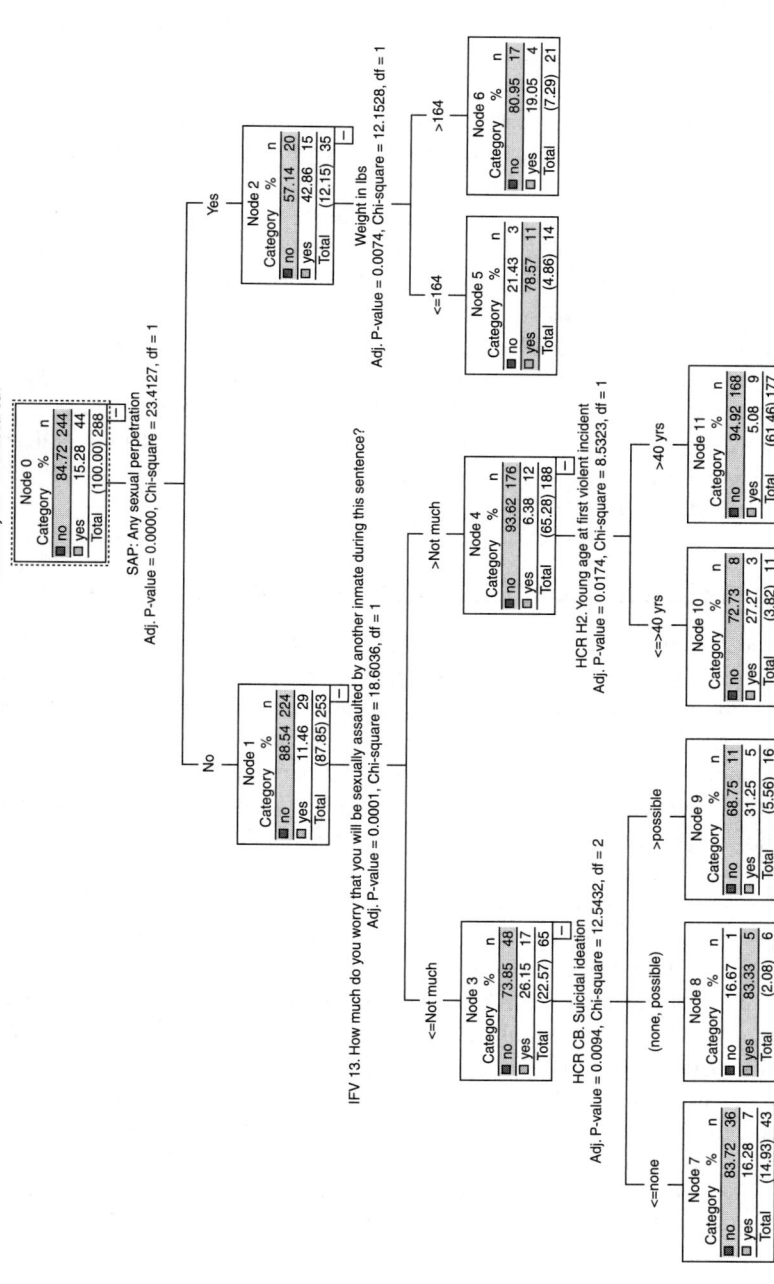

FIGURE 10.5 CHAID analyses for sexual victimization for male inmates

overall sample, 44 men (15.3%) self-reported sexual victimization in prison. Sexual predation was the best predictor of sexual victimization ($\chi^2 = 23.42$, df = 1, $p < 0.0001$). Men who self-reported sexual predation were far more likely to report sexual victimization than those who did not report sexual predation (42.9% vs 11.5%).

Among those who did not report sexual predation, worry about being sexually assaulted was the next best predictor of sexual victimization ($\chi^2 = 18.60$, df = 1, $p < 0.001$), with those reporting worry within the range of "a great deal" to "not much" being more likely to report sexual victimization (26.2% vs 6.4%). Among this group, those with possible (83.3%) or present (31.3%) suicidal ideation on the HCR-20 (experimental item) were more likely to report sexual victimization than those without suicidal ideation (16.3%) ($\chi^2 = 12.54$, df = 2, $p < 0.01$). Among those reporting no worry at all about being sexually assaulted, those who were older than 40 years at the age of their first violent incident were more likely to report sexual victimization (27.3% vs 5.1%) ($\chi^2 = 8.53$, df = 1, $p < 0.05$).

Among those reporting sexual predation, those who were less than or equal to 164 lbs were more likely to report sexual victimization in prison (78.6% vs 19.1%) ($\chi^2 = 12.15$, df = 1, $p < 0.01$).

Model Predicting Sexual Victimization for Female Inmates

The model correctly classified roughly 83 percent of all cases and had a sensitivity of 80 percent and a specificity of 84 percent. As observed in Figure 10.6, of the overall sample, 49 women (26.8%) self-reported sexual victimization in prison. Victimization by threatened physical violence was the best predictor of sexual victimization ($\chi^2 = 24.81$, df = 1, $p < 0.0001$). Women who reported victimization by threats of physical violence were far more likely to report sexual victimization than those who did not report experiencing victimization by threats of physical violence (48.5% vs 14.5%).

Among those who reported victimization by threats of physical violence, those who perpetrated relational violence were more likely to report sexual victimization in prison (60.5% vs 32.10%) ($\chi^2 = 5.20$, df = 1, $p < 0.05$). Among those not perpetrating relational violence, those who reported concerns of being assaulted by prison staff were more likely to report victimization (85.7% vs 14.3%) ($\chi^2 = 12.28$, df = 1, $p < 0.001$).

Among women who did not experience victimization by threats of physical violence, those who worried that they would be attacked by prison staff were more likely to report sexual victimization in prison (38.5% vs 7.7%) ($\chi^2 = 15.41$, df = 1, $p < 0.001$). Among women reporting concern about being attacked by prison staff, those with symptoms of Histrionic PD were more likely to report sexual victimization in prison (62.5% vs 0%) ($\chi^2 = 10.16$, df = 1, $p < 0.001$).

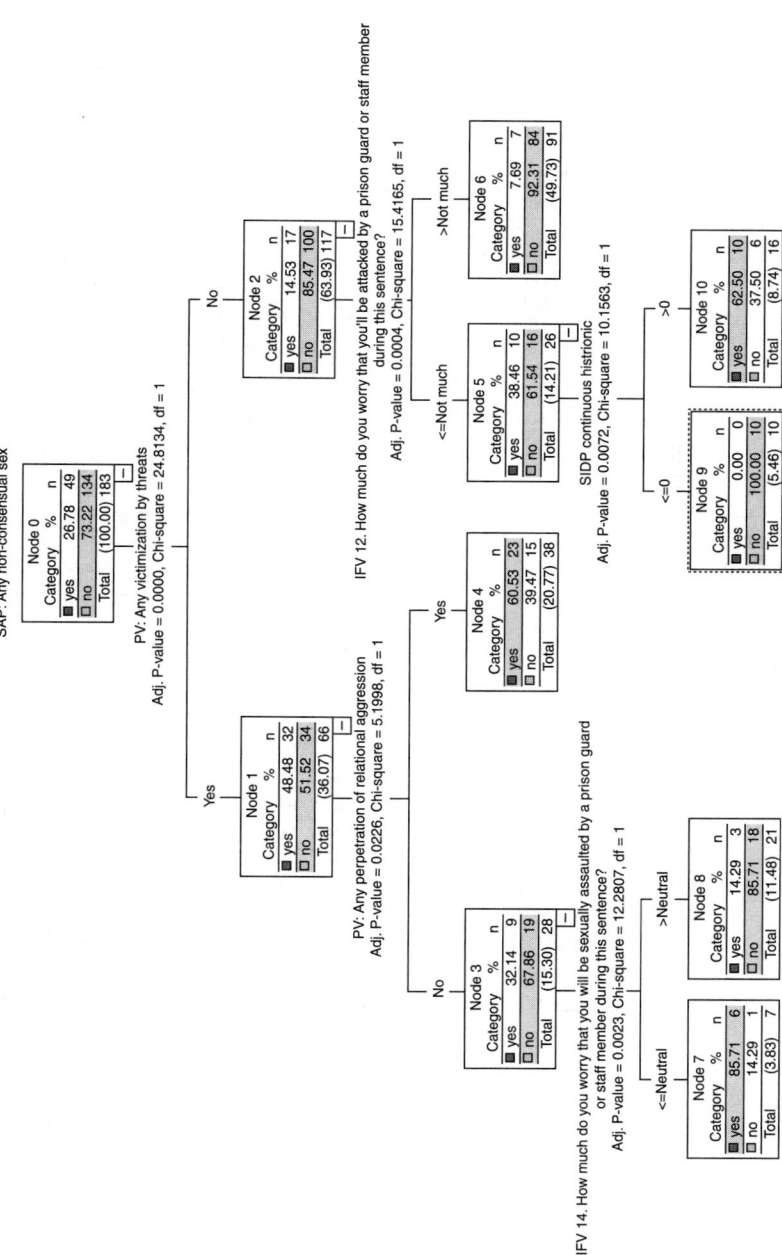

FIGURE 10.6 CHAID analyses for sexual victimization for female inmates

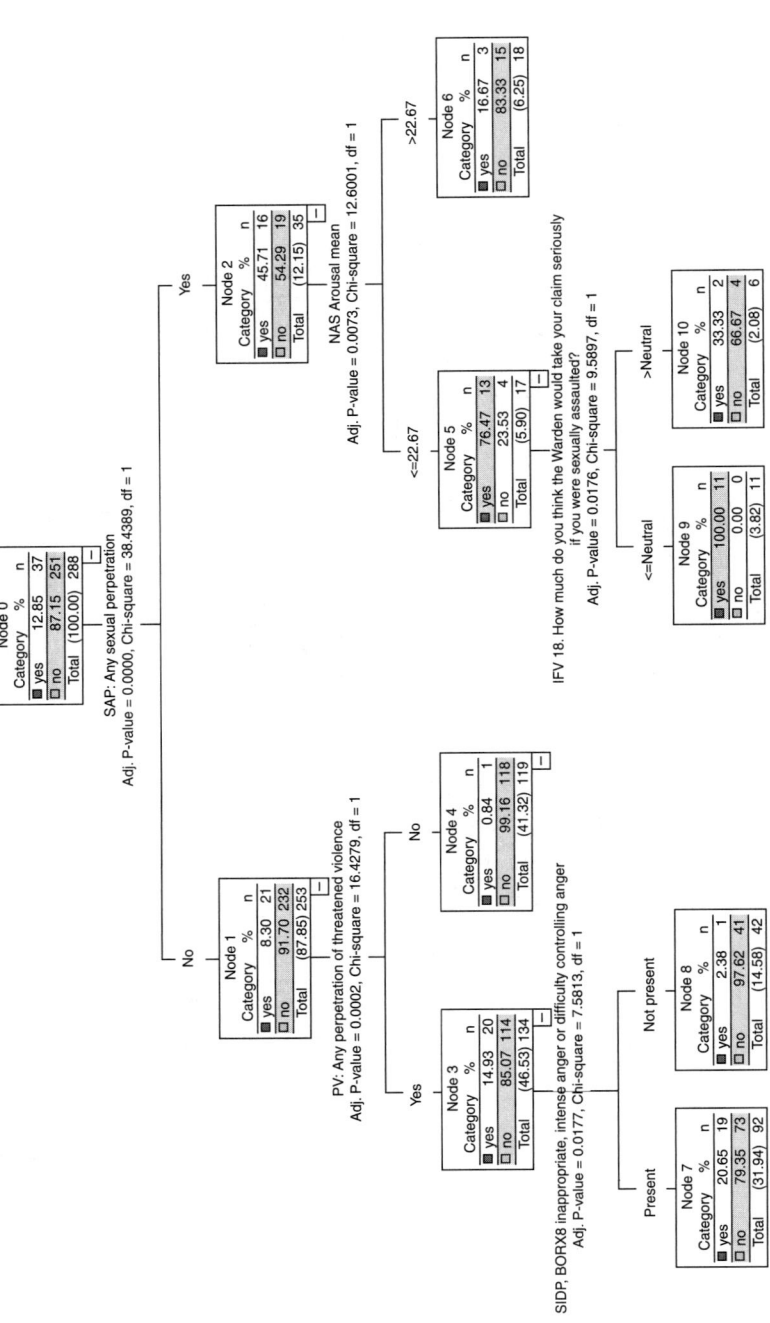

FIGURE 10.7 CHAID analyses for sexual bartering for male inmates

Model Predicting Sexual Bartering for Male Inmates

The model correctly classified roughly 91 percent of all cases and had a sensitivity of 30 percent and a specificity of 100 percent. As observed in Figure 10.7, of the overall sample, 37 men (12.9%) self-reported sexual bartering in prison. Sexual predation was the best predictor of sexual bartering ($\chi^2 = 38.44$, df = 1, $p < 0.001$). Those who self-reported sexual predation (45.7%) were more likely to report sexual bartering than those who did not (8.3%).

Among those who did not report sexual predation, perpetration of threatened physical violence was the next best predictor, with 14.9 percent of those perpetrating threatened physical violence also reporting bartering for sex as compared to 1 percent of those who did not threaten physical violence. Among those perpentrating threatened physical violence, those meeting criteria for the Borderline PD symptom of inappropriate anger were more likely to report sexual bartering than those without this symptom (20.7% vs 2.4%) ($\chi^2 = 7.58$, df = 1, $p < 0.05$).

Among those reporting sexual predation, those with NAS arousal scores less than 22.7 were more likely to report bartering sex than those with scores greater than 22.7 (76.5% vs 16.7%) ($\chi^2 = 12.60$, df = 1, $p < 0.001$). Among those with scores below 22.7, those who felt the warden was more likely to take claims of sexual assault seriously were more likely to report bartering sex than those who felt the warden would not take their claims seriously (100% vs 33.3%) ($\chi^2 = 9.59$, df = 1, $p < 0.05$).

Model Predicting Sexual Bartering for Female Inmates

The model correctly classified roughly 91 percent of all cases and had a sensitivity of 99 percent and a specificity of 17 percent. As observed in Figure 10.8, of the overall sample, 18 women (9.8%) self-reported sexual bartering in prison. Sexual predation was the best predictor of sexual bartering ($\chi^2 = 14.59$, df = 1, $p < 0.001$). Those who reported sexual predation (60.0%) were more likely to report sexual bartering than those who did not (8.4%).

Among those who reported sexual predation, perpetration of relational violence was the next best predictor, with 17.9 percent of those perpetrating relational violence also reporting bartering for sex as compared to 2.7 percent of those who did not perpetrate relational violence. Among those who did not perpetrate relational violence, a history of childhood neglect was the next best predictor, with 7 percent of women with a history of neglect reporting bartering sex as compared to 0 percent of the women without such a history.

Model Predicting Consensual Sex for Male Inmates

The model correctly classified roughly 72 percent of all cases and had a sensitivity of 72 percent and a specificity of 72 percent. As observed in Figure 10.9, of the overall sample, 127 male inmates self-reported consensual sexual activity in prison

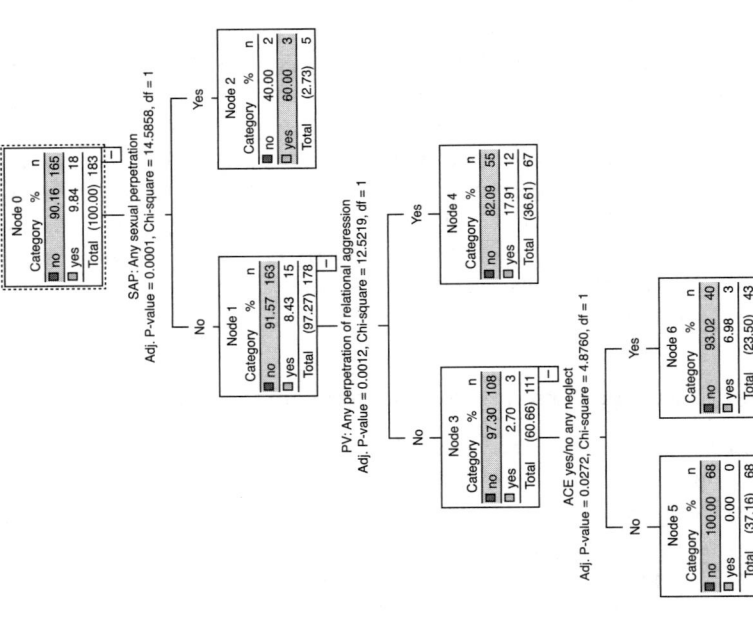

FIGURE 10.8 CHAID analyses for sexual bartering for female inmates

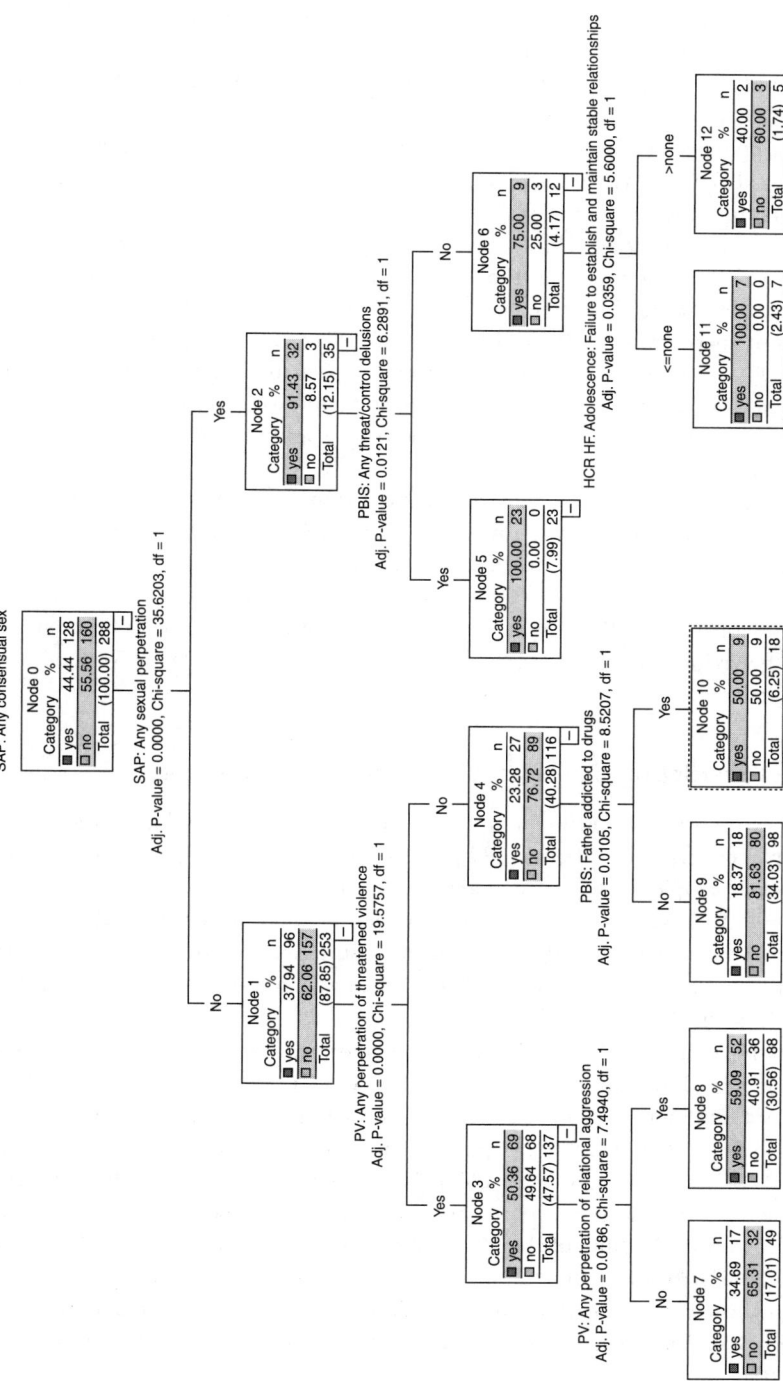

FIGURE 10.9 CHAID analyses for consensual sex for male inmates

(44.4%). Sexual predation was the best predictor of consensual sex, with 91.4 percent of those reporting sexual predation also reporting consensual sex as compared to 37.9 percent of those not reporting sexual predation (χ^2 = 35.62, df = 1, p < 0.0001).

Among those not reporting sexual predation, those who reported perpetrating threatened physical violence were more likely than those who did not report perpetrating threatened physical violence to report consensual sex in prison (50.4% vs 23.2%) (χ^2 = 19.58, df = 1, p < 0.001). Among those perpetrating threatened physical violence, those who also reported perpetrating relational violence were more likely to report consensual sex as compared to those who did not report perpetrating relational violence (59.1% vs 24.7%) (χ^2 = 7.49, df = 1, p < 0.05). Among those who did not report perpetrating threatened physical violence, those who reported paternal drug addiction were more likely than those not reporting paternal drug addiction to report engaging in consensual sex (50.0% vs 18.4%) (χ^2 = 8.52, df = 1, p < 0.05).

Among those who reported sexual predation, those who reported threat control override (TCO) symptoms were more likely to report consensual sex in prison (100% vs 75%) (χ^2 = 6.29, df = 1, p < 0.05). Among those without TCO symptoms, those who did not fail to establish and maintain stable adolescent relationships on the HCR-20 were more likely to report engaging in consensual sexual behavior in prison (experimental item) (100% vs 40%) (χ^2 = 5.60, df = 1, p < 0.05).

Model Predicting Consensual Sex for Female Inmates

The model correctly classified roughly 84 percent of all cases and had a sensitivity of 78 percent and a specificity of 89 percent. As observed in Figure 10.10, among the overall sample, 85 female inmates self-reported consensual sexual activity in prison (46.5%). Sexual orientation was the best predictor of consensual sex, with women who self-identified as homosexual or bisexual more likely to report consensual sex than women who self-identified as heterosexual (85.7% vs 32.1%) (χ^2 = 41.5, df = 1, p < 0.001).

Among women self-identifying as heterosexual, those who reported physical victimization while in prison were more likely to report consensual sex than those not experiencing physical victimization while in prison (58.3% vs 22.5%) (χ^2 = 15.56, df = 1, p < 0.001). Among women reporting physical victimization while in prison, those who were older than 39 years at the time of their current offense were less likely to report consensual sex than those who were younger than 39 years at the time of their current offense (77.8% vs 0%) (χ^2 = 16.8, df = 1, p < 0.001). Among women not experiencing physical victimization while in prision, those with thoughts of harming others were more likely to report consensual sex than those without such thoughts (63.6% vs 17.2%) (χ^2 = 12.1, df = 1, p < 0.01).

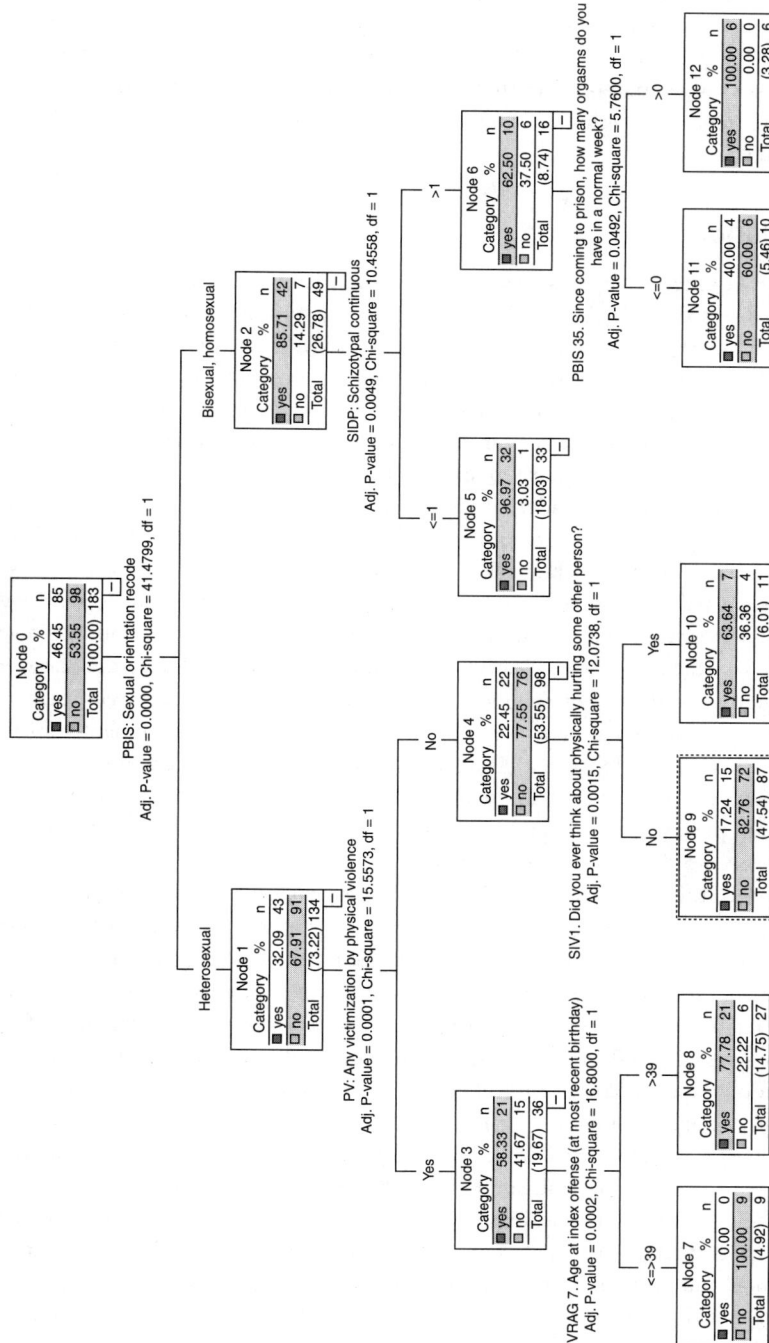

FIGURE 10.10 CHAID analyses for consensual sex for female inmates

Among women self-identifying as homosexual or bisexual, women reporting Schizotypal PD symptoms were more likely to report consensual sex (62.5% vs 97.0%) (χ^2 = 10.5, df = 1, p < 0.01). Among those with Schizotypal PD symptoms, women who reported having orgasms while in prison were more likely to report engaging in consensual sex (100% vs 0%) (χ^2 = 5.76, df = 1, p < 0.05).

Conclusions

Our decision tree analyses were exploratory in nature given the limitations of our sample size (N = 471). Yet, with this important qualification in mind, we can see that they do reflect constellations of risk markers which correlate at highly significant levels and which convey patterns of behavior consistent and explicable across an assortment of bivariate and multivariate analyses. From this perspective, they provide a framework both in terms of broad observations and specific findings that will warrant further replication and study.

The first of these broader observations involves the significance of gender differences in the risk factors that explain or predict the sexual behavior of men and women while incarcerated. Rates of any-sex, bartered sex, and consensual sex were comparable across the two genders with significant gender differences only in sexual predation and sexual victimization in the expected direction. However, these sexual behaviors were clearly not random in nature and the factors that were associated with them were gender specific and encompassing of a wide array of risk factors. The sexual behavior of the male inmates was predominantly associated with prior violence including sexual, threatening, and relational forms of aggression in prison, while the sexual behavior of women was primarily associated with personality traits and emotional states which most likely preceded their transition into the prison environment.

Second, the predictive models for the different types of sexual behavior in prison were multifaceted and included the full array of risk factors identified in prior risk research. The five types of sexual behavior were individually associated with prior historical experiences and events, personality factors and emotional states, relationships and behavior since arriving in prison, and attributes of the prison system as reflected in state differences in the any-sex model. The early childhood risk markers that reflected strong zero-order correlations in the previous analyses, however, tended to drop away in the CHAID analyses, possibly through the inclusion of personality disorders which were encompassing of these early types of traumatic events. The diversity of the relevant risk factors nonetheless underscore the importance of seeking to combine individual with relational and contextual factors in understanding the sexual behavior of incarcerated men and women and the importance of combining risk categories when seeking to identify at-risk individuals prior to their involvement in high risk sexual behavior.

Third, sexual predation and sexual victimization in prison are not the distinct phenomena suggested by traditional paradigms of sexual aggression and sexual abuse. Among the male inmates, sexually predatory behavior was most powerfully associated with sexual victimization. The relevance of threatened physical violence and diagnostic elements of Antisocial PD in the same model further supports the presence of a specific sub-culture among the male inmates in which predation and victimization tended to co-occur. For the female inmates, their sexual victimization was a far more distinct phenomenon from their sexual predation although it too was associated with involvement in relational violence as a perpetrator.

Fourth, most of our models reflected higher sensitivity ranging from 0.30 to 0.99 and lower specificity ranging from 0.17 to 0.89. These findings suggest that the models are more accurate in identifying inmates who will be involved in certain types of sexual behavior and less accurate in identifying those inmates who will not be sexually active while incarcerated. This association was reversed only in the CHAID model identifying bartered sex among the male inmates in which the sensitivity was 0.30 and the specificity was 1.00.

Finally, the sexual adaptation risk markers included in our study were largely unrelated to sexual behavior in prison. Our measures of hypersexuality (i.e., number of orgasms per week), age of first sexual experience, and number of life-time sexual partners tended not to be associated with patterns of consensual sex in prison or with sexual predation as suggested by paradigms of rape in the community. The consistency of these findings call attention to the fact that sexual behavior in prison is not a function of sexual appetite or sexual experience per se but rather a more complicated aspect of the aggressive exchanges that occur between inmates and between staff and inmates in the prison environment.

In turning to the specific models identified using our CHAID analyses, we found it was not possible to create a valid model of sexual predation for female inmates with a sample size of five women. It is interesting to note, however, that all of these women scored over 29 on the HCR-20, a structured violence risk assessment. Given the instrument's use of historical, clinical, and risk management risk markers, this finding suggests that sexually predatory women in prison are characterized by many of the same risk markers as men and women who are at higher risk for violence in the community. The predictive inclusion of having had an orgasm in prison may be tautological to the model or alternatively a marker for the hypersexuality that characterizes a minority of the women in our sample.

Of the overall sample, 44 men (15.3%) reported sexual victimization in prison. For the male inmates, sexual predation was the most powerful predictor of victimization. Men who reported sexual predation were almost four times more likely to report sexual victimization than those who did not perpetrate sexual violence. Within this group, size mattered, with men weighing less than 164 pounds being four times more likely to be sexually victimized than those who weighed over 164 pounds. Among the second group of male victims—those who were sexually victimized but who were not sexually predatory—were individuals who expressed worry and fear about being sexually assaulted by other inmates, who had experienced or were experiencing suicidal ideation at that time, and who were non-violent in their behavior within the prison environment. These distinctions between groups suggest two pathways to sexual victimization for male inmates. One appears to involve a retaliatory outcome associated with a violent and aggressive stance toward other inmates. The other reflects a more vulnerable presentation that is associated with a fearful experience of being in prison combined with suicidal ideation and/or being over the age of 40 years at the time of first violence.

The rate of sexual victimization was higher among the female inmates (26.6%). The best predictor of sexual victimization among the female inmates was having been the victim of threatened physical violence by other inmates. Among this group, a portion of the women reported having perpetrated relational violence against other inmates. Among the second group of female victims, women who had not been victimized by threatened physical violence while in prison were characterized by higher levels of fear concerning sexual assault by prison staff and with higher continuous scores on the diagnostic criteria of Histrionic PD. These findings suggest, as we found with the male inmates, that there were two pathways that lead to sexual victimization in prison. One group is victimized by threatened physical violence but appears to play a role in their own victimization through the perpetration of relational violence against other inmates. The other pathway suggests a higher endorsement of concerns about being attacked by prison staff combined with a demonstration of more symptom of Histrionic PD.

More male inmates (12.9%) than female inmates (9.8%) reported sexual bartering in prison. Male inmates who acknowledged sexual bartering are five times more likely to have been predatory in their sexual behavior than those who did not. Among this group, those who were less angry as assessed on the NAS arousal score and who were more confident that the warden would take claims of sexual assault seriously were more likely to be involved in sexual bartering. Among those inmates who did not describe themselves as being sexually predatory, most were threatening toward other inmates, and among these inmates more likely to manifest inappropriate anger as assessed by one criterion of the Borderline PD. These two pathways both confirm the impression of bartered sex being more aggressive than coercive in nature and suggests that some inmates see it as a manipulative way of obtaining both sex and goods in an environment in which sexual assault would be taken seriously by the prison administration.

As with the male inmates, sexual predation was the best predictor of sexual bartering among the female inmates. Those who reported sexual predation were seven times more likely to report bartering sex than those who did not. Among the female inmates who did not engage in sexual predation, sexual bartering was associated with relational violence among one group of women and a history of childhood neglect among the other. As with the male inmates, these pathways argue for a more aggressive interpretation of the sexual bartering that occurs in prison. However, unlike with the male inmates, it was also associated for some women with neglect in childhood and possibly the lack of familial support that might be implied by this early life experience.

Consensual sex was reported by 127 male inmates (44.4%) and 85 female inmates (46.5%). Among the male inmates, sexual predation was the best predictor of consensual sex. This group of male inmates was also characterized by at least one of the TCO symptoms (most often believing that others intended to do them harm) and having had difficulty establishing and maintaining relationships in adolescence. For those who were not sexually predatory, consensual sex was associated with threatened physical violence, relational violince, and paternal drug addiction. This suggests that male inmates engaging in consensual sex are generally more exploitative in their relationships with others, having experienced trouble in creating close relationships with others in adolescence, and more commonly having experienced their primary male figure in childhood being incapacitated because of addiction to substances.

Females who reported consensual sex more typically with other inmates similarly reported having perpetrated more threatened, physical, and relational violence and having experienced more thoughts of harming others in the past two months. Consensual sex by women was also associated with Schizotypal PD, again reflecting an association as seen with the men between social awkwardness and isolation and involvement in sex as possibly one avenue for trying to create closeness with another individual

And as embedded in the background of these findings, we can see that approximately 50 percent of the men and women in our sample self-reported no involvement in sexual behavior with others while incarcerated. This includes all types of contact and non-contact sexual encounters and exchanges with other inmates, visitors, and members of the prison staff. These data confirm that sexual activity in prison is not inevitable or inescapable and that certain protective risk factors exist which might be used to better assist individuals and institutions in understanding and addressing this important aspect of institutional life.

11
CONCLUSIONS AND RECOMMENDATIONS

In 2004, just after the passage of PREA, we undertook a project to develop a risk classification scheme for a range of sexual behavior exhibited by male and female inmates while incarcerated. The design of our study was unique in three specific ways. First, the exploratory research sought for the first time to apply empirically validated static and dynamic risk markers for violence in the community to sexual predation and victimization in prisons. Second, the study was designed to allow a direct comparison of male and female inmates across a range of domains. Finally, our study assessed a range of sexual behaviors as outcome measures in our study. These included the experience of coerced sexuality while imprisoned as either a perpetrator (predatory sex) or a victim (victimized sex), involvement in sexual exchanges that were based on the bartering of goods or protection (bartered sex), and involvement in consensual sex (consensual sex) that occurred with other inmates, visitors/others, and/or prison staff. We also included the experience of any-sex, which was defined as the experience of predatory, victimized, bartered, or consensual sex while incarcerated. This approach enabled a comparison of sexual to asexual inmates.

The empirical scaffolding of our study lay in the identification of six domains of risk factors for violent and sexually violent behavior. A review of the literature directed us to the potential relevance of a wide array of historical, criminological, clinical, and contextual risk factors that included: early adverse life experiences; community and institutional violence; hypersexuality and impersonal sexuality; affective and cognitive states including anger, impulsivity, and thoughts of harm; personality traits and disorders including psychopathy; and extant risk instruments for violence including the HCR-20 and the VRAG.

Risk Classification Schemes

Through this analytic process, we were able to build ten models that predicted five forms of sexual behavior among the male and among the female inmates using variables that did not solely rely on past incidents of sexual violence. Each model is described briefly below.

Any-sex

Male inmates engaging in any-sex were predicted by perpetration of threatened physical violence in prison, NAS behavior regulation scores under 25, being incarcerated in Texas, victimization by relational violence, and the Antisocial personality disorder (PD) symptom of irritability/aggressiveness. Female inmates engaging in any-sex were predicted by being the victim of threats of physical violence, the Borderline PD symptom of impulsivity, younger than 39 years at the time of their current offense, self-identification as homosexual or bisexual, and Narcissistic PD.

These analyses are relevant to intervention strategies as they capture the overarching set of risk markers that differentiate those inmates who are sexually active in prison from those who are not. For both the male and female inmates, these factors involved an intermingling of various forms of threatening or aggressive behavior along with personality traits associated with the Cluster B PDs. These personality traits associated with Antisocial PD, Borderline PD, and Narcissistic PD are by definition long-standing in nature and can therefore be identified at the time of admission to a correctional institution.

Sexual Predation

Male sexual predation was predicted by sexual victimization, Antisocial PD, a history of a head injury with loss of consciousness, perpetration of threatened physical violence, the state in which the inmate resided, and continuous scores on the SIDP-IV Antisocial scale less than or equal to six. Female sexual predation was predicted by higher HCR-20 Total scores and having had an orgasm with a partner in prison.

The risk factors that predict predatory sexual behavior among male inmates were found to be both individual and systemic and to reflect behavior in the present and impairments from the past. The reflective nature of these behaviors combined with the presence of an Antisocial PD and at least one head injury with loss of consciousness point towards a particular sub-group of inmates who are impulsive and somewhat reckless and who are involved in reciprocal violence with other inmates. The presence of state differences, however, also suggests that there are prison-specific differences that mediate these behaviors either through administrative edict or the racial mix of the inmates that populate the various prisons. These systemic differences converge with the BJS research, which documented some of the highest rates of sexual assault within the Texas prison system (Beck & Harrison, 2007).

Although preliminary in nature, the findings for female predatory inmates do point to the programmatic usefulness of the HCR-20 in identifying sexually violent women in prison. Theoretically, they suggest that sexually violent, incarcerated women are characterized by many of the same historical, clinical, and risk management factors that predict community and institutional violence among both males and females. The significance of orgasmic activity with a partner in prison may reflect a homosexual or bisexual sexual orientation or conversely the impact of a more intense sexual drive, two variables that were found to be associated with predatory sex by female inmates in the initial bivariate analyses.

Sexual Victimization

Male sexual victimization was predicted by sexual perpetration, weighing less than or equal to 164 pounds, worrying *a great amount* to *not much* about sexual assault, having possible or present suicidal ideation, and being over the age of 40 years at the time of their first violent offense. Female sexual victimization was predicted by threats of physical violence, perpetrating relational violence, concerns about being assaulted by correctional officers and prison staff, worrying that they would be attacked by staff, and a Histrionic PD.

The multi-tiered nature of the male and female victimization models alerted us programmatically to the multiplicity of victim types and the importance of designing programs that are responsive to the behaviors that are associated with each of them. The retaliatory nature of some victimization requires that the cyclical nature of these behaviors be addressed with the inmates and that the less egregious behaviors addressed as incubators for the more problematic types of sexual victimization. For example, promiscuity among males and relational violence among females constitute significant risk markers for sexual victimization. For the more vulnerable victims of both genders, the affective instability of the men and the provocative behavior of the women can be attended to through programs designed to create resiliency to the different types of victimization that they might experience. Each approach underscores the behaviors that increase risk and which use behavior of the victim to strengthen their position in the institution and inoculate them against multiple forms of victimization.

Systemically, these combined behaviors suggest that victimization is not only a problem for the individual but also one tendril of the network of behaviors that contribute to some of the most explosive behavior that must be handled by both the male and female prisons across the nation. Routinely, the wardens told us of the violence and bloodshed that they have encountered often traced back to the jealousy and distress that is paired with the romantic and sexual lives of the inmates. Akin to the links proposed between nuisance behavior and violence in the broken window theory of violence prevention, the behavioral risk markers for sexual violence represent viable and productive entry points for interventions that might change the inner dynamics of this sexual world (Kelling & Coles, 1997).

In research also funded as part of the PREA legislation, Fleisher and Krienert (2006) observed that the inmates' definition of victimization was quite different than that associated with the description of victimization in community settings. Based upon several hundred interviews, they concluded that coercion in prison was not defined by the sexual act per se but rather by the circumstances that preceded and followed it. For example, they observed that an inmate who voluntarily submits to threats ("Do it or I'll take you") is considered to have participated in a consensual sexual act with another. If the act is justifiable, for example retribution for a debt, it is similarly defined as justifiable and the victim is blamed for having allowed this situation to develop and for contributing to the impression of being weak. Moreover, if an inmate fails to fight back when approached sexually, it is interpreted by other inmates as being consensual and an expression of an exchange that the inmate "really wanted." These different interpretations have not been examined empirically but they do highlight the complexity of the behavior being studied and the importance of integrating the inmates' interpretation of these sexual behaviors into the programming that is designed to address it.

Sexual Bartering

Male sexual bartering was predicted by sexual perpetration, NAS arousal scores of less than 22.7, perceptions that the warden takes claims of sexual assault seriously, perpetration of threatened physical violence, and the Borderline PD symptom of inappropriate anger. Female sexual bartering was predicted by sexual perpetration, perpetration of relational violence, and a history of childhood neglect.

This model highlights the coercive behavior that is associated with bartered sex among both the male and female inmates and argues against it being interpreted as a form of exploitation elicited from the more vulnerable inmates. It also underscores the association between sexual predation and sexual bartering for both men and women and the potential use of the one behavior to predict the other.

Consensual Sex

Finally, male consensual sexual activity was predicted by sexual perpetration, threat control override symptoms, absence or failure to establish and maintain stable adolescent relationships, perpetration of threatened violence, perpetration of relational violence, and paternal drug addiction. Female consensual sexual activity was predicted by sexual orientation (homosexual/bisexual), Schizotypal PD symptoms, having had an orgasm in prison, physical victimization while in prison, younger than 39 years at the time of their current offense, and thoughts of harming others.

These two models contain risk markers that are counter-intuitive when viewed through the lens of alleged consensual sexual contact with another. Both the male and female inmates who experienced problems with interpersonal relatedness were more likely to be sexually active than those who did not. Similarly, consensual sex was associated for both genders with paranoid perceptions and thoughts of doing harm to another, emotional states that conventionally would be thought to counteract the wish for sexual intimacy. When viewed together, these similarities across sexes further illustrate the different meaning that is associated with at least some sex in the prison environment.

Overview

Three broad conclusions can be derived from this brief description of the models identified in our research. First, robust models predictive of various forms of sexual behavior in prison can be developed and potentially validated through further research. Second, there are real and meaningful gender differences that emerge from our data that highlight the importance of creating and using risk models that are unique to men and women. These are reflective of predictive diversity and accentuate the importance of developing programs that are responsive to the gender specific needs of inmates (Gover, Pérez, & Jennings, 2008). Finally, the range of variables necessary to predict various forms of sexual behavior is wide-reaching. Both static and dynamic risk factors as well as proximal and distal risk markers were predictive in our models. However, as illustrated, the different categories of sexual behavior were the best predictors of other forms of sexual behavior, suggesting that it is an interplay of sexual motivations and behaviors that contribute to the individual experience of being sexually active inmates within the prison environment.

Study Results in the Context of the PREA Commission

In 2009, the PREA Commission (National Prison Rape Elimination Commission, 2009) disseminated a report outlining the ways in which prison rape can and should be addressed. Finding 3 of the Report (p. 7) concluded that certain individuals, both male and female from all security levels, were at higher risk of sexual victimization than others. These individuals were identified as being young, of small stature, lacking in experience in the institution, having a mental disability or serious mental illness, being of a non-heterosexual orientation, and having experienced some type of sexual victimization either previously in the community or in the institution.

These conclusions prompted the development of Screening Standards 1 and 2 which endorsed the use nationally of standardized written screening tools tailored to the gender of the population being screened. The screening instrument for male sexual victimization included: mental or physical disability, young age, slight build, first incarceration, non-violent history, prior convictions for sex offenses, sexual orientation as gay or bisexual, gender non-conformance, prior sexual victimization, and the inmate's own perception of vulnerability. The screening instrument for female victimization included prior sexual victimization and the inmate's own perception of vulnerability. The sexual predation instrument for the male inmates included prior acts of sexual abuse and prior conviction for a violent offense, and only prior acts of sexual abuse for the female inmates.

All of these risk markers identified by the PREA Commission had been included in our research design but few were significant in our multivariate analyses. There were only three risk factors overlapping between the Commission-identified risk factors and our results, with only one of these risk factors operating consistently across the two reports. Both the Commission Report and our results identified slight build as a risk factor for male sexual victimization. However, prior sexual predation was identified by the Commission Report as a risk factor for male and female sexual predation, but our study revealed it as a risk factor for male sexual victimization. Similarly, while the Commission identified the inmate's own perception of vulnerability as a risk factor for both male and female sexual victimization, our study found perceptions of vulnerability were predictive only of male victimization. We further found that a robust model could be developed for sexual predation by male inmates and an interesting exploratory model for sexual predation by female inmates. Both models included a more diversified set of risk factors than suggested by the Commission's screening recommendations.

Based upon the information made available to them, the PREA Commission recommended that evidence-based screening become routine nationwide to ensure safety for all individuals under the umbrella of the criminal justice system (p. 8). They argued that this type of approach would enable correctional staff to plan for safety and needed resources while minimizing the interference of personal views and varying levels of staff experience (p. 75). Despite this recommendation, further research found that risk classification schemes were not being widely used by correctional institutions and that compliance rates with Standards 1 and 2 remained low. The consulting firm Booz – Allen – Hamilton (2010) reported that compliance with Screening Standards 1 and 2 ranged between 0 percent and 25 percent for the facilities in their sample, despite these two standards being ranked 10th in terms of their cost impact to the institution (agencies are required to modify existing tools or implement procedures where one does not exist). Programmatically, Neal and Clements (2010) and Struckman-Johnson (2011) argued that identifying individuals at risk for victimization might be used in a preventative manner in matching and cell block placements. However, the PREA Commission emphasized that isolating potential victims can have significant unintended and negative consequences for the inmate, including making the individual a target if their classification becomes widely known (Zweig, Naser, Blackmore, & Schaffer, 2007).

Gender Differences among Incarcerated Individuals

As illustrated, our ten CHAID analyses consistently confirmed differences in the characteristics and life experiences of our male and female samples. These included significant gender differences in rates of sexual behavior, the experience of childhood and adolescent trauma, community and institutional violence, patterns of sexual adaptation, affective and perceptual states, and personality disorders.

Both genders reported remarkably similar rates of consensual sex in prison (44.4% males vs 46.5% females), although the male inmates more frequently described these encounters occurring with visitors or staff and the female inmates with other female inmates. We also learned that consensual sex was initiated by female inmates within a month of arrival at the institution, whereas the male inmates reported taking a year to initiate a consensual relationship.

Homosexual males were underrepresented among the male sample and they were more likely to be sexually victimized. In contrast, homosexual women were overrepresented in the female sample and reported more predatory, bartered, and consensual sex during incarceration. Among the female inmates, sexual orientation was the best predictor of consensual sex. Women who self-identified as homosexual or bisexual were two and a half times more likely to report consensual sex than women who self-identified as heterosexual. Sexual orientation seemed to overshadow any of the physical characteristics of the women with height and weight being unrelated to these indices of sexual behavior. For the men, less weight, likely indicative of a slight build, was associated with a higher level of sexual victimization.

These differences empirically (and based upon our interviews with the inmates) consistently reinforced our impression of the profound gender differences that characterize the experience of sex in prison for male and female inmates. The female inmates were open about their sexual involvement with other women, referring to it rather lightly as "gay for the stay," and at times sharing it with their heterosexual partners during visitation as part of their shared sexual conversation and interaction. The male inmates were far more covert in their behavior and descriptions. While they would at times describe their move toward same-sex encounters or their observations of aggressive and brutal rapes within their institution, it was clear that these experiences would remain hidden within the walls of the prison and never be a part of the formal narrative of the time they spent in prison and/or the friendships that they developed within this setting.

It is not clear if this difference reflects a self-identity that existed prior to incarceration or evolved, at least for the women, as a result of their experiences while incarcerated. It may be that women tend more often to identify themselves as bisexual after a sexual encounter with a woman whereas men maintain a self-identification of being heterosexual even amidst same-sex physical contact (Man & Cronan, 2001). Alternatively, more men did report consensual sexual encounters with female correctional staff suggesting that they may, in fact, creatively develop these boundary crossing relationships either to maintain their sexual identity as heterosexual men or because of a more innate disinterest in the sexual appeal of other men. Hensley, Tewksbury, and Wright (2001) asked inmates to identify their sexual orientation prior to coming to prison and their sexual identity after incarceration. Before prison, 79 percent of respondents considered themselves heterosexual, 6 percent homosexual, and 15 percent bisexual. After incarceration, these same individuals self-identified as 69 percent heterosexual, 7 percent homosexual, and 24 percent bisexual, suggesting the fluidity of sexual orientation. Throughout our study, we were struck by this observed fluidity in the sexual orientation of these individuals and the powerful nature of the intimacy seeking behavior of some inmates. While not suggesting that object choice and sexual orientation are purely social constructs determined by social expectation, these observations did underscore for us the malleability of the human being and the powerful nature of the drive for attachment and interpersonal connectedness.

As observed by Kinsey, Pomeroy, and Martin (1948) many years ago, we found that the inmates in both our male and female samples reported sexual interests that far exceed those of the general population, although sexual interest differed significantly by gender. Almost 40 percent of the male inmates and 17 percent of the female inmates reported a level of sexual desire that is currently diagnosed as hypersexuality in the research and clinical literature. These individuals tended to experience over eight orgasms a week while living in the community and a small proportion of these individuals, primarily the males, continued this rate of orgasmic activity during incarceration. However, the presence of this high level of sexual interest was not associated with sexual predation among either the male or female inmates. As such, this finding argues against the deprivation theory of prison rape and suggests that sexual desire is not the primary factor that motivates aggressive sexual assault in a prison environment. However, these elevated levels of sexual desire were associated with higher rates of consensual sex during incarceration among the female inmates.

A Range of Sexual Activity Occurs in Prison

At the beginning of our study, we decided to step out of the mandated focus on predatory sex and sexual victimization, choosing instead to include instrumentation and interviews that assessed the full continuum of sexual behaviors that we believed occurred in prison (see Chapter 3). Auspiciously, this more inclusive approach came to constitute the foundation for many of the most important findings of our study. First, it documented with substantive detail the fact that there is a significant amount of sexual behavior occurring in prison. This sex was occurring despite firm institutional regulations prohibiting it, with accompanying criminal sanctions for violations (Saum et al. 1995; Solursh et al., 1993). The sex varied in form and intent and was found to be based upon different types of relationships between the inmates, with visitors/others, and with members of the prison staff. Some of the sex was coerced, some was not. Some involved relationships between same-gendered inmates, others illicit relationships with members of the prison staff. The intent of the sex was also found to vary at times reflecting a predatory imposition of a degrading experience upon another, at other times a bartered exchange of goods and interpersonal commodities, and at other times, the consensual exchange of sexual gratification either as a means of immediate pleasure or an avenue for future control. These different domains of sexual behavior were not substantially different from those found in the community, but they were made unique in the prison environment by the fact that they were prohibited, commonly involved single-gendered pairings by heterosexual individuals, and entailed two adults, one of whom was deemed incapable of giving consent while the other was mandated by law not to participate in the sexual exchange.

Interrelatedness of Different Types of Sexual Activity and Violent Behavior

Our study design allowed us to examine the association between different types of sexual behavior and the relationship of sexual behavior to other forms of institutional violence. From these analyses, we found that the different kinds of sexual behaviors were significantly correlated and that our sex-specific distinctions, when applied to descriptions of a single individual, were often misleading if not illusory. The female inmates that reported sexual victimization were not simultaneously involved in predatory, consensual, or bartered sexual encounters. The female inmates who reported predatory sexual behavior toward other inmates, however, did self-report involvement in other consensual and bartered sexual relationships.

The associations for the male inmates were more all-encompassing. Male inmates who reported being sexually victimized also reported being involved in predatory, bartered, and consensual sexual relationships with others. For both genders, inmates who engaged in one type of sex were far more likely to be involved in the other types of sex (with the exception of sexual victimization among the female inmates). Fleisher and Krienert (2006) came upon a similar set of observations as part of their ethnographic study of prison sex and referred to this panorama of sexual behaviors as the "sex scene" in prison.

We also found significant correlations for the male and female inmates between different types of sexual behavior and different forms of relational, threatened, and physical violence. As discussed above, male inmates who acted in a sexually predatory way toward others were at an elevated risk for being sexually victimized and being involved in bartered and consensual sex with others. Moreover, these same inmates demonstrated a higher propensity for being involved in different types of physical and relational violence with other inmates. The female inmates were far less predatory in their sexual behavior but when they were, they were similarly involved in the full array of sexual behaviors often paired with relational violence and threatened violence toward others.

Moreover, we found that many of the risk markers for sex in prison were the same as those that have been identified as predicting violent behavior in the community. Inmates who experienced conduct problems as juveniles, who had problems in establishing relationships with others during adolescence, who had a past history of early violence, and who suffered from one of the Cluster B personality diagnoses were also involved in various forms of sexual behavior while incarcerated. The HCR-20, used to predict violence risk in the community, was found to correlate with the different types of sexual behavior in prison for both the male and female inmates. Further, various affective states such as anger, impulsivity, and violent thoughts of harming self and others, often associated with reactive forms of physical violence, clustered in our sample among those who reported involvement in predatory, victimized, bartered, or consensual sex while incarcerated. This affinity between sexual and aggressive behavior in prison suggests that it is not only a "sex scene" that defines the behaviors of some inmates, but rather engagement in a turbulent set of interpersonal relationships that are sexual, aggressive, and occasionally violent. This turbulence seems to have been reflected in chaotic early lives, domestically violent relationships prior to coming to prison, and an adjustment to prison that is tinged with hostility in its many forms.

Asexual Lifestyle is Possible while Incarcerated

Our data confirmed that interpersonal sexual behavior was not an inevitable outcome of incarceration. Approximately one half of the inmates in our sample adopted a relatively asexual lifestyle and remained unattached and uninvolved in the sexual forays that were unfolding around them. These individuals tended to be older, less antisocial, less violent, and more inclined to avoid all types of aggressive interactions with other inmates. They also tended to demonstrate less trauma and exposure to violence in their childhood, less involvement in the criminal justice system as adolescents, and less violent crime prior to their current incarceration. Less sexual experience prior to coming to prison, in particular fewer lifetime sexual partners and being over the age of 18 at the time of first sexual experience, also lessened the likelihood that either the male or female inmates would be involved in sexual interactions during incarceration.

These findings, while less relevant to risk classification, might prove central to relevant programming on a systemic level. They suggest that certain protective factors can be identified which may assist in the formation of unit groups with the optimal proportion of individuals at risk for sexual activity with those who are not. The differences between these two groups also harkens to the research conducted by Byrne and Hummer (2007) and their review of studies that sought to examine the impact of classification decisions on the level of violence and disorder in prison. Based upon a review of all 14 studies conducted from 1984 through to 2006, they concluded that classification systems that were currently in use did not accurately predict prison violence, and more importantly, did not appear to reduce the risk of violence in prison. Rather, the two researchers found that new classification systems that focused on changing rather than controlling offenders were the most effective prison violence reduction strategy currently available. This research suggests that efforts to identify the sexually preoccupied inmates and to use this information to link them to active programming and treatment might serve to identify the "tipping point" between formal and informal social control mechanisms.

Sexual Relationships between Prison Staff and Inmates

In our study, we allowed the inmates to identify the nature and intent of the sexual experiences that they were reporting to us. Therefore, if the inmate reported being involved in a consensual sexual relationship with a member of the correctional staff, we included their endorsement in the consensual sex category. This decision was made with full awareness that statutory law currently defines this type of encounter as a felony offense in every state in the US. In making this determination, we were intent upon capturing the sexual experiences that were being described to us by the inmates and did not want to superimpose a socially constructed definition upon them. In time, we came to see that this decision was consistent with the research published by the BJS which identified two thirds of the staff-on-inmate incidents as being romantic in nature (Beck, Harrison, & Adams, 2007).

The rate of sexual activity between staff and inmates was relatively high in our study, although significantly different across genders. More male (8.7% non-contact and 2.8% contact sex) than female (1.1% non-contact and 0.0% contact sex) inmates reported acting in a sexually predatory manner toward staff. It was not clear if these data reflected an accurate portrayal of the inmates' predatory targets or the wish to retain a heterosexual identity when describing these incidents combined with a possible interest in demonstrating their ability to dominate institutional staff. However, these data suggest that sexual coercion of prison staff by male inmates is as much a concern as the more widely publicized incidents of inmate coercion by male correctional staff.

In contrast, more female (11.5% non-contact and 2.7% contact sex) than male (6.6% non-contact and 2.4% contact sex) inmates reported experiencing non-contact sexual victimization by correctional staff, although not significantly more contact sexual victimization. These data suggest that female inmates experience and report significantly more victimization by correctional staff through comments, looks, and innuendoes than male inmates. However, the data concerning bartered sex as described by the inmates indicated that male inmates tended to report efforts to barter with correctional staff (9.7% non-contact and 8.0% contact sex) more frequently than female (3.8% non-contact and 1.1% contact sex) inmates. Finally, sexual encounters described by inmates as consensual between correctional staff and inmates indicated that significantly more male inmates (24.3% non-contact and 17.4% contact sex) than female inmates (13.7% non-contact and 2.7% contact sex) were engaging in consensual sex with correctional staff. Consistent with the BJS study (Beck et al., 2007), many of these staff-on-inmate incidents were described as consensual and romantic in nature, further highlighting the vulnerability of female correctional officers to becoming sexually involved with male inmates.

Over the course of our study, these observations inevitably prompted our interest in the issue of consent in prison and the idea of coercion that is implicit to the status of being a prison inmate. Unlike other contexts in which consent is assumed to be lacking, the majority of these inmates have no mental illness, no impaired cognitive abilities, and no necessary assumption of vulnerability. In fact, many of these individuals are considered dangerous and powerful on the outside, but weak and vulnerable once they began living in the controlled environment of prison. It is obvious that there are strict hierarchical relationships within the prison environment, but these operate in many community settings and do not result in felony convictions for those who overstep common sense and good judgment. Ristroph (2006) offers an interesting perspective commenting that sex in the community is assumed to be consensual unless someone complains. This assumption is currently disputed in all prison settings, although it is our impression that its application to the prison setting would do much to inform the investigations that are required and minimize some of the intrigue and manipulation that distorts many aspects of our understanding and programming.

The sanctions that are being used with prison staff who become sexually or romantically involved with prison inmates also appear tinged with gender bias. Our experience suggests that female correctional officers who become sexually involved with male inmates are simply terminated from their position at the institution. In contrast, male correctional officers who become sexually involved with female inmates are often subject to a rigorous response, up to and including prosecution.

This large divide between policy and experience leaves all employees unprotected and unprepared for this important aspect of their working lives. With little training, they encounter a closed environment with young offenders who are by nature hypersexual, violent, and lacking in the ability to maintain strong, respectful interpersonal relationships, often motivated by racial tensions, and wanting in many ways to express interpersonal dominance. The nature of the laws and the implicit assumptions concerning the vulnerability of the imprisoned inmates further camouflage the seductive charms of the psychopathic male inmate and the allure of the manipulative mercenary female. While the PREA Commission chose to ignore this issue (Struckman-Johnson, 2011), laws which frame these encounters or relationships simply as an offense perpetrated by the prison employee fail to take into account this interactive aspect of the victimization and the contribution that both individuals bring to it. The difficulty that prisons have in finding qualified and educated prison staff further diminishes the cultural divide between inmates and correctional officers and emphasizes the importance of training and supervision to help prison staff avoid these inappropriate and disruptive liaisons.

It is our impression that many of these issues are inadequately addressed in the training that is offered to correctional staff and inmates within the institutional setting. Zweig and Blackmore (2008) conducted one small study of 11 state prison administrations and found that the training on sex in prison focused almost exclusively on detecting *victims* and helping to provide support and assistance to them. Only three states provided information on how to detect staff *perpetrators* (Zweig & Blackmore, 2008). These kinds of determinations fail to capture the complex interactions that can lead to both types of interactions and do not educate the correctional officers against exploitative, disruptive, and potentially violent relationships with inmates under their supervision. The BJS finding of the overwhelmingly romantic description of most staff-on-inmate incidents underscores the importance of developing programming that assists institutions in identifying and reprimanding exploitative staff while simultaneously assisting vulnerable staff from uninformed and naïve involvement with the inmate population.

Prison Policies Concerning Sexual Contact in Prison

Research has confirmed wide variation across prison systems in terms of the physical design of the institution (e.g., blind spots), the social environment (security level of inmates), and the policies promulgated by the institution (Clements et al., 2007; Austin, Fabelo, Gunter, & McGinnis, 2006; National Prison Rape Elimination Commission, 2009). However, one policy that is fairly consistent across institutions that is central to our topic of study involves the prohibition of condom distribution to prison inmates. Currently the rate of confirmed AIDS cases is three times higher among state and federal prison inmates compared to the general population (Maruschak, 2006), although the rate of disease transmission while incarcerated is largely unknown (Pinkerton, Galletly, & Seat, 2007). For the year 2004, the BJS reported that 1.9 percent of state prison and 1.1 percent of federal prison inmates were known to be infected with the human immunodeficiency virus (HIV). While condom distribution is available in four cities and two states in the US (Hammett, Maruschak, & Harmon, 1999; Spaulding, Lubelczyk, & Flanigan, 2001), condom distribution remains controversial and widely prohibited in most correctional systems. Intrinsic to this debate is a classic clash of disciplines. From a public health perspective, condom distribution is perceived as a strategy for harm reduction (or even prevention) of disease transmission, whereas from the corrections perspective, the paramount concern is safety and the eradication of all behavior that is known to be a risk factor for violence including sexual behavior. Yet, evaluations of condom distribution programs in other countries (i.e., New South Wales, Australia) have illustrated that condom distribution does not cause rape or increase rates of sexual activity and that inmates who are sexually active are likely to use a condom if it is made available to them (Dolan, Lowe, & Shearer, 2004; Yap et al., 2007).

Within our study we had inmates reporting that they did use protection when it was available and that they did have concerns about HIV transmission. When asked further about their efforts to use protections, they described various inventive solutions including the creation of condoms using supplies from the kitchen, the transfer of condoms from correctional staff, and the choice of sexual partners based somewhat on their perception of relative risk. What was often left out of these discussions were references to the community-living partners of these inmates who often assumed that incarceration was synonymous with celibacy and therefore were unaware of the need to protect themselves when their partners return home to the community.

Limitations and Future Research

Through our various analyses, we were able to build ten models that predicted five types of sexual behavior, separately for male and female inmates. These models were characterized by good to excellent (0.70 to 0.99) accuracy with high levels of sensitivity and relatively low levels of specificity. These statistics suggest that casting a wide net for predictive risk markers was successful in identifying risk markers useful in predicting various types of sexual behavior in prison. The differential ability of the models to identify sexually active individuals further underscores the value of classification models recommended in the Commission's Report (National Prison Rape Elimination Commission, 2009). However, the low levels of specificity indicate the need for replication and refinement prior to integrating risk markers into screening and investigative strategies or prosecutorial endeavors. Indeed, we must continue to emphasize the exploratory nature of our research and the preliminary nature of our findings.

Our findings will surely require replication across states and types of institutions. We recommend that this replication begin with the many significant bivariate risk markers that were identified across the six domains of potential risk markers (see Appendix D). These risk markers might well prove of predictive value in multivariate analyses that involve larger samples and we trust that the relevance of them will not be lost in a premature rush toward model testing given the complex nature of the behavior being studied. We also believe that the inclusion of personality data will be central to our understanding of the process by which early trauma is translated into turbulent sexual and aggressive behavior in prison. This type of data is very time consuming and expensive to collect and is mired in discouraging attitudes of therapeutic nihilism. Nonetheless, it is central to understanding not only the symptom-level behaviors that need to be addressed and managed, but also the individual propensities that unwittingly make some inmates particularly vulnerable to victimization or consistently prone to violence. Finally, we are convinced that time spent reviewing and reflecting upon the issues of consent, the applicability and viability of providing protections against sexually transmitted diseases to inmates, and the importance and content of boundary training for the correctional staff would benefit the integrity of all prison systems and contribute to an informed and thoughtful approach to managing the sexual behavior of some inmates. This type of preventative approach might well tame some of the passions that disturb many of the daily functions of prison life and provide a less humiliating set of experiences for inmates to conceal as they begin their process of reintegration with their families and life in the community.

Conclusions

To date, psychology has made little contribution to the social problem of prison rape (Neal & Clements, 2010). An improved classification scheme is one important part of a comprehensive prevention program using an ecological model as the guiding principle to preventing rape in prison (National Prison Rape Elimination Commission, 2009). To combat sexual exploitation in prison, there must be strong leadership at the top, training for correctional officers, risk assessment for inmates, risk assessment of the prison environment, monitoring, informing, educating new inmates about the sexual choices that they will be required to make while incarcerated, and effective and accurate responding to the different allegations and reports that come to the attention of all correctional staff (National Prison Rape Elimination Commission, 2009).

APPENDICES

Appendix A: Assessing Generalizability

TABLE A1 Comparison of Inmate Participants and Randomly Selected Group of Non-participants by Gender in Ohio

Variable	Participant Status	Males (N = 324)	Females (N = 298)
Sample Size	Did Not Participate	162	149
	Did Participate	162	149
Age	Did Not Participate	33.88 yrs	35.86 yrs
	Did Participate	35.90 yrs	37.81 yrs
		$t = 1.79$, n.s.	$t = 1.67$, n.s.
Minimum Aggregated Sentence	Did Not Participate	304.26 mo	41.32 mo
	Did Participate	498.92 mo	342.89 mo
		$t = 1.14$, n.s.	$t = 2.14, p < 0.05$
Number of Prior Imprisonments	Did Not Participate	2.31	0.56
	Did Participate	2.27	0.52
		$t = 0.09$, n.s.	$t = 0.26$, n.s.
Race	Did Not Participate Black	96	65
	White	64	82
	Asian	1	2
	Other	1	0
	Did Participate Black	85	85
	White	76	64
	Asian	0	0
	Other	1	0
		$\chi^2(3) = 2.69$, n.s.	$\chi^2(2) = 2.06$, n.s.

(*Continued overleaf*)

TABLE A1 Continued

Variable	Participant Status		Males (N = 324)	Females (N = 298)
Security Level	Did Not Participate	Level 1	2	111
		Level 2	26	38
		Level 3	61	0
		Level 4	72	0
	Did Participate	Level 1	1	123
		Level 2	28	26
		Level 3	62	0
		Level 4	71	0
			$\chi^2(4) = 1.42$, n.s.	$\chi^2(1) = 2.87$, n.s.
Gang Affiliation	Did Not Participate	None	120	149
		Passive	19	0
		Active	6	0
		Disruptive	17	0
	Did Participate	None	130	148
		Passive	16	1
		Active	6	0
		Disruptive	10	0
			$\chi^2(3) = 2.47$, n.s.	$\chi^2(1) = 1.00$, n.s.
Most Serious Offense (Dichotomous)	Did Not Participate	Violent	128	64
		Non-violent	34	85
	Did Participate	Violent	127	77
		Non-violent	35	72
			$\chi^2(1) = 0.02$, n.s.	$\chi^2(1) = 2.28$, n.s.
Most Serious Offense (Using FEIS Categories)	Did Not Participate	Violent	48	29
		Potentially Violent	43	22
		Other Crimes Against Person	16	13
		Sex	24	0
		Property	13	40
		Drug	11	38
		Minor	7	7
	Did Participate	Violent	57	37
		Potentially Violent	38	25
		Other Crimes Against Person	9	14
		Sex	31	1
		Property	7	39
		Drug	11	29
		Minor	9	4
			$\chi^2(6) = 5.98$, n.s.	$\chi^2(6) = 4.24$, n.s.

Appendix B: *Correctional Officer's State Comparisons on Key Demographic Variables*

Our circumstances in Texas varied from that of Ohio and therefore the same data collection procedures were not employed although the same instrument was administered. We found significant differences in the Ohio and Texas correctional officer (CO) samples on all but one (education) demographic variable: more female COs in Texas completed the survey, $\chi^2(1) = 36.63, p < 0.001$, COs were older in Ohio, $t = 3.42, p < 0.001$; *Ohio M* = 41.07 yrs, *Texas M* = 36.39 yrs, more COs in Texas were of minority status, $\chi^2(2) = 10.06, p < 0.01$, and more COs in Texas worked at their current facility for less than ten years, $\chi^2(1) = 74.99, p < 0.001$. COs in Ohio were more likely to interact with the general population, $\chi^2(1) = 4.88, p < 0.05$, whereas COs in Texas were more likely to interact with Holdover inmates, $\chi^2(1) = 11.32$, $p < 0.01$, and drug therapy inmates, $\chi^2(1) = 8.89, p < 0.01$. Ohio and Texas COs did not differ in the mean number of inmates with which they have daily contact.

Appendix C: Training of Interviewers and Reliability of Interview Measures

University of Virginia Coding Team

To establish consistency in coding for interview measures, coders participated in a series of training experiences followed by independent coding of ten cases by all coders. Due to institutional and logistic constraints at the participating prisons, it was not possible to gain additional reliability estimates during the data collection. We therefore estimated our consistency by coding either in-person interviews with community volunteers or coding of videotaped interviews obtained from Robert Hare.

The Structured Interview for DSM-IV of Personality (SIDP-IV)

Coders included an 11-person cohort of interviewers. Members included a doctoral-level social worker, a PhD licensed clinical psychologist, a post-masters-level social worker, and eight post-masters-level doctoral students in clinical psychology.

Coders participated in a two-day workshop regarding the proper administration and scoring of the SIDP-IV, conducted by an experienced clinical psychologist with extensive experience with the instrument. Members subsequently independently coded ten interviews of volunteers recruited from the local region.

Intra class correlation coefficients evaluated the consistency among raters for the ten interviews for continuous personality disorder scores. Results for the continuous scale scores are summarized in Table B1 and ranged from minimally acceptable (*ICC* = 0.60, Histrionic personality disorder) to very good (*ICC* = 0.92, Antisocial personality disorder). Agreement regarding diagnostic category (Meets vs Does Not Meet Diagnostic Criteria) was generally low. Further examination

TABLE C1 Reliability Estimates SIDP-IV University of Virginia Coders: Intraclass Correlation Coefficient

PD	Reliability (ICC)	
	Continuous Scale Score	Dichotomous Diagnostic Criterion
Paranoid	0.67	0.36
Schizoid	0.69	0.32
Schizotypal	0.79	0.33
Antisocial	0.92	0.68
Borderline	0.69	0.29
Histrionic	0.60	0.10
Narcissistic	0.85	0.84
Avoidant	0.78	0.63
Dependent	0.60	0.00
Obsessive-compulsive	0.70	0.85

of individual protocols revealed that the low reliability largely reflected a narrow range that was a consequence of a large number of "zero" responses.

We therefore sought another procedure to further examine our overall agreement. A "standard" was created representing a best estimate of correct diagnosis (presence vs absence) for each of the personality disorders. This standard was created by examination of the final diagnostic decisions made by two members of the interview team with the most extensive history of conducting diagnostic interviews. The two members mutually agreed on decisions regarding cases, and these decisions were compared to those of the remaining team members.

This standard was then applied to the decisions of the remaining members of the team. Results, summarized in Table B2, reflect agreement between raters for diagnostic decisions ranging from a low of 88.8 percent agreement (Antisocial personality disorder) to 100 percent (Schizotypal personality disorder).

TABLE C2 Percent Agreement for Diagnostic Category SIDP-IV

Personality Disorder	% Agreement
Paranoid	92.5
Schizoid	89.8
Schizotypal	100.0
Antisocial	88.8
Borderline	93.8
Histrionic	91.3
Narcissistic	97.5
Avoidant	96.3
Dependent	98.8
Obsessive-compulsive	96.3
Total	94.5

Psychopathy Checklist–Revised 2 (PCL-R2)

All members of the team participated in a two-day workshop regarding the Psychopathy Checklist–Revised 2 (PCL-R 2), conducted by an experienced clinical psychologist with extensive experience with the instrument. Team members independently evaluated ten cases. Cases included eight videotaped cases created by Hare, and two cases of community volunteers.

Intraclass correlation coefficients evaluated the consistency among raters. Agreement for continuous scale scores for Factor 1, Factor 2, and Total PCL-R2 scale were 0.77, 0.82, and 0.84, respectively. Agreement for the dichotomous diagnostic score (30 points Total Score cut-off) was 0.74.

As was undertaken with the SIDP-IV interviews, we also investigated the agreement of eight raters to two experienced raters for the PCL-R2 total diagnostic score. Results indicated 90 percent agreement regarding the diagnostic category (Meets Criteria: At or above 30 points Total PCL-R2 score vs Does Not Meet Criteria: Below PCL-R2 cut-off score of 30 points).

HCR-20 Assessing Risk for Violence

The eleven members of the coding team participated in a day-long workshop conducted by Kevin Douglas, one of the originators of the instrument. In addition, team members met as a group on multiple occasions to further discuss coding procedures for the instrument as described in the coding manual.

Due to time constraints, we were unable to conduct independent coding for volunteers or of videotapes prior to collecting data. We therefore devised a procedure post-interviewing to assess consistency. For each team member, one interview conducted during data collection was selected. Team members then met collectively. Each member of the team read transcribed responses of inmates and answered questions pertaining to session content. The remaining members of the team independently coded responses.

Intraclass coefficients indicated consistency among raters, as gauged in this procedure (historical composite $ICC = 0.82$; clinical composite $ICC = 0.87$; risk composite $ICC = 0.68$). As the HCR-20 does not include specific cut-off criterion diagnostic scores, we were not able to calculate percent agreements as with previous interview measures.

Sam Houston State University Coding Team

Overall, the Texas site had a total of ten coders (one PhD licensed clinical psychologist and nine doctoral students in clinical psychology), though not all coders collected data at every prison. To establish consistency in coding for interview measures, coders participated in a series of training exercises followed by independent coding of training cases. Due to institutional and logistic constraints at the participating prisons, it was not possible to gain additional reliability estimates during the data collection. Therefore, Texas coders estimated consistency by coding videotaped interviews from the Virginia reliability training.

The Structured Interview for DSM-IV Personality (SIDP-IV)

Coders participated in a two-day workshop regarding the proper administration and scoring of the SIDP-IV, conducted by an experienced clinical psychologist with extensive experience with the instrument. Members subsequently independently coded three videotaped interviews from the Virginia training sessions.

Intra class correlation coefficients evaluated the consistency and absolute agreement among raters for the three interviews using the continuous personality disorder scores. Results for the continuous scale scores are summarized in Table B3. Overall, ICC values tended to be strong (i.e., $ICCs \geq 0.85$), with the exception of absolute agreement for Schizoid, Narcissistic, and Schizotypal personality disorder ($ICCs$ of 0.70 to 0.78).

TABLE C3 Reliability Estimates SIDP-IV Sam Houston State University Coders: Intraclass Correlation Coefficients

Personality Disorder	Reliability (ICC)	
	ICC-Consistency Agreement	ICC-Absolute Agreement
Schizoid	0.96	0.70
Avoidant	0.99	0.98
Dependent	0.95	0.95
Obsessive-compulsive	0.90	0.88
Narcissistic	0.85	0.76
Schizotypal	0.88	0.78
Borderline	0.99	0.98
Paranoid	0.95	0.85
Histrionic	0.87	0.90
Antisocial	★	★

Note. ICC values can be reported as a single measure (usually lower) or an average measure (usually higher). In this table, we report single measure values because it was ultimately single rater values (not the averaged score from multiple raters) that was included in the study database for each participant. These single rater values (usually lower) therefore represent a more rigorous measure of interrater reliability. We also report Consistency agreement (which relates to covariance in scores, i.e., did all raters code participant A higher and participant B lower?) as well as Absolute agreement (in which differences *in the specific values* of scores are considered error, i.e., Did all raters score participant A as 12 and participant B as 8?). It is important to examine *consistency* agreement in those situations when it only matters whether raters agree about the relative scores, whereas it is important to consider *absolute* agreement in those situations when specific scores have specific meaning (such as a diagnostic threshold).

★SPSS did not calculate *ICC* values for Antisocial because multiple score values of zero made for minimal variance (and an error message that reads "scale or part of scale has zero variance and will be bypassed"). Qualitatively, we can report that all rater scores on the Antisocial PD scale on practice cases were within one point (on a scale for which scores could range from 0 to 24) of one another.

Psychopathy Checklist–Revised 2 (PCL-R2)

All members of the team participated in a one-day workshop regarding the PCL-R2, conducted by an experienced clinical psychologist with extensive experience with the instrument.

Intraclass correlation coefficients evaluated the consistency among raters. Agreement for continuous scale scores for Factor 1, Factor 2, and Total PCL scale were 0.60, 0.92, and 0.80, respectively. The ICC value for total score agreement is marginal, and poorer than values typically reported in the literature. However, raters demonstrated perfect agreement (i.e., 1.0) for the dichotomous diagnostic score (i.e., above/below the score of 30 conventionally used as cut-off score).

HCR-20 Assessing Risk for Violence

The coding team participated in a formal training conducted by a forensic psychologist who was experienced with the HCR-20. Team members met again as needed to further discuss coding procedures for the instrument, as described in the coding manual. Due to scheduling problems, we conducted a reliability check on only one case, thus it was not possible to calculate meaningful ICC values. However, qualitatively, we can report that all raters scored within +/− one point on the historical scale, within +/− two points on the clinical scale, and within +/− three points on the risk scale.

Appendix D:

TABLE D1 Significant Bivariate Risk Factors by Type of Sex for Incarcerated Men

Men Any Sex	Men Predation	Men Victimization	Men Trade	Men Consensual
PBIS 1. Gender	PBIS 1. Gender	PBIS 1. Gender	ACE Yes/NO any Psych abuse	ACE Yes/NO any Psych abuse
from Texas Data or Ohio Data	from Texas Data or Ohio Data	from Texas Data or Ohio Data	ACE Yes/NO any Physical abuse	ACE Yes/NO any Physical abuse
ACE Yes/NO any Psych abuse	ACE Yes/NO any Psych abuse	ACE Yes/NO any Sexual abuse	ACE Yes/NO any Sexual abuse	ACE Yes/NO any Sexual abuse
ACE Yes/NO any Physical abuse	ACE Yes/NO any Physical abuse	PBIS: LOC	PBIS-Father arrested	PBIS Lived away from home
ACE Yes/NO any Sexual abuse	ACE Yes/NO any Sexual abuse	SAP: Any Sexual Perpetration	PBIS-Father sent to jail/prison	PBIS-Father arrested
ACE Yes/NO any Neglect	PBIS: LOC	PV: Any Perpetration of Relational Aggression	PBIS-Father Psychopathology	PBIS-Father addicted to drugs
PBIS Lived away from home	HCR: young age first violence	PV: Any victimization by Relational Agg	HCR: Early maladjustment – conduct problems	HCR: Early maladjustment – conduct problems
PBIS: LOC	PV: Any Perpetration of Threatened Violence	Weight in lbs	PV: Any Perpetration of Threatened Violence	HCR: young age first violence
PBIS-Mother sent to jail/prison	PV: Any Perpetration of Physical Violence	Height in inches	PV: Any Perpetration of Physical Violence	PVRI: Any Fights since 18
PBIS-Father addicted to drugs	PV: Any Perpetration of Relational Aggression	Body Mass Index	SAP: Any Sexual Perpetration	PV: Any Perpetration of Threatened Violence

HCR: Early maladjustment – conduct problems	PBIS: Sexual orientation Recode	PV: Any Victimization by Threats	PV: Any Perpetration of Physical Violence
HCR: young age first violence	PBIS: Number of sexual partners, categorical coding	PV: Any Victimization by Physical Violence	SAP: Any Sexual Perpetration
PVRI: Any Fights since 18	NAS Behavior Regulation	SAP: Any Non-Consensual Sex	PV: Any Perpetration of Relational Aggression
PV: Any Perpetration of Threatened Violence	NAS Anger Regulation – Summary score	PV: Any victimization by Relational Agg	PV: Any Victimization by Threats
PV: Any Perpetration of Physical Violence	SIDP,ANTX4 irritability and aggressiveness, as indicated by repeated physical fights or assaults	PBIS: Sexual orientation Recode	PV: Any Victimization by Physical Violence
PV: Any Perpetration of Relational Aggression	IFV 11. How much do you worry that you will be attacked by another prisoner during this sentence?	NAS Behavior Regulation	SAP: Any Non-Consensual Sex
PV: Any Victimization by Threats	IFV 13. How much do you worry that you will be sexually assaulted by another inmate during this sentence?	IFV 10. How safe do you feel in prison? (check one)	PV: Any victimization by Relational Agg
		PV: Any Victimization by Threats	

Men Any Sex	Men Predation	Men Victimization	Men Trade	Men Consensual
PV: Any Victimization by Physical Violence	IFV 11. How much do you worry that you will be attacked by another prisoner during this sentence?	IFV 16. How much do you think the correctional officers monitor your living area sufficiently to keep you safe from sexual violence?	PBIS: Age at first sexual experience categorical coding	IFV 5. Do you belong to a prison gang?
PV: Any victimization by Relational Agg	IFV 13. How much do you worry that you will be sexually assaulted by another inmate during this sentence?	PBIS 25b. Others following you or wanting to hurt you physically?	PBIS 35. Since coming to prison, how many orgasms do you have in a normal week?	PBIS: Ethnicity Category
PBIS: Ethnicity Category	SIV1. Did you ever think about physically hurting some other person?	SIDP Diagnose Schizotypal	NAS Arousal mean	PBIS: Age at first sexual experience categorical coding
PBIS: Age at first sexual experience categorical coding	PBIS 25b. Others following you or wanting to hurt you physically?	HCR H2. Young Age at First Violence Incident	SIDP, BORX8 inappropriate, intense anger or difficulty controlling anger	PBIS 35. Since coming to prison, how many orgasms do you have in a normal week?
PBIS 35. Since coming to prison, how many orgasms do you have in a normal week?	PBIS: ANY Threat/ Control Delusions	HCR HD. Early Maladjustment: Victim of Child Abuse	HCR C4. Impulsivity	NAS Cognitive mean
NAS Cognitive mean	SIDP, CANX evidence of conduct disorder before 15 years	HCR CB. Suicidal Ideation	IFV 11. How much do you worry that you will be attacked by another prisoner during this sentence?	NAS Arousal mean

NAS Arousal mean	SIDP Diagnose Antisocial	HCR c3: Active mental illness, combined c3a c3b	NAS Behavior Regulation
NAS Behavior Regulation	SIDP Schizoid continuous	IFV 13. How much do you worry that you will be sexually assaulted by another inmate during this sentence?	NAS Total Score: Cog + Arous + Beh
NAS Total Score: Cog + Arous + Beh	SIDP continuous antisocial – includes criterion C	IFV 18. How much do you think the Warden would take your claim seriously if you were sexually assaulted?	SIDP, BORX8 inappropriate, intense anger or difficulty controlling anger
SIDP, BORX8 inappropriate, intense anger or difficulty controlling anger	HCR HC. Substance Use Problems Associated with Criminality	SIV1. Did you ever think about physically hurting some other person?	SIDP, ANTX4 irritability and aggressiveness, as indicated by repeated physical fights or assaults
SIDP, ANTX4 irritability and aggressiveness, as indicated by repeated physical fights or assaults	HCR CB. Suicidal Ideation	PBIS 25b. Others following you or wanting to hurt you physically?	SIDP, BORX4 impulsivity in at least two areas that are potentially self-damaging
IFV 11. How much do you worry that you will be attacked by another prisoner during this sentence?	VRAG 9. Any female victim (for index offense)	PBIS: ANY Threat/Control Delusions	HCR C4. Impulsivity
		SIDP, CANX evidence of conduct disorder before 15 years	

Men Any Sex	Men Predation	Men Victimization	Men Trade	Men Consensual
IFV 12. How much do you worry that you'll be attacked by a prison guard or staff member during this sentence?			SIDP, ANTX7 lack of remorse, as indicated by being indifferent to or rationalizing having hurt, mistreated, or stolen from another	IFV 11. How much do you worry that you will be attacked by another prisoner during this sentence?
IFV 13. How much do you worry that you will be sexually assaulted by another inmate during this sentence?			PCL DX – 25 cutoff	IFV 12. How much do you worry that you'll be attacked by a prison guard or staff member during this sentence?
SIV1. Did you ever think about physically hurting some other person?			PCL: Antisocial Factor	IFV 13. How much do you worry that you will be sexually assaulted by another inmate during this sentence?
PBIS 25b. Others following you or wanting to hurt you physically?			PCL Hare Total Score	IFV 14. How much do you worry that you will be sexually assaulted by a prison guard or staff member during this sentence?
PBIS: ANY Threat/Control Delusions			SIDP Diagnose Antisocial	SIV1. Did you ever think about physically hurting some other person?
SIDP, CANX evidence of conduct disorder before 15 years			SIDP Diagnose Avoidant	PBIS 25b. Others following you or wanting to hurt you physically?

SIDP, ANTX1 failure to conform to social norms w/ respect to lawful behaviors as indicated by repeatedly performing acts that are grounds for arrest

SIDP, ANTX3 impulsivity or failure to plan ahead

PCL: Antisocial Factor

SIDP Diagnose Antisocial

SIDP continuous antisocial – includes criterion C

SIDP continuous histrionic

HCR HE. Early Maladjustment: Conduct Problems

HCR R1. Plans lack Feasibility

HCR CB. Suicidal Ideation

HCR Risk Factor Traditional

HCR Total Score

VRAG 2. Elementary school maladjustment

VRAG 7. Age at index offense (at most recent birthday)

VRAG total score

PBIS: ANY Threat/Control Delusions

SIDP, CANX evidence of conduct disorder before 15 years

SIDP, ANTX1 failure to conform to social norms w/ respect to lawful behaviors as indicated by repeatedly performing acts that are grounds for arrest

SIDP, ANTX3 impulsivity or failure to plan ahead

SIDP, ANTX5 reckless disregard for the safety of self or others

PCL: Antisocial Factor

PCL Hare Total Score

Men Any Sex	Men Predation	Men Victimization	Men Trade	Men Consensual
HCR HF. Adolescence: Failure to Establish and Maintain Stable Relationships			AGE at time to interview-computed in SPSS	SIDP Diagnose Antisocial
HCR CA. Homicidal Ideation-Evidence of Serious Problems				SIDP Diagnose Histrionic
HCR CB. Suicidal Ideation				SIDP continuous antisocial – includes criterion C
HCR Risk Factor Traditional				SIDP continuous histrionic
HCR Total Score				HCR H2. Young Age at First Violence Incident
VRAG 2. Elementary school maladjustment				HCR R1. Plans lack Feasibility
VRAG 7. Age at index offense (at most recent birthday)				HCR R2. Exposure to Destabilizers
VRAG 11. Meets DSM-III criteria for schizophrenia				HCR HE. Early Maladjustment: Conduct Problems
VRAG total score				HCR HF. Adolescence: Failure to Establish and Maintain Stable Relationships
AGE at time to interview-computed in SPSS				HCR CA. Homicidal Ideation-Evidence of Serious Problems

Significant Bivariate Risk Factors by Type of Sex for Incarcerated Females

Women Any Sex	Women Predation	Women Victimization	Women Trade	Women Consensual
ACE Yes/NO any Psych abuse	ACE Yes/NO any Psych abuse	ACE Yes/NO any Physical abuse	ACE Yes/NO any Neglect	ACE Yes/NO any Sexual abuse
ACE Yes/NO any Physical abuse	ACE Yes/NO any Physical abuse	ACE Yes/NO any Neglect	PV: Any Perpetration of Threatened Violence	ACE Yes/NO any Mothers violence
ACE Yes/NO any Sexual abuse	ACE Yes/NO any Sexual abuse	PV: Any Perpetration of Threatened Violence	PV: Any Perpetration of Physical Violence	PBIS–Mother arrested
				HCR Risk Factor Traditional
				HCR Total Score
				VRAG 2. Elementary school maladjustment
				VRAG 4. Marital status
				VRAG 5. Criminal history score for nonviolent offenses
				VRAG 7. Age at index offense (at most recent birthday)
				VRAG total score
				AGE at time to interview-computed in SPSS

Women Any Sex	Women Predation	Women Victimization	Women Trade	Women Consensual
ACE Yes/NO any Mothers violence	ACE Yes/NO any Mothers violence	PV: Any Perpetration of Relational Aggression	SAP: Any Sexual Perpetration	PBIS-Mother sent to jail/prison
ACE Yes/NO any Neglect	ACE Yes/NO any Neglect	PV: Any Victimization by Threats	PV: Any Perpetration of Relational Aggression	PBIS-Mother addicted to drugs
PBIS-Mother arrested	PBIS-Mother arrested	PV: Any Victimization by Physical Violence	PV: Any Victimization by Threats	PBIS-Father addicted to drugs
PVRI: Any Fights since 18	PVRI: Any Fights since 18	PV: Any victimization by Relational Agg	PV: Any Victimization by Physical Violence	PVRI: Any Fights since 18
PV: Any Perpetration of Threatened Violence	PV: Any Perpetration of Threatened Violence	HCR C4. Impulsivity	PBIS: Sexual orientation Recode	PV: Any Perpetration of Threatened Violence
PV: Any Perpetration of Physical Violence	PV: Any Perpetration of Physical Violence	IFV 11. How much do you worry that you will be attacked by another prisoner during this sentence?	PBIS 34. Before coming to prison, how many orgasms did you have in a normal week?	PV: Any Perpetration of Physical Violence
PV: Any Perpetration of Relational Aggression	PV: Any Perpetration of Relational Aggression	IFV 12. How much do you worry that you'll be attacked by a prison guard or staff member during this sentence?	PBIS 35. Since coming to prison, how many orgasms do you have in a normal week?	SAP: Any Sexual Perpetration
PV: Any Victimization by Threats	PV: Any Victimization by Threats	IFV 13. How much do you worry that you will be sexually assaulted by another inmate during this sentence?	NAS Anger Regulation – Summary score	PV: Any Perpetration of Relational Aggression

PV: Any Victimization by Physical Violence	PV: Any Victimization by Physical Violence	IFV 14. How much do you worry that you will be sexually assaulted by a prison guard or staff member during this sentence?	NAS Total Score: Cog + Arous + Beh	PV: Any Victimization by Threats
PV: Any victimization by Relational Agg	PV: Any victimization by Relational Agg	IFV 16. How much do you think the correctional officers monitor your living area sufficiently to keep you safe from sexual violence?	HCR C4. Impulsivity	PV: Any Victimization by Physical Violence
IFV 5. Do you belong to a prison gang?	IFV 5. Do you belong to a prison gang?	PBIS 25b. Others following you or wanting to hurt you physically?	PCL DX – 30 cutoff	PV: Any victimization by Relational Agg
PBIS: Ethnicity Category	PBIS: Ethnicity Category	PBIS: ANY Threat/ Control Delusions	SIDP Diagnose Narcissistic	IFV 5. Do you belong to a prison gang?
PBIS: Sexual orientation Recode	PBIS: Sexual orientation Recode	SIDP Diagnose Dependent	SIDP continuous narcissistic	PBIS: Sexual orientation Recode
PCL-R: Promiscuity (Yes/No)	PCL-R: Promiscuity (Yes/No)	SIDP continuous histrionic	HCR H7. Psychopathy *coded from PCL	PBIS: Age at first sexual experience categorical coding

Women Any Sex	Women Predation	Women Victimization	Women Trade	Women Consensual
PBIS 34. Before coming to prison, how many orgasms did you have in a normal week?	PBIS 34. Before coming to prison, how many orgasms did you have in a normal week?	SIDP continuous paranoid	HCR CB. Suicidal Ideation	PCL-R:Promiscuity (Yes/No)
PBIS 35. Since coming to prison, how many orgasms do you have in a normal week?	PBIS 35. Since coming to prison, how many orgasms do you have in a normal week?	HCR CB. Suicidal Ideation	HCR h6 History of mental illness, combined 6a and 6b	PBIS 34. Before coming to prison, how many orgasms did you have in a normal week?
PBIS: Number of sexual partners, categorical coding	PBIS: Number of sexual partners, categorical coding			PBIS 35. Since coming to prison, how many orgasms do you have in a normal week?
NAS Cognitive mean	NAS Cognitive mean			PBIS: Number of sexual partners, categorical coding
NAS Total Score: Cog + Arous + Beh	NAS Total Score: Cog + Arous + Beh			NAS Cognitive mean
SIDP, BOR X4 impulsivity in at least two areas that are potentially self-damaging	SIDP, BOR X4 impulsivity in at least two areas that are potentially self-damaging			NAS Arousal mean
IFV 16. How much do you think the correctional officers monitor your living area sufficiently to keep you safe from sexual violence?	IFV 16. How much do you think the correctional officers monitor your living area sufficiently to keep you safe from sexual violence?			NAS Total Score: Cog + Arous + Beh

SIV1. Did you ever think about physically hurting some other person?

SIV1. Did you ever think about physically hurting some other person?

PBIS 25b. Others following you or wanting to hurt you physically?

PBIS 25b. Others following you or wanting to hurt you physically?

PBIS: ANY Threat/Control Delusions

PBIS: ANY Threat/Control Delusions

SIDP, CANX evidence of conduct disorder before 15 years

SIDP, CANX evidence of conduct disorder before 15 years

SIDP, ANTX1 failure to conform to social norms w/ respect to lawful behaviors as indicated by repeatedly performing acts that are grounds for arrest

SIDP, ANTX1 failure to conform to social norms w/ respect to lawful behaviors as indicated by repeatedly performing acts that are grounds for arrest

SIDP, ANTX5 reckless disregard for the safety of self or others

SIDP, ANTX5 reckless disregard for the safety of self or others

SIDP, ANTX4 irritability and aggressiveness, as indicated by repeated physical fights or assaults

SIDP, BORX4 impulsivity in at least two areas that are potentially self-damaging

HCR C4. Impulsivity

IFV 11. How much do you worry that you will be attacked by another prisoner during this sentence?

IFV 12. How much do you worry that you'll be attacked by a prison guard or staff member during this sentence?

IFV 13. How much do you worry that you will be sexually assaulted by another inmate during this sentence?

Women Any Sex	Women Predation	Women Victimization	Women Trade	Women Consensual
PCL: Antisocial Factor	PCL: Antisocial Factor			IFV 14. How much do you worry that you will be sexually assaulted by a prison guard or staff member during this sentence?
SIDP Diagnose Antisocial	SIDP Diagnose Antisocial	SIDP Diagnose Antisocial		IFV 16. How much do you think the correctional officers monitor your living area sufficiently to keep you safe from sexual violence?
SIDP Diagnose Narcissistic	SIDP Diagnose Narcissistic			SIV1. Did you ever think about physically hurting some other person?
SIDP continuous histrionic	SIDP continuous histrionic			SIDP, CANX evidence of conduct disorder before 15 years
SIDP continuous antisocial – includes criterion C	SIDP continuous antisocial – includes criterion C			SIDP, ANTX1 failure to conform to social norms w/ respect to lawful behaviors as indicated by repeatedly performing acts that are grounds for arrest
SIDP continuous narcissistic	SIDP continuous narcissistic			SIDP, ANTX5 reckless disregard for the safety of self or others
HCR H2. Young Age at First Violence Incident	HCR H2. Young Age at First Violence Incident			PCL: Antisocial Factor
HCR CB. Suicidal Ideation	HCR CB. Suicidal Ideation			PCL Hare Total Score

VRAG 7. Age at index offense (at most recent birthday)

VRAG total score

AGE at time to interview-computed in SPSS

VRAG 7. Age at index offense (at most recent birthday)

VRAG total score

AGE at time to interview-computed in SPSS

SIDP Diagnose Antisocial

SIDP Diagnose Narcissistic

SIDP Schizoid continuous

SIDP Schizotypal continuous

SIDP continuous antisocial – includes criterion C

SIDP continuous narcissistic

HCR H1. Previous Violence

HCR H2. Young Age at First Violence Incident

HCR HE. Early Maladjustment: Conduct Problems

HCR CA. Homicidal Ideation-Evidence of Serious Problems

HCR CB. Suicidal Ideation

VRAG 7. Age at index offense (at most recent birthday)

VRAG total score

AGE at time to interview-computed in SPSS

REFERENCES

American Psychiatric Association. (2000). *Diagnostic and statistical manual of mental disorders* (4th ed., text revision). Washington, DC: American Psychiatric Association.

Anda, R. F., Croft, J. B., Felitti, V. J., Nordenberg, D., Giles, W. H., Williamson, D. F., et al. (1999). Adverse childhood experiences and smoking during adolescence and adulthood. *Journal of the American Medical Association, 282,* 1652–1658.

Anda, R. F., Felitti, V. J., Chapman, D. P., Croft, J. B., Williamson, D. F., Santelli, J., et al. (2001). Abused boys, battered mothers, and male involvement in teen pregnancy. *Pediatrics, 107,* 19–26.

Andersen, S. L., & Teicher, M. H. (2009). Desperately driven and no brakes: Developmental stress exposure and subsequent risk for substance abuse. *Neuroscience & Biobehavioral Reviews, 33*(4), 516–524.

Aquilino, W. S. (1994). Interview mode effects in surveys of drug and alcohol use: A field experiment. *Public Opinion Quarterly, 58,* 210–240.

Augimeri, L. K., Webster, C. D., Koegl, C. J., & Levene, K. S. (1998). *Early assessment risk list for boys: EARL-20B* (Version 1 Consultation Edition). Toronto, Canada: Earlscourt Child & Family Centre.

Augimeri, L. K., Koegl, C. J., Webster, C. D., & Levene, K. (2001). *The Early Assessment Risk List for Boys (EARL-20B)–Version 2.* Toronto, Canada: Earlscourt Child and Family Centre.

Austin, J., Fabelo, T., Gunter, A., & McGinnis, K. (2006). *Sexual Violence in the Texas Prison System.* Washington, DC: JFA Institute.

Babcock, J. C., Miller, S. A., & Siard, C. (2003). Toward a typology of abusive women: Differences between partner-only and generally violent women in the use of violence. *Psychology of Women Quarterly, 27*(2), 153–161.

Bachman, R. (2000). A comparison of annual incidence rates and contextual characteristics of intimate-partner violence against women from the National Crime Victimization Survey (NCVS) and the National Violence Against Women Survey (NVAWS). *Violence Against Women, 6*(8), 839–867.

Bandura, A. (1973). *Aggression: A social learning analysis.* Oxford, UK: Prentice-Hall.

Barbaree, H. E., & Seto, M. C. (1998). *The Ongoing Follow-up of Sex Offenders Treated at the Warkworth Sexual Behavior Clinic.* Toronto, Canada: Centre for Addiction and Mental Health.

Bard, L. A., Carter, D. L., Cerce, D. D., Knight, R. A., Rosenberg, R., & Schneider, B. (1987). A descriptive study of rapists and child molesters: Developmental, clinical, and criminal characteristics. *Behavioral Sciences and the Law, 5,* 203–220.

Barnfield, T. V., & Leathem, J. M. (1998). Incidence and outcomes of traumatic brain injury and substance abuse in a New Zealand prison population. *Brain Injury, 12,* 455–466.

Barratt, E. S. (1991). Measuring and predicting aggression within the context of a personality theory. *Journal of Neuropsychiatry and Clinical Neurosciences, 3*(2), S35–S53.

Barratt, E. S., Stanford, M., Kent, T., & Felthous, A. (1997). Neuropsychological and cognitive psychophysiological substrates of impulsive aggression. *Biological Psychiatry, 41,* 1045–1061.

Beck, A. J., & Hughes, T. (2005). *Sexual violence reported by correctional authorities, 2004* (NCJ No. 020656). Washington, DC: US Department of Justice, Bureau of Justice Statistics.

Beck, A. J., & Harrison, P. M. (2006). *Sexual violence reported by correctional authorities, 2005* (NCJ No. 214646). Washington, DC: US Department of Justice, Bureau of Justice Statistics.

Beck, A. J., & Harrison, P. M. (2007). *Sexual victimization in local jails reported by inmates, 2007* (NCJ No. 221946). Washington, DC: US Department of Justice, Bureau of Justice Statistics.

Beck, A. J., & Harrison, P. M. (2008). *Sexual victimization in state and federal prisons reported by inmates, 2007* (NCJ No. 219414). Washington, DC: US Department of Justice, Bureau of Justice Statistics.

Beck, A. J., Harrison, P. M., & Adams, D. B. (2007). *Sexual violence reported by correctional authorities, 2006* (NCJ No. 218914). Washington, DC: US Department of Justice, Bureau of Justice Statistics.

Beck, A. T., Steer, R. A., & Brown, K. G. (1996). *Beck Depression Inventory–Second Edition Manual.* San Antonio, TX: The Psychological Corporation.

Belfrage, H., Fransson, R., & Strand, S. (2000). Prediction of violence using the HCR-20: A prospective study in two maximum-security correctional institutions. *The Journal of Forensic Psychiatry, 11*(1), 167–175.

Bensley, L. B., Speiker, S. J., van Eenwyck, J., & Schoder, J. (1999a). Self-reported abuse history and adolescent problem behaviors: I. Antisocial and suicidal behaviors. *Journal of Adolescent Health, 24,* 163–172.

Bensley, L. B., Speiker, S. J., van Eenwyck, J., & Schoder, J. (1999b). Self-reported abuse history and adolescent problem behaviors: II. Alcohol and drug use. *Journal of Adolescent Health, 24,* 173–180.

Bentler, P. M. (1968). Heterosexual behavior assessment: I. Males. *Behavior Research Therapy, 6,* 21–25.

Bingham, C. R., & Crockett, L. J. (1996). Longitudinal adjustment patterns of boys and girls experiencing early, middle, and late sexual intercourse. *Developmental Psychology, 32,* 647–658.

Blackburn, R. (2007). Personality disorder and antisocial deviance: comments on the debate on the structure of the psychopathy checklist-revised. *Journal of Personality Disorders, 21,* 142–159.

Blackburn, R., & Coid, J. W. (1998). Psychopathy and the dimensions of personality disorder in violent offenders. *Personality and Individual Differences, 25,* 129–145.

Blackburn, R., Logan, C., Donnelly, J., & Renwick, S. (2003). Personality disorders, psychopathy, and other mental disorders: Co-morbidity among patients at English and Scottish high-security hospitals. *Journal of Forensic Psychiatry, 14,* 111–137.

Blumstein, A., Cohen, J., Roth, J., & Visher, C. (Eds.). (1986). *Criminal careers and "career criminals": Volume I.* Washington, DC: National Academy Press.

Booz – Allen – Hamilton. (June, 2010). *Prison Rape Elimination Act (PREA): Cost Impact Analysis.* Final Report. Accessed April 30, 2012 http://www.ojp.usdoj.gov/programs/pdfs/preacostimpactanalysis.pdf

Borum, R., Bartel, P., & Forth, A. (2002). *SAVRY: Manual for the structured assessment of violence risk in youth.* Tampa, FL: Florida Mental Health Institute, University of South Florida.

Bowker, L. (1980). *Prison victimization.* New York, NY: Elsevier.

Bowlby, J. (1969). *Attachment and loss.* New York, NY: Basic Books.

Bremner, J. D., Randall, P., Vermetten, E., Staib, L., Bronen, R. A., Mazure, C., Capelli, S., McCarthy, G., Innis, R. B., & Charney, D. S. (1997). Magnetic resonance imaging-based measurement of hippocampal volume in posttraumatic stress disorder related to childhood physical and sexual abuse. *Biological Psychiatry, 41*(1), 23–32.

Brown, S. L., & Forth, A. E. (1997). Psychopathy and sexual assault: Static risk factors, emotional precursors, and rapist subtypes. *Journal of Consulting and Clinical Psychology, 65,* 848–857.

Byrne, J., & Hummer, D. (2007). In search of the "Tossed Salad Man" (and others involved in prison violence): New strategies for predicting and controlling violence in prison. *Aggression and Violent Behavior, 12,* 531–541.

Carrion, V. G., Weems, C. F., Eliez, S., Patwardhan, A., Brown, W., Ray, R. D., & Reiss, A. L. (2001). Attenuation of frontal asymmetry in pediatric posttraumatic stress disorder. *Biological Psychiatry, 50,* 943–951.

Casey, P. (2000). The epidemiology of personality disorders. In P. Tyrer (Ed.), *Personality disorders: Diagnosis, management, and course* (2nd ed., pp. 71–79). Oxford UK: Butterworth Heinemann.

Catania, J. A. (1999). A framework for conceptualizing reporting bias and its antecedents in interviews assessing human sexuality. *The Journal of Sex Research, 36,* 25–38.

Chaiken, J. M. (1998). *Compendium of federal justice statistics, 1994* (NCJ No. 163063). Washington, DC: US Department of Justice, Bureau of Justice Statistics.

Chase, K. A., O'Leary, K. D., & Heyman, R. E. (2001). Categorizing partner-violent men within the reactive-proactive typology model. *Journal of Consulting and Clinical Psychology, 69,* 567–572.

Cherek, D. R., & Lane, S. D. (1999). Effects of D- and DL- Fenfluramine on human aggressiveness and impulsivity. *Behavioral Pharmacology, 9,* 24–32.

Chivers, M. L., Rieger, G., Latty, E., & Bailey, J. M. (2004). A sex difference in the specificity of sexual arousal. *Psychological Science, 15*(11), 736–744.

Chonco, N. R. (1989). Sexual assaults among male inmates: A descriptive study. *The Prison Journal, 69,* 72–82.

Cleckley, H. M. (1941). *The mask of sanity: An attempt to reinterpret the so-called psychopathic personality.* St. Louis, MO: The CV Mosby Company.

Clements, C. B., Althouse, R., Ax, R. K., Magaletta, P. R., Fagan, T. J., & Wormith, J. S. (2007). Systemic issues and correctional outcomes: Expanding the scope of correctional psychology. *Criminal Justice and Behavior, 34*(7), 919–932.

Cohen, M., Deamant, C., Barkan, S., Richardson, J., Young, M., Holman, S., Anastos, K., Cohen, J., & Melnick, S. (2000). Domestic violence and childhood sexual abuse in

HIV-infected women and women at risk for HIV. *American Journal of Public Health, 90*, 560–565.

Coid, J. (1992). DSM-III diagnosis in criminal psychopaths: A way forward. *Criminal Behavior and Mental Health, 2*, 78–79.

Coid, J., Petruckevitch, A., Feder, G., Chung, W., Richardson, J., & Moorey, S. (2001). Relation between childhood sexual and physical abuse and risk of revictimisation in women: A cross-sectional survey. *The Lancet, 358*, 450–454.

Columbia Human Rights Law Review (2009). *A jailhouse lawyer's manual* (8th ed.). Available from http://xa.yimg.com/kq/groups/16831155/909208821/name/Jailhouse+Lawyers+Manual.pdf

Convit, A., Jaeger, J., Lin, S. P., Meisner, M., & Volavka, J. (1988). Predicting assaultiveness in psychiatric inpatients: A pilot study. *Hospital Community Psychiatry, 39*, 429–434.

Cooke, D. J., & Michie, C. (2001). Refining the construct of psychopathy: Towards a hierarchical model. *Psychological Assessment, 13*, 177–188.

Cornell, D. G., Warren, J., Hawk, G., Stafford, E., Oram, G., & Pine, D. (1996). Psychopathy in instrumental and reactive violent offenders. *Journal of Consulting and Clinical Psychology, 64*, 783–790.

Crouch, B. M., & Marquart, J. W. (1989). *Appeal to justice: Litigated reform to Texas prisons.* Austin, TX: University of Texas Press.

Dahle, K. P. (2006). Strengths and limitations of actuarial prediction of criminal reoffense in a German prison sample: A comparative study of LSI–R, HCR–20 and PCL–R. *International Journal of Law and Psychiatry, 29*, 431–442.

Daniel, A. E., Robins, A. J., Reid, J. C., & Wilfley, D. E. (1988). Lifetime and six-month prevalence of psychiatric disorders among sentenced female offenders. *Bulletin of American Academy of Psychiatry & the Law, 16*, 333–342.

Davis, A. J. (1968). Sexual assaults in the Philadelphia prison system and sheriff's vans. *Trans-Action, 6*, 8–16.

Davison, S., Leese, M., & Taylor, P. J. (2001). Examination of the screening properties of the Personality Diagnostic Questionnaire 4+ (PDQ-4+) in a prison population. *Journal of Personality Disorders, 15*, 180–194.

De Bellis, M. D., Keshavan, M. S., Clark, D. B., Casey, B. J., Giedd, J. N., Boring, A. M., Frustaci, K., Ryan, N. D. (1999). Developmental traumatology: Part II. Brain development. *Biological Psychiatry, 45*(10), 1271–1284.

De Bellis, M. D., Keshavan, M. S., Spencer, S., & Hall, J. (2000). N-Acetylaspartate concentration in the anterior cingulate of maltreated children and adolescents with PTSD. *American Journal of Psychiatry, 157*(7), 1175–1177.

De Bellis, M. D., Keshavan, M. S., Frustaci, K., Shifflett, H., Iyengar, S., Beers, S. R., & Hall, J. (2002). Superior temporal gyrus volumes in maltreated children and adolescents with PTSD. *Biological Psychiatry, 51*(7), 544–552.

De Bellis, M. D., Keshavan, M. S., Shifflett, H., Iyengar, S., Beers, S. R., Hall, J., & Moritz, J. (2002). Brain structures in pediatric maltreatment-related posttraumatic stress disorder: A sociodemographically matched study. *Biological Psychiatry, 52*(11), 1066–1078.

de Vogel, V., & de Ruiter, C. (2005). The HCR-20 in personality disordered female offenders: a comparison with a matched sample of males. *Clinical Psychology & Psychotherapy, 12*, 226–240.

Dietz, P. M., Spitz, A. M., Anda, R. F., Williamson, D. F., McMahon, P. M., Santelli, J. S., et al. (1999). Unintended pregnancy among adult women exposed to abuse or household dysfunction during their childhood. *The Journal of The American Medical Association, 282*, 1359–1364.

Dodge, K. A., Price, J. M., Coie, J. D., & Christopoulos, C. (1990). On the development of aggressive dyadic relationships in boys' peer groups. *Human Development, 33,* 260–270.

Dolan, K., Lowe, D., & Shearer, J. (2004). Evaluation of the condom distribution program in New South Wales Prisons, Australia. *Journal of Law, Medicine, & Ethics, 32,* 124–128.

Douglas, K. S., & Webster, C. D. (1999). The HCR-20 violence risk assessment scheme: Concurrent validity in a sample of incarcerated offenders. *Criminal Justice and Behavior, 26,* 3–19.

Douglas, K. S., & Weir, J. (2003). *HCR-20 violence risk assessment scheme: Overview and annotated bibliography.* University of South Florida. Available from http://www.cvp.se/publications/downloadables/hcr%2020%20annotated%20bibliography.pdf

Douglas, K. S., Webster, C. D., Hart, S. D., Eaves, D., & Ogloff, J. R. P. (2001). *The HCR-20 violence risk management companion guide.* Vancouver, Canada: Mental Health, Law, and Policy Institute, Simon Fraser University.

Douglas, K. S., Ogloff, J. R. P., & Hart, S. D. (2003). Evaluation of a model of violence risk assessment among forensic psychiatric patients. *Psychiatric Services, 54,* 1372–1379.

Douglas, K. S., Guy, L. S., Reeves, K. A., & Weir, J. (2008). *HCR-20 violence risk assessment scheme: Overview and annotated bibliography.* Available from: http://kdouglas.files.wordpress.com/2006/04/annotate10-24nov2008.pdf

Driessen, M., Herrmann, J., Stahl, K., Zwaan, M., Meier, S., Hill, A., Osterheider, M., & Petersen, D. (2000). Magnetic resonance imaging volumes of the hippocampus and the amygdala in women with borderline personality disorder and early traumatization. *Archives of General Psychiatry, 57*(12), 1115–1122.

Dube, S. R., Anda, R. F., Felitti, V. J., Chapman, D. P., Williamson, D. F., & Giles, W. H. (2001). Childhood abuse, household dysfunction, and the risk of attempted suicide throughout the life span. *The Journal of the American Medical Association, 286,* 3089–3096.

Dumond, R. W. (2003). Confronting America's most ignored crime problem: The prison rape elimination act of 2003. *The Journal of the American Academy of Psychiatry and the Law, 31,* 354–360.

Earls, F., & Barnes, J. (1997). Understanding and preventing child abuse in urban settings. In J. McCord (Ed.), *Violence and childhood in the inner city* (pp. 207–255). Cambridge, UK: Cambridge University Press.

Eaves, D., Douglas, K. S., Webster, C. D., Ogloff, J. R. P. & Hart, S. D. (2000). *Dangerous and long-term offenders: An assessment guide.* Burnaby, Canada: Mental Health Law & Policy Institute, Simon Fraser University.

Edens, J. F., Buffington-Vollum, J. K., Keilen, A., Roskamp, P., & Anthony, C. (2005). Predictions of future dangerousness in capital murder trials: Is it time to "disinvent the wheel?" *Law and Human Behavior, 29,* 55–86.

Edwards, V. J., Holden, G. W., Felitti, V. J., & Anda, R. F. (2003). Relationship between multiple forms of childhood maltreatment and adult mental health in community respondents: Results from the adverse childhood experiences study. *American Journal of Psychiatry, 160,* 1453–1460.

Eigenberg, H. M. (2000). Correctional officers' definitions of rape in male prisons. *Journal of Criminal Justice Review, 28,* 435–449.

El-Bassel, N., Gilbert, L., Schilling, R. F., Ivanoff, A., Borne, D., & Safyer, S. F. (1996). Correlates of crack abuse among drug-using incarcerated women: Psychological trauma, social support, and coping behavior. *American Journal of Drug & Alcohol Abuse, 22,* 41–56.

Ellis, L., & Walsh, A. (2000). *Criminology: A global perspective.* Boston, MA: Allyn and Bacon.

Fagan, J. A., & Wexler, S. (1988). Explanations of sexual assault among violent delinquents. *Journal of Adolescent Research, 3,* 363–385.

Fagot, B. I., Pears, K. C., Capaldi, D. M., Crosby, L., & Leve, C. S. (1998). Becoming an adolescent father: Precursors and parenting. *Developmental Psychology, 35*, 1209–1219.

Farrington, D. P. (1989). Early predictors of adolescent aggression and adult violence. *Violence and Victims, 4*, 79–100.

Fazel, S., & Danesh, J. (2002). Serious mental disorder in 23,000 prisoners: A systematic review of 62 surveys. *The Lancet, 359*, 545–550.

Felitti, V. J., Anda, R. F., Nordenberg, D., Williamson, D. F., Spitz, A. M., Edwards, V., Koss, M. P., & Marks, J. S. (1998). Relationship of childhood abuse and household dysfunction to many of the leading causes of death in adults: The Adverse Childhood Experiences (ACE) study. *American Journal of Preventative Medicine, 14*, 245–258.

Finkelhor, D., Turner, H., Ormrod, R., & Hamby, S. L. (2009). Violence, abuse, and crime exposure in a national sample of children and youth. *Pediatrics, 124*, 1–13.

Fisher, B. S., Cullen, F. T., & Turner, M. G. (2000). *The sexual victimization of college women* (NCJ No. 182369). Washington, DC: US Department of Justice, Bureau of Justice Statistics.

Fishman, J. (1951). *Sex in prison*. London, UK: John Lane, Bodley Head.

Fleisher, M. S., & Krienert, J. L. (2006). *The culture of prison sexual violence* (NCJ Publication No. 216515). Rockville, MD: US Department of Justice, National Institute of Justice.

Fleisher, M. S., & Krienert, J. L. (2009). *The myth of prison rape: Sexual culture in American prisons*. Lanham, MD: Rowman & Littlefield Publishers.

Foti, S. M. (1995). Child sexual abuse as a precursor to prostitution. *Dissertation Abstracts International: Section B: The Sciences & Engineering, 55*, 3586.

Fromuth, M. E., & Conn, V. E. (1997). Hidden perpetrators: Sexual molestation in a nonclinical sample of college women. *Journal of Interpersonal Violence, 12*, 456–465.

Gacono, C. B. (2000). *The clinical and forensic assessment of psychopathy: A practitioner's guide*. Hillsdale, NJ: Lawrence Erlbaum.

Gaes, G. G., & Goldberg, A. L. (2004). *Prison rape: A critical review of the literature*. Washington, DC: US Department of Justice.

Gaes, G. G., Wallace, S., Gilman, E., Klein-Saffran, J., & Suppa, S. (2002). The influence of prison gang affiliation on violence and other prison misconduct. *The Prison Journal, 82*, 359–385.

Gendreau, P., Goggin, C. E., & Law, M. A. (1997). Predicting prison misconducts. *Criminal Justice and Behavior, 24*, 414–431.

Gendreau, P., Goggin, C., & Smith, P. (2002). Is the PCL-R really the "unparalleled" measure of offender risk? A lesson in knowledge accumulation. *Criminal Justice and Behavior, 29*, 397–426.

Giallombardo, R. (1966). *Society of women: A study of a women's prison*. New York, NY: John Wiley.

Golden, D. M. (2006, June). *The prison litigation reform act: A proposal for closing the loophole for rapists*. Washington, DC: American Constitution Society for Law and Policy.

Gordon, M. S. (2006). Correctional officer control ideology: Implications for understanding a system. *Criminal Justice Studies: A Critical Journal of Crime, Law and Society, 19*(3), 225–239.

Gover, A. R., Pérez, D. M., & Jennings, W. G. (2008). Gender differences in factors contributing to institutional misconduct. *The Prison Journal, 88*, 378–403.

Grant, B. F., Hasin, D. S., Stinson, F. S., Dawson, D. A., Chou, S. P., Ruan, W. J., & Pickering, R. P. (2004). Prevalence, correlates, and disability of personality disorders in the United States: Results from the national epidemiologic survey on alcohol and related conditions. *Journal of Clinical Psychiatry, 65*, 948–958.

Gray, N. S., Fitzgerald, S., Taylor, J., MacCulloch, M. J., & Snowden, R. J. (2007). Predicting future reconviction in offenders with intellectual disabilities: The predictive efficacy of VRAG, PCL-SV and the HCR-20. *Psychological Assessment, 19*, 474–479.

Greenfeld, L. A., & Snell, T. L. (1999). *Women offenders* (NCJ Publication No. 175688). Washington, DC: US Department of Justice, Bureau of Justice Statistics.

Greer, K. R. (2000). The changing nature of interpersonal relationships in women's prison. *The Prison Journal, 80*, 442–468.

Grella, C. E., Stein, J. A., & Greenwell, L. (2005). Associations among childhood trauma, adolescent problem behaviors, and adverse adult outcomes in substance-abusing women offenders. *Psychology of Addictive Behaviors, 19*(1), 43–53.

Grisso, T., Davis, J., Vesselinov, R., Appelbaum, P. S., & Monahan, J. (2000). Violent thoughts and violent behavior following hospitalization for mental disorder. *Journal of Consulting and Clinical Psychology, 68*, 388–398.

Groth, A. N., Burgess, W., & Holmstrom, I. L. (1977). Rape: power, anger, and sexuality. *American Journal of Psychiatry, 134*, 1239–1243.

Hagan, M. P., & Gust-Brey, K. L. (1999). A ten-year longitudinal study of adolescent rapists upon return to the community. *International Journal of Offender Therapy and Comparative Criminology, 43*(4), 448–458.

Halleck, S. L., & Hersko, M. (1962). Homosexual behavior in a correctional institution for adolescent girls. *American Journal of Orthopsychiatry, 32*, 911–917.

Hammett, T. M., Maruschak, L., & Harmon, P. (1999). *1996–1997 update: HIV/AIDS, STDs, and TB in correctional facilities.* Washington, DC: National Institute of Justice, Bureau of Justice Statistics, and Centers for Disease Control and Prevention.

Hanson, R. K., & Morton-Bourgon, K. E. (2004). *Predictors of sexual recidivism: An updated meta-analysis* (Corrections Research User Report No. 2004–02). Ottawa, Ontario, Canada: Public Safety and Emergency Preparedness Canada.

Hare, R. D. (1978). Electrodermal and cardiovascular correlates of psychopathy. In R. D. Hare & D. Schalling (Eds.), *Psychopathic behavior: Approaches to research* (pp. 107–143). New York, NY: Wiley.

Hare, R. D. (1991). *The Hare Psychopathy Checklist–Revised.* Toronto, Canada: Multi-Health Systems.

Hare, R. D. (2003). *Manual for the psychopathy checklist* (2nd ed.). Toronto, Canada: Multi-Health Systems.

Hare, R. D., Clark, D., Grann, M., & Thornton, D. (2000). Psychopathy and the predictive validity of the PCL-R: An international perspective. *Behavioral Sciences & the Law, 18*, 623–645.

Harer, M. D., & Steffensmeier, D. J. (1996). Race and prison violence. *Criminology, 34*, 323–351.

Harer, M. D., & Langan, N. P. (2001). Gender differences in predictors of prison violence: Assessing the predictive validity of a risk classification system. *Crime & Delinquency, 47*, 513–536.

Harpur, T. J., Hakstian, A. R., & Hare, R. D. (1988). Factor structure of the Psychopathy Checklist. *Journal of Consulting and Clinical Psychology, 56*, 741–747.

Harpur, T. J., Hare, R. D., & Hakstian, A. R. (1989). Two-factor conceptualization of psychopathy: Construct validity and assessment implications. *Psychological Assessment, 1*, 6–17.

Harris, G. T., Rice, M. E., & Quinsey, V. L. (1993). Violent recidivism of mentally disordered offenders: The development of a statistical prediction instrument. *Criminal Justice and Behavior, 20*, 315–335.

Harris, G. T., Rice, M. E., & Cormier, C. A. (2002). Prospective replication of the Violence Risk Appraisal Guide in predicting violent recidivism among forensic patients. *Law and Human Behavior, 26*, 377–394.

Harris, G. T., Rice, M. E., Quinsey, V. L., Lalumière, M. L., Boer, D., & Lang, C. (2003). A multi-site comparison of actuarial risk instruments for sex offenders. *Psychological Assessment, 15*, 413–425.

Harris, G. T., Rice, M. E., & Camilleri, J. A. (2004). Applying a forensic actuarial assessment (the Violence Risk Appraisal Guide) to nonforensic patients. *Journal of Interpersonal Violence, 19*, 1063–1074.

Hart, S. D., Cox, D. N., & Hare, R. D. (1995). *Manual for the Psychopathy Checklist: Screening version (PCL:SV)*. Toronto, Canada: Multi-Health Systems.

Hart, S. D., Kropp, P. R., & Hare, R. D. (1988). Performance of male psychopaths following conditional release from prison. *Journal of Consulting and Clinical Psychology, 56*, 227–232.

Hazelwood R. R. (1987). Analyzing the rape and profiling the offender. In R. R. Hazelwood, & A. W. Burgess (Eds.), *Practical aspects of rape investigation* (pp. 169–199). New York, NY: Elsevier.

Hazelwood R. R. (2008). Analyzing the rape and profiling the offender. In R. R. Hazelwood & A. W. Burgess (Eds.), *Practical aspects of rape investigation: A multidisciplinary approach* (4th ed., pp. 97–122). Boca Raton, FL: CRC Press.

Hazelwood, R. R., & Burgess, A. W. (Eds.). (2001). *Practical aspects of rape investigation: A multidisciplinary approach* (3rd ed.). Boca Raton, FL: CRC Press.

Heilbrun, K., Hart, S. D., Hare, R. D., Gustafson, D., Nunez, C., & White, A. J. (1998). Inpatient and postdischarge aggression in mentally disordered offenders. *Journal of Interpersonal Violence, 13*, 514–527.

Hemmens, C., & Marquart, J. W. (1999). Straight time: Inmates' perceptions of violence and victimization in the prison environment. *Journal of Offender Rehabilitation, 28*, 1–21.

Hemphill, J. F., Hare, R. D., & Wong, S. (1998). Psychopathy and recidivism: A review. *Legal and Criminological Psychology, 3*, 139–170.

Hensley, C. (2001). Consensual homosexual activity in male prisons. *Corrections Compendium, 26*, 1–4.

Hensley, C. (2002). Introduction: Life and sex in prison. In C. Hensley (Ed.), *Prison sex: Practice and policy* (pp. 1–12). Boulder, CO: Lynn Rienner Publishers.

Hensley, C., Struckman-Johnson, C., & Eigenberg, H. M. (2000). Introduction: The history of prison sex research. *The Prison Journal, 80*, 360–367.

Hensley, C., Tewksbury, R., & Wright, J. (2001). Exploring the dynamics of masturbation and consensual same-sex activity within a male maximum security prison. *The Journal of Men's Studies, 10*(1), 59–71.

Hensley, C., Tewksbury, R., & Koscheski, M. (2002). The characteristics and motivations behind female prison sex. *Women and Criminal Justice, 13*, 125–139.

Hensley, C., Castle, T., & Tewksbury, R. (2003). Inmate-to-inmate sexual coercion in a prison for women. *Journal of Offender Rehabilitation, 37*, 77–87.

Hensley, C., Tewksbury, R., & Castle, T. (2003). Characteristics of prison sexual assault targets in male Oklahoma correctional facilities. *Journal of Interpersonal Violence, 18*, 595–606.

Hicks, M. M., Rogers, R., & Cashel, M. (2000). Predictions of violent and total infractions among institutionalized male juvenile offenders. *Journal of the American Academy of Psychiatry and the Law, 28*, 183–190.

Hillis, S. D., Anda, R. F., Felitti, V. J., & Marchbanks, P. A. (2001). Adverse childhood experiences and sexual risk behaviors in women: A retrospective cohort study. *Family Planning Perspectives, 33*, 206–211.

Hillis, S. D., Anda, R. F., Dube, S. R., Felitti, V. J., Marchbanks, P. A., et al. (2004). The association between adverse childhood experiences and adolescent pregnancy, long-term psychosocial consequences, and fetal death. *Pediatrics, 113*, 320–327.

Hiscoke, U. L., Langstrom, N., Ottosson, H., & Grann, M. (2003). Self-reported personality traits and disorders (DSM-IV) and risk of criminal recidivism: A prospective study. *Journal of Personality Disorders, 17*, 293–305.

Hochhausen, N. M., Lorenz, A. R., & Newman, J. P. (2002). Specifying the impulsivity of female inmates with borderline personality disorder. *Journal of Abnormal Psychology, 111*, 495–501.

Irwin, J. (1980). *Prisons in turmoil.* Boston, MA: Little, Brown, and Co.

Jackson, R. L., Rogers, R., Neumann, C. S., & Lambert, P. L. (2002). Psychopathy in female offenders: An investigation of its underlying dimensions. *Criminal Justice and Behavior, 29*, 692–704.

Jackson, S., & Warren, J. I. (2006). *Relationship violence in prison.* Unpublished manuscript.

Jacobs, J. B. (1977). *Stateville: The penitentiary in mass society.* Chicago, IL: University of Chicago Press.

Janus, S. S., & Janus, C. L. (1993). *The Janus report on sexual behavior: The first broad-scale scientific national survey since Kinsey.* Hoboken, NJ: J Wiley.

Jenness, V., Maxson, C. L., Matsuda, K. N., & Sumner, J. M. (2007). *Violence in California correctional facilities: An empirical examination of sexual assault.* Irvine, CA: University of California-Irvine, Center for Evidence-Based Corrections.

Johnson, G. M., & Knight, R. A. (1998). *Developmental antecedents of sexual coercion in adult sex offenders.* Unpublished manuscript.

Johnson, J. G., Cohen, P., Smailes, E., Kasen, S., Oldham, J. M., Skodol, A. E., et al. (2000). Adolescent personality disorders associated with violence and criminal behavior during adolescence and early adulthood. *American Journal of Psychiatry, 157*, 1406–1412.

Johnson, J. G., Bromley, E., & McGeoch, P. G. (2005). Role of childhood experiences in the development of maladaptive and adaptive personality traits. In J. M. Oldham, A. E. Skodol, & D. S. Bender (Eds.), *Textbook of personality disorders* (pp. 209–221). Washington, DC: American Psychiatric Publishing, Inc.

Kafka, M. P. (1991). Successful antidepressant treatment of nonparaphilic sexual addictions and paraphilias in men. *Journal of Clinical Psychiatry, 52*, 60–65.

Kafka, M. P. (1994). Sertraline pharmacotherapy for paraphilias and paraphilia-related disorders: An open trial. *Annals of Clinical Psychiatry, 6*, 189–195.

Kafka, M. P. (1997). Hypersexual desire in males: An operational definition and clinical implications for males with paraphilias and paraphilia-related disorders. *Archives of Sexual Behavior, 26*, 505–526.

Kafka, M. P., & Prentky, R. (1992a). Fluoxetine treatment of nonparaphilic sexual addictions and paraphilias in men. *Journal of Clinical Psychiatry, 53*(10), 351–358.

Kafka, M. P., & Prentky, R. (1992b). A comparative study of nonparaphilic sexual addictions and paraphilias in men. *Journal of Clinical Psychiatry, 53*(10), 345–350.

Kafka, M. P., & Prentky, R. A. (1994). Preliminary observations of DSM-III-R Axis I comorbidity in men with paraphilias and paraphilia-related disorders. *Journal of Clinical Psychiatry, 55*, 481–487.

Kelling, G., & Coles, C. (1997). *Fixing broken windows.* New York, NY: Free Press.

Kerbs, J. J., & Jolley, J. M. (2007). Inmate-on-inmate victimization among older male prisoners. *Crime and Delinquency, 53*, 187–218.

Kessler, R. C., Molnar, B. E., Feurer, I. D., & Appelbaum, M. (2001). Patterns and mental health predictors of domestic violence in the United States: Results from the National Co-morbidity Study. *International Journal of Law and Psychiatry, 24*, 487–508.

Kinsey, A. C., Pomeroy, W. B., & Martin, C. E. (1948). *Sexual behavior in the human male.* Philadelphia, PA: W. B. Saunders.

Kinsey, A. C., Pomeroy, W. B., Martin, C. E., & Gebhard, P. H. (1953). *Sexual behavior in the human female.* Philadelphia, PA: W. B. Saunders.

Klassen, D., & O'Connor, W. A. (1988). A prospective study of predictors of violence in adult male mental health admissions. *Law and Human Behavior, 12*, 143–158.

Klein, M. (1935). A contribution to the psychogenesis of manic-depressive states. *International Journal of Psychoanalysis, 16*, 145–174.

Klein, M. (1940). Mourning and its relation to manic-depressive states. *International Journal of Psychoanalysis, 21*, 125–153.

Knight, R. A. (1999). Validation of a typology for rapists. *Journal of Interpersonal Violence, 14*, 297–323.

Knight, R. A., & Prentky, R. A. (1990). Classifying sexual offenders: The development and corroboration of taxonomic models. In W. L. Marshall, D. R. Laws, & H. E. Barbaree (Eds.), *Handbook of sexual assault* (pp. 23–52). New York, NY: Plenum.

Knight, R. A., & Cerce, D. D. (1999). Validation and revision of the multidimensional assessment of sex and aggression. *Psychologica Belgica, 39*, 135–161.

Knight, R. A., & Sims-Knight, J. E. (1999, November). *Family and early behavioral antecedents of sexual coercion.* Paper presented at the 14th annual meeting of the Society for Research in Psychopathology, Montreal, Canada.

Knight, R. A., & Sims-Knight, J. E. (2003). The developmental antecedents of sexual coercion against women: Testing alternative hypotheses with structural equation modeling. *Annals of the New York Academy of Sciences, 989*, 72–85.

Knight, R. A., & Sims-Knight, J. E. (2004). Testing an etiological model for juvenile sexual offending against women. *Journal of Child Sexual Abuse, 13*, 33–55.

Knight, R. A., & Guay, J. P. (2006). The role of psychopathy in sexual offenders against women. In C. J. Patrick (Ed.), *Handbook of psychopathy* (pp. 512–532). New York, NY: John Wiley.

Knowles, G. J. (1999). Male prison rape: A search for causation and prevention. *The Howard Journal, 38*, 267–282.

Komarovskaya, I., Loper, A. B., & Warren, J. (2007). The role of impulsivity in antisocial and violent behavior and personality disorders among incarcerated women. *Criminal Justice and Behavior: An International Journal, 34*, 1499–1515.

Koscheski, M., Hensley, C., Wright, J., & Tewksbury, R. (2002). Consensual sexual behavior. In C. Hensley (Ed.), *Prison sex: Practice and policy* (pp. 111–132). Boulder, CO: Lynne Rienner Publishers.

Koss, M. P., & Dinero, T. E. (1988). Predictors of sexual aggression among a national sample of male college students. *Annals of the New York Academy of Sciences, 528*, 133–147.

Kosson, D. S., Kelly, J. C., & White, J. W. (1997). Psychopathy related traits predict self-report sexual aggression among college man. *Journal of Interpersonal Violence, 12*, 241–254.

Krafft-Ebing, R. von. (1965). *Psychopathia sexualis* (H. Wedeck, Trans.). New York, NY: G.P Putnam's Sons. (Originally published in Latin in 1886).

Kroner, D. G., & Mills, J. F. (2001). The accuracy of five risk appraisal instruments in predicting institutional misconduct and new convictions. *Criminal Justice and Behavior, 28*, 471–489.

Kropp, P. R., Hart, S. D., Webster, C. D., & Eaves, D. (1995). *Manual for the spousal assault risk assessment guide* (2nd ed.). Vancouver, BC: The British Columbia Institute on Family Violence.

Kunselman, J., Tewksbury, R., Dumond, R. W., & Dumond, D. A. (2002). Nonconsensual sexual behavior. In C. Hensley (Ed.), *Prison sex: Practice and policy* (pp. 27–47). Boulder, CO: Lynne Rienner Publishers.

Kury, H., & Smartt, U. (2002). Prisoner-on-prisoner violence: Victimization of young offenders in prison. Some German findings. *Criminology and Criminal Justice, 2*, 411–437.

Lalumière, M. L., & Quinsey, V. L. (1996). Sexual deviance, antisociality, mating effort, and the use of sexually coercive behaviors. *Personality and Individual Differences, 21*, 33–48.

Lalumière, M. L., & Quinsey, V. L. (1998). Pavlovian conditioning of sexual interest in human males. *Archives of Sexual Behavior, 27*, 241–252.

Lalumière, M. L., Harris, G. T., Quinsey, V. L., & Rice, M. E. (2005). *The causes of rape: Understanding individual differences in the male propensity for sexual aggression.* Washington, DC: American Psychological Association.

Langevin, R., Wright, P., & Handy, L. (1989). Characteristics of sex offenders who were sexually victimized as children. *Sexual Abuse: A Journal of Research and Treatment, 2*, 227–253.

Laumann, E. O., Gagnon, J. H., Michael, R. T., & Michaels, S. (1994). *The social organization of sexuality.* Chicago, IL: University of Chicago Press.

Link B., & Stueve, A. (1994). Psychotic symptoms and the violent/illegal behavior of mental patients compared to community controls. In J. Monahan & H. Steadman (Eds.), *Violence and mental disorder* (pp. 137–160). Chicago, IL: University of Chicago Press.

Lockwood, D. (1980). *Prison sexual violence.* New York, NY: Elsevier North-Holland.

Loeber, R., & Farrington, D. P. (Eds.) (1998). *Serious and violent juvenile offenders: Risk factors and successful interventions.* Thousand Oaks, CA: Sage.

Logan, C., & Blackburn, R., (2009). Mental disorder in violent women in secure settings: Potential relevance to risk for future violence. *International Journal of Law and Psychiatry, 32*(1), 31–38.

Loucks, A., & Zamble, E. (2000). Predictors of criminal behavior and prison misconduct in serious female offenders. *NCJRS Abstract Database.* Ontario, Canada: Canada Correctional Service [NCJ 186622].

Lusignan, R., & Marleau, J. D. (2007). Risk assessment and offender–victim relationship in juvenile offenders. *International Journal of Offender Therapy and Comparative Criminology, 51*(4), 433–443.

Lynam, D. R., & Derefinko, K. J. (2006). Convergence and divergence among self-report psychopathy measures: A personality-based approach. *Journal of Personality Disorders, 20*(3), 261–280.

Lynch, J. P. (1996). Clarifying divergent estimates of rape from two national surveys. *Public Opinion Quarterly, 60*, 410–461.

McCorkle, R. C. (1993a). Fear of victimization and symptoms of psychopathology among prison inmates. *Journal of Offender Rehabilitation, 19*, 27–41.

McCorkle, R. C. (1993b). Living on the edge: Fear in a maximum-security prison. *Journal of Offender Rehabilitation, 20*, 73–91.

McGuire, L. M., Burright, R. G., Williams, R., & Donovick, P. L. (1998). Prevalence rate of traumatic brain injury in psychiatric and non-psychiatric subjects. *Brain Injury, 12*, 207–214.

McNiel, D. E., & Binder, R. L. (1994). Screening for risk of inpatient violence. Validation of an actuarial tool. *Law and Human Behaviour, 18*, 579–586.

Maden, T., Curie, C., Meux, C., Burrow, S., & Gunn, J. (1995). *Treatment and security needs of special hospital patients*. London, UK: Whurr.

Maguin, E., & Loeber, R. (1996). Academic performance and delinquency. *Crime and Justice, 20,* 145–264.

Maguin, E., Hawkins, J. D., Catalano, R. F., Hill, K., Abbott, R., & Herrenkohl, T. (1995, November). *Risk factors measured at three ages for violence at age 17–18.* Paper presented at the American Society of Criminology, Boston, MA.

Maguire, K., & Pestore, A. L. (1997). *Sourcebook of Criminal Justice Statistics, 442.* Bureau of Justice Statistics, US Department of Justice.

Maitland, A. S., & Sluder, R. D. (1996). Victimization in prisons: A study of factors related to the general well-being of youthful inmates. *Federal Probation, 60,* 24–31.

Malamuth, N. M., Sockloskie, R. J., Koss, M. P., & Tanaka, J. S. (1991). Characteristics of aggressors against women: Testing a model using a national sample of college students. *Journal of Consulting and Clinical Psychology, 59,* 670–681.

Malamuth, N. M., Heavey, C. L., & Linz, D. (1993). Predicting men's antisocial behavior against women: The "Interaction Model" of sexual aggression. In G. Hall, R. Hirschman, J. Graham, & M. Zaragoza (Eds.), *Sexual aggression: Issues in etiology and assessment, treatment and policy* (pp. 63–97). New York, NY: Hemisphere.

Malamuth, N. M., Linz, D., Heavy, C. L., Barnes, G., & Acker, M. (1995). Using the confluence model of sexual aggression to predict men's conflicts with women: A ten year follow-up study. *Journal of Personality and Social Psychology, 69,* 353–369.

Man, C. D., & Cronan, J. P. (2001). Forecasting sexual abuse in prison: The prison subculture of masculinity as a backdrop for "deliberate indifference." *The Journal of Criminal Law and Criminology, 92,* 127–185.

Maruschak, L. M. (2006). Medical problems of jail inmates. *BJS Special Report* (NCJ 210696). Washington, DC: US Department of Justice, Office of Justice Programs.

Miller, H. G., Gribble, J. N., Mazade, L. C., & Turner, C. F. (1998). Abortion and breast cancer risk: Fact or artifact. In A. Stone (Ed.), *Science of self-report.* Mahwah, NJ: Lawrence Erlbaum Associates.

Moeller, F. G., Barratt, E. S., Dougherty, D. M., Schmitz, J. M., & Swann, M. D. (2001). Psychiatric aspects of impulsivity. *American Journal of Psychiatry, 158,* 1783–1793.

Moffitt, T. E., Caspi, A., Rutter, M., & Silva, P. A. (2001). *Sex differences in antisocial behavior: Conduct disorder, delinquency, and violence in the Dunedin longitudinal study.* Cambridge, UK: Cambridge University Press.

Monahan, J. (1981). *Clinical prediction of violent behavior* (NCJ No. 078339). Washington, DC: US Department of Health, Education, and Welfare, National Institute of Mental Health.

Monahan, J., & Steadman, H. (1994). Toward the rejuvenation of risk research. In J. Monahan & H. Steadman (Eds.), *Violence and mental disorder: Developments in risk assessment* (pp. 1–17). Chicago, IL: University of Chicago Press.

Monahan, J., Steadman, H., Silver, E., Appelbaum, P., Robbins, P., Mulvey, E., et al. (2001). *Rethinking risk assessment: The MacArthur study of mental disorder and violence.* New York, NY: Oxford University Press.

Morrell, R. F., Merbitz, C. T., Jain, S., & Jain, S. (1998). Traumatic brain injury in prisoners. *Journal of Offender Rehabilitation, 27,* 1–8.

Morrissey, C., Mooney, P., Hougue, T. E., Lindsay, W. R., & Taylor, J. L. (2007). Predictive validity of the PCL-R for offenders with intellectual disability in a high security hospital: Treatment progress. *Journal of Intellectual and Developmental Disability, 32*(2), 125–133.

Muskens, M., Bogaerts, S., van Casteren, M., & Labrijn, S. (2011). Adult female sexual offending: A comparison between co-offenders and solo offenders in a Dutch sample. *Journal of Sexual Aggression, 17*(1), 46–60.

Nacci, P., & Kane, T. (1983). The incidence of sex and sexual aggression in federal prisons. *Federal Probation, 47*, 31–36.

National Research Council. (1979). *Privacy and confidentiality as factors in survey response.* Washington, DC: National Academy of Sciences.

National Prison Rape Elimination Commission (June 2009). *National Prison Rape Elimination Commission Report* (NCJ No: 226680). Washington, DC: National Prison Rape Elimination Commission. Retrieved April 30, 2012, from https://www.ncjrs.gov/pdffiles1/226680.pdf

Neal, T. M. S., & Clements, C. B. (2010). Prison rape and psychological sequelae: A call for research. *Psychology, Public Policy and Law, 16*(3), 284–299.

Newman, J. C., Des Jarlais, D. C., Turner, C. F., Gribble, J., Cooley, P., & Paone, D. (2002). The differential effects of face-to-face and computer interview modes. *American Journal of Public Health, 92*, 294–297.

Nicholls, T. L., Douglas, K., & Ogloff, J. R. P. (1997). Risk assessments with female psychiatric patients: Utility of the HCR-20 and PCL:SV. *Canadian Psychology, 38*, 111–112.

Nicholls, T. L., Ogloff, J. R. P., & Douglas, K. S. (2004). Assessing risk for violence among female and male civil psychiatric patients: The HCR-20, PCL:SV, and McNiel & Binder's VSC. *Behavioral Sciences and the Law, 22*, 127–158.

Novaco, R. W. (1994). Anger as a risk factor for violence among the mentally disordered. In J. Monahan & H. Steadman (Eds.), *Violence and mental disorder: Developments in risk assessment* (pp. 21–56). Chicago, IL: University of Chicago Press.

Novaco, R. (2003). *The Novaco Anger Scale and Provocation Inventory Manual.* Los Angeles, CA: Western Psychological Services.

O'Donnell, I., & Edgar, K. (1999). Fear in prison. *The Prison Journal, 79*(1), 90–99.

Oliver, C. J., Beech, A. R., Fisher, D., & Beckett, R. (2007). A comparison of rapists and sexual murderers on demographic and selected psychometric measures. *International Journal of Offender Therapy and Comparative Criminology, 51*, 298–312.

Otis, M. (1913). A perversion not commonly noted. *Journal of Abnormal Psychology, 8*, 113–116.

Palmer, C. T., & Tilley, C. F. (1995). Sexual access to females as a motivation for joining gangs: An evolutionary approach. *The Journal of Sex Research, 32*, 213–217.

Patrick, C. J. (2006). *Handbook of psychopathy.* New York, NY: Guilford Press.

Pecquet, J. (2006). Gunfight in Florida prison kills 2. *USA Today.* Retrieved June 22, 2006, from http://www.usatoday.com/news/nation/2006-06-21-prison-shooting_x.htm

Pfohl, B., Blum, N., & Zimmerman, M. (1995). *Structured interview for DSM-IV personality disorders: SIDP-IV.* Iowa City, IA: University of Iowa College of Medicine.

Pinkerton, S. D., Galletly, C. L., & Seat, D. W. (2007). Model-based estimates of HIV acquisition due to prison rape. *The Prison Journal, 87*(3), 295–310.

Prentky, R. A., & Knight, R. A. (2000). *Psychopathy base rates among subtypes of sex offenders.* Paper presented at 19th Annual Meeting of the Association for the Treatment of Sexual Abusers, San Diego, CA.

Prentky, R. A., Knight, R. A., & Rosenberg, R. (1988). Validation analyses on a taxonomic system for rapists: Disconfirmation and reconceptualization. *Annals of the New York Academy of Sciences, 528*, 21–40.

Prentky, R. A., Knight, R. A., & Lee, A. (1989). Risk factors associated with recidivism among extra-familial child molesters. *Journal of Consulting and Clinical Psychology, 65*, 141–149.

Puplava, J. A. (1997). Peanut butter and politics: An evaluation of the separation of powers issues in Section 802 of the Prison Litigation Reform Act. *Indiana Law Journal, 73*(1), 329–353.

Quinsey, V. L., Warneford, A., Pruesse, M., & Link, N. (1975). Release Oak Ridge patients: A follow-up study of review board discharges. *The British Journal of Criminology, 15*, 264–270.

Quinsey, V. L., Harris, G. T., Rice, M. E., & Cormier, C. A. (1998). *Violent offenders: Appraising and managing risk.* Washington, DC: American Psychological Association.

Raine, A., & Yang, Y. (2006). Neural foundations to moral reasoning and antisocial behavior. *Social Cognitive & Affective Neuroscience, 1*(3), 203–213.

Ribet, B. (2010). Naming prison rape as disablement: A critical analysis of the Prison Litigation Reform Act, The Americans With Disabilities Act, and The Imperatives of Survivor-Oriented Advocacy. *Virginia Journal of Social Policy and the Law, 17*, 281, 317.

Rice, M. E., & Harris, G. T. (1997). Cross-validation and extension of the Violence Risk Appraisal Guide for child molesters and rapists. *Law & Human Behavior, 21*, 231–241.

Rice, M. E., Harris, G. T., & Quinsey, V. L. (1990). A follow-up of rapists assessed in a maximum-security psychiatric facility. *Journal of Interpersonal Violence, 5*, 435–448.

Ristroph, A. (2006). Sexual punishments. *Columbia Journal of Gender and Law, 15*, 139–184.

Salekin, R. T., Rogers, R., & Sewell, K. W. (1997). Construct validity of psychopathy in a female offender sample: A multitrait-multimethod evaluation. *Journal of Abnormal Psychology, 106*, 576–585.

Salekin, R. T., Trobst, K. K., & Krioukova, M. (2001). Construct validity of psychopathy in a community sample: A nomological net approach. *Journal of Personality Disorders, 15*, 425–441.

Sandler, J. C., & Freeman, N. J. (2007). Typology of female sex offenders: A test of Vandiver and Kercher. *Sexual Abuse: A Journal of Research and Treatment, 19*, 73–89.

Saum, C., Surratt, H., Inciardi, J., & Bennett, R. (1995). Sex in prison: Exploring the myths and realities. *The Prison Journal, 75*, 413–430.

Scacco, A. M. (1975). *Rape in prison.* Springfield, IL: Charles C. Thomas.

Schofield, P. W., Butler, T. G., Hollis, S. J., Smith, N. E., Lee, S. J., & Kelso, W. M. (2006). Traumatic brain injury among Australian prisoners: Rates, recurrence, and sequelae. *Brain Injury, 20*, 499–506.

Seghorn, T. K., Prentky, R. A., & Boucher, R. J. (1987). Childhood sexual abuse in the lives of sexually aggressive offenders. *Journal of the American Academy of Child and Adolescent Psychiatry, 26*(2), 262–267.

Serbin, L. A., Cooperman, J. M., Peters, P. L., Lehoux, P. M., Stack, D. M., & Schwartzman, A. E. (1998). Intergenerational transfer of psychosocial risk in women with childhood histories of aggression, withdrawal, or aggression and withdrawal. *Developmental Psychology, 34*, 1246–1262.

Shelden, R. G. (1991). Comparison of gang members and non-gang members in a prison setting. *Prison Journal, 71*, 50–60.

Singleton, N., Meltzer, H., Gatward, R., Coid, J., & Deasy, D. (1998). *Psychiatric morbidity among prisoners in England and Wales.* London, UK: The Stationery Office.

Skeem, J. L., & Louden, J. E. (2006). Toward evidence-based practice for probationers and parolees mandated to mental health treatment. *Psychiatric Services, 57*, 333–342.

Slaughter, B., Fann, J. R., & Ehde, D. (2003). Traumatic brain injury in a county jail population: Prevalence, neuropsychological functioning and psychiatric disorders. *Brain Injury, 17*, 731–741.

Slovic, P., Finucane, M., Peters, E., & MacGregor, D. G. (2002). Risk as analysis and risk as feelings: Some thoughts about affect, reason, risk, and rationality. *Risk Analysis, 24*, 1–12.

Smith, B. (2006). Rethinking prison sex: Self-expression and safety. *Columbia Journal of Gender and Law, 15*, 185–234.

Soliman, I. R. (2000). Male officers in women's prisons: The need for segregation of officers in certain positions. *Texas Journal of Women and the Law, 45*, 10–59.

Solursh, L. P., Solursh, D. S., & Meyer, C. A., Jr. (1993). Is there sex after the prison door slams shut? *Medicine and Law, 12*, 439–443.

Spaulding, A., Lubelczyk, R., & Flanigan, T. (2001). Can unsafe sex behind bars be barred? *American Journal of Public Health, 91*, 1176–1177.

Steadman, H., Monahan, J., Appelbaum, P., Grisso, T., Mulvey, E., Roth, L., et al. (1994). Designing a new generation of risk assessment research. In J. Monahan & H. Steadman (Eds.), *Violence and mental disorder: Developments in risk assessment* (pp. 297–318). Chicago, IL: University of Chicago Press.

Steadman, H., Mulvey, E., Monahan, P., Robbins, P., Appelbaum, P., Grisso, T., et al. (1998). Violence by people discharged from acute psychiatric inpatient facilities and by others in the same neighborhoods. *Archives of General Psychiatry, 55*, 393–401.

Stein, M. B., Koverola, C., Hanna, C., Torchia, M. G., & McClarty, B. (1997). Hippocampal volume in women victimized by childhood sexual abuse. *Psychological Medicine, 27*, 951–959.

Stouthamer-Loeber, M., Loeber, R., & Thomas, C. (1992). Caretakers seeking help for boys with disruptive and delinquent behavior. *Comprehensive Mental Health Care, 2*, 159–178.

Stouthamer-Loeber, M., & Wei, E. H. (1998). The precursors of young fatherhood and its effect on delinquency of teenage males. *Journal of Adolescent Health, 22*, 56–65.

Strachan, C. E. (1993). *The assessment of psychopathy in female offenders.* Unpublished doctoral dissertation. University of British Columbia, Vancouver, Canada.

Strand, S., Belfrage, H., Fransson, G., & Levander, S. (1999). Clinical and risk management factors in risk prediction of mentally disordered offenders-More important than historical data?: A retrospective study of 40 mentally disordered offenders assessed with the HCR-20 violence risk assessment scheme. *Legal and Criminological Psychology, 4*, 67–76.

Straus, M. A., Hamby, S. L., Boney-McCoy, S., & Sugarman, D. B. (1996). The Revised Conflict Tactics Scales (CTS2): Development and preliminary psychometric data. *Journal of Family Issues, 17*, 283–316.

Struckman-Johnson, C. (2011 July). *Research on prison sexual assault in American Midwestern state prisons: How findings relate to proposed policy standards from the national prison rape elimination commission.* Paper presented at the 32nd International Congress on Law and Mental Health, Berlin, Germany.

Struckman-Johnson, C., & Struckman-Johnson, D. (2000). Sexual coercion rates in seven Midwestern prison facilities for men. *The Prison Journal, 80*, 379–390.

Struckman-Johnson, C., & Struckman-Johnson, D. (2002). Sexual coercion reported by women in three Midwestern prisons. *Journal of Sex Research, 39*, 217–227.

Struckman-Johnson, C., & Struckman-Johnson, D. (2006). A comparison of sexual coercion experiences reported by men and women in prison. *Journal of Interpersonal Violence, 21*, 1591–1615.

Struckman-Johnson, C., Struckman-Johnson, D., Rucker, L., Bumby, K., & Donaldson, S. (1996). Sexual coercion reported by men and women in prison. *The Journal of Sex Research, 33*, 67–76.

Swanson, J. W., Borum, R., Swartz, M. S., & Monahan, J. (1996). Psychotic symptoms and disorders and the risk of violent behavior in the community. *Criminal Behavior and Mental Health, 6*, 309–329.

Swogger, M. T., Walsh, Z., & Kosson, D. S. (2007). Domestic violence and psychopathic traits: Distinguishing the antisocial batterer from other antisocial offenders. *Aggressive Behavior, 33*, 1–8.

Taylor, K. F. (2000). The prison litigation reform act's administrative exhaustion requirement: Closing the money damage loophole. *Washington University Law Quarterly, 78*, 955–978.

Taylor, P. J., Leese, M., Williams, D., Butwell, M., Daly, R., & Larkin, E. (1998). Mental disorder and violence: A special (high security) hospital study. *The British Journal of Psychiatry, 172*, 218–226.

Teasdale, B., Silver, E., & Monahan, J. (2006). Gender, threat/control-override delusions and violence. *Law and Human Behavior, 30*, 649–658.

Teicher, M. H., Dumont, N. L., Ito, Y., Vaituzis, C., Giedd, J. N., & Andersen, S. L. (2004). Childhood neglect is associated with reduced corpus callosum area. *Biological Psychiatry, 56*, 80–85.

Teicher, M. H., Tomoda, A., & Andersen, S. L. (2006). Neurobiological consequences of early stress and childhood maltreatment: Are results from human and animal studies comparable? *Annals of the New York Academy of Sciences, 1071*, 313–323.

Tewksbury, R. (1989a). Measures of sexual behavior in an Ohio prison. *Sociology and Social Research, 74*(1), 34–39.

Tewksbury, R. (1989b). Fear of sexual assault in prison inmates. *The Prison Journal, 69*, 62–71.

Tewksbury, R., & Collins, S. C. (2006). Aggression levels among correctional officers: Reassessing sex differences. *The Prison Journal, 86*, 327–343.

Thornberry, T. P., Huizinga, D., & Loeber, R. (1995). The prevention of serious delinquency and violence. In J. C. Howell, B. Krisberg, J. B. Hawkins, & J. J. Wilson (Eds.), *Sourcebook on serious, violent, and chronic juvenile offenders* (pp. 213–237). Thousand Oaks, CA: Sage.

Torgersen, S. (2007). Epidemiology. In J. M. Oldham, A. E. Skodol, & D. S. Bender (Eds.), *Textbook of personality disorders* (pp. 129–141). Washington, DC: American Psychiatric Publishing.

Tourangeau, R., & Smith, T. W. (1998). Collecting sensitive information with different modes of data collection. In M. P. Cooper, R. P. Baker, J. Bethlehem, C. Z. F. Clark, J. Martin, W. L. Nicholls, & J. M. O'Reilly (Eds.), *Computer assisted survey information collection* (pp. 431–454). New York, NY: Wiley.

Tourangeau, R., Rips, L. J., & Rasinski, K. (2000). *The psychology of survey response.* Cambridge, UK: Cambridge University Press.

Turner, C. F., Forsyth, B. H., O'Reilly, J. M., Cooley, P. C., Smith, T. K., Rogers, S. M., & Miller, H. G. (1998). Automated self-interviewing and the survey measurement of sensitive behaviors. In M. P. Cooper, R. P. Baker, J. Bethlehem, C. Z. F. Clark, J. Martin, W. L. Nicholls, & J. M. O'Reilly (Eds.), *Computer assisted survey information collection* (pp. 455–473). New York, NY: Wiley.

Urheim, R., Jakobsen, D., & Rasmussen, K. (2003, August). *Dimensions of inpatient aggressive behavior in a security ward: What is being "predicted"?* Paper presented at the 5th Nordic Symposium on Forensic Psychiatry, Ystad, Sweden.

Vandiver, D. M., & Kercher, G. (2004). Offender and victim characteristics of registered female sexual offenders in Texas: A proposed typology of female sexual offenders. *Sexual Abuse: A Journal of Research and Treatment, 16*, 121–137.

Vitale, J. E., Smith, S. S., Brinkley, C. A., & Newman, J. P. (2002). The reliability and validity of the Psychopathy Checklist-Revised in a sample of female offenders. *Criminal Justice and Behavior, 29*, 202–231.

Vythilingam, M., Heim, C., Newport, J., Miller, A. H., Anderson, E., Bronen, R., Brummer, M., Staib, L., Vermetten, E., Charney, D. S., Nemeroff, C. B., & Bremner, J. D. (2002). Childhood trauma associated with smaller hippocampal volume in women with major depression. *American Journal of Psychiatry, 159*(12), 2072–2080.

Walker, W. D., Rowe, R. C., & Quinsey, V. L. (1993). Authoritarianism and sexual aggression. *Journal of Personality and Social Psychology, 65*(5), 1036–1045.

Walters, G. (2003). Predicting institutional adjustment and recidivism with the Psychopathy Checklist factor scores: A meta-analysis. *Law and Human Behavior, 27*, 541–558.

Wang, E. W., & Diamond, P. M. (1999). Empirically identifying factors related to violence risk in corrections. *Behavioral Sciences and the Law, 17*(3), 377–389.

Warren, J. I. (2002). *Prison Violence Inventory*. Unpublished manuscript.

Warren, J. I. (2006a). *Paraphilic Interests*. Unpublished manuscript.

Warren, J. I. (2006b). *Self-Report Criminal History Questionnaire (SRCHQ)*. Unpublished manuscript.

Warren, J. I., Reboussin, R., Hazelwood, R., Cummings, A., Gibbs, N., & Trumbetta, S. (1998). The distance correlates of serial rape. *Journal of Quantitative Criminology, 14*, 35–58.

Warren, J. I., Bale, R., Friend, R, Burnette, M., South, S., & Chauhan, P. (2003). Personality disorders among female prison inmates: Co-morbidity and the relationship to criminality and violence. *Journal of the Academy of Psychiatry and the Law, 30*, 502–509.

Warren, J. I., Hurt, S., Loper, A. B., & Chauhan, P. (2004). Exploring prison adjustment among female inmates: Issues of measurement and prediction. *Criminal Justice and Behavior, 31*, 624–645.

Warren, J. I., South, S. C., Burnette, M. L., Rogers, A., Friend, R., Bale, R., & Van Patten, I. (2005). Understanding the risk factors for violence and criminality in women: The concurrent validity of the PCL-R and HCR-20. *International Journal of Law and Psychiatry, 28*, 269–289.

Warren, J. I., Jackson, S. L., & Loper, A. B. (2006). *Sexual Aggression in Prison (SAP)*. Unpublished manuscript.

Warren, J. I., Loper, A. B., & Jackson, S. L. (2006). *Prison Background Information Survey*. Unpublished manuscript.

Webster, C. D., Douglas, K. S., Eaves, D., & Hart, S. D. (1997). *HCR-20: Assessing the Risk for Violence* (Version 2). Mental Health, Law, and Policy Institute, Simon Fraser University.

Weinrott, M. R., & Saylor, M. (1991). Self-report of crimes committed by sex offenders. *Journal of Interpersonal Violence, 6*, 286–300.

Weiss, C., & Friar, J. D. (1974). *Terror in the prisons: Homosexual rape and why society condones it*. Indianapolis, IN: Bobbs-Merrill.

Wheeler, J. G., George, W. H., & Dahl, B. J. (2002). Sexually aggressive college students: Empathy as a moderator in the "confluence model" of sexual aggression. *Personality and Individual Differences, 33*, 759–775.

Widiger, T. A. (2006). *Dimensional models of personality disorders: Refining the research agenda for DSM-V*. Washington, DC: American Psychiatric Association.

Widom, C. S. (1989a). Child abuse, neglect, and adult behavior. *American Journal of Orthopsychiatry, 59*(3), 355–367.

Widom, C. S. (1989b). Child abuse, neglect, and violent criminal behavior. *Criminology, 27*, 251–271.

Widom, C. S. (1999). Posttraumatic stress disorder in abused and neglected children grown up. *American Journal of Psychiatry, 156*, 1223–1229.

Wiebush, R. G., Baird, C., Krisberg, B., & Onek, D. (1995). Risk assessment and classification for serious, violent, and chronic juvenile offenders. In J. C. Howell, B. F. Krisberg, J. D. Hawkins, & J. J. Wilson (Eds.), *A sourcebook: Serious, violent, and chronic juvenile offenders* (pp. 171–212). Thousand Oaks, CA: Sage.

Wijkman, M., Bijleveld, C., & Hendricks, J. (2011). Female sex offenders: Specialists, generalists and once-only offenders. *Journal of Sexual Aggression, 17*(1), 34–45.

Williams, L. M., Siegel, J. A., & Pomeroy, J. J. (2000). Validity of women's self-reports of documented child sexual abuse. In A. Stone, J. S. Turkkan, C. A. Bachrach, J. B. Jobe, H. S. Kurtzman, & V. S. Cain (Eds.), *The science of self-report: Implications for research and practice* (pp. 211–226). Hillsdale, NJ: Lawrence Erlbaum.

Williams, M. L., Freeman, R. C., Bowen, A. M., Zhao, Z., Elwood, W. N., Gordon, C., et al. (2000). A comparison of the reliability of self-reported drug use and sexual behaviors using computer-assisted versus face-to-face interviewing. *AIDS Education and Prevention, 12*, 199–213.

Wolff, N., & Shi, J. (2009). Contextualization of physical and sexual assault in male prisons: Incidents and their aftermath. *Journal of Correctional Health Care, 15*, 58–69.

Wolff, N., & Shi, J. (2011). Patterns of victimization and feelings of safety inside prison: The experience of male and female inmates. *Crime and Delinquency, 57*(1), 29–55.

Wolff, N., Blitz, C. L., Shi, J., Bachman, R., & Siegel, J. A. (2006). Sexual violence inside prisons: Rates of victimization. *Journal of Urban Health, 83*(5), 835–848.

Wolff, N., Blitz, C. L., & Shi, J. (2007). Rates of sexual victimization inside prison for inmates with and without mental disorders. *Psychiatric Services, 58*, 1087–1094.

Wolff, N., Blitz, C. L., Siegel, J., & Bachman, R. (2007). Physical violence inside prisons: Rates of victimization. *Criminal Justice and Behavior, 34*, 588–599.

Wolff, N., Shi, J., & Bachman, R. (2008). Measuring victimization inside prisons. *Journal of Interpersonal Violence, 23*, 1343–1362.

Wooden, W. S., & Parker, J. (1982). *Men behind bars: Sexual exploitation in prison.* New York, NY: Plenum Press.

Wooldredge, J. D. (1994). Inmate crime and victimization in a southwestern correctional facility. *Journal of Criminal Justice, 22*, 367–381.

Wooldredge, J. D. (1998). Inmate Lifestyles and Opportunities for Victimization. *Journal of Research in Crime and Delinquency, 35*(4), 480–502.

Yap, L., Butler, T., Richters, J., Kirkwood, K., Grant, L., Saxby, M., Ropp, F., & Donovan, B. (2007). Do condoms cause rape and mayhem? The long-term effects of condoms in New South Wales' prisons. *Sexually Transmitted Infections, 83*, 219–222.

Zamble, E., & Quinsey, V. L. (1997). *The criminal recidivism process.* New York, NY: Cambridge University Press.

Zweig, J. M., & Blackmore, J. (2008, October). *Strategies to prevent prison rape by changing the correctional culture.* [National Institute of Justice Research for Practice, NCJ No: 222843]. Washington, DC: US Department of Justice, Office of Justice Programs.

Zweig, J. M., Naser, R. L., Blackmore, J., & Schaffer, M. (2007). *Addressing sexual violence in prisons: A national snapshot of approaches and highlights of innovative strategies, Final Report.* Washington, DC: Urban Institute. Retrieved April 30, 2012, from https://www.ncjrs. gov/pdffiles1/nij/grants/216856.pdf

INDEX

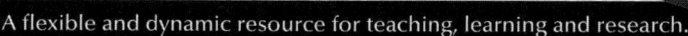